THE OTHER SIDE
OF
WESTERN CIVILIZATION

Readings in Everyday Life

Second Edition

VOLUME I
The Ancient World to the Reformation

Under the general editorship of John Morton Blum

Yale University

THE OTHER SIDE
OF
WESTERN CIVILIZATION

Readings in Everyday Life

Second Edition

VOLUME I

The Ancient World to the Reformation

Edited by

Stanley Chodorow

University of California, San Diego

 HARCOURT BRACE JOVANOVICH, INC.
New York / San Diego / Chicago / San Francisco / Atlanta

ISBN: 0-15-567648-2

Library of Congress Catalog Card Number: 78-60215

Printed in the United States of America

Picture Credits

cover   Medieval artisan and his family. Fifteenth-century
        miniature by Jean Bourdichon. Giraudon

p.   6   Alinari/EPA
p.   70   British Museum
p.   126   British Museum
p.   212   British Museum
p.   306   Alinari/EPA

For Peggy

PREFACE

The purpose of the second edition of *The Other Side of Western Civilization*, Volume I, is the same as that of the first edition: to describe and evoke the texture of life in premodern times. This new edition, however, reflects the trends in scholarship published since the appearance of the first edition in 1973. It introduces some key problems in the history of the common people of Europe before the Reformation by focusing on class structure, the nature of the economy, and patterns and aspects of everyday life. Almost two-thirds of the selections are new to this work. Some of the pieces are taken from works written in the period, but more often—because the ancients rarely described what they considered commonplace—they are historians' re-creations. They have been arranged chronologically to fit the majority of Western civilization courses, but a second table of contents provides a topical arrangement.

Courses in Western civilization necessarily focus students' attention on events and trends or ideas and culture. This book is designed to help students understand the social and institutional world in which events happened and ideas were expressed. The readings do not merely add color to the basic picture, however. They deal with fundamentally important aspects of past life.

Three selections deal with premodern travel, the extent and character of which was no less important to ancient and medieval civilization than its latest forms are to modern life. Other pieces describe life in cities, the condition of women, child-rearing practices in medieval Europe and Renaissance Italy, the impact of technological change on the life of agricultural villages and peasant families, the common soldier's experience in battle in late medieval Europe. Taken together, the readings describe the commonplace existence that formed the context in which great thinkers and artists of Western civilization lived and effected historically significant changes.

A number of people provided important assistance in the preparation of the book. I want to thank Jeremy duQ. Adams, Southern Methodist University; John F. Benton, California Institute of Technology; Elizabeth A. R. Brown, Brooklyn College; Cissie C. Fairchilds, Syracuse University; and Jeffrey B. Russell, California State University, Sacramento. These critics gave me valuable advice and helped significantly in shaping the book. I am indebted to William J. Wisneski of Harcourt Brace Jovanovich for his encouragement and aid. He has believed in the book as a teaching tool and companion to the large textbooks of Western civilization and has helped me meet the need for that kind of volume. I want also to thank my editor, Paula F. Lewis, and my copy editor, Eleanor Lahn, for their helpful criticism and editorial guidance.

Finally, and most fully, I thank my wife, Peggy. She is not only a source of encouragement and criticism, the usual things, but her own intense, productive work schedule provides a model and a goad that cures indolence and sharpens the mind.

Stanley Chodorow

CONTENTS

* For paired selections, the first page number refers to the headnote, the second to the selection proper.

3 The Peak of Medieval Civilization 12th-13th Centuries

4 The Late Middle Ages 14th-15th Centuries

5 The Renaissance and Reformation 16th-17th Centuries

Topical Table of Contents

Introduction

The aim of this second edition, as of the first, is to provide insight into the character of premodern society. The selections focus on the social life of western Europe from the ancient world through the Renaissance. They present a composite picture of urban and rural life and of the activities of the social classes and professions.

Social history was first written by the Enlightenment *philosophes*, who reacted strongly against the ancient historiographical tradition that equated history with the history of politics and government. Inspired by critics like Voltaire, who called for a history of men to replace the history of kings, ministers, and courts, writers like Montesquieu sought to describe and explain the social personalities of national groups. Others, in Germany as well as in France, began to focus on the cultural history of Europe—the history of art and literature as well as of society. But the *philosophes* were really uninterested in history even when they were ostensibly writing history. Their conviction that man was progressing toward the realization of his rational capacity underlay their historical work, so that for them, history was only a source of evidence that proved the truth of their conviction.

In the late eighteenth and early nineteenth centuries, thinkers like Goethe, Herder, and Hegel reacted against this attitude. The end product of man's progress in the eighteenth century had been the terror of the French Revolution. Man had not escaped from his history; he had only continued in its ancient course. These writers, the romanticists, thought that society is as much a product of its past as an adult is a product of his childhood and adolescence. For them, historical studies provided the key to understanding the present. The historical work of the romanticists therefore focused attention on the whole past: Social and economic history, cultural history, linguistics, and religious history became an integral part of the study of the past.

Yet the historical field that gained most from the new valuation of historical study was the old mainstay of the genre, political history. The majority of extant documents and narrative sources derived from political action and concerned political organization. It took much longer to develop methods for dealing with the cryptic sources on which social history could be founded than it took to develop methods for dealing with the literate products of the governing elite. Real progress in social history was not made until the 1920s, when Marc Bloch and Lucien Febvre founded the so-called *Annales* school—named for the journal in which they published studies of social and economic history. Inspired by Bloch and Febvre, social historians have produced studies of the social structures that provided the context in which politics, artistic creation, and other human endeavors took place.

Development of the various historical fields has paralleled growing interest in certain periods of history. Nineteenth-century historiography, founded on the romanticists' reaction to the Enlightenment, took a striking interest in the medieval period. This interest contrasts sharply with the attitude of the Renaissance humanists and Enlightenment *philosophes* toward that period. The humanists had coined the phrase "Middle Ages" as a pejorative description of the long period of European history that separated them from the ancient world. The *philosophes* shared humanist attitudes toward the barbarism and superstition associated with medieval society. But nineteenth-century historians increasingly discovered that the origins of modern Europe were to be found in the medieval communities that succeeded to the power of Rome in the sixth century. In fact, chairs of modern history in English universities, founded in the mid-nineteenth century, are often held by medievalists, and today there are about eighty major centers of medieval studies in the United States. The structure of this book reflects this attitude by focusing attention on the life of the Middle Ages. Something more should be said about this emphasis.

While most Western civilization courses begin with ancient Israel or Mycenaean Greece, the social life of these ancient peoples is not, strictly speaking, relevant to the development of European society. The ancient Greeks lived in a different world—geographically, economically, and politically—from that of the European peoples whose social and economic institutions formed the basis for modern society. The societies of Greece and the ancient Near East were antecedents of European society, not part of the edifice itself. Although the impact of Roman social life on the development of European society was, of course, much greater than that of Greece, nonetheless, before Europe became a distinct civilization, its social and economic foundations were profoundly transformed by the Germanic invasions. The urban life of the Roman Empire virtually disappeared in the fifth and sixth centuries, and while most modern Italian cities were founded on the Roman *urbs,* the same cannot be said about those in other parts of Europe. In the rural areas also, the influx of Germans changed the nature of Roman society. The provincial nobility was replaced by Germans who occupied its position but lived very differently. The peasantry changed through intermarriage and cultural amalgamation.

The organization of this book directs attention to this medieval transformation of Western society. There are five broad chronological periods. The first deals with the ancient world, the next three with the medieval world, and the last with the Renaissance–Reformation period. In choosing articles for the first section, I have focused attention on those aspects of ancient life that had the greatest impact on the growth of Western society and culture. The emphasis on the Middle Ages, to which three sections are devoted, reflects my conviction that the developments of this long period were of fundamental importance in the formation of Western society. Selections on peasant life, travel, religious life, and the experiences of the elite form the core of these sections. The last part focuses on urban life, which became in the Renaissance–Reformation period the setter of social and cultural values.

In Part I, "The Ancient World," Willard Bascom's "Ancient Ships and Shipping" sets the foundation for understanding one of the most important aspects of Western civilization—its inescapable experience of and preoccupation with the sea. As for life on land, N. J. G. Pounds describes the physical characteristics of cities in the Roman Empire. In assessing the position of women in Roman society, Sarah B. Pomeroy provides a basic description of that society, as well as an example of how historians use the scanty remains of ancient civilization to construct a coherent historical account. The final two articles, which deal with the religious life of the ancient world, place Christianity in its historical context and show how it overcame obstacles to its acceptance by people of different cultures.

The selections in Part 2, "The Early Middle Ages," deal primarily with the history of social groups that evolved after the barbarian invasions. The first article focuses on the Germans—the barbarians themselves—and provides a basis for understanding important aspects of medieval social life and ideas. Georges Duby's "Peasants and the Agricultural Revolution" is about the formation of the medieval and early modern peasant classes. Robert Chazan's article on the Jews illuminates both the life of the Jews in northern Europe and the life of the early medieval cities. In the final selection, Joshua Prawer views upper-class society from a special perspective by examining the society of the knights who established the kingdom of Jerusalem at the end of the eleventh century.

Part 3, "The Peak of Medieval Civilization," deals with the life patterns underlying the flowering of medieval art, architecture, and intellectual life, as well as commerce and government. The first article describes the training of a knight, whose special skills made him both the protector and the scourge of medieval life. In the second piece, Margaret Labarge describes the real life of upper-class women and corrects many misconceptions about them that derive from literature and earlier historical studies. In the same section, Mary Martin McLaughlin describes the experiences of children along with the experiences of women in the primary parent role, as mothers. The third article deals with an aspect of this period not generally treated in historical works: road travel. Throughout the medieval period, travel by sea or waterway was the principal means of communication, but the development of European civilization required the expansion and increasing use of roads. In "Traveling the Roads in the Twelfth Century," Urban T. Holmes, Jr., graphically describes what such a journey was like. The remaining articles in Part 3 deal with religious life. Two of these reveal the quality of life in and the organization of the two orders of ecclesiastical society—clergy-men and monks. The last piece examines the Church's treatment of heretics and, at the same time, defines the relationship between the ecclesiastical hierarchy and ordinary Christians.

Part 4 covers the late medieval period, the fourteenth and fifteenth centuries. This was a period of pestilence and war, and the selections tell us much about these conditions. The first article analyzes the causes and characteristics of the widespread peasant uprisings, which occurred with increasing frequency and violence from the late thirteenth century on. The second selection takes us along with the participants in medieval warfare and reveals the reality of battle for the common soldier. Gerald Strauss' "Organization of the Late Medieval City" describes the laws regulating urban life. These regulations grew during the medieval period because of the increasing size and complexity of social and commercial activities as well as the continuing challenge to organized life posed by famine, war, and plague. In the third article, Guy F. Lytle examines a crucial period in the history of the university, a peculiarly medieval institution that has survived nearly intact into the modern world. He shows that the problem of finding jobs for university graduates is nothing new, and that a job crisis has always had the power—realized, in this instance, in the fourteenth century—of profoundly changing the structure of the university. The last article in this section picks up the thread of Willard Bascom's piece on ships and shipping in Part 1. It describes a pilgrimage by sea from Venice to the Holy Land and proves that a fifteenth-century traveler's experiences were similar to those of the travelers of ancient times.

The final section deals with the Renaissance–Reformation period, the sixteenth and seventeenth centuries. In his piece, Carlo Cipolla reminds us that the bubonic plague remained a serious threat throughout this period, and he describes the institutions of public health that developed to meet that threat. Natalie Z. Davis turns our attention to religious change and tries to assess the impact of the Reformation on the lives of individuals, particularly women. In "Cultural Patronage in Renaissance Florence," Gene Brucker examines an important aspect of the Italian Renaissance and tries to explain why the society of Florence attracted and supported this new culture more than any other city-state in Italy. Finally, James Bruce Ross gathers material on the patterns of child-rearing and parent-child relationships that prevailed in the Renaissance cities. The significance of the experience of childhood in an urban setting is very great, for just as the family life of the rural aristocracy set the standards for child-rearing and early socialization in the Middle Ages, the urban, middle-class family was the model for the Renaissance–Reformation world—and became the model for the modern world.

BIBLIOGRAPHY

For a history of the historian's discipline and the way its focus has changed, see Herbert Butterfield, *Man on His Past: The Study of the History of Historical Scholarship* (Cambridge, Eng., 1940). See also Fritz Stern, *The Varieties of History: From Voltaire to the Present* (Cleveland, 1956). Butterfield has critically evaluated the work of one major school of nineteenth-century historians in his *The Whig Interpretation of History* (London, 1931). His critique is reconsidered in E. H. Carr, *What Is History?* (New York, 1962). The great social historian Marc Bloch wrote an appraisal of his craft which was found among his papers and published as *The Historian's Craft* (New York, 1953). In 1971, two numbers of the periodical *Daedalus* were devoted to an assessment of the discipline and fields of history. See *Daedalus*, Vol. 100 (1971), Nos. 1–2.

Part 1

THE ANCIENT WORLD

5th Century B.C. - 5th Century A.D.

Detail from mausoleum of the Aterii family. Rome, c. 90 A.D.

The five selections in Part 1 focus on ancient Greece and Rome. At the beginning of the fifth century B.C., Greece was the center of Western civilization, extending its influence over the whole Mediterranean world. In the course of the century, Athens became the hub of a far-flung empire of city-states held together by its navy and by the action of huge numbers of commercial ships. Aligned against this maritime empire was the Peloponnesian League, a league of Greek cities led by Sparta. The cities in both these configurations possessed a great deal of cultural and economic homogeneity. This pan-Hellenism reflected the great importance of seafaring, for links between the Greek communities around the Mediterranean and Black seas were maintained through continuous communication by sea. In fact, the ancient world was a Mediterranean world because sea travel was one of its salient characteristics; some historians have explained the transition from the ancient to the medieval period as the result of the collapse of Mediterranean shipping. In the first article, Willard Bascom examines the character of the ships and shipping that played this important role.

During the fifth and fourth centuries B.C., the Romans were just emerging from the effects of long subjugation by Etruscan kings. As it developed, the Roman state paralleled the Greek city-state pattern, but it retained a distinctive quality of its own. The Romans were more conscious and proud of their agricultural origins, and their conception of civic virtue preserved the ideals of life in a community of independent farmers. The social and economic changes of the first century B.C.—which brought thousands of Romans into the city—were therefore extremely important in Roman history. They altered the nature of politics and life in the state, as N. J. G. Pounds, in the second article, shows.

In ancient biographies of the Roman emperors, their relations with women hold an important place. It is clear that some women exercised extraordinary behind-the-scenes power, but the sources tell us little about the normal conditions of women's life. In the third selection, Sarah B. Pomeroy successfully uses this scanty material as the basis for an evaluation of the place of women in Roman society. The selection not only adds much to our knowledge of this aspect of Roman life, but also reveals the problems historians have in trying to use ancient sources.

Histories of the late Roman Empire focus on the evidence of decline and disintegration of institutions and economic life. But decline was not the only pattern of change in the later empire. There were also profound religious changes that can only be characterized in terms of growth and expansion. Around the time of Christ, there was a great influx of new religions to Rome and the western provinces from the Near East. In Samuel Angus' "The Appeal and Practice of the Mystery Religions," these new religions are brought into focus, and their appeal to the population of the empire is discussed. The selection by William Chaney, "The Conversion of the Germans," examines another aspect of religious change in the late antique period. Christianity competed with other Mediterranean religions for the faith of the Roman populations. Yet if it was to become the dominant religion of the modern world, it had to succeed in converting the heirs of Roman power, the Germans, whose tribal culture was no fertile seedbed for a religion created for the needs of the empire's urban society.

BIBLIOGRAPHY

For a broad introduction to ancient seafaring, see Lionel Casson, *The Ancient Mariners* (New York, 1959), and *Ships and Seamanship in the Ancient World* (Princeton, 1971). For more specialized studies, see William Culican, *The First Merchant Venturers* (New York, 1966); W. L. Rodgers, *Greek and Roman Naval Warfare* (Annapolis, Md., 1964); George Bass, ed., *A History of Seafaring Based on Underwater Archaeology* (London, 1972).

For a general history of Roman society and cities, see the classic work of I. M. Rostovtzeff, *Social and Economic History of the Roman Empire*, 2nd ed., 2 Vols. (Oxford, 1957). On ancient cities, see A. Zimmern, *The Greek Commonwealth* (Oxford, 1911); R. E. Wycherley, *How the Greeks Built Cities* (London, 1949); and Raphael Sealey, *A History of the Greek City States, ca. 700–338 B.C.*, (Berkeley, 1976). A. H. M. Jones focuses on the Greek cities of the Roman Empire in *The Greek City* (Oxford, 1940). For western cities, see Russell Meiggs, *Roman Ostia* (Oxford, 1960); A. Boëthius, "Urbanism in Italy," *The Classical Pattern of Modern Western Civilization* (Copenhagen, 1958).

For the social context of the life of women in ancient Rome, see W. W. Fowler, *Social Life at Rome in the Age of Cicero* (New York, 1909), and Jerome Carcopino, *Daily Life in Ancient Rome* (New Haven, 1940). On women, see M. I. Finley, "The Silent Women of Rome," in *Aspects of Antiquity* (London, 1965), pp. 129–42, and J. P. V. D. Balsdon, *Roman*

Women (London, 1962). For a good brief introduction to Roman law, see Barry Nicholas, *An Introduction to Roman Law* (Oxford, 1962), and J. A. Crook, *Law and Life in Rome* (Ithaca, N.Y., 1967).

For background on the mystery religions, see W. W. Fowler, *The Religious Experience of the Roman People* (London, 1911); M. P. Nilsson, *A History of Greek Religion*, 2nd ed. (Oxford, 1949); and T. R. Glover, *The Conflict of Religions in the Early Roman Empire* (London, 1909). Samuel Angus' *The Mystery Religions and Christianity* (London, 1925) is the best work on the mystery cults. For the growth of Christianity, see Henry Chadwick, *The Early Church* (Harmondsworth, Eng., 1967). On the Christian movement in the Roman Empire, see Erwin R. Goodenough, *The Church in the Roman Empire* (New York, 1931); Harold Mattingly, *Christianity in the Roman Empire* (New York, 1967); and G. E. M. de Ste. Croix, "Why were the Early Christians Persecuted?" in the journal *Past and Present*, Vol. 26 (1963), pp. 6–38.

On the conversion of the Germans, see A. H. M. Jones, *Constantine and the Conversion of Europe*, rev. ed. (New York, 1962), and J. N. Hillgarth, ed., *The Conversion of Western Europe 350–750* (Englewood Cliffs, N.J., 1969).

Ancient Ships and Shipping

WILLARD BASCOM

Willard Bascom studies ancient ships with the eye of a professional oceanographer and amateur underwater archeologist. Seafaring skills and oceanographic knowledge are of primary importance in this historical study, for the men of Crete, Phoenicia, and Greece, and the sailors of Carthage, Rome, and medieval Europe wrote little about their sea trade or the technology that made it possible. To know something of this most important part of the economies, lifestyles, and politics of these peoples, we must know about their life on their sea, the Mediterranean "mare nostrum," our sea, as the Romans called it. While the ancient sailors left almost no records, the substructure underlying the myths and literature of the ancient world is plain only to those who are familiar with the ancient shipping routes, the places of refuge and of danger around the Mediterranean. The adventures of Jason and the Argonauts, for example, relate to the experiences of Greek sailors in the Black Sea. In the *Odyssey*, Homer makes the real world of the ancient mariners the geography of a symbolic journey toward self-knowledge and self-realization. Aeneas, the figure of Rome and the model Roman in Virgil's epic, arrived at his destiny in Italy by a route patterned on that of Odysseus, and the tests of the sea were universalized by Virgil, as they were by Homer, into the basic tests of every human life. If we jump many centuries and many cultures north, to the Germans, we see that seafaring remained a crucial aspect of life and the poetic vision of life. The mythic figures of Siegfried and Brunhild lived in a world in which land and sea were nearly equal parts, and Beowulf's world was similar. In the Icelandic sagas, a long spell of adventure on the sea was the final step in the maturation of a man before he assumed the burdens of marriage, fatherhood, and political life.

None of these observations about the importance of the sea and seafaring in literature is new to those who study the actual history of the ancient and medieval worlds. Since the middle of the nineteenth century, adventurers and archeologists have tried with substantial success to identify the Homeric and Germanic sea routes as well as those of even earlier peoples. Thor Heyerdahl is probably the best known of these explorers. But Bascom wants to shift our attention away from the re-creation of ancient sea voyages to the study of ancient ships themselves. He argues that modern recovery techniques, which he has had a great part in developing, will make the study of ancient ships more fruitful than ever before. His argument rests on two assertions. First, he points out that the ship, particularly the merchant ship that plied the Mediterranean routes for months on end, was a microcosm of society. The sailors took with them all the necessaries of life: food, implements, and portable pastimes. Thus recovery of a downed ship should reveal more about the daily life of its particular civilization than any but the most remarkable and extensive excavations on land. Second, he argues that wrecks retrieved from deep water will produce by far the best archeological evidence for the study of ancient civilizations—and that the wrecks are there, in the hundreds if not the thousands. Recent advances in underwater archeology have all been concentrated on shallow-water excavations, where wave action and coastline changes—as weather, earthquakes, and the results of political change do on land—have destroyed or dismantled much of what was once there. At greater depths, where the water is still and marine life sparse or nonexistent for lack of oxygen, ships containing a veritable catalogue of Mediterranean civilization from the Bronze Age, the first great age of seafaring, to the sixteenth century wait to be lifted from the ocean floor. Bascom's book is intended to introduce students of the premodern world to the new techniques of sea recovery and to argue for a program that will put this technology into operation. His survey of what we already know about ancient ships and shipping is part of that argument.

The earliest known picture of seagoing warships was carefully carved on the tomb of a Pharaoh named Sahure in 2450 B.C.—two hundred years after Pharaoh Sneferu's forty ships brought cedars from Lebanon in the first recorded sea trade. The tomb drawing showed a fleet of troop transports carrying the Pharaoh's soldiers to some port in Asia. The ships look to be over thirty meters long, propelled by oars as well as sails. Obviously, they were the product of long years of development.

During the second millennium B.C., the people of the Aegean showed their strength at sea. The Minoans of Crete built a very high level of civilization, with cities and palaces that show no signs of defensive works. One explanation is that they relied on the same kind of "wooden walls" the oracle recommended to the Greeks during the Persian war a thousand years later. These wooden walls were fighting ships, ready to defend the island against all intruders. Thucydides wrote that "Minos is the first to whom tradition ascribes the possession of a Navy." According to Lionel Casson, "Their bold programs of overseas exploration and colonization, their far flung trade and their unwalled cities presupposes the existence of a great fleet." About 1500 B.C., the

Minoan culture seems to have suddenly disintegrated. One hypothesis is that the great sea wave from the explosion of the volcano at Santorin wiped out the defending warships on the beaches and in the harbors along the northern coast. At any rate, by 1450 B.C. the fleet that had maintained order was gone and the chaos of sea raiders prevailed.

The Mycenaean Greeks then moved across the narrow channel from the Peleponnesus in strength and took over Crete, its colonies, and its commerce. Presumably they used warships, or at least troop transports, and readily subdued the Minoans, who were unprepared for land war. Mycenaean sea power rose quickly but faded in a few hundred years, leaving little trace. We do not know what their ships looked like; the record of those ships, if it exists, is on the sea floor.

As the Mycenaean grip on the seas began to slip, the rovers and pirates of Lycia (in southwestern Asia Minor) and the nearby isles—presumably Cyprus, Rhodes, and the Cyclades—banded together and formed raiding parties that swept the shores of the eastern Mediterranean. These rovers were contemporaries with the ones who became known as the "Sea Peoples," whose great, final sea battle with Ramses III, in 1194 B.C., is recorded in considerable detail on a famous relief at Medinet Habu, in the Nile delta. Ramses won decisively, apparently by some ruse, and now the Mediterranean stage was set for the Phoenicians.

One thinks of the Phoenicians as explorers and traders, which they certainly were, but they also seem to have been largely responsible for many early developments in fighting ships. In order to maintain their famous coastal cities (Sidon, Tyre, Byblos) against raiders, as well as protect their merchantmen, the Phoenicians must have had a considerable navy. Certainly, they ventured to distant, unfriendly shores and dominated the eastern Mediterranean from 1100 to 800 B.C., although few details of their ships of that period are known. Later, in the fifth century, they minted coins showing fighting ships that were equivalent to those of the Greeks.

The first Greek ships of which we have a reasonably clear picture are the ones described by the poet Homer in the eighth century B.C. He told of the galleys of the Trojan War, in the Bronze Age, several hundred years earlier. The ships he described seem to have been a combination of those traditionally associated with Jason's Argonauts and the ships Homer saw about him. They were penteconters, long and slender, swift and black, painted with pitch except for the bow eyes. Such ships would have been about twenty meters long, low in the water and undecked. They were similar to, but probably less graceful than, the Viking ships of two thousand years later. They were built either for trading or raiding, as suited the captain's fancy. Such ships must have been light and strong, to permit frequent beachings and occasional portage. The rowing crew was fifty men, half on each side, one oar per man, and one steering oar on each side of the stern. There were also a mast and sail that could readily be stepped and rigged if there were a following wind. The crew would haul in on the forestays, raising the mast into its slot and tightening the backstay. Then they would hoist the single cross yard. The sail was square, probably of linen patches sewn checkerboard fashion between strengthening leather thongs, and supported from the yard, against which it was furled. The sail was raised and lowered by a series of lines called brails that looped around the foot, or bottom of the sail, so that it could be shortened by gathering it upward to the wooden yard, somewhat like a venetian blind.

Because the wind was contrary much of the time, the ship was often rowed. One such ship became known as the "hundred-handed giant of the Aegean"—a very apt description of fifty men rowing—not at all the mythical monster portrayed by some romantic artists. The ship would have been about wide enough to allow two men to sleep end to end on each rowing bench. With such accommodations, it is no wonder they preferred to go ashore every night to sleep on some soft beach where they could forage for food and build fires. Warships were not intended for good living even though the men that crewed them were sea rovers and adventurers used to rough conditions. Provisions, water in goatskin bags, and weapons were stowed under the benches. It must have been a hard life.

The oars were about four meters long and were levered against thole pins (vertical wooden pins that serve as lever points for the oars), being secured there by leather straps so that when the men dropped them to fight or to handle the sail the oars would not slide off and drift away. The steering oars, operated from the short, raised afterdeck, were also partly supported by leather thongs. Perhaps there was a sternpost, against which the steersman could brace himself. Because these ships were so low in the water, there may also have been a low rail along the sides to which some kind of a temporary screen of cloth or leather could be rigged—much as the Norsemen used shields two thousand years later to keep out the wind, the blown spray, and small waves. . . .

Most warships, from earliest times until after the battle of Lepanto, in 1571, were galleys. They were driven by men's muscles, pulling on oars. Although most fighting ships of early times carried masts and sails for long passages at sea, sails were not dependable enough for fighting. Men were much better-disciplined than the wind.

Most of the naval engagements of the ancient world were probably fought within a mile or so of shore. This is because the ships were essentially land-based fighting tools. They were manned by soldiers and commanded by generals. In fights between ships, ordinary swords, missiles, and spears were used and the tactics were like those on land. The soldiers slept and ate on shore, drawing the ship up on a sandy beach every night, stern first, ready to shove off in a hurry to do battle. On long cruises, headed for some distant rendezvous with an enemy fleet, they tended to follow the shore lines and stay within sight of land rather than strike off across the sea. When they sailed, they could only run before the wind or with it on the beam, because of the flat-bottomed hull and square sail.

Doubtless, there were numerous times when these early warships had to cross wide passages out of sight of land—either rowing or under sail—and this they did only when necessary and always with trepidation. When King Nestor and his men returned to Greece from the Trojan War, in about 1200 B.C., he directly crossed the Aegean from Lesbos to Euboea, a distance of a hundred and ten miles, instead of the customary flitting from island to island for nightly camp-outs. At three knots, even on a somewhat zigzag course, this risky voyage took less than two days, but the expedition members were so pleased to reach the new shore safely they made a great sacrifice to Zeus. This episode unwittingly reveals quite a bit about the dangers to warships at sea in the Bronze Age. Since Nestor's courage is undoubted, there must have been a very bad record of ship losses, perhaps caused by the sudden violent winds and poor stability, to have made him so concerned. Possibly he wasn't certain about which direction to take, or he thought the sky would be cloudy and obscure the stars so he could not navigate, or he thought his boats had too little freeboard to survive a storm. Clearly, Nestor and his associates thought their open penteconters (which probably were loaded with booty and souvenirs) had a good chance of sinking as they crossed the deep water headed for home. Perhaps some did.

There are certain difficulties in training a large crew of men to row a ship. Anyone who has watched naval cadets rowing whaleboats, or crewmen from a large passenger liner practice with lifeboats in a quiet harbor, has an inkling of the problem. Those are small craft with six to twelve rowers. Until the crew has had considerable practice, there is a great likelihood of "catching a crab" (the oar not digging deeply enough into the water and suddenly skittering along the surface when the power stroke is carelessly applied) or getting out of synchronization and tangling oars. In larger ships, with hundreds of rowers, it would be difficult to keep all the rowers in good health and a high state of training; there must have been many "crabs," bumped oars, and other foul-ups. Certainly a lot of practice was required to co-ordinate the actions of hundreds of men so that they rowed effectively in unison. The rowers had to learn to start and stop quickly, and to turn the ship in its own length by packing down on one side and pulling ahead on the other. But, in warships, they rowed as though their lives depended on it. Which they did.

War upon the sea in the early days, once it had developed beyond the stage of looting and taking slaves from coastal cities, had as its ultimate objective the control of sea-borne commerce. Piracy was the first step, but control of the trade routes and the establishment of colonies by a formal military machine were vital to expansion. The sea was the most convenient highway of the irregularly shore-lined Mediterranean, and the destruction of the ships of a city-state could cut off its food supplies and its colonies. The need for greater speed and power in sea battles led to the development of several new rowing schemes: several men on each oar, oars of different lengths on one slanted bench, and a second tier of oars mounted on the fighting deck above. The latter type of ship, the bireme, improved the speed without increasing the length or width.

Sometime in the ninth century B.C., the ram was invented. This led almost immediately to the development of the *triere*, or trireme as it is popularly known.

The trireme was a three-banked warship made specifically for fighting with the ram. It was a fast ship because it was slender and yet carried many more rowers than previous ships. This was made possible by the use of an outrigger beam to hold tholepins a bit above and outboard of the upper deck level. This arrangement permitted an entire new bank of rowers to be added without requiring longer oars or widening the hull. With this outrigger beam serving as an oar fulcrum, the oars of the upper rowers could reach out over the two banks of oars below. Now, using a one-man one-oar scheme, it was possible to add thirty-one men on each side (top row only—there were twenty-seven men in each of the other rows) and give the ship an additional ten horsepower of driving force. All oars were the same length, and the men were arranged in rows on half levels so that each bank of oars was at its most effective height. It was also necessary to position the oars so the individual rowers were not exactly one above the other. They were staggered a little so that each man (and each oar) had maximum space. One has to visualize the oar positions and motions in three dimensions for the diagrams to make sense. An additional advantage of increasing the number of rowers in the same length of ship was that this design also increased the number of fighters that could be quickly brought to bear on the enemy. The outrigger beam also squared up the deck shape with a sort of fence that held protective shields.

One limitation on going further with the idea of more oars upward and outward was ship stability—the extra weight high above the slim hull would have made it top-heavy. If there were a rush of armed men to one side to engage the enemy, such a ship would heel sharply and perhaps capsize.

Greek oared ships were carefully constructed and were much admired for their craftsmanship. The wood used for hull planking was mainly oak and poplar, often as much as eight centimeters (three inches) thick, carvel-fitted. This means the planks were joined edge to edge and held there by the mortise-and-tenon system of rectangular cavities with fitted pegs. The planks were also nailed to reinforcing ribs so the structure was secured together in two ways and would not fly apart on ramming or flex and leak after beaching. To make sure that the planks held together, it was customary to tie them together before a battle with several sets of girding cables which went completely around the ship. Before these came into use, many a ramming must have sunk the rammer as well as the intended victim.

The development of the ram reached its peak when the Athenians decided to put emphasis on a ship that would depend mainly on skillful ship handling. The ship itself, instead of the soldiers aboard, became the weapon. If it could be maneuvered to ram and sink an enemy ship, this would save much of the trouble of hand-to-hand fighting and war would be less personal.

There was real significance in the shift of strategy from trying to kill the enemy's men to that of trying to kill his ships. This had much the same kind of effect on naval warfare that the first cannon had much later. No one could ignore the new threat, and all navies began to build triremes.

Triremes were built ruggedly—able to ram or to survive ramming and, after repair, to fight another day. On many occasions, triremes were holed and capsized but remained afloat. The next day, they were towed ashore to be repaired and used again.

A good deal is known about the Greek trireme because, as the leading kind of warship for several hundred years, it was repeatedly described by historians, painted on vases, and sculptured in bas-reliefs. Unfortunately, these pictures are invariably a side view of the bow or stern of the ship and no complete representation has survived. As a result, no one knows exactly how the men were arranged or what a complete trireme looked like. The artists found that if all men and oars were shown there was too much detail, so it was customary to draw many of the oars but only a few men—and those greatly oversized.

We know what the three banks of rowers were named: thranites had the uppermost and most tiring position, zygites were between decks, and thalamites were in the lowest position (with their oars just above the water). We also know the size of Athenian triremes, because the foundations of the boathouses and launchways are still in existence. Visitors to Piraeus today can peer in basement windows on the harbor drive and see remnants of the slipways that once held these ships. Based on their size and configuration, the triremes that used them must have had flat bottoms and could not have been longer than forty meters or wider than seven. The records of the shipyard that built them, carved on stone tablets, were found lining a Piraeus storm sewer a few years ago. They list the exact amount of equipment issued to the ships: size and quantity of oars, anchors, sails, and line.

Although there must have been many varieties and sizes of triremes, most authorities agree that one set of dimensions and number of rowers predominated. The standard trireme of 500 B.C. was about thirty-five meters long, three and a half meters in the beam (five, including the outriggers) with a loaded draft of one meter and about 1.2 meters of freeboard. This meant these ships were very long and slender (fineness of 10:1), which is necessary for speed. In fact, they must have been much like an oversize racing shell, since they were light enough to be launched and dragged ashore by their crews.

The lowest oars were only about half a meter above the water line, so the hole where they penetrated the hull was sealed by a leather bag which could be bound to the oar to keep the water out. These ships had 170 rowers, each pulling an oar about 4.2 meters long. This arrangement, which permitted the use of short, standard-length oars, made the trireme a convenient ship to operate. The idea of standardized oar length for large numbers of ships suggests that somewhere there must have been a substantial production line turning out matched, interchangeable oars.

Each man was responsible for his own equipment: sword, shield, oar, and seat cushion. Sun awnings and spray shields were part of the ship's equipment, intended to keep the men as comfortable as possible.

Nearly every night, the ships were drawn up on some beach and drain plugs pulled to release the bilge water and keep the bottom planks from becoming soggy and rotten. Because the ships were light and slim, there was no way for the men to remain aboard; besides, very small amounts of stores and water were carried. This also meant that when away from their regular bases the crews had to forage for food and find entertainment; presumably, this often meant seizure and rape.

Although triremes were meant to be rowed in battle, each ship had a mast and sail that were used when there was a considerable distance to go and a wind on the stern quarter. If a battle was expected, the bulky mast and sail were left on shore. In fact, it was so much the custom for early warships to leave the sails and masts ashore, that carrying them into battle, even though they were stowed below, was regarded as a sign of cowardice, since it implied the intention to leave the battle early. Mark Antony's decision to take sails along into the great naval battle at Actium, in which he and Cleopatra VII were defeated by Octavian, is said to have demoralized his forces and contributed to his losing that battle.

The circumstances of life in the trireme fleet were not at all like most people imagine. First of all, the rowers of ancient Greece were all free men—never slaves—and no whips were used. Stroke beat was kept by a flutist, probably because the high-frequency tootling was easy to hear above the rumble and splash of the oars. Rowers who were not soldiers were well paid, with extra pay for the men who pulled the uppermost, thranite oars, where the work was hardest and the danger greatest.

Triremes were not good sea boats; in fact, they were unusable in heavy weather and a great many more were lost in storms than in battle. They were so susceptible to loss in bad weather that they rarely operated in the winter months.

Historians have noted that for one reason or another pairs of galleys were sometimes lashed together and a single sail was hoisted. On some occasions, this may have been a ruse to make the enemy think he had half as many ships to deal with. However, it seems possible this was intended to improve stability, since each hull would prevent the other from rolling over. In time, this technique may have evolved into the catamaran warships that Professor Casson has postulated.

TABLE 5.   Examples of Warship Losses in Battles and Storms

Year B.C.	Combatants		Location	Number of Ships Involved	Number of Ships Lost
	Winner	Loser			
535	Phoceans	Carthaginians and Etruscans	Corsica	180	100
480	Greeks	Persians	Salamis	1300	200
419	Syracuse	Athens	Harbor of Syracuse		350
333	Alexander	Tyre	Tyre Harbor	260	45
322	Macedonia	Athens	Amorgos (Sporades)	400	
306	Greeks	Egypt	Salamis, Cyprus		80
260	Rome	Carthage	Mylae	250	50
256	Rome	Carthage	Ecnomus	680	54
255	Rome	Carthage	Cape Hermaeum (storm)	620	284
255	Rome	Carthage	Camorina, Sicily		250
249	Rome	Carthage	Battle at Carthage and storm at Camorina	2 fleets	80
241	Rome	Carthage	Aegates Islands, Sicily	200	50
230	Rome	Illian pirates	Turkish straits	200	90
42	Agrippa	Sextus	Naulochus, Sicily	600	60
31	Octavian	Antony and Cleopatra	Actium, Gulf of Corinth	900	100

Another action that was taken to prevent these long ships from capsizing was to add ballast. Ballast may not always have been used on fighting triremes, but it was certainly used on troop transports and heavier galleys that were not intended to be drawn up on the beach. The ballast was usually in the form of sand or gravel carried in boxes in the bilges that could be removed separately to lighten the ship. Wet-sand ballast was used to keep wine jugs safe and cool as well as improve the ship's stability.

This is significant to the archaeologist. Unballasted wooden ships built for maneuvering and ramming would be "sunk" only in the sense they would fill with water and become unusable. Probably, the hulk would remain awash until it drifted ashore, was towed away, or became waterlogged and sank. But with ballast aboard, in addition to the weight of provisions in jugs, the ship fittings, the arms and armor, missiles for catapults, and souvenirs or booty from the enemy, there was a good chance a warship would go to the bottom immediately, taking these fascinating artifacts with it.

In the fourth century B.C., an arms race began when the city of Syracuse developed *tetreres* ("four-rowed" ships) to beat the Athenian *trieres* (or triremes). Although the changes in ship design came slowly at first, soon every navy in the ancient world was involved in building "fives," "eights," "tens," "thirteens," and so on up to a "forty." It is a marvelously intricate story of shifting naval power and how it was applied through great fleets of rowed ships. Ship weight, power, and stability increased at the expense of speed and convenience. Ramming became less important and instead battles were fought with catapults that flung rocks and arrows. Once again, ships grappled with each other and the rowers engaged in hand-to-hand fighting. Ptolemy II of Egypt eventually built the most powerful fleet in ancient times, which included four "thirteens," fourteen "elevens," thirty "nines," thirty-seven "sevens," and seven "fives." Unfortunately, we do not know what those numbers signify, because the exact meaning of the ending "eres," or "rowed," is lost. Presumably it is some combination of the number of tiers of oars and men on an oar.

Eventually the race subsided. After the battle of Actium, in 31 B.C., Rome ruled the Mediterranean and once again used triremes in its home fleet. In the course of the various struggles for power, especially that between Rome and Carthage, thousands of these ships were sunk. An estimate is that five thousand warships went down in deep water in ancient times. If one can be found, many of the above questions can probably be answered. . . .

Less is known about the merchant ships of the ancient world than about the warships, although there were a great many more of them. They were the slow, solid workhorses of the sea; "round ships," they were called, to distinguish them from the slender fighting craft, which were the "long ships." The fate of nations hung on how well each kind of ship did its job, but the glamorous warships were the better recorded. Information on the merchant ships that carried the trade goods cheaply and slowly from port to port is very sketchy. The appearance of seagoing merchant ships in the sixth century B.C. is known because one unusually fine Greek black-figured bowl was carefully illustrated with two scenes of a pirate ship chasing and preparing to board a merchantman. In the first scene, the unsuspecting trading ship rides high in the water with the sail on its single mast mostly reefed. Beamy and slow compared to the sleek and menacing pirate galley, it is an easy prize, idling along with a single crewman manning the steering oars. The large, rectangular opening into the cargo hold takes up most of the deck space, and its high rim rises above the deck level to keep waves sloshing over the deck from reaching the cargo below. The sides of the cargo hatch show a pattern that seems to be lashings that hold down a covering tarpaulin. Aft of the helmsman, on the upcurved sternpost, there is the customary short ladder to be used by men to get off and on a beached or anchored ship. Another ladder-like structure, which runs the length of the ship, was probably used as a gangplank for carrying cargo from ship to shore.

In the second scene, the trader's crew has became aware they are an intended victim; the sail is down, filled with wind, pulling. But the merchant-man cannot keep ahead of a pirate craft using both sails and oars. Probably the rest of the trader's crew are below, praying and getting weapons ready. Their life expectancy is short, or at least unhappy, because the pirates will likely make slaves of any who survive the takeover. . . .

Because changes in ship design have traditionally come slowly, this simple hull and sail design remained in use for many centuries. Although no good drawings of the trading ships used for the next five centuries have survived, in the first century A.D. similar vessels are portrayed by Roman artists in paintings on house walls, mosaics at Pompeii, and bas-reliefs in stone. They are still beamy and round, steered with a pair of oars, and have a single, large mainsail supplemented with a smaller sail farther forward. Their afterdeck was a little higher, the over-all size was often larger, but the appearance and sail-handling methods were about the same.

No doubt, a sailor of 500 B.C. could have stepped aboard a ship built six hundred years later and unhesitatingly sailed it to its next port. He would check out the rigging, noting that the mainsail hung from a yard made of a pair of saplings whose butts were lashed together. The top of the sail would be securely bound to the yard with twine made of esparto grass, and its foot on each side would be bound to lines (the mainsheets) that came back to be secured to chocks within the helmsman's reach. By adjusting the length of the lines, hauling in the lee sheet, and slackening the windward one, a lone sailor could set the sail on a small ship. As the ship came to anchor or if a storm threatened, the mariners aboard would shorten sail, raising it by means of brail lines. The free end of these lines was secured to a transverse bar, also convenient to the steersman; the other end went up over the top of the yard, loosely down in front of the sail, and up behind the sail to be secured to the yard. By shortening these brail lines, the sail could be crumpled upward against the yard.

Steering by means of a pair of nearly vertical steering oars, one on each side of the stern, was the standard method throughout ancient times. These oars were supported in pairs of sockets by leather thongs so that they need only be rotated about their own axes to exert a rudder-like effect. At a convenient height, a short "tiller" bar projected from each oar at right angles so that the helmsman could easily twist the oar in its socket. To steer left (to port), he would push the tiller bar in his right hand ahead and pull back on the one in his left (the bars were always moved in opposite directions to keep the oar blades parallel). This gave a lot of rudder surface and was probably quite convenient. Moreover, it was a good thing to have a second rudder so the ship was not out of control if one oar snapped or the guides holding it in place gave way.

In order to ease the forces acting on the rudder, many early sailing ships carried a small sail forward on a steep bowsprit. This spritsail, or *artemon*, was used to keep the ship from yawing—sliding sidewise and forward down the face of an overtaking wave into a dangerous position. Since these ships sailed well only when running before the wind, the pull of the *artemon* kept the bow ahead of the ship. Probably it was the only sail used during storms, since it would keep the vessel from getting sidewise to the wind and waves and being overwhelmed by a breaking wave. In any case, it made the helmsman's job an easier one.

Another common feature was the boarding ladder, which shows in many of the old drawings of both war and merchant ships. These ladders enabled the men to climb aboard when the ship was on the beach or in the shallows close to it. It was carried at the stern (which is logical, since ships beached their rounded after-ends first) and secured at its midpoint to the upswept sternpost. If a ladder was properly balanced, it could easily be swung down, used, and pushed up out of the way again.

Merchantmen also used long, ladder-like walkways for loading and unloading cargo. Significantly these are not shown on the ships after harbors with vertical stone piers came into use and a ship could tie up alongside and load or unload directly. But, in the days when cargoes were transferred across the beaches at the heads of small bays, the ship was securely moored just off the beach in very shallow water and the ladder was used as a bridge.

Like the warships, merchant vessels were beached for repair during the winter months. The bottoms were scraped to clean off the sea growth and then charred by holding blazing faggots against them to reduce marine-borer attack. The most seriously damaged planks were replaced. Teredos, the wooden hulls' worst enemy, took a heavy toll of ship bottoms that were not sheeted with lead beneath the water line. The lead was usually secured with copper tacks over a sealing fabric that was soaked in pitch or tar. If water became trapped between the lead sheeting and the planking, the wood would rot where it could not be seen, weakening the hull and sometimes causing it to break up in a storm. The results could be as bad as if borers had been there.

Many ancient ships were coated with tar and pitch and painted with colored wax to seal small holes and protect the wood against deterioration. Although the hulls were usually black from the tar, they often had bright-colored eyes and sternposts; red, violet, and gold seem to have been favored for superstructure decoration. Sails of linen or leather were sometimes assembled from multicolored patches or painted with symbols. . . .

The number of ships in use in ancient times that could have sunk along the trade routes is of great interest to the archaeologist. Fred Yallouris, a native of the island of Chios and student of classics, estimated how many ships had been in use in ancient times as follows: "The life-span of the merchant ship must have been around 40 years. The numbers we have suggest that in the fifth and fourth centuries B.C., well over 30,000 merchant ships of all sizes could have been built. Allowing for a lower building rate in the tenth to sixth centuries B.C., say 45,000, and an increase in the third to first centuries B.C., say 80,000, we arrive at an amazing 155,000 as the approximate number of merchant ships that sailed from 1000 B.C. to the beginning of the Christian era. If we were to extend our period of interest to include all the ships which sailed from the fourth millennium B.C. down to about 500 A.D., and also include warships, then that number could easily reach half a million."

Almost every port had some type of shipbuilding activity, but the larger ports, with greater merchant and naval fleets, dominated ship construction. We know that Tyre, Piraeus, Rhodes, Corinth, Alexandria, and Rome were great shipbuilding centers, but we do not know how many ships they produced. However, there are data on the docking capacity of some ports. Piraeus had, by 331 B.C., 372 docks in its three basins and could accommodate hundreds of ships, as could the harbors at Syracuse, Carthage, Rhodes, Alexandria, and the ports of Rome. The capacities of medium-sized ports such as Chios, Samos, Smyrna, Miletus, Antioch, Sidon, Tyre, Massilia, and Cyrene probably ranged from fifty to a hundred and fifty ships. The hundreds of smaller ports could probably harbor from twenty to fifty vessels.

There must have been close to four hundred ports in the Mediterranean by the end of the fourth century B.C. The average capacity of all these was probably around forty ships. Assuming that an average port was filled to about half capacity every night in the sailing season, we might reckon that from eight to ten thousand merchant ships could have been in use on the Mediterranean and the Black seas throughout the fifth and fourth centuries. The number could well have reached fifteen thousand at the height of Rome's commercial activities in the second and first centuries. . . .

Navigation must have been a serious problem for the early mariners. Although the development of navigational know-how cannot be traced precisely, we know that by the end of the fifth century B.C. most of the techniques that sailors would use for the next two thousand years were known. Of the later tools, only the magnetic compass was missing. Mainly, the early ships must have navigated by dead reckoning combined with the captain's memory.

Dead reckoning simply means that the skipper keeps track of the ship's course, its speed, and the elapsed time. From these data, he calculates how far the ship has gone and in which direction. For old sailing ships, which followed the wind and did not have a compass, a clock, or a good chart, the answer must have been, at best, a rough approximation. But perhaps because Mediterranean sailing distances are not great, the ancient mariners found their way fairly well. After years of apprenticeship, a sailor would learn the routes and how best to sail each leg of a voyage in each season. He would judge the ship's speed by tossing chips of wood overside and set its direction relative to the sun or stars if he could see them.

The knowledge of how and where to sail through the complex islands of the Aegean or across the Mediterranean to another country was largely kept in the captain's head. This special knowledge was his job security, and probably he did not want it written down so that someone else could replace him. On voyages of exploration, when new trading partners for valuable commodities were being located, the courses and distances were carefully guarded strategic secrets. At times, Phoenician vessels were followed by the ships of other countries eager to find where they traded for rare products. It is said that on more than one occasion Phoenician captains deliberately ran their ships through very dangerous waters and sometimes wrecked them in order to wreck the following ship or at least throw it off the track. Their country reimbursed them for the loss when they finally made it home.

By the fourth century B.C., a geographer named Scylax the Younger wrote a book (the Periplus), which gave the first published sailing directions for the Mediterranean. It contained the names of ports, rivers, and headlands, directions and distances from point to point, where to get water, and other useful information. Any charts of that time that may have existed were probably lost in the fires at the library of Alexandria in 47 B.C. and A.D. 640, or disintegrated over the ages.

Although there is virtually nothing in ancient literature that can tell us how many ships were lost at sea, there is no doubt that shipwrecks were a common phenomenon in antiquity. The Romans developed a code of maritime laws that eventually grew into a compendium called the Rhodian sea laws. It regarded pirates, fire, and wreck as the three normal maritime dangers, and had laws concerning all three. Three kinds of pirates were described: ". . . those who attack the merchantmen in open sea or lurk for them in harbors. Secondly there are the land-robbers, who cut a ship's cables or steal its anchors, or snap up a merchant or passenger or sailor who happens to go on land. Thirdly, there are the wreckers, and these do not merely plunder ships which have been driven ashore, but sometimes lure them to destruction by displaying false lights."

The danger of fire on board was always present. Although there is no way of ascertaining how many ships were lost in this way, it is evident from the strict laws regarding fires on board ship that loss of ship by fire was quite common.

Shipwreck was the usual way to lose a ship, however, and the sea laws discuss running aground, breaking up on the rocks, collision with other ships, seams opening up, and foundering in open water. A few excerpts from the sea laws will be of interest.

No. 28: "If a ship is hindered in the loading by a merchant or partner, and the time fixed for loading passes, and it happens the ship is lost by reason of piracy or fire or wreck, let him who caused the hindrance make good the damage."

No. 26: "If a ship in sail runs against another ship which is lying at anchor or has slackened sail, and it is day, all the damage shall be charged to the captain and those who are on board. Moreover let the cargo too come into contribution. If this happens at night, let the man who slackened sail light a fire. If he has no fire, let him shout. If he neglects to do this and a disaster takes place, he has himself to thank for it, if the evidence goes to this. . . ."

No. 45: "If in the open sea a ship is overset or destroyed, let him who brings anything from it safe to land receive instead of reward, the fifth part of that which he saves."

Cities of the Roman Empire

N. J. G. POUNDS

Cities were the focal points of ancient civilization, and, in fact, the term *civilization* is derived from the Latin *civitas,* meaning "city." Alexander the Great established and secured his empire by building Greek cities throughout its vast territories. Even the Romans, whose ancient social and political values derived from agricultural life, understood the advantage of using the city as a unit of organized political life. Like Alexander, they controlled conquered territories by enlarging existing towns and building new ones. These cities became both the centers of administration and the means of romanization, by which the leading class of subject peoples were tied to the imperial state. Even when they were developing a province as a grain-producing area, the Romans used the city as a basic unit of social and economic, as well as political, organization. In North Africa, they built hundreds of cities, of which the great majority were really just small rural towns made cities by legal definition. This type of agricultural development contrasts greatly with that undertaken in various parts of the United States, for example, where the farm has been the unit of agricultural production and rural life.

The cities built by Alexander and by the Romans were, in a sense, mass produced. Those founded by Alexander reflected an ideal of the *polis,* the Greek city-state; Roman foundations also had a regular plan. Rome itself was irregular, the center of the Mediterranean empire, whither, as Tacitus said, "all that is monstrous flows and finds a ready welcome." The city was a great, bustling emporium of goods and ideas, with a large population of foreigners. It was the largest and most varied city in the ancient world, and thus, although it served in the empire as a model city, no other city was really quite like it. In the following selection, N. J. G. Pounds describes the city in both of its aspects, as a typical and as a unique place.

Roman towns and town planning. The cities of the Empire offer a contrast between the extremes of orderly planning and the utmost urban confusion. Both aspects had been present in Italy from its earliest urban development.

From *An Historical Geography of Europe 450 B.C.–A.D. 1330* by N. J. G. Pounds (Cambridge University Press, 1973), pp. 123–32. Reprinted by permission of the author and Cambridge University Press.

Whether derived from Etruria or from the hellenised cities of the south, the idea of a planned lay-out was disseminated by the army and regularly employed in its camps. From the fourth century B.C. Greek concepts of planning began to infiltrate the Italian world. Whether directly or through the medium of soldiers' camps and veterans' *coloniae*, the idea of basing a city's plan on two streets crossing at right angles gained ground. Pompeii was one of the earliest non-Greek cities to be laid out on the basis of straight streets intersecting at right angles. Nevertheless, even if we deny that the old Italic cities—among which Rome must be counted—were planned, we have to admit, in Boëthius' words "not only a general disposition to discipline but also . . . explicit features in those untidy cities which suggested regular planning."

But only government could establish and maintain a planned development in a city. The *coloniae*, established in the first instance for veterans, seem always to have had a grid-iron pattern, but planning all too frequently ended when the governmental control was lifted. At *Alba Fucens*, near the Fucine Lake in central Italy, the centre of the city has a regular plan, but the outer area is irregular and conceptually independent of the original *coloniae*. Many similar examples can be found among the north Italian cities, notably Verona, Piacenza and Pavia, of the breakdown of planning beyond the limits of the original *colonia*.

Beyond Italy and the Mediterranean coastlands, the planned lay-out of cities was sufficiently widespread to be regarded as normal. Here, of course, the cities were founded *ab initio* by the Roman government and usually on virgin sites. The grid-iron plan was general, and is today recognisable in cities as widely separated as Cordoba and Ljubljana; Nîmes and York. In general, the Roman plan survives most completely in southern Europe, where there was a more marked continuity of settlement. In northern Europe, where the cities may have been temporarily abandoned or even destroyed, the former street pattern has been distorted and even obliterated. The street patterns of *Venta Icenorum* (Caistor-by-Norwich) and of Silchester, which were abandoned in the fifth century and never re-occupied, have been almost wholly recovered, whereas that of Trier, re-occupied after the Germanic invasions, has been very largely lost.

City buildings varied greatly in style and in their density per unit area. The Italic cities were closely built. Along their streets, often narrow and winding, were *tabernae*, rooms with wide openings, combining the functions of door and window, facing onto the street. These were the shops and the workshops of those craftsmen, who were accustomed to work under the eye of the public they served. Only a little altered through eighteen centuries, *tabernae* continue to characterise the older quarters of Naples and other Italian cities. Ruined but ossified, the *tabernae* of the first two centuries A.D. can still be seen at Pompeii, Herculaneum and Ostia. They were built of masonry; sometimes they served as living as well as working quarters: usually they opened into another room in the rear, and wherever the pressure of population on the limited space made it necessary, a second floor was added. It is doubtful whether Italian town buildings often ran to more than two storeys; the monstrous tenement blocks described by the Italian writers are not known outside Rome and Ostia. But it seems likely that, at least in the larger towns, there was an attempt to concentrate the working population near the centre, and the price of this was, of course, apartment blocks.

Local stone was generally used, and Italy fortunately had no lack of travertine, tufa and limestone. It was, however, the introduction of lime-mortar in place of clay that permitted the addition of a second floor to town houses. Even so, urban architecture took grave structural risks and was often none too secure. During the second century the use became widespread of a cement construction, faced with bricks, usually set diagonally in the style known as *opus reticulatum*. This mode of building, which was durable, water-proof and immune to fire, was just beginning at Pompeii on the eve of its destruction; it was at the height of its popularity in the age of the Antonines, and is best seen in the second-century work in Ostia.

Despite the congestion which existed in many towns, especially the Italian, there was space for large houses, on an *atrium* plan and inhabited by the rich. They were numerous at Pompeii; they are found at Ostia, and even in Rome itself they formed an "aristocratic minority" among the huge tenement blocks.

In Cisalpine Gaul, and even more in the provinces, city houses were spaciously laid out along wide streets. Buildings of two or more storeys were increasingly rare, and some variant of the *atrium* plan was common. The larger cities, in which commerce and crafts were relatively important and, doubtless, many of the small had *tabernae* in those parts which constituted the central business district. But around the periphery of the larger and over much of the area of the smaller, various types of courtyard house predominated. Some of the smaller towns, like Silchester, were in effect "garden cities."

All provincial cities, whether large or small, were the medium through which Roman civilisation was introduced to the provincials. Their public buildings, forum and basilica, temples and baths, theatre and amphitheatre, were designed to make the town attractive, and no doubt they played some part in inter-city rivalry. They covered a large part of the central urban areas, and in a small city like Caerwent must have dominated the whole settlement.

The amphitheatre was as regular a feature of the Roman city as its lineal descendant, the bull-ring, is of Spanish towns today. Often it was placed at a distance from the city centre and outside the walls, where the riots to which its spectacles sometimes gave rise could be more easily controlled. A theatre, at which one assumes a more sophisticated entertainment was offered to the provincials, was to be found in most cities. Like the amphitheatre, it was often located outside the city itself, and for the same reason.

Even more common than theatre and stadium was the temple. The religious cult of the Empire came to be that of the genius of the emperor and of his deified ancestors of the Julian house. It transcended the local cults of the Empire; it had Hellenistic and Middle Eastern overtones, but spread throughout the western Empire. Every town had its temple to the imperial cult; and in all probability most *vici*, their altars to the emperor. The emperor was a charismatic figure who had brought peace to the Empire; a pledge of allegiance to him—worship in a rather crude sense—was a symbol of loyalty to the unity of the Empire. In the western provinces the cult was "a convenient adjunct to effective administration . . . [rather] than . . . an expression of real religious policy." Other religious cults were tolerated as long as they were consistent with the unifying cult of the emperor.

The temples which began to appear in the provincial towns during the first century A.D. conformed in general to a familiar classical form: rectangular in plan, with colonnaded portico, such as the Maison Carrée at Nîmes or Temple of Augustus and Livia at Vienne.

No less characteristic of Roman cities, except those in the humid north-west of Europe, were the engineering works needed to maintain a water supply. In this respect they differed sharply from the Hellenic, and the epidemics which the Greeks endured were part of the penalty which they paid for their ignorance or their neglect. Whereas the Athenians appear to have derived an inadequate supply from possibly contaminated springs and wells within the city, the citizens of Rome tapped mountain sources far to the east and brought it to the city by an elaborate system of aqueducts.

The Romans, with their numerous fountains and bathing establishments, made heavy demands on any local water supply, and there were few cities that did not need to draw from distant sources. In the dry-summer regions of Italy, Spain and southern Gaul this frequently necessitated very long aqueducts and presented complex engineering problems. Arles was supplied from the Chaîne des Alpilles by aqueducts of which very few fragments survive. Nîmes drew its supply from near Uzès by an aqueduct which dropped only 17 metres in a course of about 50 kilometres and included the Pont du Gard and three tunnels. Fréjus (*Forum Julii*) can also show today impressive remains of its aqueduct. Even more elaborate was the water supply of Lyon. Four separate aqueducts, with a total length of 178 kilometres, brought water from the hills to the north of the city and from the Monts du Lyonnais to the west. Of these, the Gier aqueduct alone extended over 70 kilometres from near St Etienne. Paris had an aqueduct of 24 kilometres; Metz reached out 22 kilometres, and Evreux, 19 kilometres. But the most impressive of all these engineering works today is that whereby Segovia, on the dry Meseta of northern Spain, drew its water from the Sierra de Guadarrama. Scarcely less ambitious, though less well preserved, are the aqueducts at Merida and Tarragona. Even in Britain where water supply might have been expected to present little difficulty, Roman waterworks were more ambitious than any to be found again before the nineteenth century.

Not all cities had defensive walls in the time of the Antonines. Military camps had always been protected by bank, ditch and palisade, and in general the *coloniae*, peopled by veterans, followed the same pattern. The possession of a town wall became a mark of status as well as a means of protection. Many Italian towns had walls in the first century B.C. and during the following century new towns were usually walled. The period of peace which followed allowed towns to be established without walls, and doubtless many of the older defences were allowed to crumble. Only in areas that were politically insecure, such as Britain, and those which lay near the frontier were town walls maintained or strengthened. During the third century unsettled conditions returned; the danger of Germanic invasion increased, and the cities of the Empire hastened to build walls or to repair those that had fallen into decay. From this period date many of the fortifications that remain in Gaul and Spain.

During the prosperous and peaceful years of the first and second centuries some cities had built walls of more generous proportions than they were now able to maintain and defend. Foremost among these were *Augustodunum* (Autun), whose original walls, almost 6 kilometres in length, enclosed an area of about 200 hectares. How much of this area was built up is uncertain, but the whole appears to have been divided up by a grid-iron pattern of streets. In all probability much of the urban area was dotted with the villas of the romanised aristocracy of the Aedui.

The drastic reduction in the fortified perimeter of several Gallic towns may well have been accompanied by a contraction of the population. More likely the reduced area was what, in the changed conditions of the latter Empire, "it was economical to defend."

The walls which the Romans built, even in time of peace, were intended for military use. Towers and gates were designed to give the maximum cover, and the line of the walls made the greatest use of the undulations of the terrain, though there were some city entrances, among them the *Porta Nigra* of Trier, which were more decorative than defensive. To the Greeks, the walls seemed often to have been of secondary importance, mere lines of masonry thrown around an existing community, whereas the Romans appeared to have regarded the walls as dominant, anterior in planning if not also in construction, to the settlement itself, at least under the Republic and early Empire.

City of Rome. To most of these generalisations the city of Rome was an exception. "Old Athens and Old Rome," wrote Boëthius, "were both shapeless and irregular." Rome resembled the old Italic cities, clustered

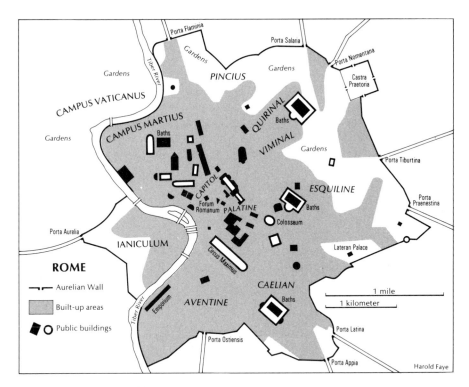

ROME UNDER THE EMPIRE

on their hilltops, but its site was a lowland one, and Rome must indeed have been one of the very few valley cities that were not regularly planned. In the age of the Antonines Rome was at the height of her prosperity. Its population may have approached a million . . . , and it was unquestionably the largest city Europe had yet known.

Growth during the Principate had been unusually fast, and the spread of buildings was subject to but little control. The city authorities, it is true, regulated through the censors the location and construction of public buildings, but private buildings were, in the main, erected by speculative builders and were maintained in good condition only as long as it was profitable to do so. It was not until the Principate of Augustus that an attempt was made to restrict the dangerous heights reached by some of the apartment blocks. Further restrictions were placed on builders under Nero and Vespasian, but these related only to the dimensions of large dwelling houses and the materials of which they were built. No attempt was made to limit their density or to provide wide, straight thoroughfares between them.

By the end of the Republic the Servian wall was ruinous, and at all points

the city had spread beyond it. Rome was, apart from the camp of the Prae-
torian Guard on its north-eastern periphery, an open city, until the Aurelian
wall was built in the third century.

Augustus had divided the city, including part of the highly urbanised areas
surrounding it, into 14 *regiones*. This administrative division of the city lasted
unchanged through the imperial period. By the time of the Antonines very
little of the area embraced by the 14 regions was free of buildings, and in the
following century the wall of Aurelian was built to enclose more than three-
quarters of it. The *regiones* covered an area of 1,783 hectares, or almost 7
square miles. Of this an excessive proportion—at least 40 per cent—was occupied by public buildings. These were scattered over all parts of the city,
with the exception of the fourteenth region, which comprised the Ianiculum
beyond the Tiber. Public buildings, especially if we include among them the
palaces of successive emperors, and the many monuments and temples,
occupied much of the area of the central regions, numbers VIII, X, and XI.
Even in outlying and mainly residential regions, the baths of Titus and
Trajan alone covered almost a square kilometre.

There were few open spaces in the central regions except those provided by the *Forum Romanum*, and the later *fora* of Augustus, Vespasian,
Trajan and others, the *Circus Maximus*, the *Stadia*, and other places of entertainment. Around the periphery of the city, however, especially on the higher
ground of the Quirinal and Esquiline to the north and east, and also west of
the river, were the luxurious villas and gardens of the rich. They had formerly
been extensive nearer the centre of the city, but had given place to the
spreading *insulae*. Nero had built his *Domus Aurea* on rising ground to the
east of the *fora*, on a site which had been laid waste by the fire. He was followed by a large part of the Roman aristocracy, driven from their traditional
seats by imperial rebuilding of the city centre. Some built gracious homes
out beyond the new house of Nero or even outside the city limits, in the hills
by Tivoli or on the coast near Ostia. It is doubtful whether the parks and
gardens of the emperors and of the rich gave much pleasure to the crowded
proletariat or contributed to the food supply of the city, though there are
instances of the more public-spirited giving their gardens to the people on their
death. But by and large, it was the baths which provided the open spaces
and garden-like courts for the masses.

The number of *domi*, of self-contained homes, commonly built on an
atrium plan, was small, probably less than 2,000. They were, as might be
expected, least numerous in the central regions, and those that had survived
in the vicinity of the *fora* must have been excessively small. The growth of
urban population, without any commensurate development of a system of
public transport, led inevitably to an appalling congestion in the central
regions, made worse by the short-sighted policy of the earlier emperors in
clearing private housing to make room for public buildings. Rows of houses

of the *tabernae* type, which under the Republic had risen at most two storeys, were made to support a third and even a fourth. Construction of mudbrick, strengthened with wooden joists, or even of lathe-and-plaster, was unstable and liable to burn. What suburbanite at Praeneste or Tivoli, wrote Juvenal, "was ever afraid of his house tumbling down . . . here we inhabit a city supported for the most part by slender props: for that is how the bailiff holds up the tottering house, patches up gaping cracks in the old wall, bidding the inmates sleep at ease under a roof ready to tumble about their ears."

This was the Rome which burned one dry July day in A.D. 64. The fire spread from the southern edge of the Palatine. "The city's narrow winding streets and irregular blocks encouraged its progress." Rome was devastated. Of the 14 regions, "only four remained intact. Three were levelled to the ground. The other seven were reduced to a few scorched and mangled ruins."

"Nero profited by his country's ruin," wrote Tacitus, "to build a new palace." This was the *domus aurea*; he was also suspected of having set the fire because he was "ambitious to found a new city to be called after himself." A new city was indeed built: the rubble was cleared and carried down the Tiber by the barges that had brought up the city's grain supply, and was dumped in the marshes at Ostia. Streets were widened and straightened; masonry construction, either of tufa or travertine, was prescribed. The dangers inherent in the architecture of the old Rome were reduced, but the problems of overcrowding and the intense summer heat were increased. Nor was the height and congestion of the tenement blocks reduced. Perhaps the greater part of a million Romans lived in these *insulae*. Six storeys were not unusual. On the street level were the *tabernae*, often with masonry vaults; above living quarters rose floor on floor. Their external walls were often of concrete, faced with brick; internal walls were generally of masonry, and the use of timber, now becoming increasingly scarce, was kept to a minimum. Sometimes such buildings enclosed small courtyards, and usually balconies projected over the streets. They were plain but functional; the danger of conflagration was kept to a minimum, and, given the number of baths and other places of public entertainment, life in them was probably no more uncomfortable than in the slums of our modern cities. Suetonius spoke of the *immensus numerus insularum*, but how many there were is not known. Many had been built before the fire, and some of these evidently survived the conflagration, and continued to be inhabited.

The ground-plan of the *insulae* is known from the *Forma Urbis*, the city plan of the third century, engraved on marble, which in a very fragmentary form, has survived. The *insulae* were grouped around the Capitoline and Palatine, and spread over the flat land of the *Campus Martius* to the northwest, where they suffered severely from flooding.

The *insulae* were a consequence of Rome's peculiar problems of overcrowding. In a sense, however, they remain with us and have become a feature of the west European city. They contributed to the dispersion of business and crafts through much of the city area. The *tabernae* were the shops and work-shops, whereas in Hellenistic cities of the Middle East, the marketing functions were concentrated in a bazaar quarter which was not at the same time residential.

The supply of food and water, of building and industrial materials to the city of Rome posed a problem which the Romans alone would have been able to solve. The surrounding Campagna had long since ceased to be the main source of essential foodstuffs. Wheat was imported, much of it from Sicily, Egypt and North Africa, and handled at the Port of Ostia . . . ; it was brought up the Tiber by barges, and again unloaded at Rome's emporium, the dock quarter that lined the waterfront below the Aventine. An enormous fleet of barges was employed, and it is estimated that 6,000 barge-trips were made each season. Tacitus recorded in A.D. 62 the destruction by storm and fire of no less than 300 barges. Warehouses, or *horrea*, lined the river downstream from the *Pons Probi*, the lowest Tiber bridge, and "a vast system of stevedores, grain measures, and warehouse guards . . . received and stored the city's food." Upstream from the grain warehouses to the *Forum Holitorium*, and accessible only by the smaller barges, were warehouses and open-air markets for all varieties of foodstuffs. Much of the wine and olive oil consumed in the city was sold here; so also were the exotic foods described by Martial; marble and ornamental building stones; metals, wool and cloth. Vegetables and fruits, grown in the Campagna, were brought into the city by cart or pack animal, and animals were driven down from the mountains to the city markets, and lumber for builders and craftsmen were floated down the Tiber from the Apennines or up the river from Ostia.

The maintenance of a steady flow of food to provision a city of a million had been handled under the Republic on a temporary and *ad hoc* basis. It formed at first part of the duties of the *aediles*. Under Augustus it was en-trusted to an office, that of the *praefectus annonae*, created for the purpose.

The supply of water presented problems of even greater difficulty in the Italian climate of long, dry summers. Mention has already been made of the aqueducts which the Romans built to supply provincial cities of even modest size. All these yield before the size and complexity of the works built to bring water to their capital. To Strabo they were among the most valuable of Rome's public works, bringing water "in such quantities that veritable rivers flow through the city and the sewers; and almost every house has cisterns, and service-pipes, and copious fountains." The oldest aqueduct, the *Aqua Appia*, had been constructed late in the fourth century B.C., and between that date and the early second century A.D., when Trajan's aqueduct was put into service, no less than nine separate works, with a total length of 264 English miles, were completed. All, except one, drew their water from the Anio and from other left-bank tributaries of the Tiber. The exception, the *Aqua*

Alsietina, was built by Augustus to deliver water from the crater lake of *Lacus Alsietinus*, 17 miles north-west of the city. Frontinus questioned the wisdom of its construction since its water is "positively unwholesome, and for that reason is nowhere delivered for consumption by the people." It was generally used for watering the gardens and supplying the fountains of the city, and only in time of dire shortage was it used domestically, and then only by settlements on the right bank of the river.

The earlier aqueducts, completed when the city was still relatively small, came in at a low level. As buildings spread up over the higher ground to the east, higher aqueducts were constructed to supply them. The earlier channels had followed the contours of the land from the Apennine foothills, frequently buried a short distance below the surface. The later aqueducts were built on or above the surface, and the last of the major works, the Claudian aqueduct, took its water from the Anio valley far above *Tibur* (Tivoli) and strode across the Campagna on giant columns, the ruins of which still stand. Even in their abandoned and ruinous condition the aqueducts of Rome are an impressive monument to the practical genius of Rome. Frontinus took a justifiable pride in the works which he was called upon to supervise: "with such an array of indispensable structures," he wrote "compare, if you will, the idle Pyramids or the useless, though famous, works of the Greeks."

Rome could not have developed without the Tiber. The ancient writers were fully aware that the river had provided protection for the infant city against the Etruscans, that its crossing points had canalised trade through the city, and that it had brought commerce, both upstream and downstream to the markets of Rome. Yet it was a dangerous and difficult river. It did not, fortunately for Rome, dry out in summer, but in winter and spring was liable to particularly severe floods. The *Campus Martius* and all the low-lying land near the Palatine is known at some time or other to have been devastated by flooding. Dio Cassius described a flood which "rose so high as to inundate all the lower levels in the city and to overwhelm many even of the higher portions. The houses . . . being constructed of brick (i.e. dried mud), became soaked through and collapsed, while all the animals perished in the flood." Disastrous floods were all too frequent. Their reason lay, not so much in the excessive rains mentioned by the ancient writers, as in the deforestation, soil erosion and consequent rapid run-off from the volcanic country to the north of Rome. Augustus was undoubtedly pursuing the correct course when he "cleared the Tiber channel which had been choked with an accumulation of rubbish and narrowed by jutting houses." There was a disastrous flood under Tiberius, with much loss of life and destruction of property. The Senate was moved to discuss the matter, and it was proposed that floods should be checked "by diverting the streams and lakes which nourished them," but, "because of the pleas from towns, or superstitious scruples, or engineering difficulties," the Senate took no action. Floods, nevertheless, became less frequent in the course of the first and second centuries. The removal of obstructions to the river's flow no doubt helped to improve the situation, but it is likely also that changes in land use in the Tiber valley . . . also played a role in reducing run-off.

The port of Rome.   The rise of Rome owed little to its navigable communication with the sea. Though tradition ascribed the foundation of Ostia to the period of the kings, archaeology can find no evidence of a settlement at the river's mouth before the fourth century B.C. and then it existed more to protect Rome from piratical attack than to handle the city's commerce. Puteoli, near Naples, was the first port of Rome, despite its considerable distance from the city. Smaller sea-going vessels sailed up the 24 miles of the lower Tiber, but the shoals of the lower river and the rapid accretion along its banks made navigation hazardous. Julius Caesar even proposed to cut a canal from the city across the Pontine marshes to Terracina to facilitate the transport of grain from the more southerly ports. The volume of food imported by Rome continued to grow; attempts by Augustus and Claudius to make a port at the Tiber mouth for the transshipment of grain met with only qualified success, and it remained for Trajan to create a network of ports and harbours of refuge and to make Ostia "not merely the harbour of the world's largest consuming centre, but an important line . . . in the great trade route from the east to west."

Ostia was rebuilt and became a populous city . . . of brick-faced *insulae*, rising in many instances to four or five storeys. The transshipment of cargoes took place at first in the river off the city. Caesar had proposed a harbour at a distance from the river, and thus free from silting. Claudius, however, constructed a port opening off the Fiumicino, a small artificial distributary of the Tiber, and Trajan added the hexagonal dock basin whose outline is apparent in the fields today two miles to the north of the ruined town. This became the harbour for the bulk-handling of grain, lumber and building materials. The old town of Ostia seems to have retained the trade in wine and perhaps also in luxury goods, many of which were probably sent on to Rome by road rather than river.

Women in Roman Society

SARAH B. POMEROY

Until very recently, historians who studied women in Roman society were almost always interested in them only in relation to men. This bias goes right back to the ancients themselves. Plutarch and Suetonius studied the character of imperial women to reveal the character of imperial men. Ancient legal sources have the same bias. While revealing a considerable amount about the legal position of women, Roman legal writings and laws nearly always focused principally on the legal status, authority, and responsibilities of men. A survey of the legal sources shows that the classical Roman law of the late Republic and early Principate strictly limited the independence of women, requiring that their property be administered by men—either their husbands or guardians—and keeping them in a position of legal subjugation to their fathers or their husbands. By the time of Justinian, however, a woman's dowry was protected from her husband's mismanagement or appropriation, and her power to act on her own behalf had increased. If a man alienated or diminished his wife's property, she could take action against him for damages. Thus, in late imperial times, women possessed significant legal rights, although their status would not meet the standards of equality being set today.

Sarah B. Pomeroy works with the same sources as other social historians, but she asks new questions of these sources. She finds ways of discovering a great deal not only about the women of upper-class families, but also about lower-class women, particularly slaves. Her study reveals much about Roman families, home life, and social relations.

The momentum of social change in the Hellenistic world combined with Roman elements to produce the emancipated, but respected, upper-class woman. The Roman matron of the late Republic must be viewed against the background of shrewd and politically powerful Hellenistic princesses, expanding cultural opportunities for women, the search for sexual fulfillment in the

Reprinted by permission of Schocken Books, Inc. from *Goddesses, Whores, Wives, and Slaves* by Sarah B. Pomeroy, pp. 153–55, 158–61, 164–66, 168–69, 190–95, 195–97. Copyright © 1975 by Sarah B. Pomeroy. Omission of footnotes, which can be found in the complete publication.

context of a declining birthrate, and the individual assertiveness characteristic of the Hellenistic period. The rest of the picture is Roman: enormous wealth, aristocratic indulgence and display, pragmatism permitting women to exercise leadership during the absence of men on military and governmental missions of long duration; and, as a final element, a past preceding the influence of the Greeks—a heritage so idealized by the Romans that historical events were scarcely distinguishable from legends, and the legends of the founding of Rome and the early Republic were employed in the late Republic and early Empire for moral instruction and propaganda. The result was that wealthy aristocratic women who played high politics and presided over literary salons were nevertheless expected to be able to spin and weave as though they were living in the days when Rome was young. These social myths set up a tension between the ideal and the real Roman matron, and were responsible for the praise awarded a woman like Cornelia, who lived in the second century B.C.

Among Roman matrons, Cornelia was a paragon. We are told that she turned down an offer of marriage from a Ptolemy. A widow, she remained faithful to the memory of her husband, Tiberius Sempronius Gracchus, to whom she had borne twelve children. She continued to manage her household and was praised for her devotion to her children's education. Only three of her children survived to adulthood, but through her two sons, Tiberius and Gaius Gracchus, Cornelia exercised a profound influence on Roman politics. Some say that she goaded her sons to excessive political zeal by insisting that she was famous as the daughter of Scipio Africanus—conqueror of Hannibal—rather than as the mother of the Gracchi. It was even rumored, though much after the fact, that, with the aid of her daughter Sempronia, Cornelia suffocated Scipio Aemilianus, Sempronia's husband, because he opposed the legislation of Tiberius Gracchus. This allegation did not tarnish Cornelia's reputation. She endured the assassination of both her adult sons with fortitude, and continued to entertain foreign and learned guests at her home in Misenum. She was herself educated, and her letters were published. A bronze portrait statue inscribed "Cornelia, daughter of Africanus, mother of the Gracchi," was erected in her honor by the Romans and restored by the Emperor Augustus.

The Letter of the Law . . . and the Reality

Looking beyond the picture of Cornelia—independent, cultured, self-assured even in her widowhood—we find a long history of Roman legislation affecting women, especially in the areas of guardianship, marriage, and inheritance.

The weakness and light-mindedness of the female sex (*infirmitas sexus* and *levitas animi*) were the underlying principles of Roman legal theory that mandated all women to be under the custody of males. In childhood, a daughter fell under the sway of the eldest male ascendant in her family, the *pater familias*. The power of the *pater familias* was without parallel in Greek law; it extended to the determination of life or death for all members of the household. Male offspring of any age were also subject to the authority of the *pater familias*, but as adults they were automatically emancipated upon his death, and the earliest Roman law code, the XII Tables (traditionally 451–450 B.C.), stated that a son who had been sold into slavery three times by his father thereby gained his freedom. Among females, however, the only automatic legal exemption from the power of the *pater familias* was accorded those who became Vestal Virgins, a cultic role reserved for a very few.

Upon the death of the *pater familias*, the custody over daughters (and prepubertal sons) passed to the nearest male relative (agnate), unless the father had designated another guardian in his will. Guardianship over females was theoretically in force until the time of Diocletian (reigned A.D. 285–305), but this power was gradually diminished by legal devices and ruses and by the assertiveness of some women interested in managing their own concerns. A guardian was required when a woman performed important transactions, such as accepting an inheritance, making a testament, or assuming a contractual obligation, and all transactions requiring *mancipatio* (a ritual form of sale), including selling land and manumitting a slave. But if the guardian withheld approval, a woman could apply to the magistrate to have his assent forced, or to have a different guardian appointed.

By the late Republic, tutelage over women was a burden to the men acting as guardians, but only a slight disability to women. The virtuous Cornelia managed a large household and is not reported to have consulted any male guardian even in her decision to turn down Ptolemy Physcon's proposal of marriage. Similarly, a century later, much is said about the financial transactions of Terentia, Cicero's wife, but nothing about her guardian.

The legislation of Augustus provided a way for women to free themselves of the formal supervision by male guardians. According to the "right of three or four children" (*jus liberorum*), a freeborn woman who bore three children and a freedwoman who bore four children were exempt from guardianship. This provision incidentally impaired the juridical doctrine of the weakness of the female sex, by expressing the notion that at least those women who had demonstrated responsible behavior by bearing the children Rome needed could be deemed capable of acting without a male guardian.

The right of three children was not a response to demands from liberated women yearning to free themselves from male domination, nor did it act as much of an incentive. As we have seen, the famous women of Roman society who had wanted to be free of the influence of guardians had managed to do so before the reign of Augustus, and without the tedious preliminary of bearing three children. Moreover, papyri from Roman Egypt, where women were less sophisticated, show a large number of women proudly announcing that they have gained the *jus liberorum*, but nevertheless availing themselves of male assistance when they transact legal business. Even after a law of Claudius in the first century A.D. abolished automatic guardianship of agnates over women, the majority of guardians or men who were present at transactions of women possessing the *jus liberorum* and who signed documents in behalf of illiterate women continued to be male relatives.

The laws of guardianship indicate that the powers of the *pater familias* surpassed those of the husband. The *pater familias* decided whether his daughter would remain in his power, or would be emancipated from his power to that of another man, and if so, who would be her guardian. The guardian was not necessarily a relative, nor was the married daughter inevitably in the power of her husband. The *pater familias* decided whether or not she would be married according to a legal form that would release her from the authority of her father and transfer her to the power (*manus*) of her husband. If the marriage was contracted with *manus*, the bride became part of her husband's family, as though she were his daughter, as far as property rights were concerned.

A wife could become subject to a husband's *manus* in three ways: either by the two formal marriage ceremonies known as *confarreatio* (sharing of spelt—a coarse grain), and *coemptio* (pretended sale), or by *usus* (continuous cohabitation for a year). In ancient times, a vital feature of *manus* marriage for the bride was the change in domestic religions. A family's religion was transmitted through males, and the *pater familias* was the chief priest. Upon marriage, a girl renounced her father's religion and worshiped instead at her husband's hearth. His ancestors became hers. The guardian spirit of the *pater familias* (known as the *genius*) and that of the *mater familias* (the *juno*) were worshiped by the household. Conversely, the woman married without *manus* was not a member of the husband's agnatic family, and hence theoretically excluded from the rites celebrated by her husband and children. In that case, she would continue to participate in her father's cult. . . .

The testimony on the issue of the husband's powers in comparison with those of the blood relatives varies. Dionysius of Halicarnassus—who, like Livy, wrote during the reign of the Emperor Augustus—states that, according to the laws of Romulus, married women were obliged to conform themselves to their husbands, since they had no other refuge, while husbands ruled over their wives as possessions. Plutarch gives the additional information that, according to the regulations of Romulus, only the husband could initiate a divorce, and then only on the grounds that his wife had committed adultery, poisoned his children, or counterfeited his keys. If he divorced his wife for another reason, she took half his property; the other half was consecrated to the goddess Ceres.

Dionysius of Halicarnassus further confuses the question by stating that her husband, after taking counsel with a woman's relations, could inflict capital punishment on a wife guilty of adultery, or of drinking, since drinking inspired adultery. The elder Pliny relates that a married woman was forced by her family to starve herself to death because she had stolen the keys to the wine cellar, but it is not clear whether "family" refers to the husband or blood relatives.

So it is uncertain whether the husband had the right to kill the wife, or merely to divorce her, or to kill her only with the agreement of her male relatives. In 186 b.c., when thousands of men and women were sentenced to death for participating in Bacchic rites, the women were handed over to their blood relatives or to those who had authority (manus) over them to be executed in private. But here, each husband merely carried out the execution ordered by the state. He did not himself condemn her.

What does emerge from this investigation is the concept that when "wives had no other refuge," as Dionysius puts it, or when they were totally under the authority of their husbands, as envisioned by Cato, marriages were more enduring. This power of husbands over wives—if, in fact, it had ever been prevalent in early Rome—was idealized and became an element in the marriage propaganda of Stoics and Augustan authors, both concerned with promoting marriage among their contemporaries.

What is also striking to anyone who lives in a society where a father's control over a daughter terminates when she reaches the age of majority, but where certain other laws make the wife subordinate to the husband, is that the situation may have been reversed at Rome, and the husband's authority more ephemeral than that of the father and blood kin. Thus, even in manus marriage, the bride's blood relatives continued to be involved in her guidance and welfare. The surveillance over her drinking is only one aspect of this. Some legends point to continued involvement by fathers of married women: among them are the raped Lucretia's appeal to both her father and husband and their joint vengeance in her behalf, and the story of the Sabine fathers who, when coming to reclaim their pregnant married daughters, were told by them that they did not want to be forced to choose between their fathers and husbands. . . .

Divorce was easily accomplished, theoretically at the initiation of either or both parties to the marriage. Beginning in the late Republic, a few women are notorious for independently divorcing their husbands, but, for the most part, these arrangements were in the hands of men. As we have seen, divorce could be initiated by fathers whose married children were not emancipated from their authority. We may note a parallel to Classical Athenian law, where the father retained the right to dissolve his daughter's marriage. . . . Not until the reign of Antoninus Pius was it made illegal for fathers to break up harmonious marriages. If the marriage had involved manus, then the manus had to be dissolved, but this situation was infrequent. The major concern was the return of the dowry, as it had been in Classical Athens and Hellenistic Egypt. If the husband were divorcing the wife for immoral conduct, he had the right to retain a portion of her dowry; the fraction varied according to the gravity of her offense. A few husbands did attempt to profit by this procedure.

In divorce, children remained with their father, since they were agnatically related to him, but, as we have seen in our discussion of manus, blood relationship was an important bond. Thirty-seven years after her divorce from Augustus, Scribonia voluntarily accompanied her daughter Julia into exile. After his parents had been divorced, and he himself adopted into another family, Scipio Aemilianus shared his wealth with his mother. Marcia had been divorced by the younger Cato because he wanted to let his friend Hortensius breed children with her. Nevertheless, after the death of Hortensius she remarried Cato, probably motivated by a wish to look after her daughters by him while Cato went off to join Pompey. After her divorce from Claudius Nero to marry Augustus, Livia's children by her first marriage lived with their father, but following his death they joined their mother.

Most of the divorces we read about were prompted by political or personal considerations. No reason was legally required, but sterility of the marriage was often a cause, and a barren marriage was considered to be due to the wife. Sulla divorced Cloelia for alleged infertility. However, a woman who died at the end of the first century B.C. won extravagant praise from her husband for offering him a divorce after a barren marriage that had lasted forty-three years. She is called "Turia," though her name is not definitely known. Her funerary encomium describes her heroism in her husband's behalf during the civil wars, and then praises her self-effacing offer to divorce her husband on the condition that she—with her fortune—would continue to stay with him and be as a sister, and treat his future children as though they were her own. Her husband indignantly turned her down, preferring to remain married although his family line would thereby become extinct. This is one of the many interesting aspects of the document. The husband regards his preference for his wife and married life over his duties to perpetuate his family line as untraditional, yet by this period morally acceptable, indeed commendable.

Some men divorced their wives for flagrant adultery. Thus, Pompey divorced Mucia, and Lucullus divorced Claudia; Caesar divorced Pompeia because her notorious involvement with Publius Clodius at the rites of the Bona Dea, which were supposed to be confined to women, created a scandal. Caesar was High Priest at the time, and proclaimed that "the High Priest's wife must be above suspicion." We have little information on wives' divorcing husbands for adultery. This may have been due to a double standard, or to the discretion of some adulterous husbands, or to the upper-class men's opportunities for involvement with women of lower social classes—liaisons that were accepted as not threatening to legitimate marriages.

Augustus declared adultery a public offense only in women. Consistent with the powers of the *pater familias*, the father of the adulteress was permitted to kill her if she had not been emancipated from his power. The husband's role, as we have seen in other areas of Roman law, was more limited than the father's. The husband was obliged to divorce his wife, and he or someone else was to bring her to trial. If convicted, she lost half her dowry, the adulterer was fined a portion of his property, and both were separately exiled. According to the Augustan legislation, a wife could divorce her husband for adultery, but she was not obliged to, and he was not liable for criminal prosecution. The law may have been more stringent than the real situation, for the jurist Ulpian later commented: "It is very unjust for a husband to require from a wife a level of morality that he does not himself achieve." Stoic theory as well condemned adultery in either man or wife. The younger Cato, a man of Stoic and Roman principles, carried the doctrine still further: he believed that sexual intercourse was only for the purpose of begetting children. Since he had a sufficient number of children and Marcia was worn out by childbearing, his second marriage to her was chaste. No doubt the long absences from home imposed by the civil wars facilitated Cato's continence in his relations with his wife during the five-year duration of the remarriage.

Like the Augustan rule on adultery, the regulation on criminal fornication (*stuprum*) perpetuated a double standard. No man was allowed to have sexual relations with an unmarried or widowed upper-class woman, but he could have relations with prostitutes, whereas upper-class women were not allowed to have any relations outside of marriage. Under some emperors, the penalties for breaking these laws were very severe. Augustus himself exiled both his daughter and granddaughter for illicit intercourse and forbade their burial in his tomb. Some upper-class women protested against the curtailment of their freedom by registering with the aediles (magistrates whose duties included supervision of the markets and trade) as prostitutes. Then the laws of *stuprum* would not apply to them, but such women were excluded from legacies and inheritance. In any case, this legal dodge was eliminated when Augustus' successor, Tiberius, forbade women whose fathers, grandfathers or husbands were Roman knights or senators to register as prostitutes.

Rape could be prosecuted—under the legal headings of criminal wrong (*iniuria*) or violence (*vis*)—by the man under whose authority the wronged woman fell. Constantine was explicit about the guilt of the victim. In his decision on raped virgins, he distinguished between girls who were willing and those who were forced against their will. If the girl had been willing, her penalty was to be burned to death. If she had been unwilling, she was still punished, although her penalty was lighter, for she should have screamed and brought neighbors to her assistance. Constantine also specified capital punishment for a free woman who had intercourse with a slave, and burning for the slave himself. This penalty was the outcome of a perpetual concern that free women would take the same liberties with slaves as men did. These liaisons were a real possibility, since unlike Athens, where women lived in separate quarters, in Rome' wealthy women were attended by numerous male slaves, often chosen for their attractive appearance. The legendary virtuous Lucretia, according to the Augustan historian Livy, was so intimidated by Tarquin's threat that he would kill her and a naked slave side by side in bed that she submitted to Tarquin's lust. Though raped, she was technically an adulteress; therefore she made the honorable decision to commit suicide.

Augustan legislation encouraged widows, like divorcées, to remarry. There was some tension between the emperor's concern that women bear as many children as possible and the traditional Roman idealization of the woman like Cornelia who remained faithful to her dead husband. The epitaphs continue to praise the women who died having known only one husband (univira), some of whom easily earned this recognition by dying young. The ideal of the univira and the eternal marriage was strictly Roman, and without counterpart in Greece. Two lengthy encomia of upper-class women of the Augustan period—one of "Turia," the other of Cornelia, wife of Lucius Aemilius Paullus—stress this ideal. In both cases, the women predeceased their husbands, who composed or commissioned the encomia. Even Livia, the widow of Augustus, although she had had a previous husband, was praised for not remarrying. Virgil, writing the national Roman epic, depicts a disastrous climax to Dido's decision not to remain faithful to her dead husband. In Rome, unlike Athens, a woman could lead an interesting life without a husband, as Cornelia, mother of the Gracchi, did in entertaining guests and pursuing her intellectual interests. But Cornelia earned praise because she bore twelve children first, and then chose not to remarry.

A further refinement of the ideal-wife motif stresses that not only should a woman have only one husband, but she ought not to survive him—especially if he has been the victim of political persecution. Thus Arria, the wife of A. Caecina Paetus, upbraided the wife of another member of her husband's political faction for daring to continue to live after seeing her own husband murdered in her arms. She also advised her own daughter to commit suicide if her husband predeceased her. When Arria's own husband was invited to commit suicide during the reign of Claudius, she plunged the dagger into her own breast to set an example, and spoke her celebrated last words, "It does not hurt, Paetus." . . .

Facts of Birth, Life, and Death

Marriage and motherhood were the traditional expectation of well-to-do women in Rome, as they had been in Greece. The rarity of spinsters indicates that most women married at least once, although afterward a number chose to remain divorcées or widows.

Augustus established the minimum age for marriage at twelve for girls and fourteen for boys. The first marriage of most girls took place between the ages of twelve and fifteen. Since menarche typically occurred at thirteen or fourteen, prepubescent marriages took place. Moreover, sometimes the future bride lived with the groom before she had reached the legal minimum for marriage, and it was not unusual for these unions to be consummated. Marriages of young girls took place because of the desire of the families involved not to delay the profit from a political or financial alliance and, beginning with the reign of Augustus, so that the bride and groom could reap the rewards of the marital legislation, although some of the benefits could be anticipated during the engagement. Sometimes one motive outweighed another. Thus there are cases of dowerless daughters of the upper class who nevertheless found social-climbing men so eager to marry them that the husbands surreptitiously provided the dowry, to save the pride of the girl's family. Another factor which we have traced back to Hesiod was the desire to find a bride who was still virginal.

Most upper-class Roman women were able to find husbands, not only for first marriages but for successive remarriages. One reason for this, apparently, was that there were fewer females than males among their social peers. As in Greece, this disproportion was the result of the shorter lifespan of females, whose numbers fell off sharply once the childbearing years were reached. There were the additional factors of the selective infanticide and exposure of female infants and, probably more important, a subtle but pervasive attitude that gave preferential treatment to boys . . . . This can be surmised from a law attributed to Romulus that required a father to raise all male children but only the first-born female. This so-called law of Romulus—while not to be accepted at face value as evidence that every father regularly raised only one daughter—is nevertheless indicative of official policy and foreshadows later legislation favoring the rearing of boys over girls. The attitude may be criticized as short-sighted in face of the manpower shortage continually threatening Rome; the policy of Sparta, where potential childbearers were considered as valuable as warriors, should be compared.

The law of Romulus incidentally shows that it was not inconvenient for a daughter to be automatically called by the feminine form of her father's name (nomen). But it was awkward when the father decided to raise two daughters, who thus had the same name, like Cornelia and her sister Cornelia.

The Romans solved the problem with the addition of "the elder" (maior) or "the younger" (minor). In families where several daughters were raised, numerals, which in earlier times may have been indicative of order of birth, were added (e.g., Claudia Tertia and Claudia Quinta). A wealthy father might decide to dispose of an infant because of the desire not to divide the family property among too many offspring and thereby reduce the individual wealth of the members of the next generation. Christian authors such as Justin Martyr doubtless exaggerate the extent to which contemporary pagans engaged in infanticide, but, on the other hand, it is clear that this method of family planning was practiced without much fanfare in antiquity. An infant of either sex who appeared weak might be exposed; in his Gynecology Soranus, a physician of the second century A.D., gives a list of criteria by which midwives were to recognize which newborns should be discarded and which were worth rearing. In deciding to expose a daughter, the provision of a dowry was an additional consideration. However, there was enough of a demand for brides, as we have mentioned, to make even the occasional dowerless bride acceptable.

Additional evidence for a dearth of females in the upper classes is that in the late Republic some men were marrying women of the lower classes. We know of no spinsters, yet upper-class women are not known to have taken husbands from the lower classes. Studies of tombstones generally show far more males than females. This disproportion is usually explained away by the comment that males were deemed more deserving of commemoration. Such a factor might discourage the erection of tombstones for those low on the social scale, but at least among the wealthier classes—the very group where small families were the trend—we could expect that, once having decided to raise a daughter, her parents would commemorate her death. In our present state of knowledge we cannot finally say that women were actually present in Rome in the numbers one expects in an average pre-industrial society, and that their lack of adequate representation in the sepulchral inscriptions is totally ascribable to their social invisibility; but it should be noted that the existence of masses of women who are not recorded by the inscriptions is, at most, hypothetical.

The traditional doctrine, enforced by Roman censors, was that men should marry, and that the purpose of marriage was the rearing of children. The example of Hellenistic Greece, where men were refusing to marry and consequently children were not being raised . . . , had a subversive influence on the ideal, although Stoicism affirmed it. A decrease in fecundity is discernible as early as the second century B.C., a time when the production of twelve children by Cornelia became a prodigy—probably because her son Gaius harped on it—although only three lived to adulthood. Metellus Macedonicus, censor in 131 B.C., made a speech urging men to marry and procreate, although he recognized that wives were troublesome creatures. The speech was read out to the Senate by Augustus as evidence that he was merely reviving Roman traditions with his legislation.

Augustus' legislation was designed to keep as many women as possible in the married state and bearing children. The penalties for nonmarriage and childlessness began for women at age twenty, for men at twenty-five. Divorce was not explicitly frowned upon, provided that each successive husband was recruited from the approved social class. Failure to remarry was penalized, all with a view to not wasting the childbearing years. Women were not able to escape the penalties of the Augustan legislation as easily as men. A man who was betrothed to a girl of ten could enjoy the political and economic privileges accorded to married men, but a woman was not permitted to betroth herself to a prepubescent male.

But the low birth rate continued, and the Augustan legislation on marriage was reinforced by Domitian and reenacted in the second and third centuries A.D. It appears that women as well as men were rebelling against biologically determined roles. One reason for the low birth rate was the practice of contraception. . . .

Abortion is closely associated with contraception in the ancient sources, and sometimes confused with it. Keith Hopkins suggests that the reason for the blurring of abortion and contraception was the lack of precise knowledge of the period of gestation. Some Romans believed that children could be born seven to ten months after conception, but eight-month babies were not possible. A contributing factor in the failure to distinguish between contraception and abortion was that some of the same drugs were recommended for both. Abortion was also accomplished by professional surgical instruments or by amateur methods. Ovid upbraids Corinna: "Why do you dig out your child with sharp instruments, and give harsh poisons to your unborn children."

The musings of philosophers on when the foetus felt life and whether abortion was sanctionable will not be reviewed. In a society where newborns were exposed, the foetus cannot have had much right to life, although it is true that in the early Empire the execution of a pregnant woman was delayed until after the birth of her child. Literary testimony, including Seneca, Juvenal, and Ovid, shows both that some men were dismayed about abortions and that some upper-class women and courtesans had them. Not until the reign of Septimius Severus was any legislation enacted curtailing abortion, and this was merely to decree the punishment of exile for a divorced woman who has an abortion without her recent hubsand's consent, since she has cheated him of his child. In the reign of Caracalla, the penalty of exile (and death if the patient died) was established for administering abortifacients, but this law was directed against those who traded in drugs and magic rather than against abortion itself.

Medical writers were concerned as well with methods of promoting fertility in sterile women and with childbirth. The writings of Soranus, a physician of the second century A.D., cover a sophisticated range of gyneco-logical and obstetrical topics. He did not adhere to the Hippocratic Oath which forbade administering abortifacients, but stated his preference for contraception. At a time when wealthy women usually employed wetnurses, Soranus declared that if the mother was in good health, it was better that she nurse the child, since it would foster the bonds of affection. Of interest are his recommendations for the alleviation of labor pains, his concern for the comfort of the mother, and his unequivocal decision that the welfare of the mother take precedence over that of the infant. In childbirth, most women who could afford professional assistance would summon a midwife, although if the procedure was beyond the midwife's ability, and funds were available, a male physician would be employed. In Rome the skilled midwives, like the physicians, were likely to be Greek. Midwives not only delivered babies, but were involved in abortions and other gynecological procedures, and as we have mentioned, they were supposed to be able to recognize which infants were healthy enough to be worth rearing.

Women—even wealthy women with access to physicians—continued to die in childbirth. Early marriage, and the resultant bearing of children by immature females, was a contributing factor. Tombstones show a marked increase in female mortality in the fifteen-to-twenty-nine-year-old group. In a study of the sepulchral inscriptions, Keith Hopkins claims that death in child-birth is to some extent exaggerated by the reliance upon evidence from tombstones. He suggests that women dying between fifteen and twenty-nine were more likely to be commemorated, because their husbands were still alive to erect tombstones. In his sample he found that the median age for the death of wives was 34; of husbands, 46.5. J. Lawrence Angel's study of skeletal remains in Greece under Roman domination shows an adult longevity of 34.3 years for women and 40.2 for men. Stepmothers are mentioned more than stepfathers, though this may reflect not only early death of mothers but the fact that children stayed with their father after divorce. . . .

How can we know about the lives of lower-class women—slaves, ex-slaves, working women, and the poor? The literature does tell us the ways in which the lower classes pleased or displeased their social superiors. The sepulchral inscriptions that owners of slaves or members of the lower classes had carved for their associates and themselves give the messages they wanted to announce to posterity. Thus an epitaph may include not merely the name of the de-ceased, but the name of her owner or former owner if she were a slave or freedwoman (especially if she had belonged to an important family), the name of her husband, the duration of her marriage and the number of children in the family, her age at death, and her métier.

For the present chapter I have drawn heavily on the recent study of

P. R. C. Weaver of the slaves and freedmen of the imperial household, which includes statistics on a control group of nonimperial slaves. Also of immense value have been S. M. Treggiari's studies of slaves and freedmen of the late Republic and the early Empire. But the essential questions of how it felt to be a female slave among the Romans, and whether—if one were an ordinary slave—it was worse to be male or female, cannot be answered.

The Exploitation of Slaves

The Roman household (*familia*) included not only kinsmen legally dependent on the head of the family, but also slaves. The number of slaves of course varied according to the means of the family, but even humble families might own a few. There is more abundant documentation on the slaves of the wealthy, as is true of the wealthy themselves. Wealthy families owned thousands of slaves, living on their various holdings, and the household of the emperor (*familia Caesaris*) was probably the largest. Owners of slaves invested in human property with the expectation that certain services would be performed, and that their own wealth would thereby be increased and their personal comfort enhanced. The complexities of Roman slavery were such that a woman might gain more prestige by marrying a slave than a free person, and that slaves and ex-slaves might be more highly educated and enjoy greater economic security than the freeborn poor.

The variety of the jobs held by female slaves was more limited than those of the males. Some women were enslaved only in adulthood, either by kidnappers or pirates, or because they were camp followers or ordinary citizens where the Romans made a conquest. In a population of captive Greeks, the Romans would find male scholars, historians, poets, and men with valuable skills. Owing to the limitations of women's education, a freshly captured woman may have been at most a midwife, an actress, or a prostitute. Most women did not have any training beyond the traditional household skills. In slavery, as in freedom, they could work as spinners, weavers, clothesmakers, menders, wetnurses, child nurses, kitchen help, and general domestics. The household duties of female slaves in Rome differed somewhat from those we observed in Greece. Because Roman engineers devised mechanical methods for transporting large quantities of water, Roman slave women did not carry water to the same extent that Greeks had done. Moreover, in Rome, unlike Greece, all clothing was not made at home. In addition, female slaves were given special training in the wealthy Roman home and worked as clerks, secretaries, ladies' maids, clothes folders, hairdressers, haircutters, mirror holders, masseuses, readers, entertainers, midwives, and infirmary attendants. Children born into slavery in a wealthy Roman home thus stood a fair chance of receiving some education.

Some female slaves, like males, were employed as attendants to enhance the splendor of the mistresses' entourage when she went out of her home. Such slaves would clear the way before their owner. If her mistress was traveling on a litter, a female slave would put her sandals on for her and place a footstool next to the litter before the mistress alighted. A slave might carry a parasol for a mistress who was taking a walk. Naturally, slaves' functions on a farm or country estate would have differed from those in the urban household, but less is known about rural slave women. However, Cato the Censor does list the duties of the *vilica*, the chief housekeeper, a slave woman who held a supervisory position of great responsibility, subordinate to a steward who was a male slave.

Women were always employable for sexual purposes, either in addition to their other domestic responsibilities, or as a primary occupation. The master had access to all his slave women. Scipio Africanus favored a particular slave girl, and when he died, his wife Aemilia, far from being vindictive, gave the girl her freedom. Cato the Censor, who was an authority on Roman virtue, was visited nightly by a slave girl after his wife died, and the emperors Augustus and Claudius consorted with numerous slave girls with their wives' explicit approval. Slave women were also available for sexual relations with the male slaves in the house, with the master's permission. Cato, who was always interested in financial gain, charged his male slaves a fixed fee for intercourse with his female slaves.

Employment in the sex trade brought great profit to the owners of female slaves. Women worked as prostitutes in brothels or in inns or baths open to the public. Exposed baby girls and daughters sold by their parents were raised for this trade. In this same category, but at a higher level, were the women trained to work as actresses and entertainers of all types. Actresses sometimes appeared nude and performed sexual acts on stage. However, actresses were not invariably employed sexually. Eucharis, a young performer who had been given her freedom sometime before her death at the age of fourteen, performed in the chorus at respectable public games given as "Greek theater," and is described as "learned" and "skilled" in her epitaph.

Marriage, Manumission, and the Law

The fact of slavery disqualified a person from entering into a formal Roman marriage, but two slaves might have an informal marital arrangement known as "cohabitation" (*contubernium*). Although the usual incest regulations applied just as if it were legal marriage, this arrangement had no legal validity: the children of the union were considered illegitimate, and the woman could not be accused of adultery. But to the slaves themselves the marriages were valid, and in the epitaphs the partners refer to each other as husband and wife. It was in the master's interest to promote family life among his slaves, for it improved morale and produced slave children who were the master's to keep in his household or to dispose of as he wished. Slaves tended to marry other slaves, and were likely to marry within their master's *familia*. With permission, a slave might marry a slave from another *familia* or a free person. However, if a male slave married a female outside his master's *familia*, the master lost the profit that might be gained from the offspring, since the children belonged to the mother if she were free, or to her master if she were a slave. Hence such a marriage might not be permitted. There was no security in a slave marriage—either partner or the children might be sold to another owner or moved to a different property owned by the original master. Broken marriages left no record. But sepulchral inscriptions show that many slave marriages survived over long periods of time, regardless of changes in habitation or changes in status from slave to freed of one or both of the partners. In lives subject to the whims of others, the stability of the marriage bond was welcome.

The study of imperial slaves and freedmen shows that almost half the marriages of freedmen whose duration is mentioned lasted at least thirty years. Moreover, their wives had married young, like the aristocrats discussed in the previous chapter. In order that the statistics on the duration of marriage be consistent with those on the age of death of wives, it is necessary to remember Keith Hopkins' hypothesis that the age of death of wives who die young is more likely to be recorded on a tombstone . . . . Over half the wives of imperial slaves and freedmen were dead before thirty, with the highest proportion dying between twenty and twenty-five. Of the nine married women buried in the tomb of a wealthy family, the Statilii, studied by Susan Treggiari, five had died at age twenty or younger. The mortality was probably even higher among the slaves belonging to poorer families.

The Roman household employed a far larger number of male slaves than female. Among children of imperial slaves and freedmen, the proportion is sixty or more per cent male, and among the adults the proportion of males is far higher, owing to the nature of the work of this elite group of civil servants. Susan Treggiari's study of the slaves and freedmen of Livia and of the Volusii likewise shows a ratio of roughly three males per female, with a slightly larger proportion of female slaves in a household owned by a woman than in the slave household belonging to a male owner. On the estates of the fictional Trimalchio were born thirty boys and forty girls in a single day. These statistics, like much in the *Satiricon*, are intended to be ludicrous, but nevertheless it is interesting to observe that all the slaves at Trimalchio's dinner are male. Boy babies were retained to fill posts as their fathers were manumitted or died, but excess female children were disposed of in various

ways. Some were sold to work as domestics in small households, many probably to brothels; others were perhaps exposed to die or be picked up by a
slave-trader. Still others were given by the master to male slaves as marriage
partners, with the expectation that children would be produced who would
be the master's property; some girls were purchased by male slaves from their
own funds. Perhaps Aurelia Philematium, a freedwoman who died at forty,
was one of these girls. Her epitaph states that her freedman husband took
her "to his bosom" when she was seven, and was like a father to her. Apparently he was kind to her when she joined the household, and then married
her. That this marriage could have been consummated when the bride was
only seven is not impossible.

Slaves were allowed to amass their own personal savings (*peculium*), and
could use this money to buy other slaves. When a male slave purchased his
wife, she had the status of a personal slave (*vicaria*) to her husband–owner—
although, strictly speaking, like all her husband's possessions she belonged to
his master—and the disaster of being sold to separate households was less
likely. This arrangement also offered a path of upward mobility for the slave
husband, since his master might free the slave's wife sooner than a valuable
and industrious male slave. . . .

Females could win their freedom through routes other than marriage.
As we have mentioned, slaves were allowed to amass their own personal
savings with a view to repaying their purchase price. A woman employed in
domestic work would have less opportunity to collect tips than a male slave
in an influential post, and her savings would grow rather slowly, although the
master's favorite bedmate might receive gifts, and a lady's maid would be
given tips from her mistress' lovers. On the other hand, as she grew older and
less attractive her value decreased, whereas the value of a highly trained male
slave increased with years. Thus a woman might eventually be able to purchase
her own freedom. In addition, Columella, who in the first century A.D. wrote
a treatise on farming, considered that a slave woman had repaid her purchase
price by bearing four children to be her master's property. Some urban slaves
might get away with fewer than this number. Freedom was often granted to
slaves voluntarily by owners, or by last testament. The manumission of the
actress Eucharis may be attributable to the good will of her owner; for example, the slave girl may have been granted freedom as she lay ill. A married
couple might be manumitted simultaneously, or the partner who was freed
first could amass enough funds to buy the partner still in slavery and manumit
him or her.

When both husband and wife had been slaves together, and the wife was
a freedwoman, the husband could in turn be manumitted by marriage. However, a freeborn woman who freed a male slave and married him was disapproved of, and such marriages were outlawed by Septimius Severus (reigned
A.D. 193–211).

The motives leading a freeborn woman or freedwoman to marry a slave are an indication of the complexity of slave society. Male slaves of the emperor or of important Roman families in administrative posts held positions of prestige and economic security. The wife had a good chance of being buried in the tomb of her husband's *familia*, and a place of burial was a concern to all Romans. The free woman who married an imperial slave was, in a sense, improving her status, while her husband also improved his. To the owner of the male slave, however, such an arrangement was detrimental, since the children were the property of the mother. Moreover, the prejudice against a free woman cohabiting with a slave extended even to slaves of high position within the slave hierarchy. Therefore a decree of the Senate was passed in A.D. 52 that discouraged freeborn and freedwomen from marrying slaves by reducing such a wife to the status of slave or freedwoman of her husband's master. This regulation was aimed at slaves of the imperial household. The loss of status gave the husband's master—the emperor in particular—financial advantages in regard to the wives and children of his male slaves.

In contrast to male slaves, female slaves in upper-class families were less likely to marry above their station. Females, even in important households, were used only for domestic service and did not hold positions of influence. There was therefore little incentive for freeborn men or freedmen outside their households to unite with them. In a lower-class family a female slave could be freed to marry her master, but in senatorial or imperial households this route of upward mobility was closed. Men of senatorial status could not marry freedwomen, although they could, of course, cohabit with them.

A few female members of the impeiial household attained positions of influence as the freedwoman concubines of emperors. These relationships were known publicly, often of long duration, and not a cause for scandal except when the woman misbehaved. Vespasian, Marcus Aurelius, and Antoninus Pius—all emperors of good reputation—lived with concubines after the death of their wives. They already had heirs to their throne, and, by choosing to live with women whom it was impossible for them to marry, they may have intended to avoid the squabbles between heirs descended from different wives which . . . characterized the Hellenistic monarchies.

The Appeal and Practice
of the Mystery-Religions

SAMUEL ANGUS

The Conversion of the Germans

WILLIAM CHANEY

Native Roman religion was family oriented, and the civic religion, as it developed, continued to rely heavily on the *gentes*, or clans. It was a practical and patriotic religion devoted to appeasing the gods who controlled the harvest, war, and civic affairs. Religious leadership was vested in a college of priests drawn from the best families and headed by the *pontifex maximus*, or high priest. With the expansion of Rome's power, the priesthood gained political influence because of its control over the religious calendar. Public business could not be conducted on holidays, and the constant necessity of adjusting the imperfect Roman calendar gave the priesthood considerable power over the timing of public action. If a crucial vote on public policy was about to be taken, for example, the priests could impose a long cooling-off period by adjusting the calendar.

Notwithstanding this power, the priesthood remained remarkably independent during the difficult years of the late Republic and the period following the assassination of Julius Caesar. Caesar did not appropriate the position of *pontifex maximus* when he became *dictator*, and Augustus, his successor, did not take the title until 13 B.C., when the holder of the office died. After that date, however, the title and power of the *pontifex* was held by the emperor, and this continued to be true even after Constantine embraced Christianity.

As the political power of the old Roman priesthood increased, the hold of the old religion over the Roman populace decreased. As the city became the center of power and commerce in an ever-widening empire, leading Romans began to show contempt for the superstitions of the old cults. After the establishment of Roman hegemony over Greece in 196 B.C., the influence of eastern religions permanently altered Rome's religious culture. Greek slaves and traders carried to Rome cults that had come to Greece from Thrace and Phrygia. These were the mysteries, cults through which men and women were initiated into a communal, mystical religious experience. As the old social associations broke down or atrophied in the altered circumstances of Roman imperial life, the new cults filled the need for community, order, and hope.

The great influx of mystery cults coincided with the early decades of the Principate founded by Augustus. After the civil wars that followed Julius Caesar's assassination and led to the annexation of Egypt and the eastern provinces, the religions of these areas gravitated toward the new center of world power in Rome and thence spread through the empire along the trade routes. Augustus and Tiberius themselves were religiously conservative, bent on restoring the ancient glory and customs of Rome. Yet even they favored the mystery cult of the Great Mother, and their successors increasingly favored or at least condoned the establishment of the other mysteries. Two of Rome's most ancient and famous churches, San Clemente and Santa Maria in Trastevere, were built over the ruins of Roman houses in which there had been Mithraic shrines. There were thousands of such sanctuaries throughout the city and the empire.

This was the religious milieu in which the Apostles and their disciples began to preach Christianity. In fact, early Christianity resembled the mystery cults in its organization. Christian churches were like cells made up of relatively few members each and organized under the Roman laws governing private associations. Though the number of Christians grew, they did not gather together in one large community, but continued to meet in small groups. The persecutions that began in earnest during the third century drove these communities underground and made them seem even more mysterious than before. Hostile outsiders suspected Christians of crude antisocial activities, and the secrecy of the communities only enhanced this image. Similar criticism was leveled at other mystery cults; for many Romans, all of them were subversive and perhaps even savage.

We know very little about early Christian communities and even less about the mystery cults. In fact, most of our information about the mysteries comes from Christian apologists who distorted the character and appeal of the rival cults. What was that appeal? What did the cultists do? Why did the cults, Christianity included, attract so many adherents among the Roman population, and why did Christianity win out over the others? In the first selection in this section, Samuel Angus elaborates on the attractions, demands, and practices of the mysteries. He uses pagan literary references and archeology to counter the effect of the biased accounts left by Christian writers. In the second selection, William Chaney focuses on a crucial aspect of Christianity's ultimate victory over other ancient religious systems—the conversion of the Germans. By the middle of the sixth century, the Germans were masters of nearly all the western territory of the Roman Empire. If Christianity was to become the dominant religion in the Mediterranean world and its northern dependencies, Christian preachers would have to deal with the Germans.

Christian leaders had to mold a religion—basically a romanized offshoot of Judaism—that would accommodate the primitive pagan tradition of the Germans. In describing how they accomplished this feat, Chaney also illuminates one of the principal features of western Germanic culture, sacral kingship.

THE APPEAL AND PRACTICE OF THE MYSTERY–RELIGIONS

A Mystery-Religion was a personal religion to which membership was open not by the accident of birth but by a religious rebirth. The hereditary principle of membership known to the state-religions of Greece and Rome and to the church–state of Israel was superseded by that of personal volition, which has been the dominating principle in religious history since the days of Alexander the Great. The religion of the *thiasos* had replaced that of the *polis*. Consequently the Mysteries, with their pronounced subjectivity and variety of impression, responded to and augmented the individualism inaugurated in the Mediterranean world by Alexander and consummated by the Roman Empire.

That religion is primarily a personal matter is a commonplace to us; it was an epoch-making discovery to the leading peoples of the Roman Empire. So strong was the racial consciousness of the Jews that they for the most part conceived God's dealings with them as moving within the Covenant. Individualism was at any time but a passing phase in their religious experience. It is true that Jeremiah and Ezekiel rescued the individual, and that Ezekiel carried individualism to such an extent as to overlook the effects of heredity and the constitution of society by which we are members the one of the other. It was in the services of the Synagogue that the personal religion and piety of Israel attained fullest expression. The religions of Greece and Rome were corporate entities—the religious experience of their social and political systems. Men worshipped for the good of all collectively rather than for the good of their own souls. These religions, like every religion that allies itself with temporal power, collapsed with the state systems which they had buttressed. In the ensuing confusion and amid the welter of centuries of strife personal needs became more clamant. These needs were at least partially satisfied by the Mysteries, which contemplated man irrespective of the polity or social conditions under which he lived. "With them," says Cumont, "religion ceases to be bound to the State in order to become universal; it is no longer conceived as a public duty, but as a personal obligation;

From *The Mystery-Religions and Christianity* by Samuel Angus (London: John Murray, 1925), pp. 65–67, 87–90, 144–48. Reprinted by permission of Charles Scribner's Sons.

it no longer subordinates the individual to the city-state, but professes above all to ensure his personal salvation in this world and above all in the next." To Orphism must be attributed in no small measure this shifting of religious emphasis. Athens, too, took a momentous religious step in the abolition before the sixth century B.C. of gentile privileges in the Eleusinian Mysteries in favour of free choice. Unlike the state religions the Mysteries as personal cults produced saints and ascetics, and martyrs. Livy records how "a multitude" of the members of the Dionysiac brotherhoods lost their lives in an attempt by the Government to extirpate them. Many and severe were the persecutions to which the Isiac faith was subjected about the beginning of the Christian era. The presence of skeletons in the Mithraic chapels testifies to this day to the martyrs who, as devoted *milites Mithrae invicti*, suffered at Christian hands. In the personal cults the worshippers were united by the ties of fellowship with the deity of their choice, by the obligation of common vows, by the duty of personal propaganda, and by revivalistic enthusiasm. The pious could in ecstasy feel himself lifted above his ordinary limitations to behold the beatific vision, or in enthusiasm believe himself to be God-inspired or God-filled—phenomena in some respects akin to the experiences of the early Christians on the outpouring of the Spirit.

One reason why the Mysteries were so long anathema to the rulers of the West was that, as personal religions, they concerned themselves little with public life, centering their attention on the individual life. They accentuated that indifference to citizenship in society at large which was charged against the Jews, and not without some justification against the Christians, and which proved one of the chief factors in the disintegration of ancient civilization. . . .

Both in preparation for initiation and in the practice of the Mysteries obligations of painful self-mortification were laid upon those celebrants who would excel in the cult, or become hierophants, or reap the fullest advantages of adherence. The period was past when men offered the fruit of their bodies for the sin of their souls, but was succeeded by another epoch when men, by personal bodily torture and discomfort, would expiate their sins and placate the deity. The naturalistic origin of the Mysteries, with violent and sanguinary survivals, rendered it too easy to retain repulsive self-mutilations against which the moral consciousness of a humaner era struggled with only partial success. The cruel elements were never wholly eliminated, though some Mysteries took on a more humane aspect than others, notably Orphism and the Hermetic Revelation Religion. Those of Phrygia and the related Anatolian cults were among the bloodiest; next came the Syrian cults, but these were gradually refined by the development of a solar monotheism. That of Isis was the most respectable, while that of Mithra was the most sober. But in each and all it was, by a true religious instinct, perceived that man must enter into fellowship of the deity's sufferings if he would participate in the deity's joy. In studying the cruel side of the Mystery-cults we must remember that the religious thought of the world was struggling with the twofold problem of the relation of the material to the spiritual, with but dim rays of that light which Christian idealism has shed upon the enigma, and of the means whereby man can most securely enter into union with God. In an era of religious excitation no price was too high to pay to attain quietude of heart. The worst forms of self-mortification were generally performed by, but by no means restricted to, the priesthood.

The religious self-multilations were of Oriental provenance. The most familiar are those of the Galli of the Great Mother (contemptuously called *semi viri* by Juvenal and *Gallae* by Catullus), which consisted in the laceration of their flesh with broken pottery, gashing of their limbs with knives during delirious dances and processions, self-flagellations or mutual floggings, and finally the perpetration of the culminating act of self-effacement in imitation of the act of their patron Attis under the pine-tree. The male servitors of the Ephesian Artemis were eunuchs, as were also the priests of Atargatis, the *dea Syria*. The rites of Bellona, identified with Ma, Isis, and Cybele, were equally bloody with those of the Great Mother. Her black-robed *fanatici* made offerings of their own blood and slashed their bodies while raving ecstatically with a sword in each hand. Blood drawn from the lacerated thighs of the priests and partaken of by the candidates was the seal of initiation.

The probation for entry into the Mithraic communion was more prolonged and the degrees of preparation more numerous and exacting than for other cults, though not so orgiastic as those of Anatolia. The number, however, and nature of the Mithraic grades are somewhat uncertain, perhaps owing to the disturbance of the original economy—whatever it was—by the introduction of the astral theology of the seven planets and the still later solar theology of the twelve signs of the zodiac. Students of Mithraism usually follow Jerome in affirming the existence of seven grades: *Raven, Hidden* or *Secret One* (? *Cryphius*), *Soldier, Lion, Persian, Sun-runner* (*Heliodromus*) and *Father*, of which the *Lion* is the most frequently met and that of *Father* the most coveted. Phythian-Adams contends for the number six as being correct and original. On the other hand, Celsus would indicate perhaps eight grades when he states that in the Persian Mysteries there is a ladder with seven gates with an eighth gate at the top. The first three stages, according to Porphyry, preceded initiation, so that the subsequent grades marked degrees of spiritual rank after initiation. Either the communicant himself or the officiating priest or those present, were obliged to wear masks corresponding to the *Raven* and *Lion*, and a garb corresponding to the other characters. By the strictest kind of freemasonry the initiate was tested at each stage, and his spiritual career was marked by ordeals, feigned or real, and by an austere discipline which demonstrated his courage, sincerity, and faith. He submitted to a baptism of total immersion. He was called upon to pass through flame with hands bound and eyes blindfolded, or to swim rivers. In some cases at least the neophyte jumped down a precipice: whether this was done in symbol merely or was an actual leap we cannot tell. If an actual jump it must have taken place outside the Mithraic chapels, which were too small to permit of such a gymnastic feat. A Heddernheim relief represents a neophyte standing in snow. Animal sacrifices, mostly of birds, were made in the chapels. At some stage the neophyte was obliged to witness or even to take part in a "simulated death to produce reverence." A case is recorded in which the emperor Commodus, on initiation, polluted the chapel by perpetrating an actual murder upon a celebrant. What was the nature of this symbolic death we may not be certain, though theologically it was perhaps viewed as vicarious rather than sacrificial, as we may infer from the evidence of the practice of animal sacrifices. Suggestive symbolic ceremonies were enacted at each stage of initiation. Tertullian records that the neophyte, on attaining the degree of "Soldier," was offered, at the point of a sword, a crown or garland, which was then put upon his head only to be thrust away with the confession "Mithra is my crown." Such a soldier was "signed" on the forehead with a hot iron. Thenceforth he renounced the social custom of wearing a garland even at a banquet. According to Porphyry, on entry upon the next degree, that of "Lion," the initiate's lips were purified with honey. . . .

At first sight it seems inexplicable that the Oriental mystic and even orgiastic cults, so humble and barbarous in their origin, frowned upon on their first entry by the governments, winning the majority of their followers from the lower, slave and artisan, classes, supported for centuries by private contributions, often exacting austerities and maintaining customs which exposed the votary to the derision of the crowd, and even endangered his health, should have exercised such an increasing sway over the Graeco-Roman world, and, but for Christianity, would have conquered. They did not afford the only religious refuge of the age: why did they afford a refuge to so many? There were intellectual systems like Greek philosophy, and Gnosticism; there were ethical forces like Judaism, while state-religion asserted itself in repeated pagan revivals and most conspicuously in the imperial cult. These entailed practically no outlay on the part of their adherents. But the mystery-cults demanded that self-sacrifice which has always distinguished Free Churches as contrasted with Established Churches or philosophic schools. Reflect on what it cost to be a regular adherent of the Isiac cult. There were the austerities and fasts, which could not be agreeable to the flesh. Festal white robes had to be procured in honour of the deity, and would regularly demand the fuller's services. The well-equipped Isaea had to be erected and the cost of maintenance met by those who used them. An elaborate and expensive priesthood had to be maintained by the offerings of the faithful. On an ostracon in the Berlin Museum, bearing date August 4, A.D. 63, a priest of Isis gives a receipt to a working man thus: "I have received from you four drachmae, one obol, as collection of Isis for the public worship." Devotion to the Egyptian Madonna resulted in costly statues adorned with abundance of precious stones. Even the inventory of the articles in one small shrine of Isis proves amazing liberality. An inscription from Delos of about 200 B.C. tells how Serapis in a dream-oracle objects to the continuance of his cult in hired premises and demands the building of a temple. Although Apuleius was the son of a rich municipal official, from whom he and his brother inherited the large fortune of two million sesterces, he was obliged to sell his scanty wardrobe to procure funds sufficient for initiation into the rites of Osiris after having been admitted to those of Isis. The frescoes of Herculaneum give some idea of the sacerdotal college attached to any regular Isaeum. There were the senior or high priest and assistant priests and acolytes. These *sacerdotes*, unlike the semi-civic priests of Greece and Rome, devoted all their time to their ecclesiastical offices, and did not generally earn their living by practising a craft or speculating in a business. The altar fires had to be supplied and tended, and the morning sacrifices to be provided. In the statutes of the Iobacchoi of Athens are regulations as to the contributions of each member and the penalty for default of payment. The museum of Thebes contains an inscription detailing the offerings to the Kabiri for one season (cir. 332 B.C.). In special cases long pilgrimages were made, which entailed absence from the ordinary means of earning a livelihood, in addition to costly fares paid to greedy ship-masters, and the still more costly land travelling. Moreover, some eager souls in pursuit of salvation sought initiation into several Mysteries, though how the cost was met by any but the rich is difficult for us to conjecture, for men had to earn their bread then as now. The prosperous Syrian merchant, the Jewish banker, the Roman landlord, the successful Greek physician, the speculating freedman could afford to indulge in any expenditure for religion; but these upper classes constituted a smaller minority then than nowadays. Of course there was much voluntary service given by slaves, artisans, and soldiers; but all this was rendered outside the long hours of toil, and is itself a testimony to the deep conviction on the part of candidates that there was something worthwhile in the Mysteries. It is true that in the religious guilds the rich members laudably realized their brotherhood with their poorer "brethren," and often bore the whole or the chief part of the expenses incurred in the maintenance of the cult and in furnishing the sacred meals. In the regular offerings the poor contributed their mite, and they that were rich brought much. Unselfishness and generosity were by no means unknown virtues among the pagans, and were not invariably conspicuous in Christian guilds, as we may infer from Paul's description of the abuses in connexion with the *Agape* in Corinth.

The *taurobolium* cannot have been other than costly. The officiating priest's stipend had to be paid, the labour supplied, the timber prepared for the trench, the bull, doubtless of exceptional quality, had to be purchased;

the sacramental garments, saturated in blood, were either fulled or kept as souvenirs of the baptismal rebirth, and so rendered economically valueless.

Some idea of the demands made upon the generosity of votaries in the construction and upkeep of the Mithraea may be gathered from the fact that the second largest Mithraeum discovered, that of Sarmizegethusa, had accommodation for a maximum of 100 members, while the majority of the chapels could not accommodate a half of this number. Upon this limited *sodalicium* fell the cost of the excavation of the grotto, the arching of the roof, the chiselling of stone benches for the worshippers, the altar with its sacrifices, the carving of the Tauroctony and the Mithraic *agape*, the sacred meals and initiations, the holy lights, and all the other cult apparatus. The "brethren" were generally legionaries whose *stipendium* was small, or oriental slaves whose *peculium* was modest indeed.

Enough has been said to make it clear that votaries in the Mysteries were not—generally speaking—prompted to seek initiation with a view to material gain, or to find a cheap religion, or to escape tithes. Indeed, these ancient initiates had recourse to religions which were costly because those religions which were provided free failed to lay hold of their imagination or satisfy their religious cravings.

As the Mysteries themselves presented a good and a bad side, so there were among their adherents and priests good, bad, and indifferent. Human nature being what it is, some initiates lived in the high latitudes of spiritual exaltation, enjoying religious serenity, while others remained content with the external pomp and symbolism, only vaguely intelligible to them, and never surmounted a superstition which saw in religion a magic or means of compulsion to be applied to the deity for selfish ends. Doubtless entrance into the Mysteries was sought from base motives by some. For the ordinary members initiation entailed financial loss rather than gain, but unscrupulous priests had abundant opportunity of using their holy office for self-aggrandizement. The sordid transaction of the senior priest of Isis, as told by Josephus, though an extreme case, is hardly solitary. The zeal of highly organized priesthoods, like that of Isis, for donations and endownments probably corresponded to a similar zeal on the part of the abbots and friars of the Middle Ages, such as is exposed, e.g. in Scott's *Fair Maid of Perth*. It is quite clear from Apuleius' account of the repeated initiations of Lucius that the Egyptian priests at Cenchreae and Rome took advantage of his credulity to enrich their cult and so benefit themselves. The initiatory fee was fixed by the goddess herself. A list of things required was furnished by the priest, which Lucius provided with even greater liberality than was necessary. At his initiation he was clad in "the cloak of Olympus," very richly embroidered, in which he was presented to his fellow-worshippers, after which followed feasts and banqueting, for which doubtless Lucius himself had paid in hard cash. A year later the goddess's grasping priests advised a further initiation into the rites of

Osiris, for which it was necessary to sell his clothes to procure the necessary fees, and shortly thereafter the goddess required a third initiation, in the preparation for which he was "guided by the enthusiasm of my faith rather than the measure of my fortunes," relying on his earnings as a professor of rhetoric at Rome. The priesthood might be sought because of the secured income attached to its functions, because of the powerful influence wielded by it over the initiates, or because of the opportunity for influencing public opinion, or even, in later days, for interfering in politics.

THE CONVERSION OF THE GERMANS

Kingship is the Anglo-Saxon political institution *par excellence* and gives cohesion to the realms established by the invading tribes. In each kingdom the royal race—the *stirps regia*—which sprang from its founder provided the source from which the individual rulers were chosen, and beyond the earthly founder was the god who was the divine ancestor of almost every Anglo-Saxon royal house, Woden. The antiquity of the monarchic institution is reflected in the developed terminology for kingship, as in the twenty-six synonyms for "king" used by the *Beowulf* poet alone, and time itself was recorded according to the regnal years of these Woden-sprung monarchs. Their accessions and deaths are recorded in such histories as have survived, which are filled above all with the deeds of kings.

In spite of the paucity of sources, even in later traditions, for the age of migrations and the Anglo-Saxon settlement in the island, it is clear that the institution of kingship was a survival from pre-conquest Germanic custom and did not arise as rule peculiar to the insular development. Tacitus records it for the Teutonic tribes of the *Germania*, in which descent-chosen kings are found sharing power with war-chiefs. *Reges ex nobilitate, duces ex virtute sumunt* [they choose kings because of their nobility, war leaders on ability], he asserts. The "king or chief" (*rex vel princeps*) speaks first in the tribal assembly, but here he rules more "by right of advising" (*auctoritate suadendi*) than by any absolute right of command. Fines are paid in part to the king or state, and the king or chief participates in the priestly office of interpreting the most sacred auguries, the neighing of the white horses. Thus, far from an autocrat, the Teutonic king of the *Germania* exercises power which is honorific and priestly but neither unlimited nor arbitrary; kingship, however, is a firm part of this generalized portrait of Germanic society, and the Tacitean distinction between *reges* and *principes* seems to rest not so much on a fixed

From *The Cult of Kingship in Anglo-Saxon England* by William Chaney (Manchester University Press, 1970), pp. 7–9, 11–12, 14–16, 156–61, 166–70, 172–73. Reprinted by permission of Manchester University Press.

division between the two titles as on multiple rulership, with more than one prince, drawn from the *stirps regia*, ruling over a single tribe. Kingly government is general to early Germanic society, though two or more kings are sometimes found sharing rule over a single tribe. Even later, in Anglo-Saxon England, there are examples of multiple-rulership. Horsa and, after Horsa's death, Hengest's son Aesc shared the rule over Kent with Hengest, as Cerdic and his son Cynric were joint-kings over the West Saxons. Sigehere and Sebbe were later co-rulers in East Anglia, and five West Saxon kings were slain in a single battle by Edwin of Northumbria. . . .

The most fundamental concept in Germanic kingships is the indissolubility of its religious and political functions. The king is above all the intermediary between his people and the gods, the charismatic embodiment of the "luck" of the folk. The relation of the divine and the tribal is primarily one of action, of "doing," and to assure the favourable actions of the gods toward the tribe the king "does" his office as mediator between them, sacrificing for victory, for good crops and for peace, "making" the year. It is not that he is the leader of the folk and the guarantor of their *heil* who acts so that the gods may bless them. Thus, later distinctions between priestly and political functions are caught up into a union, a personal embodiment of the link with the divine on which the tribe's well-being depends. In a world in which the kingdoms of men depend upon the realm of the divine, the earthly king moves in the vital strand which binds them together. In a very real sense, then, the god is first of all the god of the king, whose role it is to assume this burden of favourable relationship with the deity, and only secondarily the god of the tribe, whose "luck" is mediated by that of the ruler. When the king's "luck" or charismatic power is maintained, the favour of the god rests with the tribe; when he has lost his "luck" and is impotent to secure the divine blessings, his people are justified, even obliged, to do the only thing possible, to replace him with another who can make the office once more effective. . . . when the light of history and tradition falls on Germanic kingship of the age of migrations, the king is leader of the war-hosts but also the charismatic mediator with the divine, the sacral holder of the tribal "luck." Thus Germanic and Scandinavian history of the early Middle Ages knows no strong priesthood set apart from the secular rulers. The temples were private possessions, pagan parallels of the medieval *Eigenkirche* [private churches], and the head of the household was the temple's priest. The Germanic king himself offered sacrifices. Whether or not the *sacerdotes* [priests] of Tacitus are in reality only the *principes* in their magical and priestly role, by the time of the early migrations the chief of the *principes*—the king—has become the tribal highpriest, the "warden of the holy temple," as northern poetry calls him. Sacrificing for good crops and for victory in battle, he assured plenty among his people, but when the gods deserted him and his "luck" no longer flowed from him, he could be deposed or even killed in time of tribal disaster. So

Ammianus Marcellinus records that Burgundian kings under whom crops or victory failed were deposed, and when bad harvests continued in Sweden under the Ynglingar King Domaldi, in spite of rich sacrifices by the ruler, he was killed. His descendant, King Olaf Tretelgia of Sweden, failed to make *blot*, neglecting the rites necessary for good crops, so that the latter failed; the Swedes, who "used always to reckon good or bad crops for or against their kings," burned the king in his house as an offering to Oðin. Thus when the king maintained a proper relation with the gods, his realm was bathed in fullness, but when his "luck" left him, it was a sign that the gods themselves had deserted him; hence Odoacer, although an Arian Christian, when he was struck down by Theodoric the Ostrogoth in Ravenna, uttered his dying cry of despair at this withdrawal of the king's deity—"Where is God?"

The early Germanic king is, consequently, not a god and not all-powerful, but he is filled with a charismatic power on which his tribe depends for its well-being. This is the king's *mana*, "a force utterly distinct from mere physical power or strength, the possession of which assures success, good fortune, and the like to its possessor." This power permeates not the king alone but the entire "royal race," the whole kin from among whom the folk elect him, and its source is probably to be sought in the descent of this *stirps regia* from a god. The Woden-sprung monarchs of the Anglo-Saxons, like the god-descended royal houses of the Continent, contain within the clan the special virtue, the *mana* from on high, but hereditary as this power was, the office of kingship which embodied it might be filled by any member of the "divine race." "It was the virtue of their blood," as Fritz Kern writes, "that lifted the sons of Woden, the Astings, the Amals, and so on, out of the ranks of the folk, though without bestowing upon any individual prince a right to the throne independent of the popular will. The family's possession of the throne was as inviolable as the right of any individual prince to succeed to it was insecure." . . .

As Sir Frank Stenton has said, "throughout the country in which Augustine and his companions laboured, heathenism was still a living religion when it met the Christian challenge." The binding elements in that pagan faith, as has been observed, were the kin-group and the head of the tribe who bound the folk to the gods and the gods to the folk. The less, therefore, that a new religion attempted to isolate the converted from their group and to arouse a combined political-religious opposition, the less difficult would it be to effect a conversion to a new and more powerful God. When religious and political opposition were combined, as in King Olaf the Holy's attempted conversion of Norway, during the apostacy of Eadbald of Kent, or among the East Saxons under the sons of King Saberht, Christianity met formidable hostility; when there was little political opposition, on the other hand, the reception of the new faith was even undramatic in its lack of tension and high events. The crucial figure, consequently, in any conversion was the sacral king, and the fact that in Anglo-Saxon England the paths of the new religion were made smooth was in every kingdom due to the role played by its ruler.

The story of the English Conversion opens in Kent with the arrival in Thanet of St. Augustine and about forty companions. The mission had left Rome probably early in A.D. 596 and landed early the next year in the realms of the *bretwalda* Aethelberht, the most powerful ruler in southern Britain. Its reception was not unfriendly. The king ordered it to be provided with *necessaria*, and after some days went himself into Thanet to hear the *nuntium optimum* which the Roman had claimed to bring. Since for at least nine years Christian services had been held in the royal capital, celebrated for Queen Bertha, the Christian daughter of the Merovingian King Charibert, by her chaplain, Bishop Liudhard, the *fama . . . Christianae religionis* had, as Bede says, come to the king before, and modern historians may have underestimated his knowledge of the faith. When Pope Gregory writes that "the news had reached him that the English people wished to become Christians," the possibility is at least open that Aethelberht himself or Bertha may have acted to instigate the mission. Certainly he acknowledged in terms of his own religion (*vetere usus augurio*) the possible power of Augustine's band, "for he would not permit them to come to him in any house, lest . . . if they practiced any magical arts they might deceive him by surprise, prevailing against him." Nonetheless, the Gospel impressed him as *nova . . . et incerta* [new and uncertain] so that, as he declared, he could not abandon the faith which he and his people had observed for so long. However, he not only welcomed Augustine with all courtesy and provided for his wants but gave permission for him to "win unto the faith of your religion with your preaching as many as you may." Some (*nonnulli*) were baptized before Aethelberht, but it was only after the royal conversion that many (*plures*) turned to Christianity, so that on Christmas, A.D. 597, Gregory reports in a letter to Patriarch Eulogius of Alexandria, more than ten thousand of the king's subjects were baptized.

The dependence of the Kentish mission on the royal role is seen with equal clarity after the death of the converted Aethelberht on February 24th, A.D. 616. His and Bertha's son, the new king Eadbald, was openly heathen and, following pagan practice, married his father's widow, the second and probably heathen wife of Aethelberht. When their king moved to the worship of the old gods, so did the superficially converted folk. The very life of the Christian mission was threatened when Augustine's successor, Laurentius, agreed with the fugitive bishops, Mellitus of London and Justin of Rochester, that "it were better for them all to return to their own country and there to serve the Lord with a free mind, than to abide without profit amongst barbarous men that were rebels of the faith. It was only the conversion and baptism of Eadbald and the strong royal support for the Church thereafter which brought his people once more into the Christian fold. His son and successor, King Eorcenberht, was the "first of the kings of the English who by his princely authority ordered that idols in his whole realm should be abandoned and destroyed," and with this visible sign of the king's allegiance to the new religion, we never hear of popular apostasy in Kent again.

The loose hegemony which the *bretwalda* Aethelberht exercised over the entire territory south of the Humber facilitated the advance of Christianity. Although none of the kings who acknowledged his overlordship was forced to change his religion when the king of Kent did, yet the latter's influence on these monarchs aided the adoption of the faith by them and consequently by their people. The first kingdom to be affected was that of the East Saxons, ruled by Saberht, the son of Aethelberht's sister, Ricula. When, in A.D. 604, Augustine consecrated his follower Mellitus as bishop to preach in Essex, not only were the king and, as Bede says, the *provincia* converted, but Aethelberht himself built the church of St. Paul in Saberht's capital city, London. Again, however, royal faith and popular faith moved together, for upon the death of the East Saxon monarch his three sons, still heathen, "gave free license to the people subject to them to worship idols"; so strong was the return to paganism that not only was Mellitus driven out, but when he had returned and Eadbald had restored the faith in Kent, Essex remained true to its "idolatrous high priests."

It was not for almost half a century (A.D. 653) that a Christian mission entered Essex, when once again the baptism of its king preceded its conversion. The East Saxon king, Sigbert the Good, a friend and frequent visitor at the court of Oswiu of Northumbria, was persuaded in the North that "such could not be gods which had been made with men's hands." Following his baptism and return to Essex, the mission of Cedd was invited to his kingdom and there, since the cult-leader of the folk was now favourable to the mission, it was a success, and a "great church," increasing daily, was brought into existence. After the murder of Sigbert the Good, his successor, Swidhelm, son of Sexbald, was a Christian, having been baptized in East Anglia, and his subjects stayed firm in the faith of their monarch. However, when Sighere followed him to the throne, the great plague of 664 swept through the land, and the king himself, in his old role as guardian of the health of his folk, restored the pagan temples and returned *cum sua parte populi* to the worship of idols, "as though they could thereby be protected from the mortal sickness." It was, thus, a national calamity such as paganism had called upon the king to cure, which caused King Sighere to offer *blot* to the offended gods, and "his part of the people" apostacized with him. Wulfhere of Mercia, overlord of Sighere, however, sent a mission under Bishop Jaruman to re-christianize the country, and it turned *populum et regem* together again to Christ. Essex remained firm thereafter, but the powerful role of the king in determining the religion of his people is obvious in the long history of its conversion. When Saberht was converted, so were the East Saxons; when his sons worshipped the old gods, their subjects followed their lead; when Sigbert turned to the new religion, the conversion was again successful; when the panic of the plague swept Essex, one king and his people alike reverted to the old gods; and, finally, both together returned to Christianity. The pagan Germanic notion that the gods are primarily the gods of the king, who mediates with them for his folk, is clearly witnessed in Anglo-Saxon England. . . .

Clearly, then, the history of the coming of Christianity displays the role of the English king as the converter of his people. In no kingdom did the conversion occur without royal support, and in none do we hear of the conversion of the folk without that of the monarch previously. Even in Mercia, it was only after Peada, who ruled as sub-king under his father [Penda], became a Christian and with the permission of the great pagan war-lord himself that the Gospel was preached; the major work of the mission was done nonetheless only after Penda's death. The tribal relation with the divine still was dependent on the king's relation with the divine, and the proper *blot* was primarily the ruler's affair. Consequently, the conversion of the *folc* stemmed from the conversion of the king to the more powerful deity, since it was the king's relationship with the gods which "saved" his people as much as did the gods themselves. When the king turned to Christ, it was done *cum sua gente* [with his people].

Further, in most of the kingdoms—Kent, Essex, East Anglia, Deira, and Bernicia—royal apostasy occurred, a fact which can best be explained by the long tradition of performing essential rites for the folk. In Deira and Bernicia the one year rule of the apostate kings was so brief that we are told nothing of popular reaction. However, when Redwald of East Anglia offered sacrifice to the former gods, it would certainly have had popular support for him to have done it in the face of his conversion. In Kent, King Eadbald led his people *ad priorem vomitum* [i.e., back to paganism], and in the realm of the East Saxons, Bede tells us, the apostate folk could not be recalled to faith in Christ even after Saberht's heathen sons had been killed in battle against the West Saxons. Converted again under Sigbert the Good, they apostacized once more when Sighere returned to his ancestral gods during the great plague of A.D. 664–665. Thus, as conversion of the subjects depends on that of the ruler, so also royal and popular apostasy are closely related.

In addition, as in the pagan North improper observance of the rituals was the cause of royal deposition and even king-slaying, so apostasy from the Christian faith was regarded as bringing about the loss of kingdom and on occasion the deletion from the line of Woden-sprung monarchs who had made the proper sacrifices. Thus, when Cenwalh succeeded his father, Cynegils of the West Saxons, Bede reports that he "refused to accept the faith and sacraments of the heavenly kingdom and not long after lost even the power over his earthly kingdom." When he was converted in East Anglia, however, he was restored to his realm. We have also noted that Osric of Deira and

Eanfrid of Bernicia were removed from the king-lists because of their apostacy. However, when Eadbald of Kent apostacized after the death of his father Aethelberht, he was not stripped of his place in the line of monarchs, even though his subjects followed him, nor was Sighere of Essex. In both cases, however, they returned to the Christian faith. This cannot be said, though, of Redwald of East Anglia, who worshipped at two altars in one temple and who was nonetheless listed as a *bretwalda*. Thus, while the tribal culture was still strong enough after the Conversion to bring royal apostacy, both the old and the new religions related the fate of the kingdom to the cult of the king.

Christianity, however, even linked the destiny of king and kingdom not only with worship of God but with obedience to his priesthood. Consequently, *pax et gaudium in populis et anni frugiferi victoriaeque in hostes* [peace and joy in the people and fruitful years and victories over enemies]—the traditional rewards to rulers for pagan *blot*—were given "by the aid of God" to King Egfrith and Queen Aethelthryth, rulers of Deira and Bernicia, as long as they were obedient to Bishop Wilfrid; however, when the king was no longer at one with the bishop, his "luck" left him. Here, of course, unlike the old religion in which there was no powerful priesthood to be equated with the Divine Will and the *principes* themselves performed priestly functions, the possibility of division between two functions of the pagan Anglo-Saxon royal *persona mixta* appears. This division was to become crucial for the later concept of Christian kingship.

A final element in the royal role during the Conversion is the spiritual fatherhood of Anglo-Saxon kings over pagan rulers whose submission to Christianity they had procured. The adoption of rulers by Roman emperors was, of course, not unknown, as in the adoption by the latter of Gothic kings through the symbolic handing over of weapons. The reception by a noble foster-father was, however, a feature of pagan baptism in the North, and it was most probably from this source that the Anglo-Saxon royal custom was derived. Thus Guthorm the Earl, for example, set the eldest son of King Harald Fair-Hair of Norway on his knee and became his foster-father. Thus spiritual relationship occurs as early as A.D. 635 in England, when the Christian Oswald of Northumbria received his future father-in-law, King Cynegils of the West Saxons, as his son upon the latter's conversion. When Cynegil's grandson, Cuthred, was baptized four years later, Bishop Birinus "received him for son," in a prelude to the later expansion of this custom of the adoption of rulers. Thus, in a letter of A.D. 798 to Pope Leo III concerning the see of Lichfield, King Cenwulf of Mercia, ruling those "who dwell at the end of the world," requests "that you will especially receive me as your son by adoption, just as I love you in the person of a father, and always honour you with obedience with all my strength. For it is meet that holy faith be kept among such great persons, and inviolate love be guarded." As pagan chieftains were received as foster-sons at the hands of other rulers, so Anglo-Saxon kings desired the prestige that would come from entering into this traditional spiritual sonship with the great chief of the new religion in far-off Rome. Such personal relationships "among great persons" were honourable and customary. Indicating the cautious reception of this apparently unfamiliar custom in Rome, however, Pope Leo does not even mention the matter in his reply to Cenwulf. He speaks to the problem of the see of Lichfield but confines his suggestions for a closer relationship to exhorting the Mercian monarch to continue Offa's annual payment of three hundred and sixty-five mancuses to Rome. . . .

The king's role in conversion in England is thus well established. The theological content of the old religion, as well as its integration into the social and political background of the Germanic tribes, helped cast the mould into which Christian doctrine was poured and affected the interpretation of the finished work. As the change was more palatable to the folk if the new God were worshipped in the temples of the old, as Gregory the Great realized, so Christianity was the more readily accepted if the tribes were able to follow the sacrificial king of the old religion into the new. The totality of life and worlds made impossible the later duality of Church and State, and the interweaving of cult and culture enhanced the sacral strand of kingship which knit together the tapestry of tribal life.

Part 2

THE EARLY
MIDDLE AGES

6th–11th Centuries

Plowing scene. Luttrell Psalter. England, c. 1340

In the sixth century, the western Roman Empire fell to the Germans and was replaced by kingdoms based on the peoples making up the major elements of the migrating hordes of barbarians. In Gaul, it was the Franks; in Spain, the Visigoths; in Italy, the Ostrogoths; in North Africa, the Vandals. Under the pressures of movement and war, the small, autonomous German communities were merged under powerful kings. After the kingdoms were established, these kings consolidated their positions by assuming the mantle of Roman authority. Everywhere in Europe, the German kings sought and received confirmation of their new power from the Roman emperors in Constantinople. For their part, the emperors had nothing to lose by granting the kings Roman titles. It preserved the image of imperial power even though the reality had been gone for decades, and it helped to maintain good relations between the eastern Roman Empire and the occupants of the old imperial territories in Europe.

The new society of barbarian Europe was a compound of the old provincial society of the Roman Empire and the tribal society of the German invaders. The first selection in Part 2 deals with the lesser known of these two elements, German tribal society. The second selection deals with another aspect of early medieval social history, the formation of a new peasantry, due to an agricultural revolution that became the basis for the urban civilization of the twelfth and succeeding centuries. It is important to recognize that the introduction of new agricultural technology not only produced more food, but also changed the way of life of the largest class of the medieval population, the peasant farmers.

From consideration of the majority, we turn to consideration of a small, but important, minority, the Jews. Urbanization increased rapidly from the later eleventh century on, but the new city dwellers of that period found tightly knit, prosperous Jewish communities already well established in the north European towns. Robert Chazan's "The Jews in a Christian Society" examines these communities.

In the final selection, Joshua Prawer's "World of the Crusaders," we go to the Holy Land to look at the colonial society Europeans established there after the First Crusade (1096–1099). In fact, this colony was only the most famous of those established by Europeans during the eleventh century. Beginning in the middle of the century, northerners had pushed steadily toward reconquering the Iberian peninsula from the Arabs. The conquerors organized their new territories as colonial extensions of the ancient Christian communities that had clung to the southern flank of the Pyrenees since the time of Charlemagne. The colonial state in the Near East had much the same character as those in Spain: It was a plantation of western society in an alien world.

BIBLIOGRAPHY

On the Germans and Germanic society, see J. B. Bury, *The Invasion of Europe by the Barbarians* (London, 1928); J. M. Wallace-Hadrill, *The Barbarian West* (London, 1952); Malcolm Todd, *The Northern Barbarians, 100 B.C.–A.D. 300* (London, 1976); Lucien Musset, *The Germanic Invasions* (State College, Pa., 1975). E. A. Thompson brings his studies of Germanic society together in *The Early Germans* (Oxford, 1965) and *The Visigoths in the Time of Ulfilas* (Oxford, 1969). For contrast, see Samuel Dill, *Roman Society in the Last Century of the Western Empire* (London, 1898) and *Roman Society in Gaul in the Merovingian Age* (London, 1926). For a contemporary view of Germans in Gaul, see Gregory of Tours, *The History of the Franks*, trans. by Lewis Thorpe (Harmondsworth, Eng., 1974).

Most studies of rural life focus on the late thirteenth century and afterward because it was only in that period that adequate documentation began to be preserved. For a sociological approach, see George C. Homans, *English Villagers of the Thirteenth Century* (Cambridge, Mass., 1941). This work is built on the studies of Marc Bloch, whose writings form the basis of modern social history. See Marc Bloch, *French Rural History*, trans. by Janet Sondheimer (Berkeley, 1966). Excellent modern studies are: J. A. Raftis, *Tenure and Mobility: Studies in the Social History of the Medieval Village* (Toronto, 1964), and R. H. Hilton, *A Medieval Society: The West Midlands at the End of the Thirteenth Century* (London, 1966). For a good general survey of the field, see M. Postan, ed., *Cambridge Economic History*, 2nd ed., Vol. 1: *The Agrarian Life of the Middle Ages* (Cambridge, Eng., 1966), which has excellent bibliographies.

Robert Chazan draws much of his material from the Responsa of the medieval rabbis, and a large selection of this literature has been translated by Irving Agus in *Urban Civilization in Pre-Crusade Europe*, 2 vols. (New York, 1965). The most complete study is Salo W. Baron, *A Social and Religious History of the Jews*, 2nd ed., Vols. 3–8 (New York, 1957–58). See also Cecil Roth and I. H. Levine, eds., *The Dark Ages: Jews in Christian Europe 711–1096* (New Brunswick, N.J., 1966). An older work that is still useful is Israel Abrahams, *Jewish Life in the Middle Ages* (New York, 1896; New York, 1969). Norman Cohn focuses often on the Jews in his book on millenarianism, *The Pursuit of the Millennium* (Oxford, 1970).

There are many books on the crusades. A good general history is Steven Runciman, *A History of the Crusades*, 3 vols. (Cambridge, Eng., 1951–54). See also the studies presented in Kenneth Setton and Marshall W. Baldwin, eds., *A History of the Crusades*, Vol. 1: *The First Hundred Years* (Philadelphia, 1955). On the crusaders' kingdoms in the Levant, see Dana C. Munro, *The Kingdom of the Crusaders* (New York, 1935), and Joshua Prawer, *The Crusaders' Kingdom: European Colonialism in the Middle Ages* (New York, 1973).

German Tribal Society

E. A. THOMPSON

The Germanic society studied by William Chaney in the last selection of Part 1 was organized around a king, who was mediator between the gods and the people. The king surrounded himself with comrades-in-arms who formed his personal guard, his counsellors, and his officials. These royal friends were the great men of the society, and they themselves had men, often neighbors, who looked to them for support and protection. We should not, however, think of these Germanic societies as highly centralized or even closely organized. The king was a central figure, but he did not organize communal life nor did he interfere very much in the affairs of his subjects. We also should not think Germanic society was the same everywhere in *Germania*. Chaney notes that, in general, the western Germans—such as the Angles, Saxons, and Franks—had kings, but that the eastern Germans, such as the Goths, did not.

For the historian, this difference in social organization presents special problems because, while kings attract attention and patronize artists whose works tell us something about the communities, societies without central figures leave very little evidence of their ideas and structure. The bulk of the sources that purport to present a picture of the early Germans actually were written long after the primitive tribal life had been permanently altered by contact with the romanized population of the empire. In spite of this, scholars have constructed elaborate theories about the structure of the early communities of Germans. Some of these theories are monuments to the creative imagination.

The earliest theory, published in 1768, pictured the Germans as free farmers living in communities whose institutions were the prototypes of the liberal, democratic institutions developed in the eighteenth and nineteenth centuries. The members of these communities inhabited *Marks,* territorial units encompassing many homesteads and named for their position on the *marches,* or frontiers, of the Roman Empire. In the yearly assemblies of these *Marks,* the free warrior peasants took care of common affairs and elected their chiefs. Here was the noble savage, and in fact the original presentation of this picture was explicitly influenced by Rousseau's speculations. In the nineteenth century, those who elaborated the theory changed it slightly by making property ownership in the *Marks* communistic rather than private. The free warrior peasant and the democratic political organization remained, however.

In the late nineteenth century, the great French historian Fustel de

Coulanges attacked the *Mark* theory, pointing out that there was no evidence to support it. He argued that the word *marca* in the ancient Latin texts simply meant "boundaries," and that there was no such thing as a *Mark* or the community that was supposed to occupy it. Fustel's criticism was largely ignored, but it did force proponents of the *Mark* theory to change the name of their creation—a nonexistent *Mark* by any other name exists. Further work on the history of the Germanic communities has shown, however, that Fustel was correct. Early Germanic society was aristocratic, and the free warrior peasant did not exist. The elective chieftainries and democratic institutions were also figments.

In this selection, E. A. Thompson demonstrates the method used to reconstruct ancient German society while he analyzes the position of Christians within that society. His source is an example of a common medieval literary genre, the biography of a saint. Saints' lives were a popular type of didactic literature during the Middle Ages, and they quickly became stylized and formularized. Many of the lives were written before the saint was canonized and were in fact products of the effort to get him or her canonized. Once the requirements for becoming a saint were established, the hagiographers made certain that the demands were met by their man or woman. Even if the work was written after canonization, it had to preserve the image of the saint and thus participated in the same formularized tradition. As a result, Thompson has to distinguish between glimpses of the real St. Sabas and his society and those elements of the story determined by the hagiographical tradition. Since many of the stories were written an appreciable time after the events occurred, there is the further problem of dealing with anachronisms and misconceptions introduced into the account.

A complete text of the *Passio S. Sabae* and of certain kindred documents was published by Delehaye more than forty years ago. These works give us priceless information about early Visigothic Christianity and especially, of course, about Sabas himself, who was martyred on 12 April 372. They are also invaluable for the study of the society which produced Ulfila and the Gothic Bible. The *Passio* does what the works of Caesar and Tacitus never do—it brings us for the first time into a Germanic village and enables us to see something of how the villagers managed their own affairs. Yet it has received strangely little attention either from students of Roman history or from students of early Germanic society. . . . Here it is proposed to glance at the *Passio* as a source for the social organization of the Visigoths in the days of Ulfila.

From "The *Passio S. Sabae* and Early Visigothic Society" by E. A. Thompson, *Historia* 4 (1955), pp. 331–38. Reprinted by permission of the author and Franz Steiner Verlag.

We know from our other sources that the Visigoths, whenever they went to war, elected an over-all military leader who is called in Latin *iudex* and in Greek *dikastes*. But the *iudex* seems to have had as little personal authority as Germanic chiefs had had in the days of Tacitus. He could "advise" and "urge" his followers to accept his point of view, but he could not impose his will upon them: he had no powers of coercion. Power, such as it was, rested with the *optimates*, as Ammianus calls them, or the *megistanes*, as they are termed in the *Passio*. These no doubt formed a sort of Council and (though the point is not directly attested) they may have been the chiefs of the φυλαί of whom Eunapius speaks. For Eunapius tells us that the Visigoths were organized in "tribes" under tribal leaders, and the word φυλαί is no doubt equivalent to the Latin *pagi*. At any rate, there were tribal chiefs, as we may call them, below the general military leader of the people as a whole. But the *Passio*, as we have said, deals in the main with humbler people than the chiefs and the optimates: it is primarily concerned with the village in which Sabas lived, though it is by no means silent about the relations between this village and the central authority.

It depicts a time of persecution when the loyalty of the villagers to the pagan gods is to be put to the test: by order of the megistanes the villagers will be required to eat sacrificial meat in public. How this decision was conveyed to the villagers is unknown. But village affairs are discussed in the first instance by a village council; and this council has determined that the villagers among them who are Christian must be spared in spite of the order of the megistanes: the Christians in their midst shall merely be induced to eat unconsecrated meat rather than sacrificial meat so that a true test may be avoided and the persecutors cheated. This is the plan on which the council has decided, but it must be discussed by all the villagers assembled together before it can be put into practice. Sabas like the other villagers has the right to speak, and he comes forward on two separate occasions and uses his right boldly: he will not submit to any such subterfuge as the council had suggested—he will never deny his Christianity. Accordingly, the plan put forward by the council members has to be modified; and when a representative of the megistanes comes round to the village to see how the test is progressing, the village councillors tell him that in fact there is one Christian among them— Sabas himself.

The whole of this scene described in the third chapter of the *Passio* is a vivid representation of a clan society in action. There is no indication that Sabas' procedure in disagreeing with the council's decision was illegitimate or even unusual. He merely expressed freely an opinion which was unpopular. The scene does not quite prove that the decisions of the villagers had to be unanimous before action could be taken, though this may have been the case. At any rate, there was no machinery for suppressing Sabas' opinion or for preventing him from making his views known to the visiting chief; and still less was there any means of compelling him to change his attitude and to fall in with the opinion of the majority. Nor was Sabas an isolated case. We learn from another source that in addition to Sabas other Christians were given an opportunity of coming forward and speaking bravely on behalf of the faith in their respective villages. A further point is also noteworthy. After his first speech refusing to eat the meat the village council compelled Sabas to leave the village for a while, but shortly afterwards permitted him to come back. Now this does not in itself mean that the freedom of the villagers was disappearing and that a man who expressed an unpopular opinion was liable to be penalized. Sabas, as we shall see, had offended against the gods of the community by refusing to share their meal; and an offence against the gods was an offence against the community itself. Sabas' temporary expulsion was due to this offence—his refusal to take part in the sacrificial meal of the villagers—and not to the unpopularity of his opinions as such or to his being a Christian. The fact that he was a Christian was known to the villagers throughout the proceedings and even before the proceedings began, and was not resented by them. Indeed, when the news reached the village that the persecution had been initiated the first thought of the village councillors was how they could save Sabas. The temporary expulsion, then, was not due to Sabas' Christianity but to his unwillingness even to make a show of joining in the sacrificial meal. To that extent the expulsion was unconnected with the persecution as such.

It is a pity that it was not to the author's purpose to tell us more about the sacrifice and the sacrificial meal, which evidently formed an integral part of Visigothic village life. In a clan society the communal eating and drinking were a symbol and a confirmation of mutual social obligations. The man who refused to eat the sacrificial meat with his fellows thereby dissociated himself from their religion and from their social duties and rights: he had made himself an outcast. That is why the public eating of sacrificial meat was regarded by the megistanes as a test for men suspected of having become Christian. On the other hand, it is noteworthy that when he was first expelled from his village Sabas was soon allowed to return. On the second occasion the villagers might not have expelled him at all if pressure had not been put upon them by the visiting chief; and even then the saint might well have been spared if the village councillors could have shown to the persecutor that Sabas was a man of some property (v. infra). But even so Sabas was not lynched: action was not taken on the spur of the moment without a hearing of the merits of the case. On the contrary, the case was heard, and the action was taken by a man who had some measure of recognized authority. True, Sabas was not put to death by his fellow villagers: the men who killed him came from outside the village. Yet the villagers in the end did nothing to help him, but abandoned him to his fate. He had put himself outside their protection by his refusal to join in their sacrificial feast. Now the presbyter Sansalas, who is also mentioned in the *Passio*, does not seem to have been a Visigoth, for he is thought to bear an Asian name; and he was presumably descended from the Asian prisoners who had been carried off by the Visigoths during their great raids on Asia Minor in the mid-third century. Accordingly, it is of great interest to notice that Sansalas was not requested, so far as we know, to partake of the sacrificial meal, and although he was tortured he was not put to death. His crime was less than that of the Visigothic tribesman Sabas. Sansalas' offence was that he was a Christian, and this in a man of Asian descent was an offence during the period of the persecution but it was not a capital offence. Sabas' crime was that he had offended against the gods of his people, and for this as a Visigoth he became an outcast and was put to death.

To return to the village council: we do not know how this was chosen or who composed it. We might perhaps guess that it consisted of elders who were noted for their long experience of affairs and for their wisdom or for their prowess as warriors or hunters. At any rate, the council's two known functions were, first, that it represented the village in meetings with a member of the confederate council, and, secondly, that it discussed the business of the village before bringing it to the general assembly of the villagers. In this last point it resembles the council which pre-considered the business that was to come before the general assembly of the warriors in the first century A.D. The "national" council, as it were, which Tacitus describes in his *Germania* (xi. 1) is reproduced on a smaller scale by the village council referred to in the *Passio*. Finally, it may be observed that there is no mention of a village chief or headman, and if one had been present at these proceedings the author of the *Passio* could not well have avoided making some mention of him. The unnamed, persecuting "leader" (*archon*) of the *Passio* comes to Sabas' village from outside and knows little or nothing about the villagers. He must be the leader of some larger unit than the village, and I have little doubt that he was one of the "tribal" leaders like those referred to by Eunapius.

What light does the *Passio* throw on these tribal chiefs, as we have called them? If the confederate chief possessed few coercive powers in wartime, it is unlikely that the tribal chiefs occupied a stronger position in times of peace. True, it would be easy to conclude from one or two sentences in the *Passio* that the persecution of the Christians in Sabas' village was initiated by "the persecutor" or "the leader," that is, by an unnamed chieftain. But in fact what the *Passio* shows is that the chiefs were merely responsible for seeing that the persecution was actually enforced. A number of phrases in the *Passio* indicate clearly that the persecution was initiated not by any one ruler or chief but by the confederate council. Indeed, in one passage the author explicitly states that Atharid acted "on the order of the impious ones." The plural should be noted. It unquestionably means the confederate council, the megistanes; and that the ultimate responsibility for the persecution lay with the megistanes is shown again and again by the language of the *Passio*.

When the confederate council decided to persecute the Christians, the tribal chiefs went round the villages to see how the council's instructions were being carried out; and when a chief, as representative of the council, came to a village the members of the village council would appear before him and would give him the information which he required. This, at any rate, was the procedure in Sabas' village, and there seems to be no reason why we should not generalize from it. But the tribal chiefs were merely the instruments through which the council acted. In times of peace and indeed for the most part in wartime also even the confederate chief is not known to have had any power over the life, liberty, and property of the tribesmen except in so far as he carried out the decisions of the council. What we should greatly like to have is some information on the part which the village or at any rate the village councillors were allowed to play in the election of a tribal chief. But of this we know nothing. We cannot say whether the humble villagers had any rights at this date when it came to the choosing of a tribal leader.

However that may be, it is certain that the old egalitarian system which Tacitus had described long ago was disappearing among the fourth-century Visigoths. Quantities of property had begun to accumulate in private hands c. 370, and political power was also tending to concentrate in private hands. This is strikingly illustrated in a vivid scene depicted in the *Passio*. When the unnamed tribal chief in the course of the persecution heard that Sabas was an unrepentant Christian, he had him summoned to his presence. He then turned to the members of the village council, who were present, and asked them whether Sabas owned any property. He was told that Sabas owned nothing more than the clothes on his back. Thereupon the chief considered the saint to be of no consequence and said, "Such a man can neither help nor harm us," and ordered him to be driven out of the village. The mere fact that the author of the *Passio* turns aside to record this remark of the chief's would seem to suggest that the words were in his opinion significant and disturbing: in connexion with these words he calls the chief *anomos*—he was no respecter of tribal custom. Clearly, at that date not only had private property associated itself in the chief's mind with social power but the poor man unlike the man of property could "neither help nor harm" the execution of the confederate council's resolutions. There were sharp divisions of wealth in Visigothic society in the days of Ulfila.

In fact, the Christians in Gothia in Ulfila's time seem in general to have been drawn from the humbler strata of society. The descendants of the Roman prisoners taken in the raids on Asia Minor in the third century will scarcely have been of much social influence among the Visigoths. The Christian presbyter and his associates who were used by Fritigern as intermediaries during his negotiations with Valens in 378 are explicitly said to have been humble persons. The Audian bishop Silvanus was presumably the descendant of Roman prisoners. True, he may have been a Visigoth who adopted this

Roman name on his conversion; but to believe that is merely to multiply hypotheses, and in fact Epiphanius describes him not as a Goth but as being "from Gothia." It can scarcely be doubted that Ulfila himself, like Selenas after him, was also the offspring of a very humble family in Gothia, and not being a pure-blooded Visigoth he would not have been a member of any clan. His foreign descent would have rigorously excluded him from membership, unless he had been willing to undergo the pagan rites of initiation and adoption, which in a man of Ulfila's uncompromising Arianism can scarcely be considered as a possibility. It is true that three arguments have been put forward to show that Ulfila was a well-to-do and perhaps even noble Visigoth; but these arguments cannot stand. They are (i) that he was free to leave Gothia in 348 when the first persecution took place; but then it would follow that all those who were driven out or who fled in the persecutions were well-to-do, which was not the case; (ii) that he acted as ambassador to Constantius; but the Christian who acted as ambassador to Valens, as we have just seen, is known to have been of humble birth—these Christians were doubtless chosen as envoys because they might as Christians carry more weight with the Romans than barbarian pagans could do; (iii) that Eusebius of Nicomedia would not have made him bishop if his position among his people had not been a distinguished one; but Eusebius' action only suggests that Ulfila's position was distinguished not among the Visigoths as a whole but among the Christians in Gothia—and his distinction was due not to his birth but to his learning. Finally, the one Visigothic Christian about whom detailed information has survived, Sabas, is explicitly stated to have owned no property whatever and to have been therefore of no political account. At all events, nothing in our evidence suggests that the tribal nobility had been seriously affected by Christianity in the decades preceding 372; and indeed the *Passio* gives us positive evidence to the contrary; for it was "the megistanes throughout Gothia" who had decided on the persecution in the first place.

Finally, the *Passio* makes it clear that the confederate council, the megistanes, were able to exert stronger pressure on the villages than the latter, we may suspect, would have submitted to in the days of Tacitus. The fact is that to some extent the persecution of the Christians in 369–72 was imposed on the villages from above, and it was the megistanes who specified the test of the public eating of the sacrificial meat without any consultation, so far as we know, with the rank and file of the Visigoths. Indeed, the council in Sabas' village was reduced to a subterfuge in its effort to avoid carrying out the orders of the megistanes: they proposed to allow Christians to eat unconsecrated meat instead of sacrificial meat "so that they might keep their own men unharmed, and deceive the persecutors." In the second wave of persecution the council was actually willing to declare without ado to the prosecutor that there was no Christian in their village. They were even prepared to make this declaration on oath, a fact which suggests that enthusiasm in the village for the decisions of the megistanes was not always unbounded. But once again the obstinacy of Sabas himself foiled their well-intentioned deceit; and they admitted with some reluctance that in fact there was one Christian among them. Thereupon the chief, who had come to the village to see how the persecution was progressing, "ordered" Sabas to be driven out of the village. On the first occasion on which Sabas was expelled it was the village council who had ordered him to go. But on the occasion of the second expulsion the village council appears to have been given no voice in the matter: they simply received instructions from the tribal chief to drive Sabas out. In the final wave of persecution the henchmen of the tribal chief Atharid were able to beat and torture Sabas without any consultation with the rest of the villagers and without bringing any charge against him, though it may be significant that Sabas suffered thus when not actually present in his own village.

Clearly, political power has to some extent become concentrated in the hands of the optimates, and the village council is no longer in a position to assert its rights boldly on every issue that affects it. But individual Visigoths were not afraid to disobey outright the most stringent orders of the tribal chief who represented the megistanes. At one stage in the torturing of Sabas the saint was tied hand and foot to two axles of a cart, and was thrown on his back on the ground to spend the night in this predicament. But when his guards fell asleep an old woman, who had stayed up all night to prepare meat for the members of her household, took pity on him and set him free. Had she not been willing to defy the confederate council the saint might well have finished his career there and then. Again, when his executioners had brought Sabas to the river Musaeus (Buzău) where they were to drown him they at first proposed to set him free: Atharid, they thought, would know nothing of it. And it was only when Sabas himself insisted that they should carry out their orders that they plunged him into the water. Finally, the whole course of events in Sabas' village shows that feelings for one's neighbour—or perhaps we should say kinsman—were stronger than respect for the orders of the optimates.

It is a curious picture. The persecution was enforced by the megistanes, whose reasons for doing so will be examined elsewhere. But the Visigoths at large, it seems, did not care very much whether one of their number ate the sacrificial meat or not—if he were willing to eat any meat, that would suffice. When no persecution was on foot Christian and pagan seem to have lived on friendly terms within the one village; and in times of persecution, if we may generalize from the behaviour of Sabas' fellow villagers, regard for one's neighbour was stronger than differences of religion among the rank and file of the Visigoths. Is it a coincidence that this picture of Visigothic life dates from the very eve of the general conversion of the people to Christianity? At any rate, the brotherly and sisterly intimacy of the Christians in Gothia is reflected in the diminutive names by which they addressed one another. As a German scholar has put it, the names of practically all the martyrs, in so far as they are Germanic, are "Kurznamen, Kosenamen, Beinamen, oder Spitznamen." But no "Kosenamen" are applied to chiefs like Winguric or Atharid or even the Christian Arimerius, who is known from a somewhat later period. The simplicity of these lowly Christians and their earnest truthfulness are reflected in the one document that they have left us, the *Passio*, which is in fact a letter from the Church in Gothia to the Church in Cappadocia. It is not the work of a Goth but of a Roman living in very close contact with the barbarians, and although it was scarcely written by the presbyter Sansalas himself, it may well be based on information supplied by him, for he had friends in the Roman Empire, had fled there when the persecution was at its height, and may well have returned there after Sabas' death to await the end of the storm. The vividness and innocence of the *Passio* reveal a community in which fanaticism was confined to the powerful, and humanity to the humble. Delehaye has justly described it as one of the pearls of ancient hagiography.

Peasants and the Agricultural Revolution

GEORGES DUBY

Feudal law placed the peasant, and by extension his family, in formal subjection to his lord, and historians have created a picture of peasant life in accord with that legal status. They are seen as oppressed, subjugated, dismally poor, and tightly restricted by being tied to the land. They live in hovels and, in general, their life might be aptly described by Thomas Hobbes' famous description of life in the state of nature: It is nasty, brutish, and short.

What would the peasants have said about this portrait of peasant life? They might have looked on the progressive strengthening of the bond between a peasant and his land very differently from the way we moderns look upon it. In the chaotic conditions of the early Middle Ages, it may have been much more important to the peasant that the land was tied to him than that he was tied to it. It was an age when farms needed protection from invaders and marauders and when there were few alternatives to the agricultural life. While a peasant might aspire to the aristocracy, this goal was probably not possible for most, and if he were going to be a farmer, his security on the land was of paramount importance to him. Also, economic and political conditions did affect the lives of peasants, and they, like others involved in economic life, must have had some hope of improving their living standard when peace permitted a limited market economy to function.

Besides the minor fluctuations in the quality of agrarian life, there was a long-term improvement between the tenth and twelfth centuries. This growth in prosperity stemmed both from the advance of agricultural technology—an effective horse collar, the horseshoe, and the heavy, wheeled plow—and from the expansion of arable land. After the Viking invasions, Europeans took the offensive against the pagan tribes living around them and settled on the lands of those they conquered. At the same time, lords sought to reclaim lands that had lain fallow during the period of chaos. In order to entice peasants to migrate to areas where prospects and security were uncertain, the lords offered easy terms for holding newly cleared land. Migration to new regions and reclamation work provided the peasantry with a double reward. The productivity of the group as a whole increased, and the peasants were able to improve their status and living conditions. In this article, Georges Duby surveys the profound changes in rural life brought about by the agricultural revolution of these centuries.

I. The Condition of the Peasant

Agricultural progress stimulated certain changes in legal status. Expansion into the new lands hastened a lightening of manorial obligations and the areas of reclamation appeared usually as zones of liberty. To take an English example, in the thirteenth century free tenants made up half the peasantry of north Warwickshire, a country of assarts, but they only represented one-third in the southern part of the country; two out of five villages in the north escaped labour services, but only one in five enjoyed this advantage in the south. *Liberi tenantes* swarmed also on the lands of Ely Cathedral which adjoined the Fens in process of colonization. We know, too, that the fringes of the great forests of 'the twelfth century were invaded by small allods settled without the lord's leave and that the settlement charters created in the *villeneuves* a system of manorial rights and monopolies (*régime banale*) more flexible than elsewhere. In 1159, the settlers established on the polders of the Flemish abbey of Bourbourg enjoyed personal liberty and were directly dependent for public justice on the count; they possessed hereditary and alienable tenures, and they owed to the overlord no more than light payments of "recognition." The condition of the *Freibauern* whom the Salic kings had established in the Saxon and Thuringian forests was similar, as was that of all the rent-paying tenants freed from servitude who reclaimed the lands of the abbeys of St Dié and Remiremont in the Vosges, and the pioneers who settled the Bavarian plains and the Austrian and Styrian mountains. Finally, to prevent their men from being tempted by colonizing landowners to move out to the new lands where they were promised better conditions, lords of the old villages were forced to relax their exactions.

But has not too much been made, perhaps, of the freedom which reclamation conferred? The immigrant often arrived on new lands empty-handed, without worldly goods, even without anything to eat until his assart could yield its produce. He had first to be admitted, to be helped and to submit to the collective discipline without which the new land could not be brought into production. It is a striking fact that many settlers arriving from a distance and calling themselves free, were soon "commending" themselves to the local lord, placing themselves under his protection and falling under his sway. In Auvergne the heaviest labour services were to be found in the districts of recent occupation, and there they lingered longest. Nowhere did the manorial system show itself more tenacious than in Combraille or the Jura where reclamation was very late.

Indeed, if the weight of the lord's power did not make itself felt equally in the different regions where colonization took place, it was probably because this did not take place everywhere at the same time and in the same way. In the first phases of reclamation, in the eleventh and early twelfth centuries, free migration into the immense areas opened to cultivation by the somewhat more powerful plough teams of this time, probably caused a noticeable lightening of the lord's control by relieving demographic pressure. But what happened in the twelfth century? It is just possible that the kind of settlement characterized by the isolated farmstead favoured the personal independence of the peasant. Far from the lord's prying eye and hidden behind the leafy branches of his hedges, a tenant could more easily conceal the sheaves of which he knew he must render a share. One the other hand land became scarcer and scarcer. To receive the right to settle the peasant had now to pay a heavy entry fine, and sometimes even to surrender his own liberty and that of his descendants. It seems indeed as if, at any rate in certain parts, the settlers of that period were unfortunates cruelly exploited by the owner of the waste land.

*   *   *

The condition of the peasant was also altered in other ways. The improvements in ploughing equipment and harness, as well as the different ways of tilling the soil which formed the basis of technical progress, raised the importance of ploughing compared to other agricultural labour. From the accounts of the Hospitallers of Provence we can see that in 1338 ploughing cost four times as much as all the rest of the work on the demesne. This progress also raised the relative value of tools and equipment. In thirteenth-century Italy a pair of oxen was worth as much as all the land of a family holding. The rise of yields, the improvements in equipment and agrarian practice brought about a gradual shift in the values of farm capital in rural society. The value of land fell in relation to livestock. The effects of this shift can be observed in the terms of leases and merits further consideration.

The gap which had separated "ploughmen" from men who worked with their hands widened after the year 1000 as is shown by the distribution of manorial dues. In the eleventh century the exactions of the territorial lord did not bear as heavily on the poor peasant without a team, who worked with a hoe and got his living from the homestead toft and temporary employment in the great households, as they did on those "who perform their work with oxen or other beasts." The contrast between ploughman and manual worker became more pronounced in northern countries than in the Midi where the plough (araire) remained easy to handle, to pull, as well as to construct, and used very little iron. The devaluation of manual services in relation to those performed with the help of animals, and hence the social decline of the "cottars," "bordars" and all manual workers, can be much more clearly seen in northern manors. In every country from England to Provence the *bouvier*, i.e. the driver of the team, had since the twelfth century become the true farm servant. The "plough," by which is meant the entire team composed of the implement itself, the oxen or horses capable of drawing it and the man who drove them, ended by representing the basic economic unit, the yardstick by which the landlord could estimate the value of his dependants and the services he could expect from them. It was by "ploughs" that labour services were reckoned in the Cluniac inventory of the mid-twelfth century, as in others drawn up a little later for the English landlords.

On the other hand, manual labourers without draught animals underwent no technical progress and sustained no rise in yields: on the contrary there was a relative fall in their living conditions. At the end of the thirteenth century they formed a large proportion of village society and thanks to some documentary evidence we can say exactly how large. Lords who levied dues wished to know the movable property of their subjects and from time to time ordered surveys of their livestock. Registers in which taxes levied on the inheritance of dependants were recorded have also been preserved. Recent researches which throw a vivid light on medieval peasant life, and which are based on the records of the bishop of Winchester, show that in certain villages on these estates 40 per cent of the villeins paid their "heriot" in money, whereas normally they would have been obliged to deliver to the lord the best animal from their stable: in other words, they did not own any animals.

That the increased value of farming equipment strengthened the hold of the wealthy over the peasantry cannot be denied. By loans and advances for the purchase of cattle, or by hiring out oxen, the power of urban capital penetrated the *contado* of Italian villages. Everywhere the lord maintained his authority over his men by helping them to acquire livestock or by threatening them with its confiscation. When in some provinces in the thirteenth century servitude was born anew and flourished, it was the need to acquire agricultural equipment, efficient though costly, which led poorer peasants to bind themselves into dependence. The same needs held them in servitude, for although they had the right to decamp, to take another master, or to proclaim themselves free, they could do so only by abandoning their movable goods, in other words, by giving up their plough animals. In fact because of this, agricultural growth appears to have been a very powerful agent of social differentiation.

2. The Family Farm

Agricultural growth, by hastening the disintegration of the *manse*, broke up the ancient framework within which the daily life of the peasant family was contained. It is difficult to believe that what dissolved this fundamental unit was a change in the structure of the family or a dislocation of the kinship group. Households based on single married couples already occupied *manses* described by Carolingian inventories. The fragmentation of the *manse* resulted in part from the combined effects of demographic pressure and changes in the methods of manorial taxation. But its principal cause was undoubtedly the higher productivity of human labour. To survive, a household had no longer any need of such extensive lands. The reduction in the size of the plot of land considered sufficient to support a family, and the average dimensions of a peasant farm generally, thus appeared as one of the criteria of agricultural progress. The chronology of this process is worth establishing.

In Lorraine where the study of this process has been most detailed, the *quartier* (this fraction of the ancient *manse* did not of course always correspond to an exact quarter of its size) already appears sporadically in the *polyptyques* at the end of the ninth century. However, the lords definitely adopted this type of holding as the new basis for rents in the twelfth century. The average area of land attached to each *quartier* then reached fifteen or sixteen dayworks (*journaux*), i.e. about 7 to 10 acres. In fact, the farm was nearly four times smaller than the *manse* of the early Middle Ages. Since there is no proof of any decline whatever in the peasant group which lived on each of these family holdings we must accept that reduction in fallow periods together with a rise in agricultural yields had nearly quadrupled the productivity of the arable between the ninth and the twelfth centuries. Or else we must assume that the tenants, by assarting the fringes of the village clearings, had acquired control over free or rent-paying holdings, supplementary parcels of land which completed the *appendicia* of a *quartier*. Or again, and this is the most likely assumption, that the resources of a peasant family had been increased by reclamation and more intense cultivation simultaneously.

The breaking up of agricultural units in the early Middle Ages can be seen generally in all the regions which benefited from agrarian expansion. The course of this movement tended in its turn to disintegrate the Lotharingian *quartier*: in the country around Namur in the thirteenth century some of these new holdings supported several families each, who held them and farmed them jointly. Here and there the *manse* put up a more or less tenacious resistance. It had entirely disappeared after the eleventh century in the Norman countryside. About 1150, in one village of southern Burgundy only three *manses* out of nineteen mentioned by documents still possessed "appurtenances" which could be ploughed and formed really coherent farming units; all the others were completely fragmented and their memory was only preserved in place-names. In the thirteenth century all the ancient *manses* in the Parisian region and Flanders, as well as in Alsace and Swabia, had disintegrated and been cut up and redistributed in small plots. In other countries, however, the family farming units still firmly retained their cohesion.

They had sometimes been protected by the managerial methods of the manor or by customs of inheritance, as in Bavaria where division of holdings originating in reclamation was forbidden, or in north-western Germany, where the institution of primogeniture in the peasant class made a precocious appearance. But what is remarkable is that the most resilient *manses* which survived in the Middle Ages and whose outlines are revealed intact by modern aerial photography were usually situated either in the southern countries where the new organization was never adopted or else in the zones most recently won by reclamation, such as upper Beaujolais, Bresse, western France and the mountains of the Massif Central. In these latter areas, of course, the farming units took shape at a period when the consequences of technical progress had already made themselves felt and on the poorest of soils where productivity was unlikely to rise any further. Considerations of this nature strengthen the impression that the disintegration of the *manse* between the year 1000 and the thirteenth century was largely determined by improvements in agricultural technique.

Progress of this kind and the demographic changes which were so closely connected with it worked themselves out inside the village community itself. The most productive village lands could support more people and accommodate both immigrants and the new hearths set up by local children living in their birthplace. In this way the group of newcomers and settlers grew up outside the close and traditional circle of heads of the older households who thought of themselves as the only rightful custodians of communal rights on the common lands. Their cabins, *bordes*, and cottages, which had already appeared here and there in Carolingian inventories, multiplied in the eleventh and twelfth centuries as they were erected one after another outside the old enclosures. Then towards the middle of the thirteenth century isolated farms appeared on the edge of the cultivated land, and thereby broke up the solidarity of the village. The people who lived in them were only seen at mass; they closed their land to collective grazing and thus limited the areas where the communal flocks could roam freely. This latter form of existence profoundly modified customary ways of life. By provoking a defensive reaction on the part of the village community, they called into separate existence zones where the interests of the individual were paramount over those subject to collective control.

3. Demographic Growth

The improvements in agrarian technique increased to a very considerable extent the output of foodstuffs. It removed the obstacles which held population in check in the same way as the extension of arable. It opened the gates wide to a process which in its turn gave a further impetus to reclamation and farming methods. Nobody denies that the population of western Europe grew, but historians lack the means to measure this growth with any precision.

There is plentiful evidence pointing to a sharp growth of population during the eleventh and twelfth centuries—although factual details are vague and figures are altogether lacking. These appear in the thirteenth century, and they multiplied after 1250 when tax collection emerged from its rudimentary state. Princes and lords were anxious to know exactly who owed them taxes, and specifically how many *feux*, hearths or households there were, which from then onwards became everywhere the basis of taxation. The information found in these fiscal documents is supplemented by manorial records of various kinds, rent rolls, surveys and registers of the courts of justice, which reveal from time to time movements of land and those occupying it, and sometimes enable us to analyze the structure of the family. It is true that these sources are too imperfect for us ever to hope to follow satisfactorily the demographic trends of this period. Nevertheless they deserve close scrutiny, and in some cases scholars have begun to use them. The history of population has recently made great progress.

Most of the definite facts which have been suitably analyzed are both local and late. But they clearly indicate the vigour of the movement. I shall take Provence as an example, where the number of hearths doubled between the middle of the thirteenth and the beginning of the fourteenth century. If we accept that the census of hearths was not merely a fiscal device and that the composition of the household did not undergo significant change, this suggests that within 50 years human beings in this province became twice as numerous although many were very poor. In nine villages in the *viguerie* of Nice, 440 hearths were counted in 1263 and 722 in 1315. The rise affected different villages very unevenly; while one with 25 hearths remained stationary, another increased in two generations from 66 to 157 and a third from 30 to 103.

It is not possible to measure so precisely demographic growth over wider areas, and historians' estimates vary considerably. Recently W. C. Robinson has stated that the average annual rate of growth at that time could have been no more than 0.2 per cent for the whole of Europe, while W. Abel estimates it as 0.39 per cent for France and 0.48 per cent for Germany. The truth is that the kingdom of England appears to be the only country where demographic estimates can be supported upon a solid documentary foundation, thanks to the exceptionally abundant material such as the Domesday Book, and the Poll Tax registers of 1377. The most authoritative estimates would have us believe that the population of the kingdom rose from 1,100,000 inhabitants in 1086 to 3,700,000 in 1346. According to J. C. Russell the average rate of annual increase should be placed around 0.46 per cent. However, if we examine the facts more closely it appears again that growth was very different in the various regions. Expansion followed dissimilar trends from one village to another. Some, such as the hamlets situated on the edge of the Holland fens of Lincolnshire, were caught up in an active forward movement. It has been estimated that the number of men there increased six times in some places and twenty-four times in others during the 200 years which followed the drawing up of the Domesday Book.

Such local variations therefore invite prudence. They particularly forbid the application of rates of growth calculated for England to the whole of Europe, because this county was still backward at the time of the Norman Conquest and relatively empty compared to certain French provinces. It is far from impossible, for instance, that certain villages in the region of Paris supported almost as many men in the ninth century as they did in the fourteenth. On the other hand in one Burgundian village territory, one out of every five of the 400 inhabitants enumerated in 1248 was a settler who had come to win from the wastes the fields which supported him. Consequently, to assume that the population had trebled uniformly in all parts of the country in the twelfth and thirteenth centuries would be as fallacious as to attribute the heavy density of population of Villeneuve St Georges and Palaiseau revealed in the *polyptyque* of Irminon to the whole of Carolingian Gaul. We should do better to explore in detail the limited areas where accurate observation is possible.

★   ★   ★

Latent demographic pressure, which had only been held in check by the deficiencies of agricultural technique in the early Middle Ages, appears to have populated the empty or sparsely inhabited places as soon as it was released by improvements in equipment and the rise in productivity. In this way, it is estimated that from 20,000 to 30,000 new inhabitants spread into the forests of Brie between 1100 and 1250. From all our evidence the rate of population growth in the areas of great reclamation was much higher. In the villages of South Warwickshire, already heavily colonized in Saxon times, population increased only slightly between 1086 and 1279, and in seven parishes it had even declined. On the other hand in the northern part of the county it doubled or trebled. To begin with, therefore, the agrarian conquest encouraged large movements of rural population.

The study of these migrations in those far off times is less difficult than some. Amongst the men of the twelfth century whose names appear in manorial documents, many bore surnames which connected them with their birthplace. In this way we can recognize many peasants who emigrated and populated the outlying parts (*faubourgs*) of the growing townships of the neighbourhood. But many others also left the lands of their forefathers for pioneering ventures and assarts. Such was the case of the man who, in the eleventh century, settled in a village on the banks of the Saône and married a girl who was also not a native of the place, but had moved there without her family, from a village about 9 miles away. Rural population at this period is shown to be far more mobile than it is usually supposed to be. In 1181 in one canton of Lombardy 12 per cent of those who farmed, some of them very humble people, did not live in the village of their forebears. At this period we can also trace substantial migrations of Flemings and Dutch towards northern and eastern Germany, and of people from La Vendée and Brittany into the country of Entre-Deux-Mers between the Garonne and the Dordogne.

Nevertheless, these movements from the overpopulated areas into the empty lands, and the outflow from the ancient villages towards the *villeneuves* did nothing to equate regional densities. There were still sharp contrasts between the various counties of fourteenth-century England: the well populated parts of East Anglia and Leicestershire against the wilderness of Devon. In 1328 Hurepoix was almost unpopulated whilst the neighbouring plain of France with 19 "hearths" per square kilometre can be described as the most densely occupied countryside of Europe. Thus it can be seen that the rich, anciently settled lands, nurseries for courageous pioneers, not only supplied the colonizers of the wasteland, but also underwent an internal growth so powerful that it widened the old clearings, and stimulated technical progress and the rise in yields which fostered it. The region of Paris, already teeming with men in the ninth century, supported twice as many five hundred years later.

*   *   *

Finally, we must consider whether demographic trends were alike for all social groups. The study of these differences, in the rare instances when sources are available, is fascinating. English historians have proved that variations in mortality were more marked amongst the depressed classes of cottars, those all-but-landless people who lived by hiring themselves out on the manorial demesnes. Were not these families whose chief livelihood came from wages tempted to increase their real capital by rearing more children? Were marriage rates throughout the hierarchy of wealth the same? The study of the economy of the medieval countryside calls for detailed research into the structure of rural families of a kind which is by no means impossible.

Lastly, it must be pointed out that population movements could be either slowed down or accelerated by legal conditions, and especially, by different systems of inheritance. Very dissimilar population trends have recently been discovered at the end of the thirteenth century in two dependent villages of the Benedictine priory of Spalding, both situated on the edge of the Fens and on soils of the same quality. In one village, there were many young married couples; in the other, delayed marriages, few children and a tendency to settle elsewhere. The former village was inhabited by sokemen, free peasants who could divide their property and inheritance without restraint, and furthermore each share of the free inheritance, no matter how small, carried with it pasture rights on the neighbouring fenland. Because of this a family could exist without arable merely by owning a few score sheep, and all the children were able to have families and set themselves up in the same village. This was the source of a dynamic change within the village itself. On the other hand the people living in the other village were *operarii*, of servile status, whose lord forbade them to divide their patrimony. This ban enforced prolonged celibacy, restriction of births or else emigration.

4. Overpopulation

Though stimulated by the continued growth of population, agricultural progress appears to have been powerless in the last resort to free the peasants from food shortages, as the record of famines shows.

In the eleventh and twelfth centuries irregular harvests resulted here and there in scarcities, and hordes of famished people in search of food periodically besieged the gates of monasteries. In these religious establishments the giving of alms was an institution that fulfilled a regular economic function. The monks of Cluny every year at the beginning of Lent distributed 250 salt pork carcases amongst 16,000 people; the monks of St Benoît sur Loire fed in good years and bad anything from 500 to 700 beggars. There were some amongst the lower ranks of society who owned nothing at all, and such people suffered severely from harvest failures, falls in yields during wet seasons, or excessively hot summers, when food which had become unfit for human consumption brought on fatal epidemics of dysentery. It seems, nevertheless, as if the widespread famines, which were still terrible in the first thirty years of the eleventh century, became thereafter more widely spaced out, less intense and, at last, disappeared altogether. The last threat in old Germania was averted in 1217–1218 by importing grain from the new lands of the east. No further general shortage was felt in Germany and the Low Countries between 1215 and 1315, and only a few periods of scarcity hit relatively backward provinces such as Austria.

Nevertheless, catastrophic shortages of wheat again appear to have struck the English and French countrysides in the middle of the thirteenth century. It is true that our knowledge of famines remains somewhat doubtful, for what value can we put on the accounts of the chroniclers, who were by nature given to romance and to magnifying dramatic events, the echoes of which had already reached them in a distorted form? It seems, however, as if demographic pressure, relieved after the first 1,000 years A.D. by the opening up of new arable, once again became acute after 1250 as soon as reclamation ceased.

The sustained rise in the price of cereals from the time when sources allow us to observe it (that is, in England after about 1160) furnishes proof of the growing pressure of demand; further evidence of it can be seen in the stagnation and even gentle decline of wages. In any case the overpopulation of the countryside is obvious in the second half of the thirteenth century (although this may perhaps be due to the sudden abundance of documentary material).

The clearest signs of it can be found in manorial documents describing peasant land. Repeated division amongst heirs had by then multiplied small farming units. "In the assart of Jeannenque there are shares, a sixth of which was given to the men of Lactote; five parts were made of the other five shares, and one of these parts was divided into three, and in one of these three parts they had one half and Bertrand Carbonel the other. . . ." The fate of this parcel of land in the neighbourhood of Arles is by no means unique. At the time of Domesday there were 68 tenants living in one Norfolk village; in 1291 there were 107 sharing 935 holdings which were in turn broken up into 2,021 plots of land. One such piece measuring about 6 acres was shared by 10 tenants. In another East Anglian village a strip of land was divided between 1222 and 1277 into 20 fragments. At Rozoy in the Ile de France an inheritance comprising 160 arpents was carved up into 78 plots. Fragmentation on such a scale gives an indication of the proliferation of families which utterly broke through the administrative organization of the manor. Documents of the second half of the thirteenth century also show the rapid accumulation of population on farmholdings. Eighty-nine rent-paying tenants were counted in one Lombard village in 1248; 100 only twenty years later. At Weedon Beck in eastern England the number of tenant families increased from 81 to 110 between 1248 and 1300 without any extension of the village lands through reclamation.

Changes in mortality rates are the final and the most telling witnesses in the indictment of the excessive population which oppressed certain western countries at the end of the thirteenth century. In effect, the only important study of this kind concerns England between the years 1240 and 1350, and rests on the extraordinary series of accounts preserved in the records of the bishopric of Winchester.

It emphasizes how precarious was the existence of the peasant population, which in some districts appears by 1300 to have exceeded that of the eighteenth century by 20 per cent. In 1245 the expectation of life for a man over 20 years of age was 24. For the entire period the death rate can be estimated at 40 per 1,000. Since the evidence only takes into account adults and since we know nothing of infant mortality, the rate for the whole population might have been somewhat around 70 per 1,000, that is to say far higher than for any population, even the most backward, which is covered by modern statistics. Furthermore this rate rose after 1290. It became 52 per 1,000 for adults between 1297 and 1347 and the expectation of life therefore fell to 20 years. Fluctuations in the curve of mortalities were very frequent and expressed the sensitivity to epidemics of such a physically debilitated population; the fluctuations appeared also to be closely correlated with the curve of harvests, and an approximate analysis by social class shows that the richer peasants were less likely to die than their poorer neighbours. These statistics, imprecise as they are, provide the most striking proof of how utterly insufficient agricultural improvements were. In spite of the various changes in agriculture in the last years of the century, technical progress never succeeded in meeting the needs of a teeming population which lay at the mercy of a shortage of food as cruel perhaps as it had ever been in Carolingian times.

Jews in a Christian Society

ROBERT CHAZAN

Histories of European Jews have focused on their role in economic and intellectual life. On the one hand, historians have been concerned with estimating the importance of Jewish merchant and moneylending activities. On the other, they have traced the textual traditions of important philosophical, theological, and medical works that came to Europe through the Jewish communities of Sicily and Spain. Neither of these approaches has revealed much about the nature of the Jewish communities in Europe. Actually, there were two groups of European Jews in the Middle Ages, and today they still form distinct communities. In the south, centered in Italy and Spain, Sephardic Jews were an integral part of the society and thus a bridge between the Moslem and Christian communities there. Prior to their expulsion by Ferdinand and Isabella in 1492, the Spanish Jews had participated in one of the most interesting social amalgams in history. Medieval Spain presents a picture of a mixture of three religious and national groups that produced a brilliant civilization. This harmony between the Jews and their neighbors was in striking contrast to the relations between Jew and Christian in northern Europe.

The Ashkenazic Jews of northern Europe (*Ashkenazim* is the medieval Hebrew word for "Germans") were segregated in religious communities that formed the nuclei of the ghettos of the modern era. The Ashkenazim seem to have originated from groups of Jews brought north from Italy in the ninth century by the Carolingian emperors. It was later reported that one of the most famous communities, that of Mainz in Germany, was created when Emperor Charles the Fat brought Rabbi Moses of Lucca to the north about 887. The Rabbi naturally brought his congregation with him, and the little community expanded rapidly. Charles may have brought the Jews north in order to establish a skilled commercial group in his kingdom. In the ninth through eleventh centuries, the kings generally protected the Jews because of their importance in commerce.

The records of these Jewish communities, principally the Responsa, decisions of the rabbis in law suits, show that in the first three centuries of Ashkenazic life the Jews were borrowers of money, not lenders. The surplus capital produced on the great estates was lent to the Jews for their commercial enterprises at a time when Christians had almost no use for such capital. For example, the surplus production of the Archbishopric of Narbonne, managed by Jews, was lent to other Jews for their business operations. It was only in the twelfth century, as a result of two movements, that the Jews began to lend money to Christians and to establish the economic pattern that eventually led to the stereotype of the Jewish moneylender. The first of these movements was the crusades; the crusaders needed considerable liquid capital for the long journey to the Holy Land and borrowed against the future income of their estates. The second was the emergence of a Christian merchant class that could use business capital and sometimes turned to the Jews to get it.

The Responsa also demonstrate that although the Jews were not popular among Christians, they clung together in the medieval cities not so much because the Christians forced them to as for religious reasons. Adherence to the Talmudic laws demanded a close-knit community that could support and regulate the provisioning of the restricted diet and maintain the religious service. In some parts of Europe, the communities described by the Responsa continued to exist into this century, though the great age of the Responsa came to an end with the First Crusade.

In this selection, Robert Chazan uses the Responsa and other, narrative, sources to describe the life of the northern Jews in the "golden age," from the ninth through eleventh centuries.

During the tenth and eleventh centuries northern France slowly rose from its torpor. Population increased, the economy developed, and cities grew. This progress contributed to—and benefited from—the establishment of more effective political units. The dukes and counts of northern France carved out for themselves ever larger territories and began to control their domains with increasing authority. The most powerful of these magnates, William of Normandy, was able, during the 1060's, to muster sufficient force to conquer for himself a kingdom across the English Channel. Unobtrusively the king of France, overshadowed often by his mighty vassals, was subduing the Ile-de-France and bending it to his will, slowly laying the groundwork for the sudden expansion of royal power that materialized at the end of the twelfth century.

The revival of trade and of urban centers must have vitally affected the Jews of northern France; however, evidence from this period is sparse. Documentary records, generally meager for this early age, shed no light whatsoever on the role and position of the Jews. The only non-Jewish materials available are the random observations of churchmen, in some instances enlightening, in others misleading. Jewish sources likewise are slim, consisting of a few brief chronicles, a substantial number of rabbinic responsa, and commentaries on the classics of Biblical and Talmudic literature. While the paucity of evidence precludes a detailed reconstruction of Jewish history during this period, enough remains to sketch in outline the condition of northern French Jewry prior to the First Crusade.

A precise geography of pre-Crusade northern French Jewry is impossible. There are, however, a number of locales for which Jewish settlement is attested: Auxerre, Blois, Châlons-sur-Marne, Le Mans, Orléans, Paris, Reims, Rouen, Sens, Troyes. These are major urban centers, all the seats of dioceses. Random evidence indicates Jewish presence in smaller towns as well. Thus, in the incident of 992, the villain, a convert from Judaism to Christianity, moved from Blois to Le Mans, visiting (and duping) a number of Jewish communities in western France along the way. Likewise the so-called Rashi ordinance, which dealt with taxation procedures in the Jewry of Troyes, reflects Jewish settlement in smaller towns. The ordinance was enacted by a major Jewish community surrounded by smaller satellites: "We the inhabitants of Troyes, along with the communities in its environs. . . ." By 1096 the Jews had begun to spread beyond the confines of the major cities of northern France.

Widespread insecurity had destroyed the centralized authority of the Carolingians and had brought to power the feudal barony of northern France. Endangered French society had reconstructed itself through a network of immediate personal ties; the unity embodied in Carolingian rule gave way to a host of localized principalities. The Jews, as perhaps the most exposed element in this society, had the deepest need for the protection that only these magnates could offer. They were thus cast into permanent dependence upon a plethora of seigneurs, ranging from king to petty noble.

It is difficult to trace the implications of this dependence in the pre-Crusade period. The political status of northern French Jewry was never specified in comprehensive charters, as was the case in Germany. It is only with the passage of time and the proliferation of records that a detailed picture of Jewish political circumstances emerges. In general it is obvious that even in this early period the political authorities were responsible for basic Jewish security. This included both protection of Jewish life and property and judicial jurisdiction over the Jews. In 992, when a serious charge was leveled at the Jews of Le Mans, the count not only constituted the court before which the Jews were to be tried; he in fact stipulated the procedure to be utilized. It is also possible that even at this early stage governmental support for the Jews included aid in Jewish business affairs. Detailed information on this comes only in the twelfth century, however.

Willingness to extend to the Jews protection and aid was contingent, of course, on significant advantage to be derived from these Jews. Governmental authorities anticipated two major benefits from Jewish presence: general stimulation of trade and urban life and, more tangible, the immediate profit to be realized from taxation. Tax records from the early period no longer exist, and information in the Jewish sources is fragmentary. There can be little doubt, however, that the flow of income from this taxation was the major factor in the protective stance taken by the barony of northern France.

The dangers inherent in this alliance with the ruling class were manifested early. While the authorities were relatively successful in protecting the Jews from others, there was no power that could effectively interpose itself between the Jews and their protectors. Only two incidents of any proportion mar the calm of Jewish life in northern France prior to 1096; in both cases it was rulers with unrestricted power over the Jews who were responsible for the persecutions.

The first crisis took place in 992 in the city of Le Mans. A convert from Judaism, one Seḥok b. Esther, after earlier clashes with the Jews of Le Mans, deposited a waxen image in the synagogue ark and then unearthed it in the presence of the count of Maine, Hugh III, claiming that the Jews pierced the image regularly in hopes of destroying the count. In the face of adamant Jewish denials, Hugh of Maine ordered the Jews to be tried by combat with their accuser. The chronicle breaks off at this point, with the Jewish community seemingly on the brink of catastrophe. From the opening remarks of the communal letter which describes the incident, it is obvious that the community emerged unscathed. How this came about is unknown. Perfectly clear, however, is the danger stemming from the Jewish community's total reliance on the will of the governing authorities.

The second major incident was far more serious, both in scope and in consequences. According to a variety of extant sources, the years between 1007 and 1012 saw a series of edicts across northern Europe, posing to the Jews the alternatives of conversion to Christianity and expulsion or, on occasion, death. Most of the Jews seem to have chosen expulsion. In some cases, however, there was loss of life, the first instances of that readiness for martyrdom which became a significant characteristic of Ashkenazic Jewry. Although the factors in this persecution were of a religious nature, primarily a concern with the spread of heresy in northern Europe, the decision to convert or expel the Jews could only be made by those feudal lords who controlled Jewish fate—once more an important index of the potential dangers inhering in Jewish political status.

While the local lord exercised effective power over the Jews of his domain, there were other forces striving to make their influence felt. Chief among these was the Church. In some cases, churchmen were themselves feudal lords holding direct rights over Jews. Such overt control, however, was not so prominent in northern France as it was elsewhere. The normal channels of Church influence were twofold. The first was the Church's strong moral pressure on the barony. Clerics close to the feudal dignitaries would utilize this intimacy to further their views on the Jews. Thus, for example, in the 992 incident an anonymous churchman strongly bolstered the anti-Jewish animus by his inflammatory speech to the count of Maine. A more circuitous and less effective mode of influence was through the masses. This involved specifying the Jewish behavior which was unacceptable to the Church and threatening excommunication of those Christians having contact with recalcitrant Jews. According to Raoul Glaber, part of the early–eleventh-century program to eliminate Judaism entirely from sections of northern France was abetted by an episcopal decree outlawing all contact with Jews. The major problem with such boycotts was the difficulty of enforcement.

From the point of view of the Jews, ecclesiastical influence could be either beneficial or baneful. In the instance cited, the cleric of Le Mans much inflamed anti-Jewish passions. On the other hand, it was the awareness of potential Church protection that led a Jew of Rouen, Jacob b. Yekutiel, to deny the right of Richard II of Normandy forcibly to convert the Jews: "You lack the necessary jurisdiction over the Jews to force them from their faith or to harm them. This can only be done by the pope at Rome." The claim of Jacob was not a negation of the feudal rights of Richard over the Jews of Normandy; it was an assertion that the program undertaken ostensibly in the name of the Christian faith was in fact a perversion of Christian principles and had to be brought before the highest ecclesiastical officials for sanction or annulment. According to the Hebrew account, Jacob proceeded to Rome, pleaded his case, and secured a papal decree halting the program of forced conversion.

At this juncture the king exercised no special regalian rights over the Jews. He did, of course, possess normal baronial jurisdiction over the Jews of his own domain. Beyond this, he could on occasion exercise his prerogative as suzerain. It was on this basis that Robert the Pious intervened in the affairs of the county of Sens, deposing Count Raynaud on charges of Judaizing. In the incident of 1007–1012, the king exhibited strong moral leadership in the campaign of forced conversion. While the Hebrew chronicle emphasizes the king's central role in the affair, it also underscores the necessity of agreement by his vassals.

> Then the king and queen took counsel with his officers and his vassals throughout the limits of his kingdom. They charged: "There is one people dispersed throughout the various principalities which does not obey us. . . ." Then there was perfect agreement between the king and his officers, and they concurred on this plan.

Thus the king could suggest action; its execution, however, depended on the consent and the support of the local authorities.

Yet another potential influence on the destiny of the Jews was the municipality and its burghers. In an early stage of development at this point, its lack of authority over the Jews was already manifest. For the Jews, this powerlessness was a boon. If to the princes the Jews promised economic advantage, to the burghers they offered primarily competition. It was all to the Jews' advantage to be removed from the jurisdiction of the growing communes. Yet this removal added political animosity to the religious and economic antipathies already harbored by the townsmen towards the Jews.

During this early period, the populace at large does not appear as a major instigating force in anti-Jewish activity. This was, to be sure, an epoch of substantial violence, and the Jews felt this lawlessness on occasion. The chronicle of 992 mentions in passing economic competition between the renegade Sehok and a member of the Jewish community. This rivalry led eventually to assassination of the Jew by hired killers from Blois. The responsa literature reflects the same instability. There is, for example, an interesting responsum dealing with Jewish merchants captured and held for ransom. More striking, however, is the frequency with which governmental oppressions such as those of 992 and 1007–1012 were accompanied by outbursts of popular antipathy. This is attested by the Hebrew chronicle for 992 and by a number of the sources for 1007–1012. The breakdown of official protection allowed the overt expression of that popular hatred normally suppressed by the authorities.

The Jews of northern France were by the eleventh century already supporting themselves primarily by commerce, and, as the century progressed, this led them increasingly into moneylending. The reliance on commerce and usury is reflected in a most interesting responsum from the early eleventh century. The community had "levied on every man and woman, while under the ban, a fixed amount per pound of value of his or her *money, merchandise, and other saleable possessions*"; trade and banking were obviously primary. Despite the ordinance's orientation towards taxation of merchandise and money, the community attempted to levy taxes on a local Jewess's vineyard, demanding a portion of the value of both the land and its produce. The terms in which the issue was debated are revealing:

> They [the community] claimed that vineyards were in the same category as the capital of a loan, while the harvested crop was equivalent to the interest. One derived no benefit from the vineyard itself, nor from the capital of the loan, during the first half year or year of its investment. Since they paid taxes from both the capital and the interest of their money investments, from their merchandise as well as from its profit, they held that L should do likewise. L, on her part, pointed out that a vineyard could not be compared to the capital of a loan, nor even to merchandise. . . . Thus they argued back and forth.

What is plainly assumed by both sides in the dispute is the centrality of wares and capital in communal taxation. The reply of R. Joseph Bon Fils agreed with the position that only merchandise, money, and the profits from both are taxable.

The economic reliance on commerce and moneylending emerges also from the famous ordinance of Rashi, dating from the end of the eleventh century.

> We, the inhabitants of Troyes, along with the communities in its environs, have ordained—under threat of excommunication—upon every man and woman living here that they be forbidden to remove themselves from the yoke of communal responsibility. . . . Each one shall give per pound that which is enjoined by the members of the community, as has been practiced since the very day of its founding. We have likewise received from our predecessors the practice of paying on all possessions, except household items, houses, vineyards, and fields.

A community which exempts "household items, houses, vineyards, and fields" from taxation is obviously heavily involved in mercantile pursuits.

Jewish commerce was probably largely local. As noted, evidence for settlement shows the Jews primarily in major urban centers. A number of responsa, however, indicate Jews traveling through northern France, trading at the fairs of this period. Insecurity made such travel hazardous on occasion; Jewish traders were seized and their goods confiscated. Sometimes the inherent dangers of commerce were magnified by involvement in shady dealings. An early–eleventh-century responsum deals with the legal complications arising from the disappearance and presumed death of an unscrupulous Jewish merchant. The questionable practices, which probably led to his violent demise, are described as follows:

> A was accustomed to travel to many places and to many towns situated within a day or two of his residence. He would sell to and buy from the overlords of these towns, his regular clientele. Whenever they were short of cash, he would sell to them on credit, against pledges of gold or silver, or exchange his merchandise for cattle (or horses) which they had robbed from their enemies. These cattle he would accept at a low price, bring them home and sell them for a much higher price. His activities aroused the anger and hatred of the plundered villagers, and of their feudal lords, who would say: "This Jew, by the very fact that he is always ready to buy looted goods, entices our enemies to attack and plunder us. . . ." Moreover, occasionally the overlords quarrelled with him on account of the pledges which A would eventually sell and because of the high interest he charged.

The normal hazards of eleventh-century trade were here much enhanced. The same responsum reveals the very fluid transition which many Jews made from commerce to lending. When his customers lacked the necessary cash at hand to make their purchases, the Jewish merchant would extend credit. In fact, there is an indication of the mechanism utilized for safeguarding this investment. The debtors gained the necessary credit by depositing pledges, which were held as security for repayment of the obligation. In case of eventual nonpayment, these pledged objects could be sold. No litigation or third party was needed, and the creditor was amply protected from the moment that the loan was extended. Safeguarding loans through retention of a pledge is, of course, the simplest expedient available, and it was probably the most common method used during this period.

There are, nonetheless, fragmentary signs of more sophisticated arrangements. A responsum of Rashi deals with a dispute between a widow and her brother-in-law concerning gifts allegedly given to the widow and her deceased husband by his parents. Chief among these gifts was "the tithe collectible from a certain village, which tithe had been pledged with L and J [the parents] for a loan of seven rotl. L and J thus empowered R and A to collect the produce of that tithe and the principal of the loan in the event the original owner of the tithe should come to repay the loan and redeem his pledge." While this arrangement is also designated a pledge (mashkon), it is quite different from the pledges indicated earlier. The former were physical objects which were deposited at the time of the loan. When the debt was repaid, the pawn was returned; if the borrower defaulted, it would be kept or sold. In the case of the tithe, however, it was not a physical object that changed hands; it was a right. The difference in practical terms was twofold. First, there was constant revenue; the lender collected regular income, which was probably seen as the interest on the loan. More important, this was an arrangement that involved more than simply a creditor and a debtor; the implicit aid of a governmental agency was necessary. The creditor did not physically control the pledge; hence, should contention arise, he had to have the certainty of powerful support. Lending of the kind revealed in the responsum of Rashi is far more complex and generally more lucrative; it had as its result the further tightening of the crucial bond between Jew and baron. As Jews turned increasingly towards this kind of business operation, they began to depend on their overlords not only for physical protection but for buttressing their financial investments as well. Prior to the First Crusade this more complex method of lending may have remained rather uncommon. It was, however, destined to play an increasingly important role in Jewish economic life.

The aspect of pre-Crusade Jewish life that has attracted the most scholarly attention has been its communal organization. The Jewish communities of northern France were small, with a high level of internal cohesion and a broad range of activities. Yitzhak Baer has delineated three major functions in this community: the preservation of satisfactory relations with the ruling powers, the securing of internal discipline and order, and the establishment of necessary internal economic limitations and controls.

The alliance fashioned between the Jews and the barony was fueled by the tangible advantages realized by the feudal magnates. The most immediate expression of this was taxation. Collection of taxes was certainly one of the major functions assumed by the communal agencies. The responsum specifying those holdings open to taxation indicates that the purpose of the levy was "to collect the king's tax."

The methods for apportioning taxation were well-established and reflect the cohesiveness of the community. One method was that indicated in the above-noted responsum. This involved levying "on every man and woman, while under the ban, a fixed amount per pound of value of his or her money, merchandise, and other saleable possessions." This system depended for its effectiveness upon honest evaluation, by each member of the community, of his possessions. The likelihood of such honesty was enhanced by the religious sanctions mentioned and by the closeness of a small community, where the temptation to underevaluate would be tempered by the difficulty of concealing the truth. Occasionally, however, this arrangement broke down. R. Joseph Bon Fils was asked to resolve a complicated issue that began with the following circumstance:

> The people of T came to pay the king's tax. They complained against one another, saying: "You lightened your own burden and made mine heavier." Whereupon they selected trustees, the noble and great of the town, the experts of the land, from the community, and (agreed) to abide by their decision, for they dealt faithfully.

The role of the Jewish community organization as a liaison between the Jews and the ruling authorities was not exhausted by the collection of taxes. On occasion the organized community had to make representation before the authorities on matters affecting the security of the Jews. Thus, in 992, when faced with the danger of trial by combat, the Jewish community made vehement protestations before the count of Maine. They appealed to precedent, on the one hand, and offered substantial material inducements, on the other. While in this instance there was large-scale community response, in periods of crisis a prominent individual could take the initiative, thrusting himself to the fore as the community's spokesman. It was in this manner that Jacob b. Yekutiel ventured to step forth before the duke of Normandy and ultimately before the pope himself.

In a community desperately anxious to preserve its insulation from the local municipality within whose boundaries it lived and to achieve a measure of distance from even the more favorably-disposed feudal authorities, there was an absolute necessity for maintaining inner discipline. While the small size of the Jewish community contributed to cohesiveness, close living could on occasion produce sharp conflicts between members of the community. In the face of such conflict, the community marshaled its forces and ordained limitations on intracommunal strife. The community's goal in such cases was the preservation of peace within the community, without the intervention of outside powers.

The economic outlets available to the Jews were not extensive. For this reason the community had to exercise significant control in the area of economics also. The two major thrusts of communal limitation were the granting of exclusive commercial privileges and the restriction of the right to settle. The former usually involved business dealings with important secular lords or ecclesiastical institutions. From the slim evidence available, it seems that the arrangement was not everywhere operative and that, even where the prerogative of the community to give such privileges was recognized, the rights of exclusive trade were not widely granted. Restriction of settlement was directly related to the economic situation of the Jews. The small towns of northern France could absorb only so many Jewish traders and money-lenders. Overpopulation would simply force the available income of the community below the subsistence level. Again it must be noted, however, that the right of the community to declare a total or even a partial ban on new settlement was far from universally recognized.

To the three major functions of the Jewish community delineated by Baer at least a fourth must be added. The Jewish community of necessity had to supply certain essential religious and social services to its membership. The centrality of the synagogue in the Jewish community of this period is undisputed. It was far more than a center of worship, serving as an educational and general communal center as well. Details of Jewish schooling at the time are almost nonexistent. The literacy demanded by the business pursuits of the Jews and the already high level of cultural achievement indicate a successful educational system. Within the medieval municipality there were of course no "neutral" social welfare agencies; such facilities as did exist were Church institutions and, as such, closed to the Jews; thus the Jews had to provide for their own indigent, ill, and unfortunate. The needs of the local community were often augmented by the requirements of Jews whose business took them from town to town. In the case of the central figure in the Le Mans letter, as he proceeded through the Jewish communities of northwestern France, the Jews "supported him, as is their custom, in every town to which he came." Perhaps the most striking evidence of such concern is revealed in the following responsum:

> Jews of Rheims, while on their way to the fair of Troyes, were attacked, plundered, and taken captive by "an adversary and an enemy." The charitable Jews of Troyes risked their own lives, (negotiated with the enemy,) and agreed to a redemption price of thirty pounds. The greater part of the ransom money was paid by the captives themselves; while in order to raise

the remainder, the community of Troyes levied a tax of one *solidus* per pound on themselves, as well as on the neighboring communities of Sens and Auxerre, and on the Jews of Chalon-sur-Saone.

The locus of power in the Jewish community was the community membership itself. While the governing authorities benefited from the ability of the community to control its own affairs, particularly in the area of taxation, there was as yet no strong drive for more direct involvement in Jewish communal affairs or for more extensive exploitation of this useful and cohesive group. As noted, the community, for its part, was anxious to minimize outside interference.

The rhetoric of community enactments generally emphasized unanimous decisionmaking by the entire local Jewry: "The community of Troyes levied a tax . . ."; "the townspeople levied on every man and woman . . ."; "the community . . . heard about it and solemnly pronounced the ban. . . ." There was, in fact, even question as to the right of the majority to exercise its will over the minority.

At the same time, however, certain elements in the community did command special authority. Leadership was exercised by significant scholarly figures, such as Rashi, or by men of wealth and standing, such as Jacob b. Yekutiel. An interesting responsum indicates a more general tendency towards control by a segment of the community. In a conflict concerning the responsibility of individuals to accept the decisions of the majority, the following question was asked:

> We are a small community. The humble members among us have always abided by the leadership of our eminent members, dutifully obeyed their decrees, and never protested against their ordinances. Now, when we are about to enact a decree, must we ask each individual member whether or not he is in agreement with it?

Even at this early point a leadership class does seem to have emerged, although it certainly lacked the direct governmental support and the recognized religious authority that would later develop.

With the community itself as the fundamental authority, it is in no way surprising to find power highly localized. The question of the right of one Jewish settlement to legislate for others was raised a number of times. In general a distinction was drawn between daily administrative affairs— where each community was autonomous—and principles of Jewish religious behavior—where coercion could be exerted. One of a number of expressions of this distinction is phrased in the following way:

> As to your question whether the inhabitants of one town are competent to enact decrees binding on the inhabitants of another town, and to coerce

the latter inhabitants while they are in their own town, the following ruling seems proper to us: If the decree that they are enacting deals with the needs of their place, such as taxation, weights, measures, and wages—in all such matters the inhabitants of one town are not competent to legislate for the inhabitants of another town. Thus we quoted above the Talmudic ruling: "The townspeople are permitted," which means that only the people of the town are competent to legislate in such matters but not outsiders. If, however, the inhabitants of a town transgressed a law of the Torah, committed a wrong, or decided a point of law or of ritual, not in accordance with the accepted usage—the inhabitants of another town might coerce them, and even pronounce the ḥerem against them, in order to force them to mend their ways. In that case, the inhabitants of the former town may not say to the latter: "we are independent of you, we exercise authority among ourselves, as you do among yourselves." For all Israel is then enjoined to force them (to mend their ways); as we find in the case of the "rebellious sage," or "the condemned city," that the Sanhedrin coerces them and judges them.

Extensive authority was exercised by outstanding scholarly figures, whose enactments were generally considered binding over a wide number of settlements. Thus, Rashi affirms that the important edict of R. Gershom of Mayence would certainly be applicable in all Jewish communities.

Should it become established through the testimony of reliable witnesses who are recognized authorities on this restrictive ordinance of the great teacher (R. Gershom), that he enacted this ordinance with greater rigor and strictness than all other anathemas and restrictive measures customarily enacted in the last generations; that in this enactment he used the awesome term *shamta*; and that he solemnly prohibited to mention the disgrace (of temporary apostasy) not only to the culprits themselves who eventually returned to Judaism, but even to their descendants; and should it further become established that when A and his family were forewarned, the name of the great teacher (as author of the awesome ban) was mentioned to them—we cannot deal lightly with a ban of Rabbenu Gershom, since in our generation there is no scholar of his great eminence, capable to release a person from such a ban.

The sanctions at the disposal of the community were of course conditioned by the bases of its power. One possibility lay in the direction of the secular authority, but it was an avenue only sparingly utilized because of the danger inhering in such an approach. Thus, an early–eleventh-century Jewish community faced with the overt recalcitrance of two of its members and the support of a neighboring community for the rebels was "about to ask the king to order his constables to collect his tax directly from A and B. Upon further deliberation, however, they changed their minds and decided first to inquire whether their solemn decree was still valid, i.e., whether the cancellation thereof by the community of S was of any consequence." A turn to secular authorities was a step which most Jewish communities were reluctant to take.

Since the most tangible locus of power was the cohesive community itself, the ultimate weapon at the disposal of the Jews was the ban of excommunication. Given the importance of the Jewish community and its facilities to the individual Jew, the power of exclusion was a formidable one. The ostracized Jew was in a hazardous position politically, economically, socially, and religiously. At the same time, excommunication was not an infallible tool in the hands of the Jewish community. The realities of power within the community often limited the effectiveness of the ban. In one case, for example, "since the members of the community feared that B and his friends, living so near the synagogue, would remove the scrolls of the Law and other community articles, and that no one would be able to stop them from taking these articles, they transgressed the law on several occasions—all on B's instructions." Another limitation on the effectiveness of excommunication was the localization of Jewish authority already noted. Thus two Jews excommunicated in community T "went to S and related there the whole incident. The people of S took A and B into their homes, wined and dined them, transacted business with them, lifted from them the ban of community T, and gave them a written release of such ban." While the action of community S was judged illegal, in fact the localization of power did weaken the impact of any such ban.

The Jewish community of northern France thus emerges, from earliest times, as a remarkably cohesive and comprehensive organization. The isolation of the Jews forced them to create for themselves all sorts of agencies—political, economic, social, educational, and religious. The small size of the individual Jewish settlements precluded the independence of each of these agencies. What emerged then was a total Jewish community responsible for filling every one of the vital needs of its constituents. Therein lies the secret of the wide range of powers and the effectiveness of the Jewish community organization even at its early stage of development.

Perhaps the most persuasive index of the level of maturity reached by northern French Jewry prior to the First Crusade is its intellectual creativity. It seems reasonable to conclude that a community capable of producing extensive scholarly achievement like that of R. Solomon b. Isaac of Troyes (Rashi) must have been well-established and effectively organized. Rashi, already noted as an outstanding communal authority—one of the few whose eminence was broadly recognized—wrote copiously. His works, which quickly became classics in Ashkenazic circles, included primarily extensive commentaries on the Bible and the Talmud. While he was always revered as the beginning—and not the culmination—of a brilliant series of northern French scholars, his creations indicate that, by the last years of the eleventh century, northern French Jewry had come of age.

At the end of the eleventh century many of the creative forces that had been germinating steadily throughout western Europe burst forth into the passion, vision, and violence of the First Crusade. The Crusade was an expression of the new militance of Christendom against its external foes; it revealed also new potential for internal upheaval and disruption. While the goal of the pope and of the great barons was a military expedition against Islam, the feelings unleashed by the call to the Crusade could hardly be contained within the particular channels delineated by its instigators. Thus the First Crusade brought more than the conquest of Jerusalem; it left a path of death and destruction within Christendom itself.

The dispossessed who took up the chant "Deus lo volt" savagely vented pent-up furies upon many of their long-despised neighbors. Given the pervasive religiosity of medieval civilization and the distinctly religious hatreds that animated the Crusaders, it comes as no surprise that the prime object of the internal violence associated with the First Crusade was European Jewry.

France, particularly northern France, played a major role in the great drama of 1095–1099. It was in the French city of Clermont that Urban II issued his appeal; French barons were conspicuous in their leadership of the crusading forces; it was in the French countryside that Peter the Hermit began his preaching for a humble army of the pious to free the holy places from Moslem hands. Yet France, despite its prominence, was spared the upheavals that followed in the wake of Crusade preaching. France's eastern neighbors bore the brunt of the devastation that crusading fervor unleashed.

The relative calm with which France weathered the Crusade is reflected in the fate of her Jews. The same Jewish and Christian sources that are so copious in their description of Jewish sufferings in the Rhineland area say almost nothing of Jewish fate in France. Although arguments from silence are always suspect, it is difficult to believe that this set of Jewish and Christian chroniclers and editors would have been unaware of, or uninterested in recounting, extensive Jewish tragedy in nearby France. The Rhineland Jews who compiled the Hebrew chronicles knew the reactions of the French Jews to the organization of the Crusade, and they detailed Jewish persecution over a broad area. It is inconceivable that large-scale catastrophe in France could have gone unknown or unreported. Moreover, the longest of the Hebrew Crusade chronicles is embedded in a late–twelfth-century communal history of Spires Jewry, which includes a series of letters detailing the Blois catastrophe of 1171 and its aftermath. The Spires editor would not have omitted information on Crusade tragedy in France had it been available.

There is satisfactory evidence for but one specific persecution of Jews within the area of northern France, an attack which took place in the Norman city of Rouen. The fullest description of this assault is given by Guibert of Nogent as a backdrop to his account of a monk of the monastery of Fly.

> At Rouen on a certain day, the people who had undertaken to go on that expedition [that is, the Crusade] under the badge of the Cross began to

complain to one another, "After traversing great distances, we desire to attack the enemies of God in the East, although the Jews, of all races the worst foe of God, are before our eyes. That's doing our work backward." Saying this and seizing their weapons, they herded the Jews into a certain place of worship, rounding them up by either force or guile, and without distinction of sex or age put them to the sword. Those who accepted Christianity, however, escaped the impending slaughter.

The striking difference between the relative peace enjoyed by northern France and its Jews and the wholesale destruction, especially of Jewish life and property, further east can be accounted for in a number of ways. This difference is surely not a reflection of more benign French attitudes; as Norman Golb has argued, French Crusaders were deeply implicated in the wave of German atrocities associated with the First Crusade. In France, however, their antipathy was not translated into deed, partially because France was the very first area of organization. The problems of the undisciplined Crusader bands tended to multiply the further eastward they moved, the larger their numbers, and the slimmer their provisions. The initial rallying of these crusading groups in France and their speedy movement towards the East played a major role in the safety of French Jewry. A second factor was the protection afforded by the less pretentious, but more effective, French political authorities. While the emperor was the most exalted political dignitary of Europe, the base upon which his power rested was a shaky one. Thus, in town after town, the Jews found themselves separated from large and bloodthirsty mobs by the flimsy military and political power of the local bishop. Even the Hebrew chroniclers recognize that many of these bishops were sincere in their desire to protect their Jews; their failure resulted from a lack of the required force. In France, on the other hand, where the Capetian monarchy advanced none of the grandiose claims of the German empire, firm political power had been slowly crystallizing in a series of well-organized principalities. Within these principalities the count and his growing retinue of administrative officials exercised effective authority. It was this political stability also that aided in harnessing the violence of the Crusaders and in sparing the Jews.

Although the Jews of northern France suffered little during the tumultuous first months of the Crusade, they were hardly oblivious to the dangers. In fact they were far more aware of the impending threat than any of their fellow Jews, for it was in their land that the Crusade was called, that the first active preaching took place, and that the first crusading groups began to form. The same Hebrew chronicle that said nothing of overt persecution in France recorded faithfully the fears of the French Jews.

At the time when the Jewish communities in France heard [of the beginning of the Crusade] they were seized with fear and trembling. They then resorted to the devices of their predecessors. They wrote letters and sent messengers to the Rhineland communities, that these communities fast and seek mercy on their behalf from the God who dwells on high, so that they might be spared.

The Hebrew chronicles also reported the more immediate steps taken by French Jewry to avert the threatened catastrophe. This information is contained in the brief description of the passage of Peter the Hermit through Trèves.

> When he came to Trèves—he and the multitude of men with him—to go forth on their pilgrimage to Jerusalem, he brought with him from France a letter from the Jews, indicating that, in all places where he would pass through Jewish communities, they should afford him provisions. He then would speak favorably on behalf of the Jews.

Given the lack of destructive violence against the Jews in northern France, we can readily understand the lack of a political aftermath parallel to that which took place in Germany. Guido Kisch has carefully chronicled the evolution in Germany of safeguards designed to protect the vulnerable Jewish communities. Jewish political status in France, however, underwent no significant development in the wake of the First Crusade. There had been, after all, no major calamity to arouse among the Jews themselves or among their baronial overlords a heightened sense of the urgent need for new protective devices.

Furthermore, French Jewry never viewed 1095–1096 as a watershed in its history, as did its German counterpart. While the works of Rashi represent an early high point of French Jewish religious creativity, his successors did not see themselves as mere compilers of his legacy; they considered their efforts a continuation, not a collection. When, much later on, the sense of a chain of giant figures emerges, this series runs from Rashi through R. Samson of Sens, from the late eleventh through the early thirteenth centuries. The years of the First Crusade are in no sense construed as a major dividing line. Interestingly enough, when in 1171 French Jewry suffered what it considered its first major catastrophe, the calamity at Blois, it very movingly expressed the feelings of horror evoked by the utterly senseless death of over thirty Jews. If ever one might expect French Jewish recollection of the First Crusade, this would surely be the point. Yet significantly there is no recall whatsoever of 1096. When old memories are summoned up, they are recollections of a much earlier period. Thus, according to Ephraim of Bonn, R. Jacob Tam ordained that the twentieth of Sivan, the day of the catastrophe itself, "is fit to be set as a fast day for all our people. Indeed the gravity of this fast will exceed that of the fast of Gedaliah b. Aḥikam, for this is a veritable Day of Atonement." The fateful year of the First Crusade in no way dominated the subsequent consciousness of northern French Jewry.

Through the late tenth and on through the eleventh century, then, northern French Jewry continued to develop, benefiting from the general progress of western European civilization and making its own contribution to that progress. Already tightly allied with the powerful feudal barony, the Jews were involving themselves ever more heavily in the burgeoning urban commerce and had begun to develop viable institutions of self-government. By the end of the eleventh century, northern French Jewry was sufficiently mature to produce its first figure of renown, R. Solomon b. Isaac of Troyes. Relatively unscathed by the anti-Jewish outbreaks of the First Crusade, French Jewry proceeded into the twelfth century in a spirit of continued growth.

The World of the Crusaders

JOSHUA PRAWER

Popular histories of the crusades dwell on the formation of the crusading armies, the trek across Asia Minor to the Levant, and the revival of trade between East and West. They also indulge in endless discussions concerning the motives of the crusaders. This selection by Joshua Prawer treats an important aspect of the crusading movement that receives scant attention in most histories—the experiences and everyday lives of the Europeans who settled the new Latin principalities in Palestine and Syria. The First Crusade was successful not only in driving the Saracens out of Jerusalem, but also in establishing a feudal principality there to protect the recovered holy places. A great many of those who went with the first army were landless knights who stayed in the Holy Land to carve out baronies for themselves. Their good fortune, as well as the continual need for reinforcements to keep the new state strong against Moslem counterattack, brought in a steady stream of European knights.

What was this society of immigrants and, eventually, of second and third generation Levantines like? The Arabs of the region considered the new arrivals barbarians; brutes whose ability to fight had to be respected, but whose culture was shockingly primitive. The Europeans born in the Levant may well have had the same reaction to newcomers, but they were cultural hybrids themselves. Their kingdom produced a feudal charter, the Assizes of Jerusalem, that shows a faithful adherence to the social and political ideals of Europe. Their life style, however, absorbed much from the Arab aristocracy around them, with which they learned to live during the uneasy truces.

The noble and knight brought with them from Europe notions and ideals of the seigniorial life-style and transplanted them in the soil of the newly conquered state. Western Europe perpetuated itself under oriental skies. The French language, fashions and customs struck roots in the Levant, and soon a second and a third generation of the original conquerors and settlers had grown up in the country for whom "home" meant the Holy Land, whereas Europe—the "old home"—was a place of their ancestors' far-removed origin. This was a new breed of men and women nicknamed *Poulains*, which should probably be translated or understood in the sense of "kids." Their home life, family relations and tutors were all reflections of Europe and, more specifically, France. Yet their environment—the physical conditions of life, the daily meetings in street and bazaar—was the Levant. Thus a scion of a noble, or even a knightly, family underwent the same process of upbringing and education as his European counterpart. He was raised under the mantle of the same religion, instructed in the same tenets of faith, drew his intellectual attitudes and images from the same legends, pious tales, heroic romances and courtly poetry. A *France d'Outremer*, a "France overseas," was created.

Yet the Syrian-born Frank was not wholly European. Mixed marriages with Armenian and Byzantine ladies were a common occurrence in the upper strata of the Frankish nobility. It was thus considered quite "normal" that one's mother, grandmother or aunt was an oriental Christian. This was true not only for the nobility but even for the royal and princely Crusader houses. Such a marriage brought with it the oriental servants and attendants—whether Christian or Moslem—which abounded in every wealthy Frankish household. Members of the lower strata of Frankish society, whether simple knights or burgesses, often intermarried with oriental Christians on their own social level. A Crusader chronicler reflected upon the resultant state of affairs:

> . . . Consider, I pray, and reflect how in our time God has transferred the West into the East. For we who were Occidentals now have been made Orientals. He who was a Roman or a Frank is now a Galilean or Palestinian. One who was a citizen of Rheims or of Chartres now has been made a citizen of Tyre or Antioch. We have already forgotten the places of our birth; they have become unknown to many of us or, at least, are unmentioned. Some already possess homes and servants here which they have received through inheritance. Some have taken wives not merely of their own people but Syrians, or Armenians or even Saracens who have received the grace of baptism. Some have with them a father-in-law, or daughter-in-law, or son-in-law, or stepson or stepfather. Here, too, are grandchildren and great-grandchildren. One cultivates vines, another fields. Both use the speech and the idioms of different languages. These languages, now made common, become known to both races; and faith unites those whose forefathers were strangers.

Thus a young Frank, a *Poulain*, was accustomed from childhood to meeting and living with the Occident in the Orient. The house or citadel which he inhabited in the city was usually an oriental building which had belonged to a Moslem before the Crusader conquest and was very different from European buildings and fortifications. Timber, the most common build-ing material in the West, was almost unknown in the Holy Land. Stone was the common building material used in both the cities and villages. It was usually quarried not far from the cities themselves, like the stone cut out of the slopes of Mount Carmel for Caesarea, those of Chastel Pèlerin dug out of the nearby ridge which blocked the eastward-moving dunes, or the lovely, pink-coloured stone brought to Jerusalem from Anathot.

Two- and three-storey stone houses were the normal type of habitat, but even five-storey houses were not unknown. Their flat roofs, often dotted with potted palms or evergreen trees and shrubs, were a place to enjoy the cool breezes after the hot sun had set. Inside, the thick walls preserved warmth in the winter, when the temperature in places like Jerusalem and Safed, as well as in the mountains east of Acre, Tripoli and Antioch, descended to the freezing point. In the summer, the walls and narrow windows kept the rooms cool, even during the scorching days of the *hamsin*, the Levantine first-cousin of the *sirocco*. The ceilings were very high, and the slightly pointed arches added to the feeling of height in the atmosphere, for the narrow windows restricted the entrance of light as well as heat. The windows were not boarded up by planks or covered with parchment, but glistened with locally fabricated glass. Pure, transparent glass was rather rare, but green- or blue-tinted, semi-opaque glass enclosing air bubbles was used, unless one preferred stained glass.

The ground-floor facade of Eastern houses was usually a solid wall except for the entrance-way. The windows on the upper floors let in some light, but basically the house opened onto the inner courtyard, where the precious, life-giving well, stored rain water or, in some places, a pit connected to one of the ancient aqueducts was normally situated. In some courtyards, as we know from a description of a marvellous Crusader palace in Beirut, a fountain cooled the air and its water-jets fell back into a mosaic-paved pool.

In some houses the staircase was located outside the building, allowing access from the street to each floor. The houses of the wealthy often had a kind of out-building composed of canvas- or plank-covered arches to protect the entrance from sun and rain, like the elaborate awnings in our luxury hotels. The shafts of the arches had holes drilled into them so that horses could be tethered.

The interiors of the better-endowed houses were decorated with mosaics of exquisite Byzantine-Moslem craftsmanship. In addition, rugs, draperies or tapestries covered the walls. Mosaics were an integral part of interior decora-tion and often displayed geometric designs, flowers and animals. In wealthier households, the ceiling arches may have rested on sculpted consoles, or a display of archvaults and simple arches might have added to the decor. Furni-ture was far more elaborate than that found in Europe. At their best, tables and chairs and the legs and posts of beds were of wood carved in lace-like patterns of bas-reliefs or small sculptures of flowers or human or animal heads.

The chairs often looked like a rounded letter x, their upper part serving as a seat with handles. Oblong, cylindrical cushions covered with silk or samite that ended off in tassels were added for comfort. Mother of pearl, which became the glory of Bethlehem's craftsmanship, may already have been used in furniture decoration, as it was in some of the mosaics. Each noble household or ecclesiastical institution had a box-like writing table with accompanying chair. The writing was done on the inclined top, whereas the ink-pots, colours, quills and other paraphernalia of the scriptorium were kept on the table's lower shelves.

Kitchen utensils and tableware varied with the strata of society. Cooking was done in large earthenware pots in open ovens. Those preserved in several Crusader sites are huge pits over which meat could have been broiled or pots suspended or the pit was covered by a special iron grid to hold the pots and pans. Spoons and knives were the basic table utensils, the first normally of wood, the latter of iron or steel. One often used his dagger as a table knife (these sometimes had ornate handles of ivory or carved wood and blades of the famous Indian steel), although metal utensils were often imported from Europe. In noble households the younger squires or pages served the meal; but when the family was receiving honoured guests, the younger sons of the family would sometimes perform this duty. The carved meat was transferred on slices of round bread, which served as plates and sauce-sponges, or the bread was placed on earthenware plates which were often glazed and decorated with designs. The most common glazed crockery was a basic dark colour covered with geometrical designs of brown, green and yellow glaze. Sometimes these decorations were Christian symbols—such as crosses, fish, tiaras, mitres—but heads of animals, legendary griffons and the like were also used. The most elaborate plates would have drawings of knights or riders on their mounts.

Metal plates and goblets were part of the decor of the house. Some were purely ornamental, such as large, copper-brimmed plates engraved with verses or even scenes from the Scriptures. These seem to have been imported from Europe; but such decorative or ceremonial crockery as that on which the Crusader king's meal was served in the Mosque of al-Aqsa after the coronation must have been of precious metal designed and engraved in Syria and Palestine. Metal cups and goblets were in common use. Some were inlaid, usually with silver, in the lovely patterns of the oriental arabesque. The Arabic inscriptions which praised Allah were no impediments to their use among Christians, though they might have been used for wine-drinking (which was certainly not what their artisan-creator intended). Whereas metal cups and goblets were also in common use in Europe, glassware was far more common in the Orient. Some examples of glasses painted with scenes and inscriptions, probably made in Tyre, display excellent form and exquisite decorations.

One bears the heraldic sign of its owner, which must have been a common custom.

The oriental house and its interior decoration found their complement in the cuisine. Whatever gastronomical tradition had been imported from Europe, it could hardly compete with the local menu. Not only was oriental cuisine better adapted to the local climatic conditions, but the tantalizing spices and their use in meat, fish and sauces easily got the upper hand in competition with the abundant but rather plain dishes known to the Europeans. The oriental servants, like vendors in streets and bazaars, had no difficulty introducing their specialities into both noble and lower households. We even know about Crusader old-timers who boasted about their Egyptian cuisine, as one would boast today of having a cook with a *cordon bleu*.

Fashion and dresses also left their mark on Crusader society, but in this sphere the Franks limited their adoption. The Frank was ready to take advantage of the sumptuous textiles of the Near or Far East. Textiles which in Europe could have been found in royal and princely households only or occasionally among the ceremonial wardrobe of prelates were within the range of people of even mediocre means in the Orient. Silk, taffeta, brocade, cotton, wool and gossamer muslins were all worn by the Franks and their ladies, but they resisted the adoption of oriental style. One would wear oriental fabrics, but the cut of the dresses remained European. A Frank never wore any oriental garb, at least not in public. Sometimes he would wind a short shawl or mantle over his helmet as protection against the sun's strong rays; he might even use a white cloak, as did the Orientals and members of the military orders. But his vestments were basically European and changed with European fashions. Articles of clothing which could not be found in the kingdom, like berets, were imported from Europe. And the Franks' sense of ethnic identity went so far that they prohibited non-Franks from wearing European-style garments. This keeping to the *mores Francorum* was also expressed by the resistance to the oriental custom of growing beards. Whereas the participants of the First Crusade were bearded, as was the custom in their homelands, when beards went out of fashion in Europe two generations later (middle of the twelfth century), the Franks in the Holy Land followed suit, and their clean-shaven faces and shoulder-length hair became as much a clearly distinguishable mark of their identity as the object of oriental disgust and ridicule.

Climate and environment had their influence in the realm of hygiene and cosmetics. A nineteenth-century historian described medieval Europe as a society which had forgone washing for a thousand years. This description certainly did not apply to the Franks in the East. Soap was produced locally and may even have been exported. The partiality of the *Poulains* for baths earned them the charge of the vice of "luxury." The austere Bernard of

Clairvaux pointed out with pride that his protégés, the Templars, had no use for baths! Fifty years later, James of Vitry, the bishop of Acre, preached against this unholy institution which contaminated mores. He even hinted at some unsavoury goings on among the ladies of the Crusader upper class. The Genoese even allowed common bathing (albeit segregated by sex) in their *balneum* in Acre. Whatever the custom, Europeans who visited the kingdom returned to Europe with the impression that an effeminate society had succeeded the heroes of the First Crusade, who had since become legendary paragons of all chivalrous virtues. Today, one would probably describe such behaviour as subtlety, finesse or epicurean, but things looked different to the European newcomer. James of Vitry was rather vehement in his denunciation: "They were brought up in luxury, soft and effeminate, more used to baths than battles, addicted to unclean and riotous living, clad like women in soft robes." Beneath the heavy hand of the furious prelate, one detects a mode of life which a disgruntled contemporary observer would label as Levantine:

> They have so learned to disguise their meaning in cunning speeches, covered and bedecked with leaves, but no fruit, like barren willow-trees, that those who do not know them thoroughly by experience can scarcely understand their reservations and tricks of speech or avoid being deceived by them. They are suspicious and jealous of their wives, whom they lock up in close prison and guard in such strict and careful custody that even their brethren and nearest relatives can scarcely approach them; while they forbid them so utterly to attend churches, processions, the wholesome preaching of God's Word and other matters appertaining to their salvation, that they scarce suffer them to go to church once a year; howbeit some husbands allow their wives to go out to the bath three times a week, under strict guard.

As to Crusader womenfolk:

> But the more strictly the *Pullani* lock up their wives, the more do they by a thousand arts and endless contrivances struggle and try to find their way out. They are wondrously and beyond belief learned in witchcraft and wickednesses innumerable, which they are taught by the Syrian women.

Despite almost chronic warfare, the amenities of the Holy Land made life less grim than it was under the grey, northern skies of Europe. Houses, dress, encounters in street or market-place, the gossip and politics in the baths recalled Hellenistic cities. The Frankish knight who grew up in such surroundings, despite his speech and dress, was not French but a Near Eastern Frank. One can hardly agree with the accusation of cowardice; they were good fighters. And while not always good diplomats, thirteenth-century Crusader nobles were born politicians who loved to have a finger in every political pie and conspiracy, like the Renaissance Italians in their city-states.

The Frankish noble seldom lived in the countryside. Even the few nobles who had castles as centres of seigniories would normally maintain a household in the city (usually in Jerusalem and in the thirteenth century in Acre or Tyre). Very few nobles lived in their manors. Basically they were a class of *rentiers* who collected the income from their rural estates and spent it in their urban residences. The countryside and its villages was 'a thing one lived off, supervised, but rarely inhabited. The squire-tenant or squire-serf relationship, typical in medieval Europe, was almost non-existent in the Orient. The steward or a similar official, often a scribe or *drugeman*, would supervise the village rents, though he seldom intervened in the work itself. The Crusader noble did not go into farming on his own, very seldom kept demesne land and was normally satisfied with the third or quarter of the village crops, which were usually well supplemented by income from urban taxation. As a matter of fact, a Crusader noble's visit to his rural possessions was rather exceptional. One went out to the countryside for hunting or fishing, but seldom for economic reasons. The amenities of country life, without its burdens, were supplied by the beautiful orchards, vineyards and olive groves which surrounded all the cities. Some nobles maintained a kind of cottage or similar structure in these "suburbs" where they passed the hot summer days and cooler evenings in the company of others of their class, sometimes even Moslem nobles. From here they would pursue the chase for fox or boar or hunt with falcons. A good part of time was spent in riding and military exercises. Crusader nobles, like their Moslem antagonists, vied with each other over the beauty of their horses. A considerable amount of money was spent acquiring horses and bedecking them with trappings of finery, expensive materials and precious metals. Pasture lands around the cities were also parade grounds to display horses and horsemanship. During periods of peace, even Moslems would participate in such exercises. The crowning glory of the mounted noble was, naturally, the tournament, a mock battle of nobles or of single champions. On such occasions the ladies appeared on city or castle battlements to participate in that most-cherished of medieval shows. Here the young squire or the experienced knight could achieve prize and renown for prowess and military skill. The horses, arms and armour of the loser, often of considerable value, became the property of the winner. Still, it seems that tournaments, which were often connected with festivities, were rarer in the Crusader East than in contemporary Europe. Perhaps in a war-ridden country mock battles were too close to everyday, grim reality to exercise the attraction that was so strong in Europe, despite ecclesiastical prohibitions.

The major part of a noble's or knight's time was spent in his normal habitat, the city. A simple knight's time-table was regulated by duties of service in city garrison, manning the city's citadel, making the rounds of walls and towers or guarding the lord's palace. Higher nobility would spend a good deal of time in attendance on their overlord, often sitting in his court as councillors or judges. As councillors they would advise on matters put before them for deliberation; as judges they performed the feudal obligations judging their peers.

A short treatise entitled "On the Four Ages of Men," written by a mid–thirteenth-century Frank and describing occupations fitting to each age, gives the impression that the Franks in the East were a noble, church-going society. Unfortunately, this picture clashes too strongly with other sources—albeit of ecclesiastical origin—which give a very different version of the nobles' behaviour. Whatever the truth, whether or not one really attended daily mass, there is no doubt that a noble would participate in the great church festivities which, in a city like Jerusalem, were not only religiously moving, but offered a rich pageantry to participant and spectator.

For other amusements and social contacts, one would meet friends at home, at the bath or even in a tavern. Chess—the king's game—was known, but dice was the most popular entertainment, and one ran the risk of losing both fortune and soul. Meals and drinking—heavy drinking—were part and parcel of entertainment, and many a tavern or private house had its quota of Western-style prostitutes or Eastern-style dancing girls, sometimes slaves of an oriental *souteneur*. Prostitution, common in all medieval cities and most accentuated in ports, was quite extensive in a port city like Acre, where the pope had to warn clergy about renting houses to prostitutes. We have a vivid description of this city, recorded by James of Vitry, who was bishop of Acre for some time:

> Among the *Poulains* there is hardly one in a thousand who takes his marriage seriously. They do not regard fornication to be a deadly sin. From childhood they are pampered and wholly given to carnal pleasures, whereas they are not accustomed to hear God's word, which they lightly disregard. I found here foreigners who fled in despair from their native countries because of various horrible sins. These people, who have no fear of God, are corrupting the whole city by their nefarious deeds and pernicious examples.
>
> Almost every day and every night people are openly or secretly murdered. At night men strangle their wives if they dislike them; women, using the ancient art of poison and potion, kill their husbands so as to be able to marry other men. There are in the city vendors of toxins and poisons, so that nobody can have confidence in anyone, and a man's foes shall be they of his own household.
>
> And the city is full of brothels, and as the rent of the prostitutes is higher, not only laymen, but even clergymen, nay even monks, rent their houses all over the city to public harlots.

It is difficult to ascertain the degree of literacy among the Frankish nobility. It seems that the higher nobility was literate, and the rather few works written by them, as well as other testimonies, indicate that their level of literacy was equal to that of their European counterparts. We know of festivities where episodes from the Arthurian cycle, as well as the fabliaux popular in Europe were performed. But it is doubtful whether the same degree of literacy was common among the lower nobility. Likewise, we know very little about the nobility's intellectual interests. Very few seem to have been interested in the rich oriental heritage around them, and few mastered Arabic, the common language of the Orient and the key to its treasures. On the whole, this breed of Europeans in the East does not strike one as being bent on an intellectual adventure.

The general lack of intellectual interests is stressed by the fact that no scholarly or intellectual centre, no university or school was ever created in the Crusader colonies—and this in an age when all major European centres were dotted with colleges or universities. A man bent on acquiring a wider education went to Europe, as did the only historian of the kingdom, William, bishop of Tyre, a *Poulain*, who easily ranks among the greatest historians in the Middle Ages. This phenomenon in itself explains why the Crusader colonies never became bridges between the Orient and Occident, despite the fact that for two hundred years they were the outposts of Europe in the Eastern Mediterranean. . . .

If Frankish nobility could usually trace their origin to a noble house in their European homeland—though not to the famous houses of Christendom—the burgesses, despite their title, were hardly descendants of European burghers or city dwellers. The lower strata of Frankish population was predominantly of peasant stock, villeins and serfs. They had left Europe either with one of the crusades or as part of a wave of migration. And it was this strata of society which made up the majority of the Frankish population. The transition from their basically rural life-style to the mastery of urban occupations was not an easy one. The native craftsmen, oriental Christians or Moslems, could offer far superior products which were better adapted to local needs and were certainly more elegant than anything usually produced in the manorial worksheds of Europe. The burgesses, however, had the advantage of being able to produce goods according to European tastes and create fashions more easily acceptable to the new settlers. They also enjoyed the fact that the new immigrants preferred their own kin; but this advantage quickly disappeared—as it always does—in the face of the competitive prices of local talent.

It was this strata of immigrants which made up the new society's middle class of craftsmen and merchants, occupations which were seldom distinct. They filled the demand for tailors, shoemakers, goldsmiths, carpenters, smiths, millers, cooks, bakers, confectioners, and candle-makers. In the ports and anchorage places, the new profession of catering, to assure ships provisions for the three-week voyage to Europe, developed. And other new occupations appeared, like the muleteers and camel-drivers; porters of water; spice, incense and perfume vendors; and, naturally, guides, suppliers of holy relics, and publicans. The latter were notorious throughout Christendom. Pilgrim and immigrant alike constantly complained of being cheated. Some taverns which served as hostelries in the ports and in centres of pilgrimage were often also bawdy houses. It was here that prostitution and dice games flourished to the outrage of those who were bent on penitence and spirituality.

On another plane, the burgesses filled the ranks of the kingdom's lower officialdom, whether in the city or in the lordship's rural administration. Some acquired enough Arabic to serve as dragomans; others, more literate, filled the office of scribes or petition-writers. We can visualise them squatting near the lord's or bishop's dwellings, with their portable tables, ink-pots, quills and strips of parchment, penning (for remuneration) the humble requests of the simple people. Then there were the administrative tasks proper. Both lordly and ecclesiastical institutions needed stewards to run their estates and their revenues, assure provisions for their households and to supervise their servants. At the gates of cities and entrances to the ports, a swarm of scribes, customs and tax collectors performed these duties in the din of haggling and recriminations.

The Crusader burgesses in the triple bazaars of Jerusalem or the souks of Antioch, Tripoli and Acre rented their nooks, stalls and benches from the city lord or an ecclesiastical institution. Here they sold their wares, the agricultural yield of their gardens and orchards or products purchased in the countryside to be resold to the city dwellers. Another typical burgess occupation was that of the money-changer. It was often connected with lending money and was the nearest the Frankish burgess ever came to the realm of high finance. Serious activities in high finance were beyond his reach because historical circumstances during the earliest period of conquest made the field a de facto monopoly of the Italian (later also Provençal and Catalan) merchants.

Beginning with the First Crusade, but especially during the following first decade of the kingdom, when the crusaders were fighting the Moslem powers from Cilicia to the Red Sea, the fleets of Venice, Pisa and Genoa— the great European emporia—were instrumental in the conquest of the maritime cities of Syria, Lebanon and the Holy Land. The Italians, whose participation in the Crusades was motivated by a mixture of religious ideals and material calculations, asked to be remunerated for their services. The pious declaration that they sailed to the East to fight the Holy War and in the service of Christianity did not prevent them from assuring themselves a share in the conquest—not only the immediate, tangible booty (which was not negligible), but more permanent gains in the form of streets or quarters in the cities, exemptions from tax and customs and privileges of immunity and autonomy in ruling their nationals and managing their possessions. Thus every major Frankish city in the Levant—and with the exception of Jerusalem, all of them were maritime cities—had at least one, but usually several streets or quarters which belonged to the various Italian communes. The Italians were the third distinctive class among the Franks (along with the nobles and burgesses), and their presence added to the variety of nations and to the Babel of languages.

The Italian settlements were not created immediately after the conquest. Few merchants settled during the early years of the kingdom, but the administrative nucleus sent from the Italian metropolis to safeguard its rights and privileges was a permanent fixture even then. It represented a foothold, but its future depended on the ability to use possessions in Antioch, Tyre or Acre as a basis for business. Realities never matched their expectations because even the great Crusader cities were not centres of production, or at least could not compare with Constantinople or Alexandria. Neither were they outlets for a rich hinterland. Consequently, European commerce could not forgo direct contacts with such Moslem or Byzantine centres. Nonetheless, the privileged position of the communes in the Crusader establishments counter-balanced the obvious economic handicaps. For example, the customs exemptions enjoyed by the communes made the Crusader centres an ideal depot for merchandise imported from the Moslem hinterland—like medieval free ports on the Mediterranean. With the growing volume of trade and more daring penetration of the Moslem hinterland, Italian merchants who had used the Crusader ports only as way-stations began to prolong their stay in the Levant, and fairly sizeable Italian-merchant settlements were founded in all the major ports of the Crusader establishments in the East.

The communes, as such settlements were called, were a strange world— sort of colonies within colonies. A minority surrounded by a French-speaking majority, the Italians used and abused the "foreign language," as did every one else, in their contacts with their fellow Franks. But inside their quarters, in the precincts of the "fondaco," one was transported to beloved Italy. Once Byzantine or Moslem merchandise was acquired, business was often transacted between the Italian merchants themselves. Here each spoke his peculiar dialect of Venetian, Tuscan or Ligurian. Notaries wrote Latin, or sometimes thirteenth-century French, but thought in Italian. The Italians had all the conditions to preserve their identity. The commune overlord was not only of the quarter but also proprietor of all real estate within it. Large and often resplendent buildings—once the lodgings of a Moslem, Byzantine or Turkish governor or official—or houses which belonged to the Moslem merchant aristocracy of the city became *palazzi* in the Italian inventories and were taken over by the commune's administration. Buildings too large to serve any practical needs were divided into *camerae* (rooms rented for limited periods) and *magazini* (rooms to store merchandise). They often stood empty for the greater part of the year, but filled to overflowing when a *stola* (fleet of ships) arrived from Europe at around Easter time.

The main street or square of the quarter became the market-place, and the houses which surrounded it usually contained shops, stalls and magazines where the oriental merchandise waiting to be exported to Europe or imported European merchandise waiting for buyers were deposited. The merchants lodged in the upper floors. Taverns and hostelries catering to the Italian palate were to be found everywhere. In addition, *banci* (benches) were set up by money-changers and vendors of perishable foodstuffs. Besides shops and magazines, a market-place and usually a vaulted bazaar, each quarter had its bakeries, ovens and baths. Some Italian banking families even saw fit to open subsidiaries in the Crusader cities, and big business, still being family business, sent members of the trading class to Palestine.

The center of the quarter was the *palazzo* of the commune, which housed its administration. It housed the *vicomte* or consul, the governor sent from the mother-city. Supported by a council, he represented the commune's interest vis-à-vis the city's lord, ruler or king and was responsible for the management of the commune's possessions and privileges in the city. The notaries attached to him would draft agreements between merchants and marriage contracts; the jurors would sit in judgement or arbitration in cases regarding their own nationals, but in some cases they would also judge other inhabitants of the quarter. Crimes punishable by death, such as homicide or rape, were sometimes excepted from this system, and the guardians of peace— beadles or sergeants—would arrest the accused and turn him over to the seigniorial authorities. There was always some bickering in such cases as the Italians were naturally reluctant to hand over one of their own to external jurisdiction. The law of the communal courts was not that of the kingdom but that of the Italian mother-city. The proceedings were held in the merchants' native language, the procedure was familiar from homeland and the judgement was made by their peers. The head of the commune had his contingent of scribes and sergeants. The first were responsible for the inventory of the commune's property and for collecting rents, which were duly registered in "*quaterna*" (account books) and guarded in the community chest. The town crier and sergeants announced the ordinances of the commune's council and supervised their execution. Time and again ordinances prohibiting prostitution and gambling were issued, but in such communities of travelling salesmen, they were of doubtful effect. . . .

The degree to which the settlers of Italian origin mixed with the local Franks is rather difficult to ascertain. We know of Italians who looked for brides in Europe, but marriages with the local Frankish population were common. A Frankish family may well have seen it as advantageous to marry off their daughters to the Italian and Provençal merchants. Such a union was not considered a *mésalliance*, and it normally meant a step up on the social and economic ladder. The story of the wealthy merchant from Pisa who married a member of the Frankish aristocracy in Tripoli must have made the rounds of oriental *souks*. To receive the permission to marry the young lady, the merchant paid to the maiden's noble warden her weight in gold! A hundred and twenty or so pounds of pure gold could weigh down many barriers.

Some other families entered Frankish life not through marriage but through feudal positions. A Genoese family like the Embriaci, to whom the commune rented its property in the city of Gebal, severed its links with the mother-city and became part and parcel of the Frankish aristocracy. That they continued to favour their compatriots in the city, however, was to be expected. On a lower level, Italian families entered the Frankish *bourgeoisie* through marriage, which we know from documentation of the legal bickering over whether the marriage contract should follow local or Italian custom. Whatever the degree of assimilation through marriage, the Italians remained a power unto themselves, maintaining the customs, language and institution of the Rialto or Porto Vecchio in the Holy Land.

Part 3

THE PEAK OF MEDIEVAL CIVILIZATION

12th–13th Centuries

Author in his study.
Miniature from Vincent de Beauvais'
Miroir Historial.
Flemish, late 15th century

The eleventh century was a turning point in the history of Europe. For the first time in more than a millennium, Europe was not attacked by outside invaders, and its social and political life was not disrupted by massive migrations. European monarchs now began the long process of consolidating their power, and the Church succeeded in establishing its independence from the secular powers. In the same period, the various elements of early medieval society achieved a maturity marked by stability and increasing institutional consistency throughout Europe. This century of change and development was followed by one of cultural rebirth, the so-called twelfth-century renaissance. Scholastic philosophy, Gothic cathedrals, the revival of jurisprudence and of medical studies, all are products of the twelfth century and were carried over into the thirteenth. Medieval civilization flowered, and the selections that follow deal with the major social institutions that underlay this flowering.

The selection by Sidney Painter recounts the youth of one of the most famous knights of the period. The knightly class dominated feudal society—aristocrats, knights, and peasants. All noblemen outside the Church were members of this class, and whatever differences—and they could be vast—existed between the great feudal baron and the landless knight, both belonged to the order of knighthood and shared a common code of behavior and system of values. The origins of feudalism must be traced back into the early Middle Ages; the golden age of the system and of the class of knights was the eleventh and twelfth centuries. William Marshal, the subject of Painter's piece, lived at the end of this period.

The next two selections return to a theme taken up in Part 1, the position of women. In "The Role of a Baron's Wife," Margaret Labarge suggests that neither the common literary image of the noblewoman as a protected, precious being nor the gloomy portrait of woman's lot depicted in much historical work is accurate. Noblewomen presided over large households and often participated in the political and economic life of their class. In the second piece in this section, Mary Martin McLaughlin describes eleventh- and twelfth-century child-rearing practices and examines the relationship between mother and child. Such a study relies perforce on the accounts of a few educated churchmen who reflected on their early lives, and it presents a very different view of medieval women than Labarge's work.

Many features of twelfth- and thirteenth-century life contributed to the growth of commerce and intellectual activity—for example, political stability and the improvement of agriculture—but one factor rarely if ever mentioned was the expansion of effective communication between urban centers. As we saw in Willard Bascom's article in Part 1, the ancient civilizations of the Mediterranean basin depended on maintaining sea travel for such communication. The rise of European civilization also depended primarily on water transport, but from the eleventh century, road systems expanded rapidly and steadily increased in importance as links between the markets of goods and ideas. Urban T. Holmes relies on the diary of a twelfth-century scholar to describe what it was like to travel along these roads.

During the eleventh century, monastic reformers gained control of the central ecclesiastical institutions, the papacy and bishoprics, and transformed them. Battling against clerical illiteracy and immorality, the new leaders found that the root of these evils was secular interference in the Church. Parish priests, bishops, and other ecclesiastical officers were appointed by laymen who had little concern for the care of souls; they wanted to control the wealth of the Church and its political power by controlling its personnel. The reformers succeeded in reducing secular influence to a minimum—although they could not get rid of it alto-gether—and created a respectable ecclesiastical hierarchy in which the conscientious bishop was a common rather than a rare occurrence. In the selection from the register of Archbishop Eudes of Rouen, we see such a bishop at work, and we see that, while the reformers had striking success among the higher churchmen, the work of improving the lower ranks was a struggle that continued long after the reform movement ended.

Eudes gives us a glimpse of the lives and foibles of many monks who inhabited tiny monastic communities, cells, or priories in which fewer than ten persons practiced their devotions. The flowers of medieval monasticism, however, were the great houses where hundreds of monks lived. The selection from the chronicle of the monk Jocelin of Brakelond reveals the community of Bury St. Edmunds, one of the greatest Bene-dictine abbeys in England.

The final selection in Part 3 deals with another aspect of medieval religious life—heresy and dissent. The intellectual revival inevitably produced some people who failed to observe the boundaries of religious orthodoxy as they became caught up in the excitement of speculative philosophy and theology. In general, the Church tried errant intellectuals in its councils. Here their errors would be exposed and corrected before a wide and influential audience of men who had to be able to deal with erring parishioners at home. The problem of heresy grew beyond this cumbersome system of justice, however. A secondary effect of the eleventh-century reform movement was that it encouraged some lay people to attack the Church hierarchy—as leading churchmen themselves were doing—and to drift into anticlerical heresy. What began as criticism of immoral or worldly priests often turned into questioning of the sacraments and basic doctrines of Christian religion. During the twelfth century, this problem of popular heresy grew steadily, and, at the end of the century, the Church created a new institution to counter the danger. This institution was the infamous Inquisition; Austin P. Evans' article examines its methods of investigation and trial.

BIBLIOGRAPHY

For the history of feudalism and the social, economic, and political world of the medieval knight, see F. L. Ganshof, *Feudalism* (New York, 1961), and Carl Stephenson, *Feudalism* (Ithaca, N.Y., 1940). Sidney Painter's little book *French Chivalry* (Baltimore, 1940) provides a good survey of the cultural milieu of the knights. See also Georges Duby's excellent article "In Northwestern France: The 'Youth' in Twelfth Century Aristocratic Society," trans. by F. Cheyette, in F. Cheyette, ed., *Lordship and Community in Medieval Europe* (New York, 1968). Duby focuses on knights errant—a class in which William Marshal spent many years—and he tries to assess their place in, and impact on, twelfth-century society. The classic work on feudal society is Marc Bloch, *Feudal Society*, trans. L. A. Manyon, 2 vols. (Chicago, 1961); see especially Parts IV, VI, and VIII. Lynn White argues that feudalism was based on technological innovation rather than on social or legal changes. See Lynn White, Jr., *Medieval Technology and Social Change* (Oxford, 1962).

A remarkable amount of literature about women was published in the 1890s, perhaps as a response to the women's suffrage movement. See, for example, A. R. Cleveland, *Woman Under English Law from Anglo-Saxon Times to the Present* (London, 1896); and M. A. R. de Maulde La Clavière, *The Women of the Renaissance; a Study of Feminism* (London, 1900). Eileen Power, a highly regarded economic historian, wrote a fine article on women in C. G. Crump and E. F. Jacobs, eds., *The Legacy of the Middle Ages* (Oxford, 1926). She also portrayed two women in her book of characterizations, *Medieval People* (London, 1924; 10th ed., rev. and enl., 1963). Power's articles on women have now been collected in *Medieval Women* (Cambridge, Eng., 1975). See also the articles in Susan M. Stuard, ed., *Women in Medieval Society* (Philadelphia, 1976), and in R. T. Morewedge, ed., *The Role of Women in the Middle Ages* (Albany, N.Y., 1975).

The quotation from the tenth-century traveler in the introduction to Urban T. Holmes' "Traveling the Roads in the Twelfth Century" comes from a good article by Robert S. Lopez, "The Evolution of Land Transport in the Middle Ages," *Past and Present,* Vol. 19 (1956), pp. 17–29. See also Margaret N. Boyer, "Roads and Rivers: Their Use and Disuse in Late Medieval France," *Medievalia et Humanistica,* Vol. 13 (1960), pp. 68–80. A short commentary on the same topic is T. W. Parratt's "On Northern Roads in the Middle Ages," *Ryedale History,* Vol. 5 (1970), pp. 3–11. Irving Agus' *Urban Civilization in Pre-Crusade Europe,* 2 vols. (New York, 1965) contains a lot of material on Jewish merchant travelers, and later Christian entrepreneurs are the subject of E. M. Carus Wilson, *Medieval Merchant Venturers* (London, 1954). Jonathan Sumption describes a long journey in *Pilgrimage: An Image of Mediaeval Religion* (Totowa, N.J., 1975).

On the early history of the ecclesiastical hierarchy, see J. Danielou and H. Marrou, *History of the Church: The First Six Hundred Years* (London, 1964); Henry Chadwick, *The Early Church* (Harmondsworth, Eng., 1967); and R. W. Southern, *Western Society and the Church in the Middle Ages* (Harmondsworth, Eng., 1970). See also Geoffrey Barraclough, *The Medieval Papacy* (New York, 1968). On the origins of monasticism, see D. J. Chitty, *The Desert a City* (Oxford, 1966); A. Vööbus, *A History of Asceticism in the Syrian Orient,* Vol. 2 (Louvain, Belgium, 1960); and Helen Waddell, *The Desert Fathers* (Ann Arbor, 1957), a translation of early medieval lives of the first monks. For the Benedictine constitution, see *The Rule of St. Benedict,* trans. A. C. Meisel and M. L. del Mastro (New York, 1975). On the later history of monasticism, see David Knowles, *Christian Monasticism* (London, 1969). On the culture of medieval monasticism, see Jean Leclercq, *The Love of Learning and the Desire for God: A Study of Monastic Culture* (New York, 1961); see also J. F. Benton, ed., *Self and Society in Medieval France: The Memoirs of Abbot Guibert of Nogent* (New York, 1970).

For an attempt to understand the nature of heresy in the Middle Ages, see Jeffrey B. Russell, *Dissent and Reform in the Early Middle Ages* (Berkeley, 1965); Gordon Leff, *Heresy in the Later Middle Ages: The Relation of Heterodoxy to Dissent c. 1250–c. 1450,* 2 vols. (Manchester, Eng., 1967); Robert E. Lerner, *The Heresy of the Free Spirit in the Later Middle Ages* (Berkeley, 1972). The standard work on the history of the Inquisition is Henry C. Lea, *A History of the Inquisition of the Middle Ages,* 3 vols. (New York, 1955 [reprint of 1888 edition]). W. L. Wakefield and A. P. Evans, eds., *Heresies of the High Middle Ages* (New York, 1969) contains a substantial collection of translated sources.

The Training of a Knight

SIDNEY PAINTER

The knight in shining armor is mostly a figment created by medieval romance writers and refurbished and given new impetus by nineteenth-century authors. The real knight lived a life not so far removed in its material aspects from that of prosperous contemporary peasants. He was almost constantly on the move, living the hard life of a traveler and engaging in tournaments or real campaigns. The rules governing his life, so embellished by the romance poets, were largely responses to the demands of his existence and served to make its hardships bearable. Most of the rules evolved out of the conditions of feudal warfare; they regulated the treatment of prisoners taken in combat and the relations between the ranks in the feudal army. In the constant round of fighting, one week's victor might be next week's victim, and the economics of knightly life dictated a refined treatment of captured knights. A dead knight was not worth very much, but a live one might ransom himself at a considerable price. If a knight was one of the majority in his class who did not possess any landed estate and therefore had no stable income, collecting ransoms constituted a livelihood. Other aspects of the chivalric code, as the rules were called, were aimed at preserving the social and political structure of feudalism, although these too were related to military activities. The feudal system depended on the loyalty of vassals to their liege lords, and this loyalty was the cohesive element of the feudal army. Loyalty was won and kept by open-handedness, so generosity too was a knightly virtue.

It is important to study the training of a knight in order to understand the character of the class. In this selection, we observe the early training of William Marshal, a man who achieved the ideal of knighthood according to the writings of his time. He was born about 1146 in England, the fourth son of a petty baron, John, who was marshal for King Henry I. The marshal was originally in charge of the royal stables and the provisioning of the household, but by John's day these duties had been delegated to others, and the marshal was a hereditary post in the king's entourage. William, as a younger son, had little chance of inheriting his father's position, but he was trained as a knight anyway, since he could make his way in the world as a feudal soldier. As it turned out, his talent won him one of the premier places in the feudal hierarchy of England.

There were several stages in the life of a successful knight. In his early youth, he was taught to ride and perhaps given the rudiments of his education in chivalry. But his real training began around the age of thirteen, when he was sent to a relative's or lord's household as a squire. There he learned to handle a knight's weapons and to be part of a feudal army. He also learned the details of the life style he was expected to adopt. After the squire became a knight, he began an often long period of itinerancy, traveling from tournament to tournament and joining in real campaigns when the opportunity arose. Sometimes knights errant, as such men were called, joined the entourage of great lords or kings and became part of their "team" in the tournaments. William became a member of Prince Henry of England's (son of Henry II) entourage and quickly rose to a preeminent position within it. In William's time, the tournaments were not the controlled combats of the later Middle Ages so often described in popular literature. They were virtual free-for-alls in which knights teamed up and fought as armies. One of these melees is described in this selection.

For the knight who did not inherit a position within the feudal hierarchy, the period of errancy often lasted until he was past forty. At this point, if he was lucky, he would marry into the hierarchy. William achieved this goal in 1190 when Richard I of England (son and successor of Henry II) permitted him to marry the heiress of the great earldom of Pembroke. The marriage made William one of the first lords of England, and when Richard's successor, John, died in 1216, William became one of the regents of the realm. He himself died in 1219.

William's career demonstrates that there was mobility within the feudal ranks during the twelfth century. He was clearly the outstanding example of the possibilities that existed, but many others had similar if not so illustrious careers. In the later Middle Ages, the possibility of rising in the ranks became increasingly restricted as the feudal elite found its position challenged by the kings on one side and by the burghers on the other. In its heyday, the knightly class exhibited vitality and adaptability. Once it was forced to take a defensive stance, it became rigid and regressive in its social, economic, and political attitudes.

William Marshal was the fourth son of John fitz Gilbert and the second of those born to the castellan of Marlborough by the sister of Earl Patrick of Salisbury. Our knowledge of William's youth is confined to a few brief glimpses through the fog of time—scenes which made so vivid an impression on his mind that he could recount them years later to his squire and biographer, John d'Erley. The earliest of these recollections concerned a comparatively unimportant incident in the contest between Stephen and Matilda.

From *William Marshall* by Sidney Painter, pp. 13–29. Copyright 1933 by The Johns Hopkins University Press, publisher. Reprinted by permission of The Johns Hopkins University Press.

In the year 1152 King Stephen at the head of a strong force suddenly swooped down on John Marshal's castle of Newbury at a time when it was inadequately garrisoned and poorly stocked with provisions. The constable, a man both brave and loyal, indignantly refused the king's demand for the immediate surrender of the fortress. When the garrison successfully repulsed an attempt to take the place by storm, Stephen prepared for a regular siege and swore that he would not leave until he had captured the castle and hanged its defenders. The constable, realizing that his lack of provisions made an extended resistance impossible, asked for and obtained a day's truce so that he might make known his plight to his lord, John Marshal. This was the customary procedure for a castellan who found himself in a hopeless position. Once granted a truce, he would inform his master that unless he were relieved by a certain day, he would be forced to surrender. If no assistance appeared within the specified time, the commander could surrender the castle without failing in his duty to his lord. The besieging force was usually willing to grant a truce in the hope of obtaining the castle without long, wearisome, and expensive siege operations. When John Marshal learned of the predicament of his garrison of Newbury, he was sadly perplexed. As he could not muster enough men to drive off Stephen's army, his only hope of saving his fortress lay in a resort to strategy. John asked Stephen to extend the truce while he sought aid from the Countess Matilda in whose name he held the castle. The king did not trust his turbulent marshal, but he finally agreed to give the garrison of Newbury a further respite if John would surrender one of his sons as a guarantee that he would observe the terms of the truce. John was to use the days of grace to communicate with Matilda—the hostage would be his pledge that he would not reinforce or provision the castle. Acceding to Stephen's demand, John gave the king his son William as a hostage. Then he promptly sent into Newbury a strong force of knights, serjeants, and archers with a plentiful supply of provisions. Newbury was prepared to withstand a siege—the cunning of John Marshal had saved his castle.

His father's clever strategem left William in an extremely precarious position. By the customs of the time his life was forfeited by his father's breach of faith. Stephen's entourage urged him to hang William at once, but the king was unwilling to execute the child without giving his father a chance to have him by surrendering Newbury. But John Marshal, having four sons and a fruitful wife, considered the youngest of his sons of far less value than a strong castle. He cheerfully told the king's messenger that he cared little if William were hanged, for he had the anvils and hammers with which to forge still better sons. When he received this brutal reply, Stephen ordered his men to lead William to a convenient tree. Fearing that John planned a rescue, the king himself escorted the executioners with a strong force. William, who was only five or six years old, had no idea what this solemn parade portended. When he saw William, earl of Arundel, twirling a most enticing javelin, he asked him for the weapon. This reminder of William's youth and innocence was too much for King Stephen's resolution, and, taking the boy in his arms, he carried him back to the camp. A little later some of the royalists had the ingenious idea of throwing William over the castle walls from a siege engine, but Stephen vetoed that scheme as well. He had decided to spare his young prisoner.

For some two months William was the guest of King Stephen while the royal army lay before Newbury. One day as the king sat in a tent strewn with varicolored flowers William wandered about picking plantains. When the boy had gathered a fair number, he asked the king to play "knights" with him. Each of them would take a "knight" or plantain, and strike it against the one held by the other. The victory would go to the player who with his knight struck off the clump of leaves that represented the head of his opponent's champion. When Stephen readily agreed to play, William gave him a bunch of plantains and asked him to decide who should strike first. The amiable king gave William the first blow with the result that the royal champion lost his head. The boy was vastly pleased with his victory. While Stephen, king of England, was playing at knights with the young son of his rebellious marshal, a servitor whom Lady Sibile had sent to see how her son fared glanced into the tent. As war and enemies meant nothing to William, he loudly welcomed the familiar face. The man, utterly terrified, fled so hastily that the pursuit ordered by the king was fruitless.

This story of William and King Stephen is, no doubt, merely reminiscence recounted years later with the embellishments usual in such tales, but it bears all the ear-marks of veracity. It serves to confirm the statements of the chroniclers as to Stephen's character—that he was a man of gentle nature, far too mild to rule the barons of England. Furthermore the incidents of the tale are essentially probable. It was quite customary to give young children as hostages to guarantee an agreement and equally so to make them suffer for their parents' bad faith. When Eustace de Breteuil, the husband of a natural daughter of Henry I, put out the eyes of the son of one of his vassals, the king allowed the enraged father to multilate in the same way Eustace's daughter whom Henry held as a hostage for his son-in-law's good behavior. Again in the year 1211 when Maelgwyn ap Rees, prince of South Wales, raided the marches, Robert de Vieuxpont hanged the prince's seven-year-old son who was in his hands as a pledge that Maelgwyn would keep the peace. The fact that Earl William of Arundel is known to have taken part in the siege of Newbury and might well have twirled his javelin before the fascinated William tends to confirm this story still further. Hence one can accept as essentially true this pleasant and very human picture of a dark age and an unfortunate king.

When peace was finally concluded between Stephen and Henry Plantagenet, William was returned to his parents who, according to the *History*, had been very unquiet about him. While John Marshal had probably counted to some extent on Stephen's notorious mildness, he had had plenty of justification for any fears he may have felt for his son's safety. Meanwhile the boy was growing rapidly. Within a few years the Marshal family would be forced to consider his future. If the romances of the time are to be believed, it was customary for a baron of any importance to entrust his sons' education to some friendly lord. John Marshal decided to send William to his cousin, William, lord of Tancarville and hereditary chamberlain of Normandy. The chamberlain was a powerful baron with a great castle on the lower Seine and ninety-four knights to follow his banner. Being himself a well known knight and a frequenter of tourneys, he was well fitted to supervise the military education of his young kinsman and to give him a good start on his chivalric career. When he was about thirteen years old, William started for Tancarville attended by a *valet*, or companion of gentle birth, and a servant. The fourth son of a minor English baron was setting forth to seek his fortune.

For eight years William served as a squire to the chamberlain of Tancarville. During this time his principal duty was to learn the trade of arms. The squire's body was hardened and his skill in the use of weapons developed by frequent and strenuous military exercises. While the chain mail of the twelfth century was far lighter and less cumbersome than the plate armor of later times, the mere wearing of it required considerable physical strength. To be able, as every squire must, to leap fully armed into the saddle without touching the stirrup, was a feat which must have required long and rigorous training. The effective use of the weapons of a knight—the spear, sword, and shield—was a highly intricate science which a squire was forced to master if he wished to excel in his chosen profession. In addition a knight should know how to care for his equipment. A squire spent long hours tending his master's horses and cleaning, polishing, and testing his arms and armor. William's success in battle and tourney will show how thoroughly he mastered these fundamentals of his profession. But while it was essential that a knight be brave and skillful in the use of his weapons, other quite different qualities were also expected of him. God and Woman, the church and the troubadour cult of Courtly Love, were beginning to soften and polish the manners of the feudal aristocracy. For a long time the church had demanded that a knight be pious, now ladies were insisting that he be courteous. If a squire hoped to be acceptable to such devotees of the new movement as Eleanor of Aquitaine and her daughter, Marie of Champagne, he must learn some more gentle art than that of smiting mighty blows. If he could not write songs, he could at least learn to sing them. Finally the professional creators and distributors of the literature which embodied these new ideas, the trouvères and the jongleurs, were formulating another knightly virtue—generosity. Their existence depended on the liberality of their patrons, and they did not fail to extol the generous and heap scorn on the penurious. Every time the squire confessed to a priest, he was instructed in the church's conception of the perfect knight. As he sat in the great hall of the castle while some trouvère or jongleur told of Tristan and Iseut or of Lancelot and Guenevere, he was imbued with the doctrines of romantic chivalry. The squire himself might be expected to while away the leisure hours of his lady and her damsels with one of the gentle songs of the troubadours. Possibly William owed his love for singing which remained with him to his death to the advanced taste of the lady of Tancarville.

By the spring of 1167 William was approaching his twenty-first year. As a squire he seems to have given little promise of future greatness. He gained a reputation for drinking, eating, and sleeping, but for little else. His companions, who were jealous of the favor shown him by the chamberlain, made fun of his appetite, but he was so gentle and debonnaire that he always kept silent and pretended not to hear the remarks. A hearty, healthy, good natured, and rather stupid youth was young William. The author of the *History* furnishes a personal description which probably belongs to this period of William's life. "His body was so well formed that if it had been fashioned by a sculptor, it would not have had such beautiful limbs. I saw them and remember them well. He had very beautiful feet and hands, but all these were minor details in the ensemble of his body. If anyone looked at him carefully, he seemed so well and straightly made that if one judged honestly, one would be forced to say that he had the best formed body in the world. He had brown hair. His face even more than his body resembled that of a man of high enough rank to be the Emperor of Rome. He had as long legs and as good a stature as a gentleman could. Whoever fashioned him was master." Is this a purely conventional portrait or a true one of William Marshal as he reached man's estate?

In a military society, be it that of the early Germans or the feudal aristocracy, the youth comes of age when he is accepted as a full-fledged warrior. Every squire burned to end his apprenticeship by receiving the insignia of knighthood. The squire followed his master to battles and tournaments, cared for his horse and armor, nursed him if he were wounded, and often guarded his prisoners, but he himself could not take an active part in the combat. Being simply an attendant, the squire had no opportunity to win renown. As eight years was, at least according to the testimony of contemporary romances, a rather long time to remain a squire, William must have been extremely impatient for the day when he would be admitted into the chivalric order. He longed for the time when the approach of a promising war or a great tourney would move the chamberlain to dub him a knight and give him a chance to show his worth.

The occasion for which William had hoped came in the summer of 1167. King Henry II was at war with his suzerain Louis VII of France. While Louis himself occupied Henry's attention by ravaging the Norman Vexin, the French king's allies, the counts of Flanders, Boulogne, and Ponthieu, invaded the county of Eu. Count John of Eu, unable to hold his own against the invaders, was forced to retire to Neufchatel-en-Bray, then called Drincourt. There he encountered a force of knights which Henry had sent to his assistance under the command of the constable of Normandy and the lord of Tancarville. The chamberlain decided that this was an auspicious time for knighting William. A goodly array of Norman barons was at hand to lend dignity to the occasion, and the future seemed to promise an opportunity for the young knight to prove his valor. William's induction into the order of chivalry was attended by little of the ceremony usually associated with the dubbing of a knight. Dressed in a new mantle, the young man stood before the chamberlain, who girt him with a sword, the principal emblem of knighthood, and gave him the ceremonial blow.

William had not long to wait for an opportunity to prove himself worthy of his new dignity. As Drincourt lay on the northern bank of the river Bethune at the southern extremity of the county of Eu, it was directly in the path of the army which had been ravaging that district. Count John of Eu and the constable of Normandy had no desire to await the advance of the enemy. On the morning following William's knighting they left Drincourt by the road which led south toward Rouen. Before they had gone very far, they were overtaken by a messenger with the news that the counts of Flanders, Boulogne, and Ponthieu, and the lord of St. Valery were marching on Drincourt at the head of a strong force of knights and serjeants. As the two barons halted their party to consider what they should do, they saw the chamberlain followed by twenty-eight knights of his household riding toward them from the direction of Drincourt. As soon as he was within speaking distance, the chamberlain addressed the constable, "Sire, it will be a great disgrace if we permit them to burn this town." "You speak truly, chamberlain," replied the constable, "and since it is your idea, do you go to its defence." When they saw that they could hope for no assistance from either the count of Eu or the constable, the chamberlain and his knights rode back toward Drincourt. Between them and the town ran the river Bethune. When they reached the bridge which spanned this stream, they found it occupied by a party of knights under the command of William de Mandeville, earl of Essex, who, lacking sufficient men to dispute the enemy's entrance into the town, had retired to hold the passage of the Bethune. The chamberlain hurried to join Earl William, and William Marshal, anxious to show his mettle, spurred forward at his leader's side. The chamberlain turned to the enthusiastic novice, "William, drop back; be not so impatient; let these knights pass." William, who considered himself most decidedly a knight, fell back, abashed. He let three others go ahead of him and then dashed forward again until he was in the front rank.

The combined forces of the chamberlain and the earl of Essex rode into Drincourt to meet the enemy who were entering the town from the northeast. The two parties met at full gallop with a thunderous shock. William's lance was broken, but drawing his sword, he rushed into the midst of the enemy. So fiercely did the Normans fight that they drove the French out of the town as far as the bridge over the moat on the road to Eu. There the enemy was reinforced, and the Normans were pressed back through Drincourt to the bridge over the Bethune. Once more the Normans charged, and once more they drove the French before them. Just as their victory seemed certain, Count Mathew of Boulogne came up with a fresh division. Four times the enemy beat their way into the town, and each time the Normans drove them out again. Once as William turned back from a charge, a Flemish serjeant caught him by the shoulder with an iron hook. Although he was dragged from his horse in the midst of hostile foot-soldiers, he managed to disengage the hook and cut his way out, but his horse was killed. Meanwhile the good people of Drincourt had been watching from their windows the fierce battle being waged up and down the streets of the town. Hastily arming themselves, the burghers rushed to the aid of the Norman knights, and the enemy was completely routed.

That night the lord of Tancarville held a great feast to celebrate the victory. The burghers of Drincourt were loud in their praises of the chamberlain and his knights. While the constable and the count of Eu had deserted the town, the chamberlain and his household had saved it from burning and pillage. As the revelers discussed the incidents of the battle, someone remarked that William had fought to save the town rather than to take prisoners who could pay him rich ransoms. With this in mind the earl of Essex addressed the young knight—"Marshal, give me a gift, a crupper or an old horse collar." "But I have never possessed one in all my life." "Marshal, what are you saying? Assuredly you had forty or sixty today." The hardened warrior was gently reminding the novice that war was a business as well as a path to fame.

The war was soon brought to an end by a truce between King Henry and Louis of France. As their services were no longer needed, the chamberlain and his entourage returned to Tancarville. Since no true knight would willingly rest peacefully in a castle, the lord of Tancarville gave his followers leave to seek adventure where they pleased. William now found himself in a most embarrassing position, for he had lost his war horse at Drincourt, and the cost of a new one was far beyond his resources. While he still had his palfrey, this light animal could not be expected to carry him in full armor through the shocks of a battle or tourney. The chamberlain, who normally would have seen to it that William as a member of his household was properly equipped, felt that the young man should be taught to take advantage of his opportunities to capture horses in battle and hence showed little sympathy for his predicament: By selling the rich mantle which he had worn when he was dubbed a knight, William obtained twenty-two sous Angevin with which he purchased a baggage horse to carry his armor, but while this arrangement allowed him to travel in comfort, it would not enable him to take part in a tourney. One day word came to Tancarville that a great tournament was to be held near Le Mans in which the knights of Anjou, Maine, Poitou, and Brittany would oppose those of France, England, and Normandy. The chamberlain and his court received the news with joy and prepared to take part in the sport, but William, who could not go without a horse, was very sorrowful. The chamberlain, however, decided that his young cousin had had enough of a lesson in knightly economy and promised to furnish him with a mount. After a night spent in making ready their arms and armor, the knights gathered in the castle court while their lord distributed the war horses. William received a splendid one, strong and fast. He never forgot the lesson taught him by the chamberlain and William de Mandeville. Never again did he neglect to capture good horses when he had the opportunity.

On the appointed day a fair sized company assembled to take part in the tournament. King William of Scotland was present with a numerous suite while the chamberlain himself took the field at the head of forty knights. This tourney was not to be one of those mild affairs in which everything was arranged beforehand even to the price of the ransoms, but a contest in which the vanquished would lose all they possessed. After the knights had armed in the refuges provided at each end of the field, the two parties advanced toward one another in serried, orderly ranks. William wasted no time in getting about the business of the day. Attacking Philip de Valognes, a knight of King William's household, he seized his horse by the rein and forced him out of the mêlée. Then after taking Philip's pledge that he would pay his ransom, William returned to the combat and captured two more knights. By his success in this tourney William not only demonstrated his prowess, but rehabilitated his finances as well. Each of the captured knights was forced to surrender all his equipment. William gained war horses, palfreys, arms, and armor for his own use, roncins for his servants, and sumpter horses for his baggage. His first tournament had been highly profitable.

This success sharpened William's appetite for knightly sports. When word came to Tancarville of another tourney to be held in Maine, he asked the chamberlain, who had decided to stay at home, to allow him to attend. He arrived at the appointed place just as the last of the contestants were arming in their refuges, and leaping from his palfrey hastened to put on his armor and mount his charger. In the first onslaught the young knight handled his lance so skillfully that he was able to unhorse one of his opponents, but before he could complete the capture of the fallen knight he was attacked by five others. Although by drawing his sword and smiting lusty blows on every side William managed to beat off his enemies, he received a stroke on his helmet which turned it around on his head so that he could no longer breathe through the holes provided for that purpose. While he was standing in the refuge repairing this damage, two well known knights rode past, Bon Abbé le Rouge and John de Subligni. "Sir John," said the first, "who is that knight who is so capable with his weapons?" "That is William Marshal" replied the other. "There is no man more true. The device on his shield shows that he hails from Tancarville." "Surely," said Bon Abbé, "the band which he leads should be the gainer in valor and hardiness." Much pleased by these words of praise, William put on his helmet again and re-entered the contest. So well did he bear himself that he was awarded the prize of the tourney—a splendid war horse from Lombardy.

William now felt that he was well started on his chivalric career. He had achieved the dignity of knighthood and had shown his prowess in the combat at Drincourt and in two tournaments. It was high time that he visited England to parade his accomplishments before his admiring family. John fitz Gilbert had died in 1165 while William was still a squire at Tancarville. Of his two sons by his first wife the elder had outlived him but a year, the younger had predeceased him. Hence John, the eldest son by Sibile of Salisbury, had inherited the family lands and the office of marshal. When William sought the chamberlain's permission to go to England, the lord of Tancarville feared that his young cousin, being the heir presumptive to the family lands, might be tempted to settle down at home. He gave him leave to go, but urged him to return as soon as possible. While England was a good enough country for a man of mean spirit who had no desire to seek adventure, those who loved the life of a knight-errant and the excitement of the tourney should stay in Normandy and Brittany where such pastimes were appreciated. If one were to acquire the prizes of battle, one must live in a land of tourneys. England seemed to the chamberlain to be an orderly, dull, spiritless country. Carried across the channel by a fair wind, William traversed Sussex and Hampshire on his way to his Wiltshire home. At Salisbury he found his uncle, Earl Patrick, who received him joyfully as a gallant young knight and his own sister's son.

William's vacation in England was destined to be a short one. In December 1167 Earl Patrick was summoned to the continent to aid the king in suppressing a revolt of the nobles of Poitou led by the counts of La Marche and Angoulême and the house of Lusignan. Being in all probability heartily tired of his quiet life in England, William was only too willing to follow his uncle to Poitou. King Henry captured the castle of Lusignan, garrisoned it, and then turned north to keep an appointment with Louis VII in the Norman marches near Mantes. His wife, Eleanor, who was by right of her birth duchess of Aquitaine and countess of Poitou, stayed at Lusignan with Earl Patrick. Their position was far from comfortable. Of all the restless nobility of Poitou none were more turbulent than the five de Lusignan brothers, and none played so great a part in the history of their day. Two of the brothers, Hugh and Ralph, became respectively counts of La Marche and Eu, while Guy and Aimery, expelled from Poitou for their perpetual rebellions, both attained the throne of Jerusalem. Such a family was unlikely to stand by quietly while an enemy held their ancestral castle, even if that enemy was their liege lord. One day near Eastertide as the queen and Earl Patrick were riding outside the castle, they were suddenly confronted by a strong force under the command of Geoffrey and Guy de Lusignan. Although Patrick and his men were unarmed, the earl was unwilling to flee. Sending Eleanor to shelter in the castle, he called for his war horse and ordered his followers to prepare for battle. Unfortunately the de Lusignans were not sufficiently chivalrous to wait while their foes armed. Just as Earl Patrick was mounting his charger, a Poitevin knight killed him with a single blow at his unprotected back. Meanwhile William had donned his hauberk, but had not had time to put on his helmet. When he saw his uncle fall, he jumped on his horse and charged the enemy, sword in hand. The first man he met was cut down at a single stroke, but before he could satisfy his thirst for vengeance on the slayers of his uncle, a well directed thrust killed his horse. When he had freed himself from the saddle, William placed his back against a hedge to fight it out on foot as the loss of his horse made flight impossible. For some time he managed to hold his own by cutting down the chargers of his opponents, but at last a knight crossed the hedge, came up behind, and leaning over the barrier, thrust his sword into the young man's thigh. Disabled, William was easily made prisoner.

His captors mounted him on a mare and set off. No one paid any attention to William's wound, for, according to the *History*, they wanted him to suffer as much as possible so that he might be the more anxious to ransom himself. William took the cords which bound his braies and tied up his wound as best he could. Dreading the king's vengeance, the rebel band kept to the wooded country and made its halts in secluded spots. Henry Plantagenet was not a monarch who would permit the slayers of his lieutenant to go unpunished. One night while they were resting at the castle of one of their partisans, a lady noticed the wounded prisoner. She cut the center out of a loaf of bread, filled the hole with flaxen bandages, and sent the loaf to William. Her kindness enabled him to dress his wound properly. Another evening William's captors amused themselves by casting a great stone. William joined in the game and defeated all the others, but the exertion reopened his wound, and as he was forced to ride night and day with little rest, he grew better very slowly. Finally Queen Eleanor came to his aid. She gave hostages to his captors to guarantee that his ransom would be paid, and he was delivered to her. To recompense him for his sufferings, she gave him money, horses, arms, and rich vestments.

The Poitevin campaign had a far-reaching effect on William's life. In it lay the origins of his intense hatred for the house of Lusignan and his close personal relationship with the Plantagenet family. To understand his bitter feud with the Lusignans one must realize that the killing of Earl Patrick, which seems to us a normal act of war, was in William's sight a dastardly crime. The author of the *History* calls the earl's slayer felon and assassin. Not only did he strike down an unarmed man, an unknightly act in itself, but he slew the lieutenant of his feudal suzerain. The first of these offences probably did not trouble William greatly. Some years later when Richard Plantagenet was in rebellion against his father, William came on that prince when he was unarmed and slew his horse. William afterward insisted that it would have been no crime had he slain Richard himself. To attack an unarmed man was at worst merely a breach of knightly courtesy. But for a rebel to kill the representative of his suzerain was the most serious of feudal crimes—treason. William held Geoffrey de Lusignan responsible for his uncle's death. Whether he simply blamed Geoffrey as the leader of the party and responsible for his men or whether he believed him the actual slayer is not clear. Geoffrey himself denied his guilt, and one chronicler places the blame on his brother, Guy. One is inclined to believe that the two de Lusignan brothers were in command of the party, but had no intention of killing Earl Patrick. Some careless or over-enthusiastic subordinate struck down the earl whom the leaders were simply hoping to capture. This view is confirmed by the care exercised by the rebels to take William alive when, as he was fighting without his helmet, he could have been killed easily. But, rightly or wrongly, William never forgave the house of Lusignan.

The same brief combat which made William the mortal enemy of the de Lusignans brought him to the attention of Queen Eleanor, the ideal patroness for a young knight. The richest heiress of Europe by reason of the great duchy of Aquitaine which she had inherited from her father, Eleanor had at an early age married Louis VII of France. Divorced from him, she had promptly given her hand to Henry Plantagenet. As ruler of more than half of the homeland of the troubadours, as patroness of such artists as Bernard de Ventadour, and as the mother of the countesses of Champagne and Blois whose courts were centers of romantic literature, Eleanor was the high priestess of the cult of courtly love. Unfortunately little is known of William's relations with this great lady. One cannot say whether she became interested in him because of his fondness for singing and his knightly courtesy, or simply because he had undergone hardships in her service. But whatever its origin, her favor was an invaluable asset. Normandy and England were full of brave young knights, but there were few who could say that they had suffered wounds and imprisonment in the service of Queen Eleanor and had been ransomed and reequipped by her.

When William Marshal left Poitou in the autumn of 1168, he may well have considered with satisfaction the accomplishments of his twenty-two years. While he had followed what the contemporary romances tell us was the usual course of a young man's education, he had done so with rare success. At the age of thirteen he had left home to seek his fortune in the service of

William of Tancarville. At the chamberlain's court he had served his apprenticeship in the trade of arms and from his hand he had received the boon of knighthood. In the combat at Drincourt and in at least two tourneys he had shown himself a brave and capable warrior. The campaign in Poitou had not only given him a taste of the hardships of a soldier's life, but had gained him the favor of Eleanor of Aquitaine. William could with justice believe that he was on the high road to fame and fortune.

The Role of a Baron's Wife

MARGARET LABARGE

Mother and Child

MARY MARTIN MCLAUGHLIN

Historians have assumed that women of the medieval noble classes were little better off than their Roman counterparts, described by Sarah B. Pomeroy in Part 1 of this volume. Little space is devoted to women in the standard histories of the Middle Ages. It is often said that only literature gave medieval women an escape from the restrictions and drudgery of their lives, and some scholars have suggested that the literary genre of courtly love romances was created for women by the *jongleurs* (minstrels) of the twelfth century. During the long absences of their husbands, who were occupied with the rounds of tournaments and wars, women sought entertainment by patronizing these singers, who naturally catered to the dreams of their audience. But while the romances do place the women in an unaccustomed position of importance, they also focus on the men and their exploits, and, consequently, they were popular with men as well as with women. In addition, recent research has indicated that the wives of barons did not conform to the stereotype presented by the romances or by storytellers trying to imagine the character of their audiences.

Women of the peasant class undoubtedly worked hard alongside their husbands, and while there were differences in the work done by each of the sexes, those differences were dictated more by the demands of the job than by socially defined sex roles. An assessment of the position of upper-class women, however, is more difficult. In the eleventh and twelfth centuries—at about the same time that the romance literature came into being—aristocratic women emerged from the shadows and began to play an active role in politics. Agnes of Poitiers (c. 1024–77), wife of Henry III of Germany, was an active queen who was regent of her kingdom for almost ten years after the death of her husband in 1056. Countess Mathilda of Tuscany (1048–1115) governed one of Italy's most populous and richest provinces for more than four decades and held the difficult middle ground between the papacy and the German empire during the Investiture Contest. Another Mathilda (1102–67), daughter of the English king Henry I (1100–35), waged a long civil war in England on behalf of her son Henry II. Henry II's succession to the largest domain in Europe in 1154 was largely due to the persistence and abilities of his mother. Henry's power was also significantly increased by his marriage to the famous Eleanor of Aquitaine (1122–1204), heiress to the largest duchy in France. It might be that mention of such women in contemporary documents resulted not from a new status for women, but from the growing literacy of the aristocratic class during the twelfth-century renaissance. It is certainly possible, however, that the rise in the cultural level and the relative stability of the European communities did affect the position of women for the better.

Political activity was not, of course, the normal occupation of medieval women—as it was not the normal occupation of medieval men either. Women spent the bulk of their time running the household and administering the landed estates of their families during the frequent absences of their husbands. These tasks could be formidable; the baronial household was a large and complex organization almost always on the move or getting ready to move. Because large supplies of food and forage could not be transported appreciable distances, large households were forced to move from manor to manor, eating up the surplus produce of each in turn. Middle-class urban households were also substantial in size and required managerial skills. One of the most famous medieval works pertaining to the role of women is the *Goodman of Paris,* a thirteenth-century treatise written by a merchant for the edification of his young wife. It deals with all aspects of managing an urban household—for example, buying food and supplies, governing servants, and the social obligations of a merchant's spouse.

The first of these articles, by Margaret Labarge, deals with these household duties among upper-class medieval women. It focuses on the role of a great baron's wife because the household of such a person was so large and complex that it produced records, almost as if it were a department of state. Eleanor, the main character in Labarge's study, was the sister of King Henry III of England and wife of Simon de Montfort, son of a famous leader of the crusade against the Albigensians in 1215.

It is obvious that the role of a woman as wife depended on the kind of household she presided over, but it is perhaps not so obvious that a woman's role as mother also depended on her class. In aristocratic families, wet nurses were employed and, often, young children were sent to be raised in the household of a higher lord. Charlemagne's household became the school, a kind of boarding school, for the children of his greatest subjects. William Marshal, the subject of the previous selection, was sent to his cousin's house at about thirteen years of age. Legal sources reveal that aristocratic children were often betrothed very young, and the young couple, to be married when they reached thirteen or fourteen, was raised in the house of the boy's parents. Urban middle-class families also used wet nurses, but their children were raised at home until they entered apprenticeships. The apprentices, who were of course all male, lived with their masters. Girls were simply raised at home. This picture of medieval urban families contrasts somewhat with that constructed by James Bruce Ross in his study of child-rearing in the urban families of the Italian Renaissance (see Part 5). Finally, peasant families shared the characteristics of poor families everywhere and in nearly every age. The children were not given out to wet nurses unless the mother had difficulty producing milk or died in childbirth—and then the nurse was likely to be a neighbor or relative in the same village. Peasant children lived at home until adulthood and became part of the family's work force early in life. In addition, the differences in work between the sexes were less extreme in this class than in the upper classes, so the training of male and female children differed less than it did higher up the social and economic scale.

These remarks are very general and rest on snatches of information gleaned from chronicles, treatises like the *Goodman of Paris,* and legal records. How can we get a closer view of childhood and child-rearing in the Middle Ages? In the second of these articles, Mary Martin McLaughlin uses another source, the reminiscences of some eleventh- and twelfth-century men, to uncover their childhood experiences and to delve into the relationship between mother and child.

THE ROLE OF A BARON'S WIFE

If it is difficult to think of the castle as a home, it is even harder to estimate fairly the position of the lady of the house. The evidence is varied and conflicting. On the one hand, the moralists and the writers on manners underline the basic, divinely-ordained subordination of women; they emphasize their foolishness and the need of their obedient submission to man in the person of their husbands. On the other, the romances present the ideas and standards of courtly love; they describe amazing heroines for whose supercilious smile any right-minded knight would brave death innumerable times. But the ladies of the romances generally seem to be only cardboard figures, cut to an identical pattern. The description of the heroine of *Jehan et Blonde* illustrates the accepted type.[1] Blonde was the ideal heroine with hair of shining gold, dark, straight eyebrows, and white unwrinkled skin. Her tiny mouth

[1] *Jehan et Blonde,* by Philippe de Beaumanoir, was one of the most popular French romances of the thirteenth century. It has a special interest for English readers because its central situation, of a French younger son gaining love and fortune in England, parallels the true life story of Simon de Montfort. The author probably formed part of Simon's household for a time, and certainly was familiar with English ways. This romance was a product of his youth, when he was known as Philippe de Remi; many years later, as sire de Beaumanoir, he wrote *Coutumes de Beauvaisis,* the most famous lawbook of thirteenth-century France.
From *A Baronial Household of the Thirteenth Century* by Margaret Labarge (London, Eyre & Spottiswoode, 1965), pp. 38–52. Reprinted by permission of Eyre & Spottiswoode (Publishers) Ltd. and Curtis Brown Ltd.

had full red lips over little white teeth, and her breath smelt pleasantly sweet. Her throat was so long and white that the author poetically insisted that you could see when she drank red wine. The catalogue goes on, but even this brief sample is sufficient to illustrate the medieval requirements for the fashionable beauty.

Neither the moralists' nor the romancer's descriptions of women had much relation to reality, for the chroniclers quite incidentally provide occasional glimpses of women who did not fit into these stock categories. There was Nicolaa de la Hay, for example, who held the castle of Lincoln for the boy king Henry during the desperate siege of 1216. The redoubtable countess of Arundel, who in 1252 reproved Henry III for his refusal to do justice to his barons and taunted him with his failure to keep his oaths to uphold the Great Charter, was a woman of great force, praised for her outspokenness. Even more impressive was Blanche of Castile, queen and regent of France and the backbone of French administration for a quarter of a century. These women were obviously neither cardboard beauties nor foolish, submissive sheep. Indeed the roster of independent active and capable women could be greatly extended at many levels of the social scale. Contemporary evidence affords considerable insight into the actual relation of the female stereotype to the reality, and enables us to evaluate more accurately the true place of women in thirteenth-century society.

It must be remembered that there was an enormous gulf between the occupations and status of the young girl and the married woman. At this time fourteen was generally considered the normal marriageable age for a girl. An important heiress, or a royal relative, who served as a pawn in the absorbing game of feudal politics, might be betrothed much earlier. The Countess Eleanor had been married at the age of nine in the hopes of assuring the loyalty of her first husband, Earl William Marshal the younger. Her elder sister Joanna had been betrothed at the age of four, as part of a peace settlement between King John and the Lusignan family of Poitou. Even the less well born unmarried girl was likely to be both young and foolish, and often in need of all the stringent protection the moralists insisted on. The single girl had no real tasks and little social standing; she therefore looked forward to marriage which brought her prestige and an independent establishment. The married woman was charged with the considerable responsibility of directly supervising the affairs of the household. This was particularly true in less extensive establishments than that of the countess of Leicester. The initiative and ability of the wife of a lesser baron were at once more obvious and more necessary.

Apart from her domestic responsibilities, the woman had a recognized legal position; though her lands and goods were theoretically under the control of her husband, she was in fact the equal of a man in all matters of private law. Frederick Maitland, the great legal historian, puts the matter most clearly:

The woman can hold land, even by military tenure, can own chattels, make a will, make a contract, can sue and be sued. She sues and is sued in person without the interposition of a guardian; she can plead with her own voice if she pleases; indeed—and this is a strong case—a married woman will sometimes appear as her husband's attorney. A widow will often be the guardian of her own children; a lady will often be the guardian of the children of her tenants.

Thus the wife of any great baron would expect to cope with her own property and lands; also to understand and carry on the many legal and financial affairs of the barony during her husband's absence or after his death. Robert Grosseteste, the great bishop of Lincoln, wrote a brief treatise on administration for the countess of Lincoln after her husband's death in 1240. He took for granted her ability to supervise the seignorial and manorial officials, as well as her own immediate household, and merely wrote down some instruction on the accepted methods. The best evidence for the independence and initiative of women is to be found in the numerous court cases in which they figure. Countess Eleanor's legal struggle for her full dower rights, which dragged on for over forty years, is only a particularly long-drawn-out instance of the persistent litigiousness of both sexes in thirteenth-century society.

Obviously the wife of a great baron often played an extraordinarily important part in the marriage partnership. Her varied activities were such an accepted fact that contemporary writers usually ignore them as too ordinary for comment. Nor do they refer to the bond of unity and affection which frequently developed in medieval marriages even though these were primarily arranged to increase wealth or power. Husband and wife often worked together in a common purpose, and showed a mutual respect which was not echoed by the woman-hating moralists.

Surprisingly these didactic writers seem blinded by their clerical animus, and singularly remote from practical affairs. They pay little attention to the legal and financial responsibilities of a baron's wife, or the important position of middle-class women in many of the town trades. Instead they fall back on the trite statement that a good wife is man's greatest gift from heaven, although they hasten to add that this is only true if she behaves herself and obeys him.

The writers of the treatises on etiquette are equally conventional and uninformative. Stephen of Fougères, chaplain of King Henry II and later bishop of Rennes, had a narrow conception of the proper employments of a great lady. To judge by his praise of the countess of Hereford, the best way for a gentlewoman to occupy her time was in building chapels, decorating altars, caring for the poor, and honouring and serving high personages—to which the bishop thoughtfully added, "especially churchmen." One wonders what he thought of the extremely secular activities of Eleanor of Aquitaine, Henry II's indomitable queen. Fortunately not all the didactic writers were quite so pious, or so limited. Robert of Blois,[2] for example, breathes a welcome air of common sense in his discussion of the matter. He admitted that he would like to teach ladies how to behave, but he realized that it was very difficult for a lady to conduct herself well in the world.

> If she speaks, someone says it is too much. If she is silent, she is reproached for not knowing how to greet people. If she is friendly and courteous, someone pretends it is for love. If on the other hand she does not put on a bright face, she passes for being too proud.

The problem of contradictory advice to women is obviously not a modern development.

About 1265, Philip of Novara[3] wrote a little treatise called the *Four Ages of Man* in which he dealt with the proper education of upper-class boys and girls. His work provides convenient clues to what the age expected of them. Philip, like most other medieval writers, emphasized the importance of largess as the prime virtue of kings, princes and the nobility. Generosity could cover a multitude of sins, and any man with pretensions to noble blood must practice it as part of his duty to his class and himself. However, largess was not a suitable virtue for a girl, or even a woman. A maid had no need to make gifts, Philip thought, and he quoted approvingly the common saying, "poorer than a maid." His disapproval of gift-giving by married women stemmed from strictly practical reasons:

> If the wife and husband are both generous, it is the ruin of the house, while a wife's greater generosity shames her lord. The only kind of largess suitable for a woman is the giving of alms, provided she has her husband's permission and the household can afford it.

In Philip's opinion, obedience and chastity should be a girl's main virtues, and were the only ones strictly required. They were aided by a "fair countenance," that is, the habit of looking straight ahead "with a tranquil and measured air, not too high and not too low, modestly and without affectation." This question of a woman's style of walking and regarding others was one on which all the writers on manners laid great emphasis. Ladies were to walk erect, with dignity, said Robert of Blois, neither trotting nor running, nor dallying either, with their eyes fixed on the ground ahead of them. They were to be particularly careful that they did not regard men as the sparrow-hawk does the lark. Anger and high words would also inevitably injure their reputations.

[2] Robert of Blois was a French poet who wrote in the middle of the thirteenth century. His treatise on manners has perhaps some element of satire in it but generally echoes the accepted requirements of the times.
[3] Philip of Novara was a Lombard crusader who settled in the East and wrote a chronicle favourable to the Ibelin family. His treatise on manners was written when he himself was seventy-five.

The feminine range of accomplishments was not expected to be very great. Every girl should learn to spin and weave, Philip of Novara insisted, because the poor will need the knowledge and the rich will better appreciate the work of others; but should not be taught to read and write unless she was to become a nun. Many evils, said Philip disapprovingly, have come from the fact that women have learnt such things, for then men dare to write follies or supplications which they would not dare to say or send by messenger. Philip ended his injunctions with the rather patronizing remark that even old women might be useful, for "they can manage and watch their houses, raise the children and arrange marriages." At least, the good ones occupied themselves in these ways, but the bad "plaster their faces, dye their hair, waste their patrimony in seeking love when they are old."

The requirements for the ideal woman put forward by such writers as Robert of Blois and Philip of Novara probably have as much relation to the realities of their time as the formalities of present-day writers on etiquette have to ordinary social life. They mirror the contemporary French ideals of polite behaviour carried to extremes. But, in the thirteenth century too, a good wife was rather more than the bloodless embodiment of the virtues preached by the moralists, or even the competent administrative helpmeet. The Knight of La Tour Landry, in the prologue of his fourteenth-century book of deportment for his daughters, describes most eloquently the bond of love and respect that bound him to his dead wife. According to the Knight, she was:

> Both fair and good, which had knowledge of all honour, all good, and fair maintaining, and of all good she was bell and the flower; and I delighted so much in her that I made for her love songs, ballads, rondels, virelays, and diverse things in the best wise I could. . . . And so it is more than twenty years that I have been for her full of great sorrow. For a true lover's heart forgetteth never the woman that once he has truly loved.

This was indeed a noble compliment, although perhaps influenced by literary convention. It is a useful counterbalance to the belief that marriage and love were quite incompatible in the Middle Ages.

The countess of Leicester did not altogether conform to the patterns laid down by writers on morals and manners. Her character and activities can afford one example of how thirteenth-century theory about the place of women was carried out in practice. Certainly the countess was no cipher. Eleanor brought Simon de Montfort great wealth, as she was the widow of one of the greatest earls of the realm; also great prestige because she was the king's sister. These two facts alone would have ensured her importance. In addition her character was assertive—she was not the meek, submissive, dove-like type so highly praised by the moralists. Several years earlier, the Franciscan Adam Marsh had found it necessary to write to her reprovingly, suggesting that she lay aside all contentions and irritating quarrels and act in a spirit of moderation when she had to counsel her husband. Obviously a high-spirited woman, she was also unfailingly loyal to Earl Simon through good times and bad. She shared many of her husband's travels—to Italy, France, and Gascony, but she was also capable of handling their many concerns alone. The evidence of the household account shows the countess at a period when she was, of necessity, in charge. The earl was away, engaged on his campaigns, and the management of all their affairs lay in her hands. The role of the countess at this time was more than ever that of the woman of affairs. Even the sober items of the account show how much political initiative Eleanor displayed, and how the executive ability and practical foresight of a capable woman were extended to their furthest limits.

On the domestic side the countess had many officials to take care of the immediate requirements of the household, though she herself had to oversee their accounts and agree to their expenditures. For female companionship she had certain women, who also served as ladies-in-waiting and were referred to as the countess's damsels. Her daughter Eleanor was now almost thirteen, but she still had her own nurse and took an unimportant place in the life of the household.

Indeed the medieval magnates had surprisingly little to do with their children. Almost immediately after birth, they were handed over to the care of a nurse whose duties, as described by Bartholomew the Englishman,[4] included not only the physical care of the child, but also the display of affection which is now considered essentially maternal. According to Bartholomew the nurse's duties were very extensive. She was ordained to nourish and feed the child, to give it suck, to kiss it if it fell, and comfort it if it wept, and to wash it when it was dirty. The nurse was also to teach the child to speak by sounding out the words for him, to dose him with medicines when necessary, and even to chew the toothless child's meat so that he could swallow it. The mother must have been a rather remote figure. Discipline was always considered the father's primary duty. Bartholomew specifically insisted that the father must treat his child with harshness and severity. He should teach him with scoldings and beatings, put him under wardens and tutors, and, above all, show "no glad cheer lest the child wax proud." The old adage of "spare the rod and spoil the child" was firmly entrenched in all medieval treatises on the proper upbringing of children.

The earl and countess of Leicester had taken care to put these precepts into practice. In 1265 they had six living children, ranging in age from twenty-six to thirteen. Two of their sons had been sent when young to the household of Bishop Grosseteste to be instructed in good manners and some learning. It was a recognized medieval practice to send both boys and girls away to

---

[4] Bartholomew the Englishman was a thirteenth-century Franciscan who wrote an immensely popular encyclopaedia, *Concerning the Nature of Things*. He dealt with a multiplicity of subjects, ranging from the nature of God and the angels to the size of the cooking pots. His work was widely used as a textbook until the sixteenth century.

more important or more learned households as a way of furthering their education. Now the two eldest boys, Henry and Simon the younger, had been knighted and were a valued part of their father's army. Guy was also a fighting man with his father. The fourth son, Amaury, was a clerk; he had profited handsomely by his father's success for he had been appointed, at the age of twenty-one, to the rich office of treasurer of York. Richard, the youngest of the sons, is a shadowy figure who flits briefly through the records before his departure for Bigorre in September when he disappears completely. The only daughter, Eleanor, remained with her mother during this period, but her father was busy trying to arrange a marriage for her with Llywelyn, prince of Wales. Earl Simon hoped to reinforce the alliance between the baronial troops and the wild Welsh tribesmen. However, the catastrophe of Evesham changed all this. Young Eleanor accompanied her mother into exile in France, and the betrothal to Llywelyn was postponed. Finally the countess succeeded in having it carried out by proxy in France just before her death in 1275. Even then complications of policy forced a further postponement of three years before Eleanor's marriage was solemnized and, at the age of twenty-six, she was finally free to join her Welsh prince.

It seems to have been the usual practice for each child in an important household to have his own nurse. In the countess's account, besides the payment for young Eleanor's nurse, there is also mention of the nurse of William de Braose.[5] This multiplicity of nurses is also evident in the household of young Henry, the son of Edward I. There were three children in that household: Henry himself, his elder sister, Eleanor, and their cousin, John of Brittany; each of these children had his own nurse. These ladies were of some standing, since their robes, a considerable addition to their annual wages and a gauge of social position, were of the same value as those of the official guardian of the household. Henry's account also underlines the fact that it was the nurse, not the mother, who was constantly present. The queen sent messengers enquiring after the health of the sickly lad, but affairs of state and the pattern of behaviour of the time kept them apart even in his final illness. The thirteenth century regarded children's deaths as a frequent, and inevitable, example of the inscrutable will of God.

It is obvious that the duties of the countess, or of any great baron's wife, were not restricted to her home and family in the sense in which later centuries have understood these terms. A great magnate's wife was not expected to be a very domestic woman—her duties dealt with a wider sphere. The account shows very clearly two fields in which the countess's personal initiative was particularly important. Eleanor entertained a great number of

---

[5] William's place in the household remains in doubt. Probably he was a relation of the famous marcher family to which Earl Simon's great-aunt, Countess Loretta of Leicester, belonged, and may have been a hostage for father or uncle, as a William de Braose holding lands in Dorset and Kent was a vigorous loyalist.

people, both at Odiham and Dover, during the spring and summer of 1265; she also had an extraordinary wide range of correspondence.

Visitors were a common and welcome feature of medieval social life. Indeed one of the primary duties of the gently-born, and especially of the heads of a household, was to greet all their guests with enthusiasm and courtesy. Grosseteste counselled the countess of Lincoln that all guests, secular and religious, should be received "quickly, courteously, and with good cheer," and then they should be "courteously addressed, lodged and served." It is an interesting peculiarity of the Montfort household account that the clerk each day listed by name those guests of importance who ate with the countess. This gives us valuable clues to the nature of people who came on varying errands, and, with the marshal's daily accounting for the number of horses, shows the fluctuations in size of the countess's household.

A considerable number of visitors were listed—over fifty names are mentioned in the seven months of the account—and many of them were accompanied by large retinues. However, it should be remembered that everyone whose normal place was not in the countess's household was specified on the roll as an outsider. For example, when Earl Simon came with his own large army to spend the two weeks before Easter at Odiham, he was listed as a visitor; so, too, were the elder sons, on their occasional appearances to see their mother. Others who appear frequently are the senior officials of the household, whose business led them back and forth between the earl and the countess, wherever they might be, and also took them up and down to London for purchases.

The true guests were of many types: royal officials, knights of the shire who were staunch supporters of the earl, and men who had previously served as local officials for the earl and now had a share in the administration of the country. It is interesting to note that in a period which might reasonably seem to discourage unarmed travellers, the countess also entertained a large number of religious personages. Some were definitely friends of the Leicesters and supporters of the baronial cause, such as the abbot of Waverley, the Cistercian abbey so close to Odiham. Others, such as the prioress of Wintney and the prioress of Amesbury, seem to have been trying to complete business for their convents.

But nuns were not the only women travelling, either for business or for pleasure. Some of the greatest ladies of the realm were among the countess's visitors. Isabella de Fortibus, for example, spent the Easter weekend at Odiham, and the countess of Oxford visited in May. Her appearance is less surprising since her husband was a strong supporter of Earl Simon.

The titled and the wealthy are easily classifiable, but sometimes it is possible to trace the lines of self-interest and feudal relationship which lie behind the unexplained and unfamiliar names in the roll. Margery de Crek is a particularly good example of the many possible ties. Margery came to visit the countess at Odiham in March, travelling with a retinue of twelve horses.

She was almost certainly a widow. Her husband, Bartholomew de Crek, had been in Ireland in 1224 in the service of William Marshal, the Countess Eleanor's first husband, and in 1232, after the earl's death, was described as Eleanor's yeoman. By 1235 he had married Margery, held lands in Norfolk and Suffolk and, like many others richer than himself, was deeply in debt to some Jews of London. His upward social climb was ultimately crowned by knighthood. The date of Bartholomew's death is not ascertainable, though his name disappears from the records after 1251. Margery, however, lived many years as a widow, dying in 1282 when she must have been at least in her sixties. By this time she had retired with a fairly large household to the Augustinian convent of Flixton. She was quite a wealthy woman, and her will disposed of many of her goods in favour of the Flixton community. Her son John died seven years after his mother, still holding Creake in Norfolk of the earl marshal, and Combe in Suffolk of the king in chief. The original connection of Margery and Bartholomew de Crek with the countess of Leicester was undoubtedly due to Bartholomew's service of William Marshal, who may have rewarded him with his original landholding. In any case ancient acquaintance, and perhaps the hope of present favours, kept Margery in friendly touch with the Countess Eleanor in the troubled year of 1256. This one case, in which the connecting links are reasonably easy to uncover, illustrates very clearly the involved tangle of political self-interest, feudal relationships, and even natural human companionship which formed the fabric of thirteenth-century feudal society.

Apart from her overnight guests, the Countess Eleanor seems to have been well aware that hospitality could serve political ends. During her trip from Odiham to the greater safety of Dover she entertained the burgesses of Winchelsea as she passed through their town. Only three days after she arrived at Dover she invited the burgesses of Sandwich to dinner, and both groups of burgesses were again asked to dinner at Dover castle in July. The reason for these invitations is abundantly clear, as the support of the important townsmen of the Cinque Ports was essential for the baronial cause. It was imperative that Eleanor should keep them loyal to Earl Simon, for they could guard the coast against French invasion, and keep out mercenaries recruited for the king overseas.

Correspondence, as well as hospitality, was put to political uses. An analysis of the Countess Eleanor's correspondents shows very clearly the wide-ranging interests of a great magnate and his wife, though its unusual extent was influenced by their extraordinary situation. The frequent use of letters was nothing new, for in more peaceful years Eleanor and Simon had corresponded with Bishop Grosseteste and Brother Adam Marsh, who was a fluent, if enigmatic, letter-writer. In the spring and summer of 1265 an unusual number of messages went back and forth between husband and wife. These were undoubtedly accounted for by the exigencies of the political and military situation. Indeed the messengers who carried the letters were among the busiest members of the household. Besides her husband, the countess corresponded with Richard Gravesend, bishop of Lincoln and enthusiast for the baronial cause, Thomas Cantilupe, the baronial chancellor, and her officials and favourite merchants among many others. Nor was this activity limited only to England. Messengers went back and forth between England and Bigorre, where the earl still claimed the title of count, and Laura de Montfort, Earl Simon's niece, wrote from the family castle at Montfort-l'Amaury. The frequent entries on the account are sufficient to show that the countess was extremely active in many fields, and that constant communication was possible whenever political or personal needs required it.

After the earl's defeat and death at Evesham, the countess's role was even more important and demanding. The responsibility for salvaging any fragment of the Montfort fortunes was hers alone. The account shows how she armed her intercessors with letters for her unforgiving brother the king when he held his first parliament after his return to unfettered power; and how she also wrote, with greater success, to Richard of Cornwall to ensure his good will and promise of assistance. Not only did she arrange the departure of her youngest son for Bigorre, she also seems to have succeeded in smuggling 11,000 marks out of England to France. In a final agreement made at Dover with the Lord Edward, Eleanor ensured the return to grace and favour of most of her household, though she herself had to leave the kingdom. All these various achievements illustrate the many facets of the countess's executive ability and capacity for planning.

The household account gives glimpses of a great lady's many activities. From its evidence it is easy to see that many, in fact most, of her occupations were not particularly domestic, or even feminine in the restricted sense. The primary duty of a great baron's wife was to produce the heir necessary to carry on the line, and then to serve as an active partner with her husband in the many enterprises of feudal life. She might even, when necessary, take sole charge. The purely domestic routine of the lady of the house in such a vast establishment was discharged by a well-planned and carefully detailed organization which was responsible for the smooth running of the domestic machinery.

MOTHER AND CHILD

"In her despair, his mother wholly rejected her baby, weaning him before he had hardly begun to nurse, and refusing to hold or touch him with her own hands."

John of Lodi, *Life of St. Peter Damian*,
late eleventh century

From "Survivors and Surrogates: Children and Parents from the Ninth to the Thirteenth Centuries" by Mary Martin McLaughlin, in *The History of Childhood*, edited by L. deMause (New York: The Psychohistory Press, 1974), pp. 101–41. Reprinted by permission of The Psychohistory Press.

"Yet thou knowest, Almighty One, with what purity and holiness in obedience to Thee she raised me, how greatly she provided me with the care of nurses in infancy and of masters and teachers in boyhood, with no lack even of fine clothes for my little body, so that I seemed to equal the sons of kings and counts in indulgence."

Guibert of Nogent, *Memoirs,* 1115

Some Introductory Reflections on Two Eleventh-Century Childhoods

For the period from which these voices speak, as for all but the most recent times, the realities of early life must remain a largely hidden world, accessible to us only partially and indirectly, through the recollections, portrayals and fantasies of those who were no longer children. Among such fragile if indispensable witnesses, the two works just quoted have for our period and purposes a singular importance. Offering us the fullest, the most intimate and revealing accounts of infancy and childhood in Western society during the time-span of this study, they lead us most directly into the virtually uncharted hinterland of childhood during these distant centuries. To suggest that much of this terrain is still unexplored is by no means to undervalue the contributions of modern scholarship in many areas that impinge upon it. Studies concerned with the family and its changing structure, with medieval demography, law and education, with the history of medicine and especially pediatrics, with religious movements and cultural transformations, as well as essays on the "idea" and the "cult" of childhood: all of these and many others help us in some measure to recreate both the immediate and the social settings of children's lives in the remoter past. Still in its own infancy, however, is the effort to approach more closely the psychic realities of these lives, to gain some understanding, however tentative and incomplete, of the experiences of childhood, the modes of rearing and the relations of parents and children, with all of their profound implications for the development of both individuals and societies. Whatever may be the verdict on the various hypotheses advanced in this volume, the discovery of childhood in these and in other centuries must inevitably, like all such novel ventures, pose fresh and formidable questions that will leave almost no field of history uninvaded. . . .

The man whose childhood John of Lodi describes was, indeed, no ordinary person. For Peter Damian, who was born in the early eleventh century, perhaps in 1007, in the Italian city of Ravenna, to respectable but evidently far from prosperous parents, was destined to become one of the great spiritual reformers of his age and one of its most notable saints. An eloquent preacher and zealous ascetic, head of a congregation of hermits dedicated to the contemplative life, a powerful opponent of abuses and in later life a cardinal-bishop of the Roman Church, he played a major part in the most important ecclesiastical movements of the century. He also wrote copiously and sometimes brilliantly on many subjects; but his writings, though variously self-revealing, contain little that is directly autobiographical. For our most substantial and sequential knowledge of his life, in both its earlier and its later phases, we must turn to John of Lodi, a devoted disciple of Peter Damian's last years, who wrote at the request of his fellow-monks of Fonte Avellana a biography that was, like other such works, intended above all to demonstrate the sanctity of its hero.

No doubt John's story of Peter Damian's early life reflected also his own ideas and fantasies of childhood and it is perhaps this concern, as well as the immediacy of his sources and his intense devotion to his subject, that explains the vividness, empathy and apparent veracity in which this biography markedly transcends the conventions of the medieval saint's-life. Strikingly absent from it are the visions, dreams and portents that commonly attended the births of saintly children and the glorification of their parentage that was also a tradition of this genre. In keeping with its principles, however, John did wish to stress those experiences which formed and tested the heroic virtues of his subject, and so, perhaps, he did not hesitate to record a childhood of almost unrelieved misery and deprivation. Peter's adversities began, in fact, at the very moment of his birth, to a mother "worn out by child-bearing," into a family already so numerous and so impoverished that when this son was born, an adolescent brother bitterly reproached their mother for having added yet another child to an overcrowded household, to the "throng of heirs" competing for a meagre inheritance.

Enraged by this attack, the mother fell into what John of Lodi describes as "a violent fit of feminine malice" (in which we may perceive the symptoms of postpartum depression), wringing her hands and declaring that she was utterly wretched and unworthy to live any longer. In her despair, she wholly rejected her baby, refusing to nurse him and "to hold or touch him with her own hands." Cast away "before he had learned to live," disinherited from the maternal breast that was his only possession, this tiny creature began to grow dark with hunger and cold, and so weak that he could hardly cry; "only the barest whisper came from his scarcely palpitating little chest." At this point, when the baby seemed about to perish from maternal neglect, he was rescued through the intervention of a certain priest's wife, or concubine, who had been a domestic servant in his father's family and who had perhaps assisted at the child's birth. Clearly hers was also an important role in the symmetry as well as the sensibility of John's story, for she is the "good" foil of the "bad" mother in a pairing that is later balanced by the contrast between Peter's "good" and "bad" brothers. Appalled by the inhuman harshness of his mother, this compassionate woman vehemently reproached her, asking how a Christian mother could behave as no lioness or tigress would do. If these mothers faithfully nurse their cubs, she cried, how could human mothers reject children formed in the image of God and shaped in their own wombs? Clinching her argument with the stern warning that to continue in this way would be to risk being judged guilty of filicide, the priest's wife contrived to soften the mother's heart and restore the dying child to life.

To set an example of proper maternal solicitude, in whose details John of Lodi took evident pleasure, she freed the baby's withered limbs from their swaddling bands, warmed the naked little body at the fire and cured the rash or scabies that covered it by rubbing it lavishly with oil. Then, he exclaimed, "you would have seen the tender little limbs, wrapped in poultices soaked in melted fat, begin to grow rosy as their vital heat returned, and the beauty of infancy flower again." So, we are told, the compassion of a "sinful little woman" snatched a desperate child from the jaws of death and saved his mother from "the dreadful sin of infanticide." Indeed, restored to that maternal self and feeling which "an alien savagery had driven out," Peter's mother from that time on showed unstinting diligence and love in the nursing of her baby, who flourished under this care until he was weaned.

Shortly after this, however, when he was still a very young child, Peter was prematurely orphaned by the death of both of his parents. Left to the care of his family, he was, unhappily, adopted by the very brother, probably the eldest, who had been so angered by his birth and who, with a wife equally harsh and cruel, now treated the little boy, according to his biographer, in a savage and "stepmotherly" fashion. Fed grudgingly with slops fit only for pigs, he was forced to go about barefoot, clad in rags, a "battered child," frequently kicked and beaten. Subjected to this brutality for some years, compelled to live "like a slave," he was eventually turned out to become a swineherd. From this period of Peter's boyhood only one episode, which John considered highly significant, is reported at length. One day the miserable boy chanced to find a gold coin and, delighted by this unexpected wealth, he reflected for a long time on what he might buy with it. After long inner debate, he was at last divinely inspired to renounce his dreams of transitory pleasure and to give up his cherished coin to a priest for a Mass to be offered for his father's soul. If to his biographer this renunciation of the ephemeral for the eternal seemed to presage his later sanctity, to us it may seem not without meaning that only his father and not his rejecting mother was included in this generous offering.

Concluding his tale of childhood misery on a happier note, John reports that when Peter was perhaps twelve years old, he was delivered from his tormentors and placed in the care of another brother, as kind as the first was cruel, who lavished on the boy so much affection that "it seemed to exceed a father's love." It was to this brother, Damian, who later became an archpriest of Ravenna, that Peter owed the education that made possible his career first as a secular teacher and then as a distinguished churchman. To this brother, whose name he adopted, Peter remained deeply devoted in later life, as he was to a nephew, also called Damian, for whose education he in turn provided, and to the sisters of whom his biographer says nothing. To this last attachment Peter himself testified in a fashion that adds suggestively to our knowledge of his childhood and the lasting effect of his sufferings in it. In a letter written when he was perhaps sixty, he described an earlier visit to the deathbed of a beloved sister, who had been "like a mother" to him; as he crossed the threshold of the family house for the first time since his youth, he declared, such a "cloud of timidity" hung over his eyes that he could see almost nothing of the household during the time he spent there. Although John of Lodi failed to mention this affectionate sister and her role, perhaps because her presence would have disturbed the symmetry of his story, its essential truth is supported by Peter's own revelation of the enduring anxieties aroused by this visit to the home of his childhood and the painful memories associated with it.

Unlike Peter Damian, Guibert of Nogent was neither particularly influential nor, if we may judge by his account of himself, very saintly. Born a half-century or so after Peter, in Clermont-en-Beauvaisis in northern France, into a noble family of only local importance, he was destined from the first for the monastic life, which he entered at the age of twelve or thirteen. Much later, he became the abbot of a small monastery, Nogent-sous-Coucy, and also, though his role on the larger scene was never more than modest, an acute observer, recorder and critic of his turbulent society. No less fascinated by himself than by the world in which he moved, he distinguished himself most strikingly from all but a few of his contemporaries by telling his own story in his *Monodiae* or "songs for one voice," a somewhat miscellaneous collection of memoirs which has been described, with some exaggeration, as "the first comprehensive autobiography of the middle ages." Although these memoirs are by no means so encompassing autobiographically as we might wish, there is no work of these centuries that gives us so immediate a sense of what at least one medieval child and childhood might have been like. Indeed, his intense, perhaps obsessive, concern with his early life reveals to us not only the young Guibert in his strangely isolated and rigorously disciplined childhood, but the child living still in the man of fifty. Remarkable as his memoirs are in their portrayal of the dramas of his world, and the wealth of insights they offer into the details of its life, the true singularity of his work lies in its major theme and inspiration, that passionate attachment to his mother which remained the central and apparently the only emotionally significant relationship of his existence.

Dominating all that is most personal in his story, this possessive and somewhat ambivalent devotion is first clearly disclosed in Guibert's uncommonly precise account of the shared dangers and deliverance of his birth. For, like Peter Damian's, Guibert's early hold on life had been extremely tenuous and his entrance into the world even more dramatic, in circumstances of great peril to both mother and child. In reporting them he took, in fact, considerable retrospective pleasure, dwelling at length on his mother's prolonged and painful labor and the dangers that led his father, in hope of a safe delivery, to promise him to the monastic life even before he had been born. When at last he appeared, "a weak little being, almost an abortion," and was on that same day, Holy Saturday, brought to the baptismal font, he was, as he was often told jokingly in later years, tossed from hand to hand by "a certain woman," probably the midwife, who exclaimed: "Look at this thing! Do you think such a child can live . . . ?" After his lively picture of this important occasion, Guibert tells us disappointingly little of his very early childhood. The youngest child in a family that included at least two brothers, whom he barely mentions throughout his memoirs and for whom he apparently felt little affection, at the age of about eight months he lost his father, at a time when he had, he says, scarcely begun to cherish his rattle. After his father's death, which Guibert later saw as a stroke of good fortune, his mother remained a widow, devoting herself to the rearing of this, in his view at least, her favorite child, "truest to me," he insists, "of all that she bore."

What sort of woman was this whom her son regarded throughout his life as his "sole personal possession among all the goods I had in the world"? In his portrayal of her, "beautiful, yet chaste, modest, steeped in the fear of the Lord," we glimpse faintly the influences of another childhood, formative perhaps for both mother and son. And we see more clearly the effects of the marriage of which he was the offspring. For terrified from her earliest years by fears of sin and sudden death, she had been given in marriage to Guibert's father, himself a mere youth, when she was still a child, "hardly of marriageable age." Probably because of their youthful ignorance and inhibitions rather than through the "bewitchments" to which Guibert attributed their failure, his parents' marriage remained unconsummated for several years. During this time the impotent young husband and his still virginal wife were subjected to heavy and humiliating pressures from their families and neighbors, until at last the "bewitchment was broken," probably, as their son suggests, by his father's successful liaison with another woman. Thereafter his mother submitted, though clearly not eagerly, to those wifely duties for which, according to Guibert, she had little taste. Still a young and handsome woman when her husband died, she resisted with formidable determination the self-interested efforts of his kinsmen to persuade her to remarry so that they might gain control of her children and property. Continuing for the rest of her life in what was to her and to many other women in this period the highly desirable state of widowhood, she showed herself the conventionally dutiful, efficient, extraordinarily pious, in some ways generous but, it seems emotionally inhibited woman whose image emerges from Guibert's recollections. Illiterate but practically gifted, burdened with all of the responsibilities of governing a noble household, she was evidently assiduous in her concern for the physical and spiritual welfare of her son, providing him, he says, with nurses in his infancy, dressing him in fine clothes and, when she had leisure from her household cares, teaching him how and for what to pray. From his earliest years Guibert appears to have been powerfully influenced by his mother's piety and sense of sin, and particularly by her uncommonly rigid standards of sexual purity and control. He was also strongly affected by her concern for his education, for as soon as this child who was destined for the monastic life had begun to learn his letters, at the age of four or five, she procured the services of a teacher who became his private tutor for at least six years, living in the household and giving his full attention to his pupil, whom he worked very hard and whose every waking moment he supervised.

Between his mother and his tutor, who "guarded him as a parent not as a master," Guibert was evidently brought up with excessive, indeed, repressive care, kept, he says, from ordinary games, never allowed to leave his master's company or to eat anywhere but at home, or to accept gifts from anyone without his leave. "While others of my age wandered everywhere at will and were unchecked in the indulgence of such inclinations as were natural at their age," says Guibert, "I, hedged in by constant restraints and dressed in my clerical garb, would sit and look at the troops of players like a beast awaiting sacrifice." Rarely permitted a holiday, he was constantly driven to study by an assiduous but poorly educated teacher who tried to compensate for his own deficiencies with scoldings and frequent beatings. Persuading himself, at least retrospectively, of the genuine concern, the "harsh love," underlying this rough treatment, and himself returning this love, mingled with a certain contempt, Guibert was also pleasurably aware of the rivalry for his affections between his master and his mother, who was grieved and distressed, according to her son, when she saw the evidence of excessive beating. On one occasion when, he says, "she threw off my inner garment and saw my little arms blackened and the skin of my back everywhere puffed up with the cuts from the twigs," she was "grieved to the heart" and protested bitterly, "weeping with sorrow," that he should never become a cleric or "any more suffer so much to get an education." Yet when she offered to give him the arms and equipment of a knight, when he had reached the age for them, Guibert proudly refused, insisting that "if I had to die on the spot, I would not give up studying my lessons and becoming a clerk."

Different as their childhoods were in many ways, Guibert evidently shared with Peter Damian not only heavy physical punishment but also the experience, or the feeling, of maternal rejection, although Guibert's came at a much later time, when in fact, he was past twelve and his mother, in her growing obsession with her own spiritual welfare, decided to withdraw from the world and undertake the life of a recluse. Regarding this decision as desertion, Guibert thought of her in putting her salvation before his well-being as, for all her devotion to him, a "cruel and unnatural mother."

> She knew that I should be utterly an orphan with no one at all on whom to depend, for great as was my wealth of kinsfolk and connections, yet there

was no one to give me the loving care a little child needs at such an age; though I did not lack for the necessities of food and clothing, I often suffered from the loss of that careful provision for the helplessness of tender years that only a woman can provide. . . . Although she knew that I would be condemned to such neglect, yet Thy love and fear, O God, hardened her heart . . . the tenderest in all the world, that it might not be tender to her own soul's harm.

Clearly, as this passage suggests, what is extraordinary in Guibert's reminiscences of his childhood is his capacity to convey not only its significant details but the intense, if ambivalent, emotions that were persistently evoked by his profound attachment to his mother. Living constantly, it seems, under the scrutiny of her critical and demanding eye—for even in her retirement she continued to supervise his life and to show her anxiety about him—he never ceased to feel the sense of guilt she had apparently instilled and to long for the love and approval that were, perhaps, never fully given. Throughout his recollections he shows himself as always, essentially, the jealously possessive and dependent child to whose self-concern we owe what is certainly our fullest and most intimate account of the relationship of a medieval mother and son. . . .

To Live or to Die: The Dramas of Birth and Survival

Racked by pains long endured and her tortures increasing as her hour drew near, when she thought I had at last in natural course come to birth, instead I was returned within the womb. By this time my father, friends and kinsfolk were crushed with dismal sorrowing for both of us, for while the child was hastening the death of the mother; and she her child's in denying him deliverance, all had reason for compassion.

Guibert of Nogent, Memoirs

If Guibert gives us some sense of the emotional atmosphere surrounding childbirth, he also provides as realistic a description of this occasion as we are likely to find in any but the medical writings of this period. The reason for the lack of direct description is simple; the authors of most such works, being men, were rarely, if ever, present at the actual occasion of birth, which was customarily attended only by women. Until the appearance of popular, vernacular treatises fairly late in our period, moreover, the obstetrical and pediatric knowledge available in medical works of this period, can hardly have affected more than a very small minority of mothers and children. This knowledge appears in any case to have been an amalgam of theoretical learning with the customary and empirical practices which were the stock in trade of the midwives or "sages femmes" who commonly supervised labor and childbirth, and we have almost no trustworthy evidence regarding their training.

It was the midwife, Bartholomew of England writes in the early thirteenth century, who knew how to soften the uterus with unguents and fomentations so that the child might be delivered with less difficulty and pain. It was she who received the infant from the womb, severed and tied the umbilical cord at a length of four fingers, washed or bathed the baby, rubbed it with salt and sometimes crushed rose leaves or honey "to comfort its limbs and free them of mucus," and with her finger rubbed the palate and gums with honey to clean the insides of the mouth and to stimulate the infant's appetite. Bartholomew strongly recommended the frequent bathing of newborns, as well as anointing with oil of myrtle or rose and the massaging of all their limbs, especially those of boys, which should be more strenuously exercised. He also provided a rationale for what was in most regions of Europe the apparently universal practice of swaddling the limbs of newborn and young infants; this should be done, he says, not only to prevent the deformities likely to occur because of the "fluidity" and "flexibility" of infantile limbs, but also to ensure that "natural heat might be restored to the interior of the body" and aid in the digestion of food, which was further encouraged, he thought, by the gentle rocking of infants in their cradles. . . .

Once having made the hazardous passage from the womb, the infant's survival depended upon one thing above all else: its access to breast milk of good quality. In these centuries this meant, for all but the small minority of the noble and prosperous who could afford wet-nurses, the mother's milk. For all classes the mother who nursed her own children reflected the ideal maternal image. Celebrated in contemporary representations of the Virgo lactans, the nursing Mother of Christ, and in the poignant Eve nursing her child portrayed on the bronze doors at Hildesheim, and later at Verona, this essential maternal function was emphasized and extolled in literary and didactic works of various kinds. Praising it on both scientific and emotional grounds, Bartholomew of England explained that "while the foetus exists in the womb it is nourished on blood, but at birth nature sends that blood to the breasts to be changed into milk." Its own mother's milk, therefore, was better for the newborn child than another's. Anticipating modern views on the subject, he stressed also the emotional bonds thereby strengthened; "for the mother loves her own child most tenderly, embraces and kisses it, nurses and cares for it most solicitously." Repeating these themes, another thirteenth century writer stressed also the idea that as every plant draws its strength from its roots, and maternal milk best shapes the child's nature, that mother does ill who cuts her child off from these fostering sources.

If the nursing mother represented the ideal of these centuries, she was also to a very large extent the reality; for the vast majority of children, except in cases of dire necessity, must have been dependent on their mother's milk. But it also seems clear that among women of the noble classes—again, it must be emphasized, a small but highly visible minority—the practice of resorting to wet-nurses became increasingly common. What has been called perhaps over-enthusiastically the "nursing revolution" of this period may thus have made some contribution to a growing population, since the use of wet-nurses is thought to have shortened the interval between pregnancies and, in general, to have encouraged the production of more children. The practice of wet-nursing was, in fact, fairly common throughout this time; in the mid-eleventh century, for example, Guibert's mother provided nurses both for her own son and for the child whom she adopted in expiation of her husband's sins. As this case and many others show, however, the infant was not ordinarily, so far as I have been able to discover, sent out to nurse, after the fashion of later centuries; the wet-nurse was, rather, brought into the household to the child. That the use of wet-nurses in general was resisted in some noble circles is suggested by the story, intended as exemplary, of the Blessed Ida of Boulogne, which in its most inflated version describes how violently this saintly and devoted mother of three sons, who had never permitted them to be nursed by anyone but herself, reacted to the flouting of her wishes in this matter. . . .

But there is more to the care of babies than nursing, and here again what evidence we have points largely to the habits and practices of the noble class and to the prominent role of the nurse. By the early thirteenth century, in a work of "popular science," she was assigned the functions doubtless performed by the mother in households farther down the social scale. Assuming the maternal role in nursing the baby, she also rejoiced with the child when he was happy and sympathized with his sorrows; she bathed, cleaned and changed him when he was soiled; she chewed the meat in her own mouth for the toothless child and fed him with her finger. Hers was the hand that rocked his cradle and hers the voice that soothed him with lullabies; it was she who began teaching him to speak, "lisping and repeating the same words." She was, it seems, something more like a "nanny" than a wet-nurse and by this time such nurses in some noble households remained with their charges throughout their childhood years.

Whether or not it was rocked by a nurse, one accoutrement of infant life assumed a growing importance during these centuries, and this is the cradle. Although our earliest pictorial representations of the rocking-cradle date from the thirteenth century, the cradle in simpler forms must certainly have been in use very much earlier; there was, for example, a deep basket-like cradle, easily portable, in which the baby was held in place by bands, and there are many literary references to cradles of one kind or another, among them the silver cradle that figures in the life of St. Elizabeth of Hungary. But if this object might be something of a "status-symbol," its use could also be regarded as a matter of life and death, as is clear from numerous injunctions of ecclesiastical authorities directed at keeping children out of the parental bed and thus avoiding the danger of "overlaying" and suffocation. In a series of such exhortations extending through the thirteenth century the English bishops strongly urged that children be kept in cradles at least until the age of three. Quite apart from its other implications, which will be more fully considered elsewhere, this legislation is suggestive regarding the sleeping arrangements of many parents and children in this period.

Babies who spent their days playing and sleeping and their nights demanding the attention of their mothers or nurses were doubtless no less trying, if less comprehensible, in this period than in later times, and the difficulties of soothing them might even encourage thoughts of demonic possession. But there are also clear signs, especially from the twelfth century onwards, of tenderness towards infants and small children, interest in the stages of their development, awareness of their need for love, and active responsiveness to that "beauty of infancy" which John of Lodi had earlier portrayed. Hildegard of Bingen, for example, explains at length, in terms favorable to the dignity of the species, why human infants are so slow to walk, compared with animals, and why they must crawl or creep on hands and feet before they walk. Several poets show us, though without noting its age at this momentous advance, the child taking its first steps, holding on to benches and stools, or standing by a table, being tempted by pieces of bread held just out of its reach; another writer pictures a child playing "peek-a-boo," covering its eyes and thinking no one sees it. There is also Caesarius of Heisterbach's story of the affectionate nun to whom Jesus appeared as a child of three, "just beginning to talk," and, regarding speech, Salimbene's well-known tale of the babies in Frederick II's experiment, who all died when cut off from human speech, "because they could not live without the petting and the joyful faces and loving words of their foster mothers, or without those "swaddling songs" which a woman sings to put a child to sleep and without which "it sleeps badly and has no rest." . . .

After birth and baptism, the best milk, the most careful nursing and, after weaning, sufficient food might, as we have seen, markedly improve the chances of survival and thus explain why, as David Herlihy puts it, "those blessed with the goods of this earth were also blessed (or burdened) with children; in contrast, the deprived, the heavily burdened, the poor left comparatively few heirs." If this is true, it is probably not because the poor produced fewer children, but because they could not support them. For they were most directly and constantly at the mercy of the chronic cycles of famine, malnutrition, disease and death, and their children were by far the most common victims of the parental negligence and despair, of the abandonment, exposure and even infanticide, which must be counted among major threats to young life in this period.

If all of these practices were related to the pressures, material and psychological, of a society living often at the limits of subsistence, they are related most specifically to the problem of population, or "family," control in a time when the means of limiting births were totally inadequate, if not, for practical purposes, virtually non-existent. That there were attempts at such control through contraception and abortion is evident from the records condemning these practices, as well as in works recommending the means by which they might be achieved. That they were largely ineffective is demonstrated by the incidence of other practices to which the records of this period also bear substantial testimony. The problem of infanticide in Western society during this period has only very recently become the subject of the serious investigation which will doubtless increase our knowledge of what, insofar as it was a secret sin, or crime, must in large measure lie beyond our closest scrutiny. As the case of Peter Damian's mother suggests, simple failure or refusal to nourish may well have been the most common form of infanticide. There is, in any case, considerable evidence, especially from the earlier medieval centuries, that wherever selective or neglective factors were at work, they were likely to work to the disadvantage of girls, who were not highly valued in a predominantly military and agricultural society, and even more drastically to the disadvantage not only of the illegitimate but of the physically deformed and mentally retarded, of those children who were regarded as "changelings," the works of another powerful enemy of children, the Devil. . . .

The Exiles: Perspectives on the Experience of Childhood in the Eleventh and Twelfth Centuries

Although Guibert of Nogent's relationship with his mother may seem in its intensity, as well as in the fullness of its portrayal, very much a special case, her qualities appear with significant frequency in other maternal portraits drawn or sketched in our sources. Like her, the noble mothers of these centuries are commonly depicted as the efficient administrators of their often extensive households, prudent yet generous and charitable to the poor, distinguished for their piety and their devotion to the physical and spiritual welfare of their children. All of these virtues, and others, were impressively displayed, according to his biographer, by the mother of St. Bernard of Clairvaux, who combined "gentleness with firmness" in the rearing of her seven children, six boys and one girl, all of whom ultimately entered the monastic life. "As soon as a child was born to her," we are told, "Aleth would offer it to the Lord with her own hands," and it was for this reason that, unlike many mothers of her class, she refused to allow her children to be nursed by anyone else; "for it almost seemed as though the babes were fed with the qualities of their mother's goodness as they drew the milk from her breast." By contrast with Guibert's mother, she offered her children, when they were older, only plain and simple fare, "never allowing them to acquire the taste and habit for elaborate and delicate dishes." As in her case and many others, an active concern for the education of their children was another prominent feature of the maternal portraits of our sources: the saintly Queen Margaret of Scotland, for example, was famous for having taught her children herself, as was Countess Ida of Boulogne, who had received some training in letters.

If we look for the realities behind this doubtless idealized image, Guibert's more penetrating observations concerning his mother's background and experience offer us some clues to the preparation of such women as these for the arduous responsibilities of marriage and motherhood. Illiterate, as he tells us, she had evidently received little or no education as a child, and this lack of concern for the education of daughters, unless they were destined for the monastic life, was probably more common among noble families in the eleventh century and before than it was thereafter. But even in this earlier period, a number of royal and noble ladies had learned at least enough Latin to read the Psalter, and a few of them were considerably further advanced in their learning. By the twelfth century the level of literacy was probably higher among women of the nobility than it was among their husbands and brothers, unless these last were monks or clerics. Illuminated Gospel books and Psalters were often prized possessions of such ladies, and their texts and illustrations were, it seems, a major channel through which the newer currents of piety circulated. We may assume, therefore, that the religious devotion of our mothers and their early instruction of their children had a growing basis in reality. Some of them may, in fact, have made use of the alphabet cards and similar teaching games and devices to which Peter Damian, among others, refers.

Whatever the extent of their education, early marriage was the destiny of those girls who did not enter the religious life, and in either case the choice was rarely theirs to make; the decision almost always lay with their parents, for whom practical considerations and advantages commonly outweighed the desires and feelings of their children. An unusual and illuminating instance of successful resistance to parental authority is the story of Christina of Markyate, a famous English recluse of the twelfth century, whose biographer paints a picture of contemporary parents much less favorable and perhaps more realistic than that offered by many of our sources. Although this girl had early shown marked signs of her spiritual vocation, conversing with God in her bed as a little child, and had later vowed herself to virginity, the determination of her rich and worldly parents to force her into a desirable marriage led to a long and often violent struggle in which she was finally victorious. In explaining why they were ready to stop at nothing, from bribes and threats to beating and imprisonment, to gain their end, her biographer makes it clear that, though she was "very dear" to them, they regarded her essentially as a valuable property and "feared losing her and all they could hope to gain through her."

Most parents were evidently more successful than Christina's in arranging the futures of their children and most girls were, like Guibert's mother, married off by their fathers to husbands not of their own choosing and often, as in her case, at an age when they were barely nubile, if not still children. According to canon law, the minimum ages at marriage were twelve for girls and fourteen for boys, and many, it seems, were married or at least betrothed below these ages, although a growing ecclesiastical opposition to child-marriage may have had some effect as a deterrent. So also, apparently, did the emphasis of canon lawyers on consent and "marital affection" as important, if not essential, elements in a valid marriage and even more perhaps, in the long run, an increasingly powerful effort to exalt the sanctity and sacramental character of Christian marriage. We need not assume that all marriages were as miserable as that of Guibert's parents seems to have been to suspect that, in the setting of feudal society, conjugal affection was more often a happy accident than a natural condition and that his mother's sexual and emotional inhibitions may have been shared by many women who came as frightened children to marriages in which physical brutality and rejection were evidently far from uncommon. Whatever the realities may have been, in theory and in law the husband's power and authority were supreme. Even in what his biographer regarded as the "model marriage" of St. Bernard's parents, not their mutual affection but his mother's submissiveness is emphasized; "in so far as a woman can and may who is submissive to her husband's authority and who does not even have rights over her own body, she anticipated her husband's every wish." That marriage was quite widely regarded by women of this period as a state to be endured rather than enjoyed is strongly suggested by the readiness, often the determination, of many of them, once widowed, to remain in that admirable condition, and by the alacrity with which many also, like Guibert's mother, turned to the consolations and securities of the religious life. . . .

Whatever the virtues and deficiencies of actual mothers may have been, there can be little doubt that, as in Guibert's case, maternal example and maternal values were dominant in the lives and ideals of those children of whose experience we have some knowledge. When Bernard of Clairvaux, for instance, was still living the life of a carefree and worldly youth, "the memory of his holy mother was always in his mind, so that he seemed to see her coming to him, reproaching and upbraiding him that she had not brought him up with such love and care that he could adopt this empty kind of existence." If by the standards of their time the success of these mothers was judged by the spiritual distinction of their children, we may consider remarkable, too, in view of contemporary prospects, the numbers of sons and daughters they succeeded in rearing to maturity. What is still more impressive, however, is the enduring devotion that some of them seem to have inspired. To this there is in the literature of this period no more eloquent testimony, not even Guibert's, than Peter the Venerable's epistolary portrait of his dead mother, in whose lovingly depicted life and character—she was not only saintly, compassionate and incessantly anxious for her children but "always happy and gay"—are reflected every facet of the contemporary maternal ideal.

By contrast with this emphasis on the maternal figure and her influence, fathers and their relations with their children assume a more modest and sometimes ambiguous place in our sources. If the father was not virtually absent from the child's early life, as he frequently was in a military and expansionist society, he is often depicted as the worldlier, less admirable figure, drawing the child away from his religious vocation, or more rarely, displaying the outright hostility that drove Anselm to renounce his patrimony and his native land and to find, at length, a more satisfactory father in Lanfranc at Bec. Among the records examined here, only briefly in Abelard's *Story of Calamities* and more fully in the life of St. Hugh of Lincoln is the early relationship of a father and son portrayed sympathetically and even in the latter there are distinct overtones of deprivation. For, "deprived of a mother's care" by her death, Hugh was barely eight years old when he and his father together entered a community of canons regular. As he himself later reported, in "talking confidentially" with his companions: "Truly, I never tasted the joys of this world. I never knew or learnt how to play." When Hugh was "learning to read," his father divided his patrimony by lot among his children, and gave the portion that fell to this youngest son to the community which he then entered by his father's choice. They evidently remained closely associated in their life there, and as his father grew old, Hugh devoted himself almost entirely to his care. According to his biographer, "he often used to relate with great pleasure how for the rest of his father's life, he used to lead him and carry him about, dress and undress him, wash him, dry him and make his bed, and, when he grew feebler and weaker, prepare his food and even feed him."

Although nearly all of the children with whom we are here concerned found their way eventually, like Hugh, into some form of the religious life, they did not all enter it so early or so involuntarily or by the same route. St. Anselm, for example, was perhaps twenty-seven when he became a monk at Bec, and Peter Damian was also in his twenties at the time of his conversion, as was Bernard of Clairvaux when he renounced the pleasures of the knightly life and eventually persuaded all of his brothers to do the same. Intended for a secular career, like many boys of whose childhood we know nothing, Ailred of Rievaulx, a priest's son, had served in his boyhood at the Scottish court before his conversion to the monastic life. But others, like Guibert, were much younger, often destined for this life from the outset and entering it as "oblates," children offered to monasteries by their parents, usually at an early age. It was such children as these who faced most acutely the separation and the exile poignantly recalled by Orderic Vitalis when as an old man he wrote . . . :

> And I, a mere boy, did not presume to oppose my father's wishes, but obeyed him in all things, for he promised me for his part that if I became a monk I should taste of the joys of Heaven with the Innocents after my death. . . . And so, a boy of ten, I crossed the English channel and came into Normandy as an exile, unknown to all, knowing no one.

When Orderic entered his Norman monastery in the late eleventh century, the practice of oblation was already on the wane, and its sharp decline during the next fifty years is yet another symptom of the transformations of this time. But for at least two centuries and perhaps longer, the offering of noble children by their parents had been a major, indeed, probably the principal means of monastic recruitment, and its history and the motives that inspired it are most revealing of the attitudes of parents as well as the experience of children during this period. Few aspects of this experience are, as Dom Knowles observes, more repellent to modern sensibility than the rearing of children "from infancy in the cloister, without home life, or the free society of other boys and girls, and without entry into many wide areas of innocent life." To us this custom may seem, in fact, the most distressing instance of child-rearing practices which, though diverse and variable over this long period, frequently involved, at least among the noble classes, the early separation of children from their parents and siblings. . . .

Entrusted to the care of masters, one of whom was to remain between every two boys wherever they went, they were always to sit apart from one another "in such a way as to prevent any physical contact, never making signs or speaking to anyone or rising from their places without the master's permission." In their relations with each other and with other monks they were not to hand anything to anyone or receive anything from anyone except the abbot, prior or masters and no one but these was ever to "make a sign to them or smile to them." None of the other monks was to enter their school or speak to them anywhere without the permission of the abbot or prior. In the dormitories, their beds were to be separated by those of their masters and often one of these was to keep watch throughout the night by the light of candles or lanterns; no child was ever to visit the lavatory or the latrine unaccompanied by a master. Since, as at least one custumal put it, "children everywhere need custody with discipline," the children were not only beaten in their school and elsewhere, but in their own chapter, as the older monks were.

Plainly intended, among other things, to prevent sexual activities among the children and the development of dangerous intimacies with their elders, this rigorous watchfulness reflected, and no doubt enhanced, fears that were evidently well founded. Testimony to the facts and fantasies of sexual temptations of every variety abounds in the monastic sources of this period, which also invite serious reflection on the impact of this environment on young minds exposed to no other experience. The omnipresence of the Devil and his minions, the lurid visions and nightmares that might haunt their over-charged imaginations, are vividly described by Guibert of Nogent, among many others, and with perhaps greater penetration by his older contemporary, Otloh of Saint-Emmeram. Seeking self-understanding through the recording of his temptations, dreams and hallucinations, this extraordinary monk dis-closes with particular clarity how deeply he had been affected by the experi-ences of his childhood and youth and especially by his fear of beating, which fostered his own later belief in the moderate discipline of the young, with words rather than with blows.

But no criticism of the abuses affecting children in monasteries is more revealing and significant than St. Anselm's admonition to a certain abbot who had complained to him of his difficulties in controlling the obstreperous boys in his charge, declaring that "we never give over beating them day and night, and they only get worse and worse." Even the barest summary of Anselm's remarkable answer may convey the import of an argument that not only underscores the weaknesses of a system, but offers an impressively positive statement of a new and more sympathetic approach to the rearing of children. Pointing to the destructive effects of the use of force and "injudicious oppression" upon the personalities of their young victims, Anselm declared that "feeling no love or pity, good-will or tenderness in your attitude towards them, they have in future no faith in your goodness but believe that all your actions proceed from hatred and malice against them; they have been brought up in no true charity towards anyone, so they regard everyone with suspicion and jealousy." Then he demanded, urging his benighted colleague to greater empathy, "Are they not human? Are they not flesh and blood like you? Would you like to have been treated as you treat them, and to have become what they are now?" Finally, stressing, as did Peter Damian and others, the importance of firm but gentle molding and shaping in the rearing of the young, he insisted that they must have "the encouragement and help of fatherly sympathy and gentleness" and that teaching and discipline should be adapted to the temperaments and capacities of individuals. . . .

Concern for the physical care and training of young children becomes more articulate and specific in a growing number of didactic works of the thirteenth century; such treatises, displaying often also some sense of the needs of children at different stages of development, point to ways in which, with increasing literacy among laymen, more favorable values and attitudes, as well as useful pediatric information, may have become more widely diffused, at least among the more prosperous classes. Despite the obvious limitations of these writings as mirrors of childhood realities, their popularity suggests a felt need for works offering guidance for parents, and while some of them reflect the clerical perspectives which have dominated this study, in others, more novel, parental views are directly stated.

Representing the churchman's approach, Bartholomew of England provides, in one of the earliest and most influential of popular encyclopedias, a precise description of the physical constitution, emotional qualities and habits of children, and conveys as well a now more articulate sense of early childhood as a carefree and playful stage of life. Little boys (*pueri*), he tells us, echoing a common though by no means universal opinion, are so called because of their "purity," since at this age the insufficient development of their organs makes them incapable of sexual activity and they are not ashamed of their nakedness. Despite their innocence, however, they are capable of guile and deceit, and so in need of discipline and teaching. Painting what will seem to many a fairly lifelike picture of small boys, he describes them as "living without thought or care, loving only to play, fearing no danger more than being beaten with a rod, always hungry and hence always disposed to various infirmities from being overfed, wanting everything they see, quick to laughter and as quick to tears, resisting their mothers' efforts to wash and comb them, and no sooner clean but dirty again." Little girls, in Bartholomew's hardly original view, are better disciplined, more careful, more modest and timid, and more graceful; because of the likeness of sex they are also, he thought, dearer to their mothers than boys.

Strongly urging the careful education of girls in reading and writing, Vincent of Beauvais maintained that these pursuits would keep them busy and thus distracted from "harmful and idle thoughts." They should, in his view, be trained in the "womanly arts" as well as in letters, and both boys and girls should be carefully instructed in the duties and responsibilities of marriage. As a theorist of education and an adviser in the rearing of the young, this most zealous of medieval encyclopedists was not particularly original, but he drew on traditional and contemporary learning in the development of ideas that display a genuine concern for the actual needs and capacities of children at different stages of early life. Like his contemporary, Master Aldobrandino of Siena, Vincent repeats with slight variations the Soranian precepts concerning the physical care of children, ideas now readily accessible in learned circles. In a suggested regime for the young child, he provides for frequent baths, at least two daily, careful feeding and ample playtime; to similar recommendations Aldobrandino adds the advice that the child should be given what he asks for and relieved of what displeases him. When at six the child begins school, he should be taught slowly and without forcing, being allowed plenty of time for sleep and for diversion. With others among his fellow-clerics, Vincent of Beauvais advocates a moderation in instruction and discipline in which we may perceive the significant assimilation and diffusion of ideas expressed by St. Anselm and his contemporaries a century and a half earlier. Teaching without beating is the ideal commonly stated, although Vincent suggests that in the matter of discipline distinctions should be made between those children for whom physical coercion is unnecessary and disastrous and others whose temperaments seem to require it; even in this case discipline should never be sudden and unpremeditated but should spring from motives of love and foresight rather than a mistaken sense of kindness. It is this attitude and this conception of the child's sensitive nature that were poetically summed up, around 1200, by Walther von der Vogelweide:

> "Children won't do what they ought
> If you beat them with a rod.
> Children thrive, children grow
> When taught by words, and not a blow. . . .
> Evil words, words unkind
> Will do harm to a child's mind."

In some ways less enlightened are several works representing a paternal view of child-rearing, which may in their stress on the importance of discipline and correction provide a closer reflection of the actual practice of parents. For the elderly Philip of Novara, the infant and small child possesses three great gifts: he loves and recognizes the person who nurses him, he expresses pleasure and affection for those who play with him, and he inspires a natural love and sympathy in those who rear him. Like the great Jewish philosopher, Moses Maimonides, in the preceding century, this father believed that parental love increases as children grow older, but he cautioned strongly against the excessive and indulgent display of affection, which may encourage children to be bolder in their naughtiness. They should not be permitted to do everything they wish, but should be firmly corrected while they are young, first with words, then if necessary, by beating, and as a last resort by "imprisonment." Parents and their surrogates should, he advised, be especially watchful for early signs of tendencies to such vices as theft, violence and blasphemy which may lead the child to a bad end. . . .

Some Concluding Reflections

If a central issue of this history, abstractly viewed, has been the enduring conflict between destructive or rejecting and fostering attitudes, this issue was stated with extraordinary, almost prophetic clarity in John of Lodi's story of Peter Damian's early years. Throughout our period and beyond, it is true, the power of destructive forces may seem little diminished. Certainly, the fundamental menace of infant and maternal mortality continued, apparently unabated; here there was to be little substantial progress before the early years of our own century. The neglect, exploitation and abandonment of children continued also, but these practices were now more widely and consciously opposed and in efforts at control or suppression, however immeasurable their effects, may be discerned clear signs of the awakening consciences and sensibilities of this time. The idea of the child as the possession and property of its parents continued to dominate parental attitudes and actions in these, as in earlier and later centuries. But the dangers inherent in this conception had achieved wider recognition and the salutary intervention of external authorities had made some modest advances. The proprietary notion had also been joined by more favorable conceptions, by a sense of the child as a being in its own right, as a nature of "potential greatness," and by a sense of childhood as a distinctive and formative stage of life. That churchmen should have been pre-eminently active in the diffusion of more humane attitudes and ideas is, given the character of medieval society, hardly surprising. Nor is the fact that attempts to translate law and precept into practice were in this sphere, as in many others, faltering and often ineffective. The fostering role of churchmen as pastors and preachers, reformers and surrogates, has been noted in this study, but it deserves more coherent and critical attention, in the setting of contemporary spiritual and religious movements, than it could be given here.

Clearly, as the cases of Anselm and Hugh of Lincoln suggest, in many matters affecting the lives of children the example and influence of a few great figures may have counted for a good deal, not least in giving powerful expression to the new impulses and currents of feeling whose growing strength is displayed in numerous works of this period, among them the two with which we began. In Guibert of Nogent's recollections of his early life, a new awareness is written large; and if he offers us our fullest insight into the realities of childhood during these centuries, he also draws us most deeply into that world of ambivalence and wishful thinking which encompasses the relations of parents and children, introducing us to what appear to have been, in both fact and fantasy, certain dominant experiences of many children in this time. Among the many great changes that emerged during the century and more spanned by the lifetimes of Peter Damian and Guibert, none was more profound than the slow transformation in modes of consciousness and expression with which the relationships and experiences of childhood were inextricably bound up. Tenderness, compassion, the capacity to comprehend the needs and emotions of others: these are fragile and late-maturing plants of feeling and they flowered slowly in the hard and sometimes violent lives of this period, especially in the lives of parents who were themselves often literally, as well as emotionally, little more than children. Yet it is in this realm of feeling that the most deeply rooted and fruitful developments of our centuries are likely to be found.

Traveling the Roads
in the Twelfth Century

URBAN T. HOLMES, JR.

The importance of roads in Western history has varied. The Greeks seem to have done the bulk of their traveling by ship, and they planted their colonies along the shores of the Mediterranean. Road systems connected these cities with their hinterlands, but none of the networks was very extensive or impressive. Conversely, the Romans made the road a central part of their transportation and communication systems, and their roads are justly famous for their engineering. But the Roman road was designed for the specific purpose of military communications and movement, and it went straight to its goal without regard for the convenience of travelers. The military engineers paid no attention to the needs of commerce and built narrow roads that were often ill suited for carts or even pack animals. Often the Roman roads ran precipitously over ridges and mountains instead of following the valleys and winding over the plains. The roads, however, were well built: Over a foundation of large stones went one or more layers of gravel topped by large paving stones. A large supply of slave labor was needed to repair the cracking and settling that was common in the rigid pavement. By the Middle Ages, lack of care and theft of the paving blocks for roadside construction had stripped the Roman highways to their foundations. Yet, even in this condition, many Roman roads became the basis for medieval and modern ones; the Roman foundations are still there under the asphalt.

In Roman times, there were severe restrictions on land transport that had nothing to do with the character of the roads. Until the ninth century, draft animals were unshod and could not travel long distances without damaging their hooves. The weakness of horses' feet virtually eliminated them from any serious use and thus deprived the Romans and their German successors of potentially their best animal power. At the same time, the collars used in pre–ninth-century harnesses severely limited the weight of loads. If an animal pulled much more than its own weight, the soft collar would constrict its windpipe and choke it. When the rigid collar was introduced in Carolingian times, it became possible for animals to haul very large loads even though there were few roads and not enough of an economy to make use of the new technology.

That traveling any distance by road in the Middle Ages was a formidable feat is proven by the comments of men who did it. As one tenth-century traveler remarked of his journey from the Greek city of Lepanto to Constantinople (with some exaggeration perhaps), "On mule-back, on

foot, on horseback, fasting, suffering from thirst, sighing, weeping, la-
menting, I arrived after forty-nine days." No wonder the chief means of
transport in medieval Europe was the river system, which, while often
indirect and difficult, was easily maintained and permitted the shipping
of heavy and bulky loads.

By the thirteenth century, however, the road had again become a
major avenue of commerce and communication in Europe. An English
law of 1285 indicates the importance of the road system: It required the
clearing of trees, large rocks, and other possible hiding places for robbers
to a distance of 200 feet on either side of the country's main roads.

The roads of the Middle Ages were considerably different from the
ancient Roman roads. On the whole, medieval roads followed foot and
animal paths that had been worn between the fields. Since these roads
led from village to village, they were a boon to the commercial traveler,
who was thus provided with easy access to the region's markets. At the
same time, many of the remains of Roman roads were controlled by
feudal lords who demanded tolls. The traveler could keep costs down by
avoiding these highways. This economy was important not only to the
merchants but also to the many noncommercial travelers who used the
roads from the twelfth century on.

One of the scholars who regularly traveled from one school to another in the late twelfth century has left an account of his experiences.
Urban T. Holmes used the account of Alexander Neckam (1157–1217) as
the basis for a description of the trip from southern England to Paris.
Alexander made the journey in 1177, and his experiences were typical of
those encountered by most people who traveled to the famous schools
of Paris in this period.

The trip to London was an easy one along the somewhat battered Roman
pavement of Watling Street. A traveler who rode seriously could average some
thirty-five miles a day, making six miles an hour on his horse or mule. He
would mount in the morning at six-thirty or seven, modern time, and would
ride until the dinner hour at eleven. Usually he rested immediately after this
meal. It would be nearly three o'clock, after relevée, before the traveler would
once more mount his steed, and this time he would continue till nearly six
o'clock. In the time-reckoning of the twelfth century we would say that the
rider began his journey at basse prime, or at break of day, and went on till
dinner at haute tierce. After relevée he continued till Vespers.

Alexander was a cleric in lesser orders, or perhaps he had only the simple
tonsure. We will assume that his mount was a mule, borrowed for the occa-

From *Daily Living in the Twelfth Century* by Urban T. Holmes, Jr., pp. 19–25. Copyright
1952 by the University of Wisconsin Press. Reprinted by permission of the University
of Wisconsin Press.

sion, to be left at the Augustinian priory of St. Bartholomew's in Smithfield, London. The harness worn by such an animal was not unlike what we know today. The headstall was of cloth strips, or perhaps of leather. Like modern harness, the chin strap of this headpiece was slipped under the animal's chin and the metal bit was placed in his mouth. The upper strap looped over the ears. But, unlike what we see today, the headband continued around the head and was tied in the rear with long loose ends. Alexander describes the harness of a palfrey or mule, but his language is not very specific:

> Let the horse's back be covered with a canvas, afterwards with a sweat pad or cloth; next let a saddle be properly placed with the fringes of the sweat cloth hanging over the crupper. The stirrups should hang well. The saddle has a front bow or pommel and a cantle. . . . Folded clothing may be well placed in a saddlebag behind the cantle. A breast strap and the trappings for the use of someone riding should not be forgotten: halter and headstall, bit covered with bloody foam, reins, girths, buckles, cushion, padding . . . which I intentionally pass over. An attendant should carry a currycomb.

We can do better than this, at eight hundred years' distance, by describing what we find in illuminations and sculptures of the time. The bit was always single, but double reins were attached to it. A *culière*, or crupper, passed under the horse's tail and fastened to the cantle of the saddle. The traveling pack was tied onto this. Over the seat of the saddle a third cloth was usually draped. This was called the *baudré*, and we are told that it was often a rich brown material, well embroidered. It could be very long, almost touching the ground. The bows of the saddle were of wood and, more often than not, were ornamented with plates of ivory, hammered metal, or elaborately painted leather. Supposedly such decoration should be added after purchase from the saddler, but John of Garland mentions the sale of painted saddles. Precious stones could be soldered onto the surface of the pommel and cantle, producing, in our modern eyes, a very tawdry effect. Alexander refers to buckles on the saddle girths, usually two. In the illuminated Bible page of the Morgan Library, the girths of Absalom's saddle seem to have hard knots at the end which slip into openings on the two straps hanging down from under the right side of the saddle. In brief, metal buckles existed, but it is evident that they were expensive enough to be avoided when possible. Metal pendants or little bells jangled from the *peitrel*, or breast strap, of the mount. Women had a sidesaddle (*sambue*), but whether they used it invariably is not clear.

Alexander lists also the clothing that was best worn by a traveler:

> Let one who is about to ride have a *chape* with sleeves, of which the hood will not mind the weather, and let him have boots, and spurs that he may prevent the horse from stumbling, jolting, turning, rearing, resisting, and

may make him *bein amblant*, "possessed of a good gait," and easily manageable. Shoes should be well fastened with iron nails.

Most of the traveling at this date was done at a good walk. There are excellent examples of the twelfth-century spur in both Cluny and the British Museum. It had a single prong or prick, which could give the horse quite a wound if improperly used. The heavy shoe worn by a traveler might have a high top of soft leather, when it was called a boot (*heuse* or *ocrea*). This is the type of footwear which Alexander has in mind. A peasant, however, might wear a heavy shoe of undressed leather (*revelins*) and drape his legs in baggy cloth which he would then bandage on with leather thongs. This arrangement also could be referred to as *ocreas*. Men of all classes often wrapped their legs with spiral puttees, which are visible to us in hunting scenes or on the legs of knights. As a clerk in minor orders Alexander would have worn dark clothing, perhaps black, and his hair was cut shorter than was customary among the laity. It was nonetheless a little shaggy about the neck and ears. A simple tonsure, or small shaven spot, was visible on the crown of his head. His face was more or less clean shaven. He could have worn a peaked felt hat, with a very narrow rolled brim, but it is not likely that he did. We will picture him as bareheaded.

Although Alexander was traveling without a retinue, he must have made chance acquaintances along the road. When traveling on a walking mule there was ample time for companionship. For our story's sake we will assume that Alexander fell in with a Scot who likewise was on his way to London town. This man, like all his countrymen, wore "Scottish dress and had the manner of the Scot." He frequently shook his "staff as they shake the weapon which they call a *gaveloc* at those who mock them, shouting threatening words in the manner of the Scots." Alexander "closely examined his clothes and boots . . . and even the old shoes which he carried on his shoulders in the Scottish manner." We should like some details on these Scottish peculiarities of dress and manner, but Jocelin of Brakeland, whom we are quoting, gives nothing further. Englishmen were considered "cold of disposition" inwardly.

As the two rode along they would be joined by others, and they would continue conversing in the "common language" of England, the Anglo-Norman dialect of French. This tongue was careless in its use of cases, and cultivated speakers were ashamed of this laxity; they yearned to improve their speech by a sojourn on the Continent. Like most members of the clerical class, Alexander lapsed freely into Latin when he had complicated thoughts to express. Years of habit in the schools had brought this about. But the Norman speech was his mother tongue and he enjoyed speaking it with the "simple gent," and on occasion with brother clerics. Living in England as he did, Alexander could understand a little English, but the memories of it which remained from childhood, when he spoke it with his nurse and the kitchen knaves, had grown rusty. A few common words such as *welcomme* and *drinkhail* were used by everyone, often for comic effect. Alexander could barely understand the Scottish phrases and oaths with which the Scottish traveler frequently salted his remarks.

It was customary to travel in company for two reasons. First, there was the matter of protection from wild beasts and bad men. Both of these annoyances sometimes appeared out of the woods, which came down to the very edge of the road. The region to the north of London was rather heavily forested. A second reason was one of pride. Much importance was placed on external appearances. One of the greatest compliments that could be paid was to say that a man looked *fier*. This meant that he looked every inch a man of quality. A person traveling by himself did not attract much attention, and his dignity could be slighted. We assume, therefore, that as Alexander rode along Watling Street he drew together with other voyagers.

On such an occasion it was customary to sing. "He came sitting on his horse, a song echoing to his voice; in the manner of travelers he thus shortened his journey." If the company were friendly enough, they might exchange tales. The common types of song were the *virelai*, the *rondeau*, and the *rotrouenge*. Such verse forms had considerable repetition of melody and lines, which made it possible for all to join in. The *virelai* ran *AbbaA*, capital letters indicating repeated words or refrain. The *rondeau* had the form *ABaAabAB*. The repetition in the *rondeau* was so considerable that it lent itself admirably to group participation. The English members of Alexander's traveling party probably thought of singing in unison, but the Scotsman, if we are to believe Giraldus, would break forth into a free separate part in his quavering treble. Alexander, like Giraldus, would be astonished at the ease with which those who dwelt north of the Humber could chime in with a free organum, or second moving part. They learned to do this as children. If there had been Welshmen in the company, they would have added a third, and even a fourth part, but we will not burden our company with all those Celts. Welsh music was frequently not pleasant to English ears.

Alexander's mule sometimes had to pick its way carefully over the worn Roman pavement, which was in frightful repair. Too often a neighboring farmer would have removed a few flat paving stones to build him a wall or the corner of his house. This kind of theft left a layer of rubble which was hard on an animal's feet. An occasional hole was deep enough to cause a broken neck. Along this road to London were scattered clearings, and a village or two. Groups of detached houses, usually of wood (unpainted), and rarely of small stones cemented together, stood along the road. Farmyards were seldom, if ever, contiguous to the houses. These yards were detached enclosures, walled with pales or tall wooden stakes, squared and sharpened at the top. Briars or other thorn branches were intertwined over the entire surface of such a fencing, to keep out intruders. The yards were built sufficiently near to the house to allow the tenant to hear any disturbance among his chickens or his cattle. The houses themselves consisted of little more than a doorway and one window. The roof was thatched with straw or reeds. A large wooden shutter, hinged at the top, perhaps with leather thongs, was held open by a stick placed between it and the sill. Because of the constant wear of feet, each house was apt to have a depression in the unpaved ground before its door. This was too often filled with stagnant water. Houses such as these were occupied by villeins and bordars (serfs). Well-to-do peasant farmers would occupy manor houses of a kind set farther back from the highway.

The Workday of a Bishop

From *THE REGISTER OF EUDES OF ROUEN*

The Operation of a Monastery

From *THE CHRONICLE OF JOCELIN OF BRAKELOND*

The Church of the Middle Ages grew slowly during the first millennium of Christian Europe. The Apostles spread out through the Roman Empire, establishing Christian communities in its great cities. At the end of the third century, the successors of the Apostles, the bishops, emerged as the rulers of the Christian communities, patterning their government of the Church on the imperial system established by the Roman emperor Diocletian. The diocese and its bishop became the basic unit of ecclesiastical organization. From the reign of Constantine on, the great decisions concerning the life of the Church—the definition of its faith and the establishment of its discipline—were made in general councils of bishops.

The centers of episcopal power were in the cities. Only very slowly did Christian preachers penetrate the countryside, where the conservative peasant population held to its pagan religion. Each bishop had a *familia*, a group of helpers who gradually formed the clerical orders of the Church and who administered the diocese under the bishop's direction. The *familia* lived with the bishop in the city, but as the Church made progress in rural areas, the *familia* divided into two groups. One group continued to help the bishop in the diocesan administration, while the other spent more and more of its time in the outlying areas, preaching and ministering to the peasants. This arrangement might have persisted if the development of feudalism had not taken place. In the chaos created by the breakdown of the Carolingian government and the Viking invasions, feudal lords saw in the Church a tool for controlling their territories and extracting from them all the financial resources they possessed. By building churches in their villages, lords could use the Church's ancient tithing powers to their own advantage. They appointed their own men to these "proprietary churches" and paid them a pittance out of funds produced by the ecclesiastical taxes, while retaining most of the wealth themselves. Ecclesiastical ordination was a mere technicality in the appointment of village priests.

This system of private churches, the basis of the parish church system that still exists, strengthened the hold of Christianity on the peasants, but it also created a corrupt and incompetent clergy. Feudal lords were not interested in providing well-trained and honest pastors for their churches, and although the parishes were ostensibly subject to the bishops, the bishops themselves were the appointees of great lords and kings. By the eleventh century, the use of the Church by secular rulers had brought the hierarchy to one of the lowest points in its history. This situation in turn produced one of the Church's most powerful reform movements, the Gregorian reform of the eleventh century. Under the direction of the papacy, which itself had been rescued from secular control, the reformers were to turn the elaborate system of churches and bishoprics to the cause of religion. In the twelfth and thirteenth centuries, churchmen still played an important role in the political life of the secular kingdoms, but they also spent considerable time fulfilling their role as pastors.

The register of Archbishop Eudes of Rouen is a monument to the figure of the bishop as pastor. Rouen was one of the greatest dioceses of Europe, the primatial see of Normandy. Eudes, bishop from 1242 to 1267, was a conscientious administrator, and in his register we can see the pattern and character of his activities. He traveled constantly to check up on his clergy, and he seems to have had periodic obsessions with certain aspects of clerical misbehavior—concubinage, gluttony, drunkenness. From his record, it is clear that although Eudes held a spiritual office, he was an effective ruler of the community contained within his diocese. There was also a secular ruler, and one of the most interesting questions raised by the register is how the roles of the secular and ecclesiastical rulers were distinguished in the day-to-day life of the community.

The second of the two selections presented here comes from the other major sector of the Church, the monastic orders. The earliest monks were desert-dwelling anchorites in Egypt and Syria. By the middle of the third century, there were hundreds, perhaps thousands, of such men, many of whom were not even Christian. The increasingly burdensome obligations placed on city-dwellers by the Roman government drove men of all creeds away from their homes. Cenobitic—that is, communal—monasticism first arose in Egypt during the third century, when the monk Pachomius formed a community of monks on an island in the Nile. He wrote down the monastic traditions of the anchorites as a guide for his monks. From the beginning, the ideals of these communities consisted in helping men achieve an easier path to God through withdrawal, asceticism, and prayer. Pachomius and his successors tempered the extreme asceticism practiced by some of the most famous anchorites—such as Macrobius and Simon Stylites—and instead aimed at a moderate standard to which all might aspire.

Withdrawal, prayer, and asceticism continued to be the aims of monastic life when it was transported to the West. Romans, including members of the ecclesiastical hierarchy, did not immediately accept the monastic ideals; but gradually the monks brought western Europeans to understand and sympathize with their spiritual program, and by the sixth century monasticism was well established in the western part of the empire. In the first part of the sixth century, St. Benedict of Nursia (490–540) wrote his rules for monastic communities, the end product of the development begun by Pachomius and the basis of Western monasticism since that time. Benedict stressed an orderly pattern of prayer, manual labor, poverty, and withdrawal and created a community based on humility and paternalistic authority. His simple constitution is one of the great communal plans in Western history.

The Benedictines, as followers of Benedict's rule are called, began almost immediately to attract attention. Under the auspices of Pope Gregory the Great (590–604), the Benedictines spread through Europe. Although time and growth changed and sometimes corrupted Benedictinism, the movement produced periodic reform groups that revitalized its ideals and gave it new life. The monks had a varied and profound effect on European society. Some withdrew to wild areas and became expert and progressive farmers who significantly improved Europe's agricultural technique. Others built great churches and advanced the art of building. They patronized art and developed a rich musical tradition to go along with their liturgical activities. They preserved the Latin classics for posterity and produced a prodigious literature of their own to which all Western literature owes a great debt. And they attracted to their ranks some of the most forceful and brilliant men in their society. For a long time, the monasteries were the seat of Europe's intellectual and administrative talent, and when the general reform movement began, in the eleventh and twelfth centuries, the monasteries furnished the men who led it.

Thus the monks withdrew from the world only to find that the world had come with them. The regular round of prayer and fasts became only the background pattern of a communal life focused on the monastery's responsible position in the world. The monks found that wealth and power were two of the results of their holiness.

The monastic chronicle—"diary" might be a more accurate term—written by the monk Jocelin of Brakelond reflects the focus of monastic life in a great congregation. Jocelin was a member of Bury St. Edmund's in England, and he presents a picture of life in the great monastery at the juncture of the twelfth and thirteenth centuries. He portrays a highly organized community complete with internal struggles and complex relations with its abbot on the one hand and the king on the other. Jocelin's eye is keen and his judgment good. His chronicle fills a large gap in our knowledge of monastic life in the Middle Ages.

THE WORKDAY OF A BISHOP

1249

June 30. We visited the deanery of Meulan at Chars. We found that the priest at Courdimanche has occasionally celebrated Mass though he is under suspension and that he has kept a concubine; he rides horseback dressed in a short mantle, and he runs about too much. Item, the priest at Courcelles does not keep residence well nor is he in the habit of wearing his gown. Item, the priest at Hérouville only rarely wears a gown. Item, the priest at Valmondois sells his services; he is noted for having money, is contentious, and is given to drinking. Item, the priest at Vaux is a trader and had, and still has, a certain vineyard which he holds as security from a certain wastrel to whom he has loaned his too precious coins; he does not say his Hours well and sometimes he comes to Mass straight from his bed. Item, the priest at Chars is ill famed of a certain widow; he runs about too much. Item, the priest at Courcelles does not keep residence well, nor does he wear a gown. Item, the priest at Longuesse is ill famed of Eugénie, his parishioner, and has had children by her; he promised us that if he should be ill famed of these matters again he would regard his church as resigned.

We spent the night at Sérans, at our own expense.

July 1. We visited the priory at Parnes.

July 2. At Parnes. We visited the priory and received our procuration from it. They have but one chalice and one missal. They do not confess every month as required by the Statutes of Pope Gregory; we enjoined them to confess as the said Statutes require. They have an income of two hundred pounds; they owe about fifteen pounds. They use meat; we prohibited the eating of meat altogether, saving as the Rule permits. They use feather beds; we forbade the use of these, except in cases of necessity.

This day we visited the deanery of Magny, at Magny. We found that the priest at Lainville is a drunkard and incontinent. Item, the prior of Magny is grievously ill famed of a certain woman who is known as "The Mistress" and of the wife of a knight at Etres. The priest at Magny is ill famed of drinking too much, especially with laymen, and of incontinence, and about a year ago he begot a child because of it. Item, the priest at Genainville is ill famed of drunkenness and is useless to his church. The priest at Lierville does not attend the synods. Item, the priest at St. Clair is publicly known for drinking too much at the tavern. We warned them.

This day we visited the priory at Magny. There are three canons there, and they have made profession in their order. They do not observe the fasts of the Rule very well. They receive money for clothing. They have an income of eighty pounds and are in debt up to eighty pounds. The prior is publicly known for incontinence, as we have already been informed by several priests during our visitation of the deanery of Magny. This day we visited the priory at Magny; there were three canons there. They do not observe the fasts of the Rule; they have money to buy clothes. They have an income of eighty pounds of Paris; they owe about eighty pounds.

From *The Register of Eudes of Rouen*, edited by J. F. O'Sullivan, translated by S. M. Brown (New York: Columbia University Press, 1964), pp. 43–46, 292–95, 514–16. Reprinted by permission of Columbia University Press.

From the prior of Magny, whom we found grievously ill famed of incontinence, we have a letter stating that if any further ill fame should arise against him and is supported by the truth, or is of such a nature that he cannot purge himself, he will regard his priorate as resigned by that very fact. And this he swore to us. Item, he also swore to set out for Rome before the octave of the Assumption of the Blessed Virgin and to bring us a letter from any one of the Lord Pope's penitentiaries which made mention of this matter, and furthermore, neither to remain in the said priory nor to return to it until recalled by us.

July 3.   We visited the priory of Notre-Dame-de-Chaumont. Only two monks are there, and there should be three. They do not confess every month as the Statutes of Pope Gregory require. They have no written copy of their Rule, nor a copy of the Statutes. They do not hold chapter, nor do they receive the minor penances. They do not keep the fasts of the Rule; they eat meat when it is not necessary. They use feather beds, though we had warned them about this before. Instead this time, and in the presence of their own abbot of St-Germer, we enjoined them with firmness to correct their deficiencies. They have an income of one hundred pounds; they owe about thirty pounds.

July 4.   We visited the priory at Liancourt. Three monks are there. They have an income of one hundred twenty pounds; they owe seventy pounds of Paris. We found some things amiss, to wit, that they eat meat and use feather beds though we had prohibited these things before. This time we forbade them more severely. They owe us a procuration fee of only four pounds of Paris.

July 5.   We visited the monastery of St-Martin-de-Pontoise, where there are twenty-five monks. They have nine priories, and two monks are in each. On Sundays, women and laymen enter the cloister, marching in procession; we forbade them to enter henceforth. They owe pensions up to sixteen pounds of Paris. They have the patronage of thirty churches. In the outside priories they eat meat at any time. We enjoined them to abstain from the eating of meat, save as the Rule permits. They owe about twelve hundred pounds; they have an income of one thousand pounds. We spent the night there and received our procuration. . . .

1256

October 22.   We visited the chapter of St.-Sépulcre-de-Caen. One dignitary is there, that is to say, the dean. There is as yet no certain number of canons. Luke, called Capet, runs about the town disgracefully and gets intoxicated very easily; but then he is weak in the head. Total for procuration: nine pounds, fourteen shillings, six pence.

October 23. We visited the monastery of nuns at La-Trinité-de-Caen. The abbess was in England at the time. We found seventy-two nuns there. One does not accuse another [in chapter]. The rule of silence is not well observed; we enjoined them to correct this. They take three vows at the time of their being blessed; to wit, the vows of obedience, chastity, and poverty, but no other vow. The young nuns keep larks, and at the feast of the Innocents they sing their Office with farcical improvisations; we forbade this. They have paid three hundred fifty marks to the Roman Curia. About as much is owing to them as they owe. Total for procuration: seven pounds, six shillings, four pence.

October 24. We visited the abbey of St-Étienne-de-Caen, where there are sixty-three monks. All but three are priests. In one of the priories there are rabbit dogs; we forbade the monks who are staying there to become hunters. There are some who do not confess every month; we enjoined them to correct this. It used to be their practice that all those ministering [to the celebrants] at all Masses, save those [Masses] for the dead, received Communion, but this practice, through negligence, has gradually been abandoned; we enjoined the abbot and prior to have this custom more fully observed by all. The cloister is badly kept; we enjoined them to correct this. Traveling monks do not observe the fasts of the Rule; we enjoined them to correct this. In the priories they do not observe the fasts of the Rule and they eat meat freely; we enjoined them to correct this. They owe fifteen hundred pounds, but about as much is owed to them; they have an income of four thousand pounds. Total for procuration: seven pounds, ten shillings, ten pence.

October 25. We visited the Maison-Dieu at Caen. Seven canons are there. The prior was not there. The brethren receive Communion and confess twice a year, to wit, at Advent and at Lent. They have an income of one thousand pounds and another five hundred for daily alms; they owe two hundred pounds, and they have their annate money on hand.

This day we spent the night at Troarn, at our own expense.

October 26. We visited there, finding forty monks. All but six are priests. Those who are not priests receive Communion every Sunday. Traveling monks do not observe the fasts of the Rule. In the priories they do not observe the fasts of the Rule, and they eat meat freely; we enjoined them to correct this. They owe about four hundred pounds; they have an income of about three thousand pounds. Total for procuration: eight pounds, twelve shillings, eight pence.

When we were visiting in the diocese of Bayeux, we warned Brother Henry, prior of Cahagnes, of the diocese of Bayeux, to receive us for visitation and procuration, but he refused to do this, stating that he was not under obligation to do so, and alleged in justification that, in his time, the bishop of Bayeux had never visited him, nor had he ever received procuration there from him nor, as far as he knew, from any of his predecessors. However, the prior swore to abide by our decision in this matter, and we, after diligent investigation, discovered that the bishop of Bayeux had visited there many times and had received procuration. This being the case, we peremptorily cited the said prior to appear before us at Troarn on the Thursday before All Saints to hear our judgment, and the said prior having come before us at the said time and place, we gave orders that the prior and his successors should be obliged to receive us there for visitation and procuration. We ordered the prior to pay us a fine for having given us offense by unjustly refusing to receive us on the aforementioned business. Present were: Peter, archdeacon of Grand-Caux; Richard of Sap, canon of Rouen; the prior of Ste-Barbe; Hugh, rector at Foucescalier; Reginald, rector at Giverny; Morel of Us; Robert Scansore; . . . [lacuna in MS], the abbot of Troarn; and many others. Thereupon, and at the said time and place, the said prior recognized that he was obligated to the foregoing and to the payment of full procuration if we should desire to exact it. He agreed to pay whatever fine we should desire for the offense shown to us. However, we forbore to exact this penalty until such time as we should think best. Present were the aforesaid archdeacon, Richard; William, the prior of Troarn; Brother Harduin of the Friars Minor, and Morel and Robert, our abovementioned clerks. The said prior, before the aforementioned witnesses, swore that he would pay the said fine to us, whenever we should ask him to do so.

October 27. At Pont-l'Évêque, at our expense. October 28. At Pont-Audemer. October 29. At Bourg-Achard. October 30. At Déville. October 31. At Rouen. November 1. At Rouen. We celebrated the feast of All Saints. November 2–5. At Déville. November 6. We held the sacred synod at Rouen, and spent the night at St-Matthieu. November 7–8. At Rouen. November 9. At Frênes. November 10. At St-Germer-de-Flay. November 11. At Bulles. November 12. At Gournay-sur-Aronde. November 13–23. At Noyon, on the business of the inquest held on the body of St. Eloi. November 24. At Verberie. November 25. At Louvres, in the diocese of Paris. November 26–28. At Pontoise. November 29. We received procuration at Gasny. Total for procuration: one hundred nine shillings, three pence. . . .

1262

January 26. With God's grace we visited the priory at Bures. There was a certain monk from Pré, near Rouen, there, not as prior, but acting as a custodian for the prior of Pré. He holds the administration at the prior's pleasure. There should be at least two monks there. We did find two who had arrived with the said custodian, to convalesce, and with the prior's permission. They used feather beds and ate meat when there was no need, nor did they observe the fasts of the Rule very well. They owed nothing, nor was anything owed to them, since the prior of Pré collected everything and kept what remained after paying for the sustenance of the monks and the household. We received procuration there this day. Total: . . . [*lacuna in MS*].

January 27.   We visited the house at Nogent, near Neufchâtel, and spent the night at Neufchâtel, where the lessee of the abovementioned house gave us procuration. Total for procuration: eleven pounds, nine shillings, five pence.

This day we visited the local Hôtel-Dieu, or hospital, where were two canons with their prior. One of them, to wit, Hugh, called Dominus, was useless and broken down by age, wherefore we were pleased to order him [the prior] to receive into the hospital and give the habit to two suitable men as soon as possible; he [the prior] should receive Communion at least once a month. There were three lay brothers and six lay sisters there. The prior has the cure of all those in residence. They have an income of two hundred pounds and more; they owed fifty pounds; more than one hundred pounds was owed to them. With the exception of wine, they had sufficient provisions to last out the year.

January 28.   To wit, Septuagesima Sunday. With God's grace we celebrated Mass and preached at St. Mary's church at Neufchâtel. We spent the night at Mortemer-sur-Eaulne, where we received procuration from the lessee of the local house or priory. Total for procuration: thirteen pounds, eleven shillings.

January 29.   We visited the said house, where there were two monks from Lewes. They receive twenty shillings of Tours every week for their sustenance from Master Eudes of St-Denis, who holds the said house for life.

This day we spent the night at Aumale, at our own expense.

January 30.   With God's grace we visited the abbey of this said place. Nineteen monks were in residence; three were in England. All but four were priests. One did not accuse another [in chapter]. Four lay brothers were there; we ordered the abbot to urge them to make frequent confession and to see that they confessed and received Communion four to six times a year. Silence was badly observed; we ordered this corrected. Item, we gave orders that lay folk be kept out of the cloister and that some monk be appointed to guard the cloister gate so that women and laymen could not have free access as they had had up to this time. Item, we expressly forbade anyone to remain away from Compline or to drink after Compline. Item, we ordered them to dismiss their present baker and to secure someone else who would be more upright and suitable. Item, we ordered the abbot to inspect and take away all keys of coffers and boxes of the monks before Ash Wednesday, lest they should be in the possession of any property. He had been negligent in this matter. Item, we ordered them to have the income written down in registers. They owed five hundred pounds; they had sufficient provisions for the year, and at present some eighty pounds from last year's wool was still owed to them. We advised them to increase both their alms donations and the number of their monks, if they could do so. The abbot's sister sometimes dined with him at the abbey, a thing which displeased us. We forbade him to invite her in the future. He may invite his brother-in-law without his wife. Item, we expressly forbade him, as well as all the monks of the place, and as we had done before, to allow any secular clerics, priests, or laymen to dine in the refectory as had been the custom. Item, we enjoined the monks to obey their abbot in all legitimate and proper things as they were bound to do, or that otherwise we would severely punish those whom we should find guilty of disobedience. Item, Ralph of St-Valery was suspected of owning property; we ordered the abbot to have a careful investigation made into the truth of this, and then to take such action as seemed fitting under the Rule. Item, we found that Enguerrand, the prior, was defamed and that an evil report had been raised against him; but since we were not at that time able to get any definite evidence concerning the truth of the matter, we ordered the abbot to make an inquiry into the evil report as well as into the truth of the matter, as cautiously and honestly as he could, and then to handle it in a proper manner. Furthermore, we were much displeased that the abbot had promoted the said E[nguerrand], as prior, for he had been behaving badly for many years, and an evil report of long standing had never been cleared up. We received procuration there this day. Total for procuration: nine pounds, eight shillings.

THE OPERATION OF A MONASTERY

I have been at pains to set down the things that I have seen and heard, which came to pass in the Church of St. Edmund in our days, from the year in which the Flemings were taken prisoner outside the town, that being the year in which I assumed the religious habit, and Prior Hugh was deposed and his office given to Robert; and I have included certain evil things for a warning, and certain good as an example to others. At that time Abbot Hugh was grown old and his eyes waxed somewhat dim. Pious he was and kindly, a strict monk and good, but in the business of this world neither good nor wise. For he trusted those about him overmuch and gave them too ready credence, relying always on the wisdom of others rather than his own. Discipline and religion and all things pertaining to the Rule were zealously observed within the cloister; but outside all things were badly handled, and every man did, not what he ought, but what he would, since his lord was simple and growing old. The townships of the Abbot and all the hundreds were given out to farm;

From *The Chronicle of Jocelin of Brakelond*, edited and translated by H. E. Butler (Thomas Nelson, Publisher, 1949), pp. 1–5, 7–9, 20–23. Reprinted by permission of Oxford University Press.

the woods were destroyed, the houses of the manors threatened to fall in ruin, and day by day all things went from bad to worse. The Abbot found but one remedy and one consolation—to borrow money, that thus at least he might be able to maintain the honour of his house. No Easter nor Michaelmas came round during the eight years before his death but that one or two hundred pounds were added to his debt; the bonds were continually renewed, and the interest as it grew was turned into capital. This infirmity spread from the head to the members—from the superior to his subjects. And so it came about that each obedientiary had his own seal and bound himself in debt to Jews and Christians as he pleased. Often silken copes and flasks of gold and other ornaments of the church were placed in pawn without the knowledge of the Convent. I saw a bond given to William FitzIsabel for one thousand and forty pounds, and have never known the why or the wherefore. I saw another bond given to Isaac the son of Rabbi Joce for four hundred pounds, but I know not why; and yet a third to Benedict the Jew of Norwich for eight hundred and fourscore; and the cause of this last debt was as follows: our chamber was fallen in ruin, and the Sacrist, willy-nilly, undertook to restore it, and secretly borrowed forty marks at interest from Benedict the Jew and gave him a bond sealed with the seal that used to hang from the feretory of St. Edmund, and with which the instruments of the guilds and fraternities used to be sealed: it was broken up afterwards, at the bidding of the Convent, but all too late. Now when this debt had increased to one hundred pounds, the Jew came with letters from our lord the King concerning the Sacrist's debt, and at last that which had been hidden from the Abbot and the Convent was revealed. The Abbot was angry and would have deposed the Sacrist, alleging a privilege granted him by the Lord Pope, enabling him to depose William his Sacrist when he would. But someone came to the Abbot and speaking on the Sacrist's behalf, so deluded the Abbot that he allowed a bond to be given to Benedict the Jew for four hundred pounds, to be paid at the end of four years, to wit, for the hundred pounds already accumulated at interest and another hundred pounds which the said Jew had lent the Sacrist on the Abbot's behalf. And the Sacrist undertook in full chapter to repay the whole debt, and a bond was given sealed with the Convent's seal: for the Abbot dissembled and would not set his seal to the bond, as though the debt was no concern of his. But at the end of four years there was not the wherewithal to pay the debt, and a new bond was made for eight hundred and fourscore pounds, to be paid off at stated times at the rate of fourscore pounds a year. The same Jew also held a number of bonds for smaller debts and one that was of fourteen years' standing, so that the total debt due to him amounted to twelve hundred pounds not counting the accumulated interest. And R. the almoner of our lord the King came and made it known to the Abbot that a rumour had reached the King concerning these great debts. So after the Abbot had taken counsel with the prior and a few others, the Almoner was brought into the Chapter; and, while we sat by in silence, the Abbot said: "Here is the King's Almoner, my lord and friend and yours also, who led by his love of God and of St. Edmund, has told us that our lord the King has heard something untoward concerning us, and that the affairs of our Church are ill-managed both within and without. Wherefore it is my will, and I charge you on your obedience that you should say and openly acknowledge how matters stand." The Prior therefore arose, and speaking as it were on behalf of us all, he said that the Church was in good state, and that the Rule was well and religiously observed within our house, while without our affairs were well and wisely handled, though none the less we had incurred some small amount of debt, like others of our neighbours; but that there was no debt of sufficient magnitude to be a burden to us. Hearing this the Almoner replied that he was very glad to have heard the testimony of the Convent—that is to say, the Prior speaking as he did. The Prior said the same thing on another occasion, and with him Master Geoffrey de Constantine, both of them speaking and excusing the Abbot, when Arch-bishop Richard came to our Chapter in virtue of his office as legate, before we possessed such exemption as we now enjoy. But at that time I was a novice and, when the opportunity offered, I spoke concerning these matters with my master, who used to teach me the Rule and to whose care I had been assigned—to wit, Master Samson, who was afterwards Abbot, "What is this," I said, "that I hear? Why are you silent, who see and hear such things as these, you who are a cloister monk and have no desire for office and fear God more than you fear man?" But he made answer and said, "My son, a child newly burned dreads the fire; thus it is with me and many others. Hugh the Prior has of late been deposed from his priorship and sent into exile. Denys and Hugh and Roger of Hingham have but lately returned from exile. I like them was imprisoned and afterwards sent to Acre, because we had spoken on behalf of the common good of our Church against the will of the Abbot. This is the hour of darkness; this is the hour in which flatterers pre-vail and are believed; their power is made strong and we can do nothing against it. We must for a time shut our eyes to these things. Let the Lord behold and judge."

A rumour reached Abbot Hugh that Richard, Archbishop of Canter-bury, desired to come to us and hold a scrutiny in our Church, by virtue of his authority as legate; and after taking counsel the Abbot sent to Rome and obtained exemption from the power of the said legate. When our messenger returned from Rome, we had not the wherewithal to pay the sums that he had promised the Lord Pope and the cardinals, except, under the circum-stances, the cross that was above the High Altar and the little image of the Virgin and that of St. John, which images Stigand the Archbishop had adorned with a great weight of gold and silver, and had given to St. Edmund.

Some of our brethren who were close friends of the Abbot went so far as to say that even the feretory of St. Edmund ought to be stripped of its plating to pay for such a liberty as this, not noting the great peril that might arise from such a liberty. For if there should arise some Abbot of ours who desired to dilapidate the property of our Church and to treat his Convent ill, there will be no man to whom the Convent will be able to complain of the wrongs done by the Abbot, who will fear neither Bishop or Archbishop or Legate, and his impunity will make him all the bolder to do wrong. . . .

In the twenty-third year of his abbacy it came into Abbot Hugh's mind to go to the shrine of St. Thomas to pray; and on his way thither upon the day after the Nativity of the Virgin he had a grievous fall near Rochester, so that his knee-cap was put out and lodged in the ham of his leg. Physicians hastened to him and tortured him in many ways, but healed him not; and he was carried back to us in a horse litter and devoutly received as was his due. To cut a long story short, his leg mortified and the pain ascended even to his heart, and by reason of the pain a tertian fever laid hold on him, in the fourth fit of which he died and gave up his soul to God on the morrow of the day of St. Brice. Before he died, everything was pillaged by his servants so that nothing was left in his house but three-legged stools and tables which they were unable to carry off. The Abbot himself was scarce left with his coverlet and two old torn blankets which someone had placed over him after removing those that were whole. There was nothing worth a single penny that could be distributed to the poor for the benefit of his soul. The Sacrist said that it was no business of his, asserting that he had found all expenses for the Abbot and his household for a whole month. For the tenants of the townships refused to give anything before the appointed time and his creditors would lend him nothing, when they saw that he was sick even unto death. None the less the tenant of Palgrave found fifty shillings for distribution to the poor, since he entered on his tenancy of Palgrave on that day. But those fifty shillings were later given back to the King's bailiffs who demanded the whole rent on behalf of the King.

When Abbot Hugh had been buried, it was resolved in the Chapter that a messenger should announce his death to Ranulph de Glanvill, Justiciar of England. Master Samson and Master R. Ruff, monks of our house, crossed the sea and bore this news to our lord the King: and from him they secured letters to the effect that the property and revenues of the Convent, which were separated from those of the abbot, should be wholly in the hands of the Prior and the Convent, while the rest of the Abbey should be in the hands of the King. The custody of the Abbey was given to Robert de Cockfield and Robert de Flamville, our Steward, who straightway placed under gage and pledge all the servants and kinsfolk of the Abbot, to whom he had given anything before he fell sick or who had taken anything from his property; and they did this even to the Abbot's chaplain, one of our monks, for whom the Prior stood security: and entering our vestry they caused an inventory to be made of all the ornaments of the church.

While the abbacy was vacant, the Prior was above all things zealous for the maintenance of peace in the Convent and the preservation of the honour of our Church in the entertainment of guests, desiring neither to disturb anyone or provoke any to anger, so that he might keep all men and all things in peace. Yet none the less he shut his eyes to certain things that deserved correction in the conduct of our obedientiaries, above all of the Sacrist who, during the vacancy, as though he did not care what he did with the sacristy, paid not a single debt nor built anything at all, but oblations and chance incomings were foolishly squandered. Wherefore the Prior who was the head of the Convent was thought blameworthy and called remiss. And our brethren spoke of this among themselves, when the time came for the election of an Abbot. . . .

But the Prior and the twelve with him, after much toil and delay, at length stood before the King at Waltham, a manor of the Bishop of Winchester, on the second Sunday in Lent. Our lord the King received them kindly and, declaring that he wished to act according to God's will and for the honour of the Church, he commanded the brethren by the mouth of his intermediaries, Richard Bishop of Winchester and Geoffrey the Chancellor, afterwards Archbishop of York, that they should nominate three of our Convent. Whereupon the Prior and the brethren went aside, as though to speak on this matter, and drew out the seal and broke it, and found the names in the following order: Samson the sub-sacrist, Roger the Cellarer and Hugh the third prior. Whereat the brothers who were of higher rank blushed. Moreover, all marvelled that the same Hugh was both elector and elect. But since they could not change the facts, by common consent they changed the order, putting Hugh first, because he was third prior, Roger the Cellarer second, and Samson third, making, on the face of it, the first last and the last first. But the King, after first enquiring whether those nominated were born in his realm and within whose domain, said that he did not know them and ordered that three others of the Convent should be nominated as well as those three. This being agreed, William the Sacrist said, "Our Prior should be nominated because he is our head." This was readily allowed. Then said the Prior, "William the Sacrist is a good man." The same was said of Denys, and it was allowed. These being nominated without delay before the King, he marvelled saying, "They have done this quickly; God is with them." Afterwards the King demanded that for the honour of his realm they should nominate three more from other houses. Hearing this the brethren were afraid, suspecting guile. At length they agreed to name three, but on this condition that they should accept none of them without the counsel of those of the Convent who remained at home. And they nominated three: Master Nicholas of Wallingford, later and at the present time Abbot of Malmesbury, Bertrand, Prior of St. Faith, afterwards Abbot of Chertsey, and the Lord H. of St. Neots, a monk of Bec, a man of great religion and very circumspect both in matters temporal and spiritual. This done, the King thanked them and gave orders that three out of the nine should be struck off the list, whereupon the three aliens were at once removed, to wit, the Prior of St. Faith afterwards Abbot of Chertsey, Nicholas, monk of St. Albans, afterwards Abbot of Malmesbury, and the Prior of St. Neots. William the Sacrist withdrew of his own free will: two of the remaining five were struck off by order of the King, and then one of the three remaining, two only being left, namely the Prior and Samson. Finally the intermediaries of our lord the King whom I have mentioned above, were called in to take counsel with the brethren. And Denys, speaking for us all, began to commend the persons of the Prior and Samson, saying that both were literate, both good, both of praiseworthy life and of unblemished reputation; but always in the corner of his speech thrusting Samson forward, multiplying the words he uttered in his praise and saying that he was a man strict in his behaviour, stern in chastising transgressions, a hard worker, prudent in worldly business, and proved in divers offices. The Bishop of Winchester replied, "We understand clearly what you mean; from your words we gather that your Prior seems to you to be somewhat slack and that you desire him whom you call Samson." Denys replied, "Both of them are good, but we should like, God willing, to have the better." The Bishop made answer, "Of two good men you must choose the better. Tell me openly, do you wish to have Samson?" And a number, making a majority, answered clearly, "We want Samson," not a voice being raised against them, though some of set purpose said nothing, because they wished to offend neither the one or the other. Samson then having been nominated in the presence of the King, and the latter having taken brief counsel with his advisers, all the rest were summoned, and the King said, "You have presented Samson to me: I do not know him. If you had presented your Prior, I should have accepted him; for I have seen him and know him. But, as it is, I will do what you desire. But have a care; for by the very eyes of God, if you do ill, I will be at you!" He then asked the Prior, if he agreed to this and desired it. The Prior answered that he did desire it and that Samson was much more worthy of honour. The elect therefore fell at the King's feet and kissed them, then rose in haste, and in haste went to the altar with the brethren, singing "Miserere mei, Deus," his head held high and his countenance unchanged. And when the King saw this, he said to those who stood by, "By God's eyes, this elect thinks himself worthy to be the guardian of his Abbey."

Hunting Subversion in the Middle Ages

AUSTIN P. EVANS

      One of the focal points in the debate between critics and defenders of the medieval Church is its treatment of heretics. The principal ecclesiastical institution set up to deal with dissenters was the Inquisition, which flourished from the thirteenth to the sixteenth century. But heresy was not a problem of that period alone. It had been a persistent problem in the early days of the Christian movement and became very serious after the conversion of Constantine. Many of the early heresies arose from theological debates in which the orthodox position became accepted as such only after authoritative decisions had been made by general ecclesiastical councils. Thus, the council of Nicaea rejected Arianism after a lengthy discussion of its tenets, and many other theological positions received the same treatment during the following centuries. The abstruseness of some of these positions should not prevent appreciation of their importance in the history of the ecclesiastical community. Theological differences often split the Church and created alternative authority structures to challenge the orthodox hierarchy.

      The decline of intellectual life after the establishment of the Germanic kingdoms in Europe caused a sharp decrease in the number of heretical movements based on the teachings of errant intellectuals. There were few condemnations of such men until the eleventh and twelfth centuries, when the revival of learning again produced an intellectual atmosphere in which heresy born of sophisticated speculation became a problem for ecclesiastical authorities. Charges made against men like Berengar of Tours and Roscellinus in the eleventh century and Peter Abelard and Gilbert de la Porée in the twelfth century repeatedly referred to the danger that their heterodox ideas would mislead the masses and become a threat to the ecclesiastical community. But the threat that had been real in the third, fourth, and fifth centuries was no longer very serious in the twelfth century. By that time, the ecclesiastical authorities had become so well established and so much a part of the secular as well as religious authority structure in Europe that their attacks on the errant intellectuals appear unjustified, even in a period when the ideal of freedom of thought attracted few adherents.

      The concern of the hierarchy with the effect of new and questionable theological positions was not so incomprehensible as it may seem. There was a dramatic increase in the incidence of popular heresy in the eleventh and twelfth centuries that presented considerable difficulties for those in power. The lower-class heretics had little to do with theological debates, but for orthodox churchmen, the connection between errant theological ideas and popular heresy appeared real and dangerous. Until the late nineteenth century, in fact, most historians treated the popular heresies as religious protests, despite the provocative Marxist interpretation that they were really manifestations of the class struggle. Non-Marxist historians began to take this interpretation seriously only at the end of the last century, when their own researches had shown that heretics often attacked the authority of the Church and often had social grievances. It eventually became common to regard heretics as social dissenters. What with the blurring of the distinction between the medieval Church's religious and worldly functions, it is to be expected that dissent against it would unite social, political, and religious issues.

But it is important to note that while many of the heretical movements had extensive social and political consequences, almost none of them included a specific social or political program. All the sources indicate that the main concern of the heretics was in the religious sphere, and only one mid-twelfth century group, led by Arnold of Brescia in Rome, is known to have had a definite political platform. Similarly, there appears to be no decisive correlation between social groups and heresies. Most of the heretics of the early Middle Ages and most of those brought before the Inquisition were peasants or members of the urban lower classes; but this is to be expected, since these groups comprised 70 to 80 percent of the population. Heresy was also common among the clergy and the nobility, who were presumably satisfied with the social situation. The validity of the sociological and Marxist theories explaining the nature and origins of heretical dissent, therefore, seems questionable.

Professor Jeffrey Russell (see Bibliography) has suggested that the dramatic increase in the incidence of heresy during the eleventh and twelfth centuries was connected with the great reform movement often called the Gregorian Reform. The reformers attacked the worldliness of the Church and sought to free it from the power of secular lords. It was natural that the spirit of this movement would spill over the confines of the Church hierarchy and inspire many to attack the ecclesiastical authority and its doctrine without regard to orthodoxy. In the selection presented here, Austin Evans describes the methods used by the Church to combat popular heresies. These methods, associated with the Inquisition, were developed slowly during the century and a half after the papal reform movement.

As theme of the present discussion I here set down four quotations, taken from documents of the first half of the thirteenth century and bearing upon the problem of heresy and its suppression:

From "Hunting Subversion in the Middle Ages" by Austin P. Evans, *Speculum* 33 (1958), pp. 1–15. Reprinted by permission of *Speculum*.

"The Apostle enjoins upon us the avoidance not alone of evil, but the very appearance thereof."

"Lest the innocent be punished for the guilty, or the stain of heresy be imputed to some through the malice of others, we order that no one shall be punished as a heretic or a believer in heretics unless he has been adjudged such by his bishop or other ecclesiastic who has that authority."

"The question should not be asked whether anyone may be condemned for this crime [i.e., heresy] on the testimony of one witness and common report. The answer obviously is no. . . . For, especially in a criminal action, the proofs should be clearer than light. . . . And for this crime no one should be condemned on presumptive evidence, but should be allowed canonical purgation."

"You should not proceed to the sentencing of anyone except on his own confession or on transparently clear proofs. For it is better to leave a crime unpunished than to convict the innocent."

These precepts, chosen somewhat at random, and others like them, run through the official literature dealing with heresy during the thirteenth and early fourteenth centuries. They afford illustration of the best thinking of the time relative to restraints which should be exercised in dealing with "subversion" of that day, despite the fact that, as treason to God, heresy was then considered the most terrible of crimes, by which men's souls were damned for all eternity in the world to come and not merely their bodies in this world. The first excerpt is from a letter of Innocent III to his lieutenants in Languedoc, counseling care and moderation in dealing with Raymond VI of Toulouse; the second and fourth are from decrees of councils called to devise measures to bind up wounds, after two decades of the ravages of the Albigensian Crusade, and to aid in fixing the procedure of the newly established papal Inquisition; the third is from a series of replies, by Guy Foulques, archbishop of Narbonne and soon to be Pope Clement IV, to questions raised by inquisitors after some twenty-five years of experience with the new instrument devised to hunt out and bring to justice the men and women who were unsettling the faith of simple folk. They say, in effect, let us now have done with drumhead courts and impromptu bonfires where people are done to death by the score with only the slightest trace, if any, of legal procedure or the attempt to separate the guilty from the innocent. Let us see to it that, by proper procedure, irrefrangible proofs of guilt are established, or, failing this, let us release the suspect or at least delay sentence until better evidence may be obtained.

This, it must be borne in mind, was the ideal. How far was it possible to hew to the line in the actual conflict with the heretic? How far did procedural expedients, which at the time seemed necessary to cope with an ever present danger, vitiate the ideal? How far did strong and sometimes hard men, thrown into positions of power by the rough and tumble of the fight, succeed in stilling their consciences and in justifying, under the cloak of over-whelming necessity, practices which ill accorded with the principles just expressed? We have been troubled over the past few years, in our preoccupation with subversive elements in our own society, with these and similar questions. It has seemed, therefore, of some interest to devote a few moments to asking how men dealt with them some seven centuries ago. As the subject is obviously too vast for a brief discussion, attention will here be directed primarily to certain questions which occupied the minds of men responsible for the conduct of the inquisitorial courts and which have troubled men over the past few years: the use of anonymous informers or spies; imputation of guilt by association and guilt by kinship; failure to assure adequate counsel to the accused; failure to allow the accused an adequately clear, full, and specific statement of the charges and testimony against him; failure to allow the accused to confront his accusers and those who witnessed against him or even to know who they were. Useful evidence is much more abundant on some of these points than on others, but they will all be included in the discussion which follows; the reader is asked merely to bear in mind that this is intended only as a partial picture of inquisitorial procedure of the thirteenth century and that illustration is drawn almost entirely from the region of southern France.

The use of informers has over the years been such a common practice by judicial or semi-judicial bodies that it may seem hardly worth the time it takes to allude to it here. The extent and quality of such use does, however, hold some interest. We are doubtless all familiar with Trajan's commendation of Pliny, his governor in Bithynia, for refusal to entertain anonymous charges against the Christians. "Such accusations," he said, "ought to have no place in any prosecution. For this is both a dangerous kind of precedent and out of keeping with [the spirit of] our laws." Precedents against the employment of informers are numerous, in both the Jewish and the Christian tradition, for the centuries preceding and following this pronouncement. But in the Middle Ages, as in some later periods, these seem to have been abandoned. The use of informers was common procedure in the hunt for heretics, particularly in connection with the Inquisition, and the informer more often than not was supposed to remain anonymous.

Indeed, many generations before the founding of the papal Inquisition, in connection with the heresy uncovered at Orléans in 1022, our sources tell us an interesting tale of a Norman noble who got wind of a nest of heresy in this town in the Loire valley, reported it to King Robert and, under his direction, insinuated himself into the group, won the confidence of its members, learned their secrets, denounced them, and had the satisfaction of seeing his work crowned with success in their burning. There is no mention of a reward for this activity other than that of having accomplished a good deed, unless his later appearance as one of the canons at St. Peter of Chartres may be interpreted as such. But with the Inquisition rewards, material or other, were not long in coming.

Clauses which illustrate the use of informers and show the length to which Church and State were prepared to go in their efforts to erase heresy, specifically from Languedoc at the close of the Albigensian Crusade, appear in the articles of the Peace of Paris ending the Crusade in 1229 and in the decrees of the Council of Toulouse held later during the same year. By the former all males of fourteen years and above, females of twelve and above, were to take oath to eschew heresy and to report suspects to the authorities, this oath to be renewed biennially; and a bounty was offered for such information if and when it led to actual conviction for heresy. By the latter, in each parish a team composed of a priest and two or three laymen of good repute was to search out heretics, their believers and supporters, and report them to the proper ecclesiastical or lay authorities. This was denunciation on a mass scale and it became a regular element in the procedure of the Inquisition; popes, councils, and inquisitors united in inculcating the duty of the faithful thus to assist in the work of rooting out heresy. But we are still short of the actual employment of informers as a regular element in inquisitorial procedure.

Informers were not long in appearing, however. Guillaume de Puylaurens tells of one Guillaume de Solerio who had been a perfected heretic, had of his own volition withdrawn from the sect, and had been reconciled with the Church. During the Council of Toulouse he had been fully reinstated (*restitutus ad famam*) that he might validly testify against his former associates "concerning whom he knew the truth." The clergy were assembled that they as a body might be briefed by Guillaume.

This incident illustrates one usual form of denunciation, the revelation by a converted heretic of the names of associates with whom he had attended heretical meetings, together with the times and places of those meetings. Councils and inquisitors were constant in their insistence that names of heretics and of their believers should be given to suspects before the Inquisition, and inquisitors spared no pains to secure the co-operation of the converted heretic. Inquisitorial registers surprise the reader by the mass of detail drawn from the witness, covering a period in some instances of twenty-five, thirty, or even forty years, and giving the time and place of heretical gatherings, together with the names of those attending. For example, Saurine Rigaud, who had been a perfected heretic in Languedoc about the middle of the thirteenth century, tells of numerous meetings over a period, in this case of only twelve years, wherein she foregathered with a total of some one hundred suspects whose names she divulged. Witnesses with memories such as hers would gladden the heart of more than one member of some of our hard pressed congressional committees. And there was then no troublesome bill of rights by the terms of which the witness might claim the right to silence.

In addition to the converted heretic, or indeed any suspect who came voluntarily or was cited before the Inquisition and required under oath to testify concerning all those, at the time living or dead, whom he had seen at heretical meetings, there were the regularly employed agents or spies of the inquisitors who were used to uncover heretics and, if they had fled the jurisdiction of the court, to hunt them out and entice them back into territory where they could be apprehended or to arrange for their extradition. Two illustrations of men of this type may be briefly sketched.

The first is that of Arnaud Sicre of Ax, a village in the foothills of the Pyrenees. Arnaud's mother, Sybilla, had been a notorious heretic, whose property had been confiscated, and Arnaud himself was not entirely free from suspicion. Being anxious to regain the family estate, he accepted the counsel of his brother, who felt that the delivery of one or more heretics might net him that boon. Arnaud, thereupon, crossed the Pyrenees and searched throughout Aragon and Catalonia, on the trail of Guillaume Bélibaste, one of the last of the Catharist leaders in the region south of Toulouse, who had in 1312 sought asylum over the Pyrenees and had gathered about him some remnants of the faithful. After a long hunt Arnaud found them, succeeded in winning their confidence, and developed a ruse whereby he hoped to lure them into the territory of Foix. For nearly a year he absented himself on the ground that he was searching out some relatives in Aragon whom he wished to bring into relationship with Bélibaste. The time of his absence he spent not at all in Aragon but in the region of Pamiers, France, arranging with the bishop of that place, Jacques Fournier, the details of his plan for delivering the heretics into the hands of the Inquisition. Receiving the full approval of the bishop, together with a sum of money to aid him in carrying out his plan, he returned to his friends at San Mateo, in the province of Tarragona. To them he told a story of the illness of one relative, who was thus unable to journey to San Mateo but who besought Bélibaste to come to her that she might receive the consolation of his ministrations.

There is no need to recount the rest. The ruse worked. On the journey they had to cross a corner of the county of Foix, where officers of the Inquisition were waiting to arrest them. Taken to Carcassonne, Bélibaste proved obstinate and was relaxed to the secular arm and burned. Arnaud Sicre was warmly congratulated for his fine work by Jacques Fournier and the inquisitors, Bernard Gui and Jean de Beaune, who salved his conscience by the assurance, if that were needed, that such people could be caught only by the aid of one of their number who would betray them or by agents who succeeded in securing their trust.

Arnaud had spent some three years, from 1318 to the spring of 1321, in trapping his heretic. In the fall of the latter year Bishop Fournier, feeling that he might still further aid the Inquisition by recounting what he had learned, invited him to depose before that body. His deposition fills some thirteen folios of the register of Jacques Fournier (MS. Vat. lat. 4030), one of the fullest and most informative of the inquisitorial registers now extant. It is a long and, as may well be imagined, a pretty story. But Sicre did not end there his service to the Inquisition. Throughout the following two or three years he continued the search for heretics, with satisfactory results. The little group of Bélibaste's followers was hounded down to the last man. Unfortunately, however, we are not informed whether Sicre finally regained the family property, the lust for which had started him on his career.

The other illustration concerns the person and activity of Blaise Boyer, a tailor and prominent citizen of Narbonne of about the same period as the preceding. He had been suspected of cultivating the Spiritual Franciscans, had confessed at Carcassonne in 1325 before the inquisitor Jean Duprat, was given a light penance, involving freedom from prison, from confiscation of property, and from the necessity of wearing crosses, and was sent off to Sicily to search out heretics and bring them to justice. He operated, not only in Sicily, but in Provence, Italy, and even as far east as Cyprus, in at least one case returning a suspect from Sicily to southern France at his own expense. So exemplary was his conduct over a period of three years, and so favorable were the letters from inquisitors in Sicily that Henri de Chamay, then inquisitor of Carcassonne, in 1328 gave him final absolution, requiring only that he make a pilgrimage to Nîmes and give twenty livres for the founding of a chapel. Boyer's slight brush with the Inquisition seems not to have lessened the esteem of his fellow citizens, for he appears as a member of the town council of Narbonne in 1331, 1338, and 1346. However, under date of 5 November 1351 Pope Clement VI wrote to the archbishop of Narbonne stating that four citizens of the city had petitioned him to have the case of Boyer before the Inquisition re-opened. It was rumored, they said, that he had escaped judgment from the Inquisition by "prayers, gifts, and favors,"—i.e., by bribes—to the scandal of simple Catholic Christians. The pope urgently requested that the archbishop inquire into the truth of the matter and correct anything that was amiss. It would be interesting to learn how Blaise Boyer fared under this investigation, but on this our sources are silent.

There was some risk involved, however, in reporting heretics. We learn from a letter, written in 1234 by Gregory IX to the bishop of Toulouse, that a priest by the name of Hugh, in the bishopric of Cahors, had appealed to the pope for protection from the relatives of two women whom, in obedience to the injunction of the Council of Toulouse (1229), he had haled before his bishop; by the latter they were adjudged heretical and turned over to the secular arm to be burned. Being now threatened with death, he petitioned for transfer to a safer spot. Gregory asked the bishop to look into the matter and to arrange a suitable transfer if conditions warranted.

This was a simple case, illustrative of what apparently happened frequently, particularly during the early years of the Inquisition. But let us consider one much more involved from 1324–1325, a period almost one hundred years later. In the foothills of the Pyrenees, south of Pamiers, one Guillaume Traverii, priest in Verdun-sur-Ariège, charged before the Inquisition that six people of the region were tainted with heresy, and he secured nine others to join with him in this charge. The six were forthwith apprehended and held in custody, under the ban of excommunication when they refused to confess and seek absolution. Testimony was taken, but was of a nature to arouse the suspicions of the acting inquisitor Jacques Fournier, as noted above bishop of Pamiers and later Pope Benedict XII. Finally, under questioning, one of the witnesses broke down, and the truth then came out. Guillaume Traverii, so the record runs, "seduced by a malign impulse and a hateful spirit" had manufactured the charges against the six and had suborned his confederates. Our knowledge of the whole episode comes only from the record of the deliberations of the commission of *jurisperiti*, called to assist in the case, and from the final sentences imposed upon the false accusers and witnesses. But what we have is sufficient to give a lively impression of the possibilities in the situation. Peter Marenges, one of the group against whom charges had been brought, had been a heretic, had confessed, and had received absolution. Were he convicted again of heretical acts, that conviction would automatically entail relaxation to the secular arm for burning. All of the accused had been under sentence of excommunication for a year and were thus without the consolations of the Church. They were also in danger of being declared heretics, without further proof, under the rule that a suspect who remained excommunicate for a year became by that fact alone a heretic. The question arose in the commission, then, what penalty should be recommended for the false priest, Guillaume. On this there was some difference of opinion. The general feeling was that he should receive the judgment which would have been imposed upon Peter had he really fallen again into heresy, but some thought strict imprisonment enough. The final sentence declared by the inquisitor consigned him to *murus strictus*, in chains and on "the bread of sorrow and the water of tribulation," with no hope of amelioration of sentence at a later time. Of the others all, except Bernard Faber who had confessed and broken the case, were condemned to prison, either mild (*murus largus*) or harsh (*murus strictus*); all without exception were to be exhibited in all the towns and villages of the diocese, with yellow crosses and red tongues sewed to their clothing, as awful examples of the sin of falsely testifying. Those whom they had traduced were to be suitably indemnified from the assets of the guilty.

Were this an isolated case, it would hardly be worth mentioning in the present context. But the records of sufficient incidents of like sort have come down to us to create the impression that such framing of innocent people was by no means rare. The temptation thus to meddle in other people's affairs or to dispose of a rival or an enemy was always present. The very harshness of the judgment meted out to the guilty may be taken as some indication of the seriousness of the problem for the inquisitors. It should, one would think, have operated as a deterrent to one tempted thus to settle an old grudge. It might even have given pause to those officials, lay or ecclesiastical, who opened the gates for this sort of thing by inviting all to spy upon their neighbors.

Among other questions involved in the problem of the suspect and getting him before the court is that of the definition of heresy. Could the charge of heresy be brought against one who habitually associated with heretics, actual or presumed, or was related by family ties to a heretic? In law one was not a heretic until he had been declared such by competent authority, after his error had been pointed out to him and he had refused to recant. But in discovering these the Inquisition found it expedient to spread wide its nets, to bring before it all manner of men, guilty or not, and to ask them sweeping questions in order to secure clues regarding those actually implicated in heresy. Illustration of this is to be found abundantly in a manuscript of Toulouse from about 1250, where are recorded some five thousand auditions, frequently, so far as one can judge, including testimony from practically the whole adult population of villages in the region southeast of that city. In these the witnesses were instructed under oath to tell anything they knew about heretical beliefs or activities, of themselves or anyone else, living or now dead. This was obviously a fishing expedition, the questioning turning at times upon who was present at small gatherings, attended by the witness, at which heretical leaders were present and what was the degree of involvement of each, at other times the center of interest seeming to shift to following the activities of certain families more or less prominent among the lesser nobility of the region. Information thus gathered could serve for more searching questioning of those who appeared to be the more deeply involved in heresy.

That association with heretics, either chance or prolonged, might raise a suspicion of heretical tendencies can hardly be a matter of surprise or comment. Prudent men tried to assure themselves against possible unfavorable future report by appearing during the "time of grace," or the period at which, in the opening of the court in a given region, the inhabitants were invited to appear freely before it, confess any commerce they may have had with heretics, name their associates, and receive light penances. Thus we find that a peasant, who discovered that two men whom he had hired as harvest hands were heretics, appeared before the inquisitor, confessed the fact, and was cleared. Another who had inadvertently accepted heretics as passengers on his river boat between Moissac and Toulouse, when he learned they were heretics reported to the inquisitor and was penanced to a pilgrimage to St. James of Compostella. Or, again, there were the witnesses before the court who thought a suspect was probably a heretic because, among other things, he was friendly with suspects and believers or with those defamed of heresy.

Just how much weight was given this sort of testimony in actually assessing the guilt of any individual, it would be difficult to judge; that the court allowed it some weight is attested by the fact that the notary recorded it. But in the questioning of suspects the inquisitor was definite in his inquiries whether the defendant, or those whom he might name, were by specific beliefs or acts implicated in heresy. The suspect was asked if he had "adored" perfected heretics, had accepted their blessing, listened to them teaching or preaching, had eaten of food blessed by them, had given anything to or accepted anything from them, had escorted them anywhere, had protected or hidden them; that is, was he a believer, receiver, defender, or protector of heretics. Any of these acts constituted proof of belief in heresy and made one liable to severe penalties. But it was only upon his own confession—and this accounts for the introduction of torture into the procedure of the Inquisition—or the concordant testimony of at least two witnesses that a man could be adjudged guilty of heresy.

Much the same is true of family connection as ground for considering a man or woman a heretic. There are a good many illustrations of suspicion of heresy being lodged, either popularly or officially, against an individual on nothing more tangible than this. One of the best advertised cases is that of the count of Foix, who was under grave suspicion of heresy quite largely because he harbored his sister Esclarmonde, a notorious heretic. According to the anonymous author of the second part of the *Chanson de la croisade albigeoise*, he defended himself stoutly against the charge before the Fourth Lateran Council, on the ground that in harboring her he was merely honoring his feudal oath. However, though he was never actually convicted of heresy, the suspicion remained. There is another illustration, better authenticated, of a man called before the Inquisition in 1254 on suspicion of heresy. It was charged that his mother had been hereticated a short time before and, since he visited her frequently and occasionally gave her provisions, he seemed to give assent to her evil ways. He was required, under oath, to promise obedience in all things to the inquisitor and to pledge all his property. Six others, including his wife, went surety for him to the amount of 50 livres. There appears to have been no room for filial piety in face of the danger threatened by the spread of heresy. My last illustration of this point concerns one Raymond Amélius, a monk of Saint Polycarp in the diocese of Narbonne. Three of the nine counts alleged against him at his trial for heresy in 1337 concerned the conviction for heresy of his paternal grandfather, of his grandmother, and of his maternal uncle. Such heredity was held to place him under grave suspicion of heresy.

The wife and offspring of a convicted heretic were also liable to serious disability in regard to inheritance and right to hold public office. As in confiscation in other criminal actions, the dower rights of the wife were respected provided she had married prior to her husband's commerce with heretics and was not herself a heretic. On the other hand, the heir of a deceased heretic had no right to the property unless he could show that he had held it for a period of forty years and that he was not himself a heretic. Moreover, wife and heir of one convicted of heresy, who knew and acquiesced in the heresy of husband and father, were deprived of all right to the property, including the dower, and the heirs were rendered incapable of holding any ecclesiastical benefice or public office—to the second generation in the male line, to the first in the female line. Documents containing appeals for restitution of property confiscated in southern France by officials of Alphonse of Poitiers and King Louis IX fully illustrate the financial disabilities suffered by the heirs of heretics.

These few illustrations may suffice to show how tempting was the charge of heresy and how all-pervasive was the action of the court of the Inquisition. Much injustice was probably done as the result of the testimony of ignorant, overzealous, or hostile neighbors or of the action of inquisitors who considered themselves prosecuting attorneys rather than judges. None the less, it would be hazardous to conclude that men and women were in the thirteenth century widely condemned as heretics on the basis of association or kinship with heretics, however much common report may have tarred them with that stick and however much such connection may have drawn unfavorable attention to them on the part of ecclesiastical or lay authority and operated to deprive them of rights in property or office.

Let us now turn to consideration of some of the disabilities suffered by the man who found himself actually before the court of the inquisitor. He stood alone. Apart from the opportunity afforded him to mention the names of persons who might support his allegations of enmity toward him on the part of some members of the community, and the opportunity to secure, if he could, those who would stand surety for his appearance when called by the inquisitor, there was no one upon whom he normally could rely for assistance. Only rarely do we read of witnesses in his behalf; except under the most limited conditions he could employ no counsel; under the rules he did not know the names of his accusers or of those whom the court called as witnesses, nor could he confront them. He was allowed to see the charges and the testimony against him, but these were generally communicated to him in summary rather than in full text.

Let us examine these points. Little time will be spent upon the question of witnesses in his behalf. For a witness to appear before the court, at the call of a suspect and openly favoring his cause, would lay him open to the charge of defending a heretic. Had the procedure of the court provided for such appearance few would have been found willing to risk the danger involved. As I mentioned above, a man whose case was before the Inquisition could escape imprisonment provided he could find sureties who would pledge a certain sum to guarantee his appearance when called. But he was not always successful in finding such sureties. It might also be his good fortune to find support, partial or complete, on the part of one or more witnesses called by the court. Of this the best illustration which has come to my attention is that of the trial of Bernard Otho, together with his mother and three brothers, held at Carcassonne in 1236–1237. Starting with no less a person than the archbishop of Narbqnne, one hundred and eleven witnesses were examined on four specific points. There was much variation in the answers. The archbishop, as Bernard's "diocesan," had no hesitation in declaring him a heretic; others were not so sure. Two, both clerics, held there was no truth in any of the charges against him, one asserting that "they proceed more from hate than from a spirit of love." The document merits careful study, but the only point I wish here to make is that, in the course of a hearing, testimony in favor of the accused might sometimes be heard. But such categorical statements as those of the two clerics are not usual.

I have indicated as a further disability of the defendant before the court his lack of counsel. Innocent III in 1199 had forbidden advocates to represent heretics and notaries to prepare legal papers for them. Were this rule infringed, they would make themselves liable to prosecution and deprivation of the right to practice longer their professions. Six years later, in the bull *Si adversus*, he was even more explicit in his insistence that no lawyer or notary should serve any heretic or one of their believers, defenders, or protectors. Since this prohibition was specifically against those who were "still in their contumacy and error" the presumption is that it would not apply to the counseling of suspects before the court of the Inquisition, after its establishment a generation later, at least until their heresy had been proved. That this is the correct interpretation is implied in a letter of Gregory IX, written in 1234 to the papal legate and five bishops of southern France, advising them to investigate certain charges made by Count Raymond of Toulouse against inquisitors in his lands. Among these was the claim that "certain men, proceeding to make inquest in his lands about the said crime [of heresy], put aside normal legal procedure . . . and . . . on their own authority deprive those concerning whom inquest is being made of all means of defense and advice of counsel." It may be inferred, also, from a formulary of the Inquisition, drawn up about 1245. In this the authors, two inquisitors, state that they deny to no one proper defense; their procedure accords with that of other courts except in their refusal to divulge the names of witnesses. Since in other contemporary courts counsel was permitted, and even under certain conditions provided, it seems reasonable to conclude that there was no existing law forbidding counsel to suspects before the Inquisition. In the actual records of the Inquisition, however, no evidence of the presence of advocates before the court, either to advise the accused or actually to argue the cases, appears prior to the third decade of the fourteenth century. Indeed, it would have been a courageous man who would have accepted the risk

involved in representing one charged with heresy, and by this incurring the
threat of implication in heresy. By the middle of the century theory was,
rather, in the other direction. The business of the court should be carried on
"simply and directly without the loud speaking and sophistry of lawyers and
the ordinary courts of law." With the fourteenth century we see indication of
an amelioration of this rule. In 1323 the Inquisition, in the person of Jacques
Fournier, bishop of Pamiers, had under consideration the case of one Bernard
Clerc, which had already been before the court over a period of two years and
was to continue for one and one-half years longer before its final disposition.
To Bernard was granted the right to have "an advocate, or advocates, if he so
desired, in accord with the form of law and the manner and practice of the
court of the Inquisition." A decade later, in the trial of Raymond Amélius,
to which reference was made above, the same privilege was accorded by the
inquisitor in substantially the same terms.

The whole question seems to turn on the meaning of the phrase "juxta
juris formam ac stylum et usum officii inquisitionis." The fact of its insertion
into the record of these trials seems again to indicate that allowing advocates
to the accused was, under certain conditions, normal procedure, though no
other cases have, to my knowledge, come to light, except from a later period.
Bernard Clerc, however, found that no lawyer would represent him except
by formal order of the court. When one was finally appointed he devoted
himself largely to attempting to persuade Bernard to plead guilty and thus
gain the mercy of the court. Vidal, in his discussion of this case, concludes
that the "stylum et usum officii inquisitionis" consisted in the court designat-
ing a lawyer as advocate for the defendant. He was not expected to appear
before the court, but confined himself to advising the accused and aiding him
in drawing up any papers he might wish to present to the court. He was to
be constant in his endeavor to induce the defendant to tell the truth. And
he must dissociate himself from the case the moment he became convinced
of the guilt of his client. Vidal concluded that the counsel of Bernard Clerc
was rather the advocate of the court than of the defendant. Bernard refused
his aid on these terms and resigned any attempt at defense. Eymeric clarifies
somewhat this situation. He argues that if the accused confesses his fault,
whether or not he has been convicted by the testimony of witnesses, the
services of counsel are useless, but where there is doubt of his guilt or he
insists upon defending himself he may have counsel, "honorable, beyond
suspicion in the eyes of the law, with knowledge of both laws, and zealous for
the faith." Such a man may be given a complete record of the trial, with
names of witnesses and accusers suppressed if there be threat of danger, otherwise they also are given. Elsewhere he holds that the inquisitor may proceed
against advocates or notaries who render aid to heretics. Thus his position is
that a man may be assisted by counsel so long as valid proof of his guilt is
lacking, but when guilt has been established there is no further utility in

allowing such assistance. He bases his judgment upon *Si adversus* of Innocent III, to which reference has been made above, and seems to be fully in accord with the principle there laid down.

The actual procedure of the inquisitorial courts during the thirteenth century was, however, not in accord with this principle. Indeed, at almost the same time that Bishop Fournier was allowing counsel to a suspect before his court, Bernard Gui was writing his *Practica inquisitionis,* wherein he states procedure without the delay and irritation of advocates to be one of the prerogatives of the inquisitor. We may conclude, therefore, that during this period of approximately seventy-five years the inquisitors, under stress of the urgent need to root out heresy and with the acquiescence of popes and councils, departed from the normal procedure of the courts in the matter of counsel and only returned when, in the early fourteenth century, pressure was relieved through the decline of the Catharist heresy.

We have now come to the last point under discussion, that of the anonymity of informers and witnesses. This was much debated at the time and has been the subject of sharp criticism on the part of modern historians. From the earliest days of the Inquisition it appears to have been a sore point. Prior to the founding of that tribunal the custom in both lay and ecclesiastical courts was to make known the names of accusers and witnesses. Defendants before the court were allowed to confront their accusers. It was difficult enough, at best, for a man accused of heresy to present a useful defense, given the reluctance or absolute refusal of witnesses to testify in his behalf, the difficulty if not impossibility of securing counsel, and his lack of knowledge of the exact nature of the charges against him. To keep him in ignorance also of the names of those who had given evidence against him and to deprive him of all opportunity to cross-examine them may well have seemed an intolerable handicap.

The matter arose in 1229 in connection with the Council of Toulouse and those there brought under suspicion of heresy by Guillaume de Solerio. When these were cited before the pope's legate to answer the charges, some readily admitted their guilt and were reconciled with slight penances; others with "tougher minds" resisted for a time, but finally sought absolution; a third group elected to defend themselves against the charges and asked for the names of those who testified against them, "because," they said, "mortal enemies might be among them to whose testimony no credence should be given." The names the legate refused to divulge, though they importuned him from Toulouse to Montpellier, because he feared for the safety of the witnesses. But he finally yielded to the point where he let them have a single list including the names of all those who had testified against any of the suspects. This proved of no value, since no individual could tell from the list who had testified specifically against him. Hence they felt themselves unable to prepare a proper defense and in disgust abandoned the attempt.

The question was not then settled, however, for five years later we find Pope Gregory IX writing to the legate and bishops in southern France asking them so to conduct themselves, and so to watch over the process of uprooting heresy in the lands of the count of Toulouse, that "innocence may not suffer and iniquity may not remain unpunished." On the particular point under discussion he wrote: "It has been made known to us by our beloved son, the noble count of Toulouse, that certain men, proceeding to make inquest in his lands about the said crime [of heresy], put aside normal legal procedure, hear witnesses concerning heresy in secret, and, entirely withholding the names and testimony of the witnesses, on their own authority deprive those concerning whom inquest is being made of all means of defense and advice of advocates. From this it comes about that sometimes those conscious of guilt turn to shrewd falsehoods and denounce to the Inquisition those men of good repute, by whom they fear that they may be anticipated in bringing accusation. At times, forsooth, in secret confessions they freely accuse their own enemies, and thus it often happens that the innocent are condemned and wickedness is passed over without punishment." It would not be accurate to present this as typical of Pope Gregory's attitude toward heresy and the means taken to uproot it. It probably reflects rather the criticisms of Raymond VII of Toulouse, with whose mood the pope for the moment was in sympathy. It does, however, make clear some of the objections already being raised against inquisitorial procedure, and specifically this question of the difficult position in which a suspect was placed before the inquisitor's court.

Part 4

THE LATE MIDDLE AGES

14th-15th Centuries

Genoese bankers.
Miniature from *De Septem Vitiis*,
late 14th century

Many studies of social life in premodern Europe focus on the four-teenth and fifteenth centuries, for two main reasons. First, during the late thirteenth and early fourteenth centuries, record-keeping by govern-mental and private institutions became a standard practice. Studies of rural society, which are so dependent on records of landholding, naturally end up focusing on this record-rich period. Studies of the cities follow the same pattern, and even legal history assumes a new dimension when it concerns itself with the period of the Yearbooks—reports of cases brought before the royal court in England, which were first circulated in 1292. Second, war and pestilence profoundly disrupted the society of this period. The Hundred Years' War, originating in sporadic conflicts be-tween England and France in the early fourteenth century, created a new nationalism in Europe's kingdoms and caused destruction on a scale that could not fail to affect the character of both rural and urban communities. The Black Death, recurrent in Europe from the middle of the fourteenth century, drastically reduced the population at all levels and created in-stability throughout the society. The selections in Part 4 reflect both the record-keeping proclivities of fourteenth- and fifteenth-century institu-tions and the effect of war and plague on those institutions.

R. H. Hilton's article "The Peasants in Revolt" deals with the causes and the character of mass movements, which often were connected with war, famine, and plague as well as adding to these miseries and disrup-tions. Mass movements occurred throughout Europe and expressed a variety of grievances and troubles.

John Keegan's powerful description and analysis of the famous battle of Agincourt turns our attention to an aspect of war, especially medieval war, rarely treated: the experience of the common soldier. He creates an appreciation for the strength of medieval soldiers, and he puts us in the very midst of the fear and pain of medieval battle.

Gerald Strauss reveals the daily life of a late medieval German city. The urban communes were small, self-contained units, with a varied pop-ulation living in close quarters. Such conditions presented serious threats to the peace and safety of citizens. The city government took cognizance of hygiene, fire protection, and police functions, as well as of matters pertaining to the city's prosperity.

In the twelfth and thirteenth centuries there was an ever-increasing market for educated men. Royal and ducal governments employed university graduates in their growing bureaucracies; the apparatus of ecclesiastical government grew to enormous proportions; every town had a demand for teachers. The boom ended in the mid-fourteenth century, and Guy F. Lytle, in "The Relevance of a University Education in 14th-Century England," analyzes both the job crisis for graduates and its impact on the universities of Oxford and Cambridge.

Finally, H. F. M. Prescott's "Touring the Holy Land" brings to life the experience of travelers and sailors in the Mediterranean. It is a story that would have been familiar to the men who went down to the sea two thousand years earlier, in ships that oceanographer Willard Bascom ("Ancient Ships and Shipping" in Part 1) seeks along the deep-water routes.

BIBLIOGRAPHY

On the peasant rebellions and other late medieval mass movements, see R. H. Hilton, *Bond Men Made Free: Medieval Peasant Movements and the English Rising of 1381* (London, 1973), the work from which the selection in this part is taken. See also Wallace K. Ferguson, *Europe in Transition, 1300–1520* (Boston, 1962), and Michel Mollat and Philippe Wolff, *The Popular Revolutions of the Late Middle Ages* (London, 1972). On specific rebellions, see Charles Oman, *The Great Revolt of 1381* (Oxford, 1906); Eileen Power, "The Effects of the Black Death on Rural Organization in England," *History*, Vol. 3 (1918), pp. 109–16; Steven Runciman, *The Sicilian Vespers* (Cambridge, Eng., 1958); and Howard Kaminsky, *A History of the Hussite Revolution* (Berkeley, 1967).

For a general history of war in medieval Europe, see the classic book by Charles Oman, *A History of the Art of War in the Middle Ages* (London, 1924). See also John Beeler, *Warfare in Feudal Europe, 730–1200* (Ithaca, N.Y., 1971); R. C. Smail, *Crusading Warfare (1097–1193): A Contribution to Medieval Military History* (Cambridge, Eng., 1956); Sidney Toy, *A History of Fortification from 3000 B.C. to A.D. 1700* (New York, 1955). On medieval weaponry, see Claude Blair, *European Armour, circa 1066 to circa 1700* (New York, 1959), and R. Ewart Oakeshott, *The Archaeology of Weapons: Arms and Armour from Prehistory to the Age of Chivalry* (London, 1960). For a general history of the Hundred Years' War, see Eduard Perroy, *The Hundred Years' War* (London, 1957). See also H. J. Hewitt, *The Organization of War Under Edward III* (Manchester, Eng., 1966), where traditional ideas about the limited destructiveness of medieval armies and strategy are challenged. For a general introduction to the character of medieval warriors, see A. Vesey B. Norman, *The Medieval Soldier* (New York, 1971).

The study of medieval cities has flourished in recent decades, See J. W. F. Hill, *Medieval Lincoln* (Cambridge, Eng., 1948); G. A. Williams, *Medieval London* (London, 1963); David Herlihy, *Medieval and Renaissance Pistoia* (New Haven, 1967); and Robert Brentano, *Rome Before Avignon* (New York, 1974). On the planning and founding of towns in the Middle Ages, see M. W. Beresford, *New Towns of the Middle Ages* (London, 1967), and F. Haverfield, *Ancient Town Planning* (Oxford, 1913). For an introduction to the urban populations, see, in addition to the works cited above, Fritz Rörig, *The Medieval Town* (Berkeley, 1967).

On the history of education in general, see Henri Marrou, *A History of Education in Antiquity* (New York, 1956); M. L. W. Laistner, *Thought and Letters in Western Europe A.D. 500 to 900* (Ithaca, N.Y., 1957, 1966); Pierre Riché, *Education and Culture in the Barbarian West: Sixth Through Eighth Centuries,* trans. J. J. Contreni (Columbia, S.C., 1976). For background material on the schools of the twelfth century, see the classic work of Charles Homer Haskins, *The Renaissance of the Twelfth Century* (Cambridge, Mass., 1927). On the universities, the basic work is H. Rashdall, *The Universities of Europe in the Middle Ages,* ed. F. M. Powicke and A. B. Emden, 3 vols., rev. ed. (Oxford, 1936). Two good short introductions are Charles Homer Haskins, *The Rise of the Universities* (New York, 1923) and Lowrie J. Daly, *The Medieval University, 1200–1400* (New York, 1961). On the internal organization of the universities, see Pearl Kibre, *The Nations in the Mediaeval Universities* (Cambridge, Mass., 1948). On later developments, see Gordon Leff, *Paris and Oxford Universities in the Thirteenth and Fourteenth Centuries* (New York, 1968).

There is a study of ships of the period of Friar Felix's journey in M. E. Mallett, *The Florentine Galleys in the Fifteenth Century* (Oxford, 1967). Mallett includes a ship's log from the period as well. See also E. L. Guilford, *Travel and Travellers in the Middle Ages* (New York, 1924). On the pilgrimages of the Middle Ages, see A. Kendall, *Medieval Pilgrims* (London, 1970). See also Robert S. Lopez, "The Evolution of Land Transport in the Middle Ages," *Past and Present,* Vol. 19 (1956), pp. 17–29. Irving Agus, in *Urban Civilization in Pre-Crusade Europe* (New York, 1965), includes an entire section on travel. His material focuses on the period from the ninth to the eleventh centuries, when political conditions kept most people off the roads.

The Peasants in Revolt

R. H. HILTON

France in 1251 and 1358; Sicily in 1282; Flanders in 1255, 1267, 1275, 1280, and 1302; and England in 1381 all experienced violent lower-class rebellions. And these are only the major uprisings; there were many others. In 1251, Louis IX of France, on a crusade in Egypt and recently defeated at Cairo, sent home a call for help. All over France, peasants rose to form a huge army that would bring succor to the king, but within a short time segments of this army forgot their mission and went rampaging through manors and cities. Under Louis's mother, Blanche of Castille, the royal government had at first supported the peasant army, but when Blanche and her counselors recognized the anarchic character of the movement, they acted in concert with city authorities and feudal lords to put a bloody end to it. In 1358, after twenty years of war with England and several plague epidemics, the peasants of France again rose in revolt. The immediate cause of the uprising was an order that the hard-pressed peasants must help rebuild the castles and manor houses of the rich in preparation for further fighting. The rising was incredibly vicious and bloody on both sides.

In Flanders the rebellions were mostly urban, since that area was, and still is, one of the most densely populated regions in Europe. The weavers and other lower-class groups in the cities rose against the patriciate, which had allied itself with the hated French king. The worst of these uprisings was the Matins of Bruges, which took place on May 17, 1302. When the town's church bells sounded matins, the first prayer service of the day at 2 A.M., the population rose to slaughter the French garrison and officials. Under the leadership of the count of Flanders, an army of weavers and workers devastated a French army sent to put down the rebellion. All the rebellions of Flanders were tied up with the political competition between the count and the French king. During the Hundred Years' War, the count sided with the English and further deepened the political divisions.

The Sicilian Vespers was also a popular uprising with political overtones. The people rose to drive out the French conquerors of the island, leaving the way open to Spanish intervention. But politics and social grievances were inextricably mixed up in the rebellion, and hundreds of French citizens, including women and children, lost their lives. Castles and other buildings occupied by the ruling class were also destroyed.

Perhaps the most famous insurrection, however, was the Peasants' Rebellion of 1381 in England. There had been unrest among the lower classes of the country for years following the plague (1348–1349). The drastic population decrease caused a severe labor shortage and led to a general disruption of the economy. Workers demanded higher wages, peasants left their farms to seek higher-paying jobs in the cities. The nobility, whose income depended on the rents received from peasant farmers, and the merchants, whose profits were being squeezed, took action against this movement in the Statutes of Laborers, which fixed wages and prohibited migration from the farms. That these provisions were not effective is shown by the complaints brought out in the parliaments of the period.

Why was late medieval society so prone to these upheavals? Was there some characteristic or set of characteristics that permeated all European society and would explain these events? In this selection, R. H. Hilton gives an overview of the movements, their causes, and their programs.

The best known of the late medieval peasant rebellions are: the revolt in maritime Flanders 1323–1327; the Jacquerie in the Paris region in 1358; the Tuchin movement in central France, from the 1360s to the end of the fourteenth century; the English rising of 1381; and the wars of the *remensas* in Catalonia during the 1460s and the 1480s. This is not an exhaustive list. Other specifically peasant movements on a smaller scale included the strike of the vineyard workers of the Auxerrois in the 1390s; and, more difficult to evaluate, movements involving peasants, in which the peasants might have formed the majority of participants, but which aimed at goals other than theirs or theirs specifically. The peasants might be full participants, or they might be being used by others for their own purposes.

The Taborite movement in Bohemia (the militant wing of the national Hussite movement against German and papal domination) was clearly to a considerable degree a peasant one in its composition and there were millenarian elements in its religious outlook, but it was led by gentry and clerics and there was a considerable artisan element. It hardly aimed, then, to fulfil specifically peasant demands. Peasants also participated in the risings in various parts of England in 1450, of which the most important was that in Kent led by Jack Cade, but their motivation was to such a degree political, and even dynastic, that there is some doubt as to whether they can be designated as peasant movements. In some ways they more resemble the provincial risings in parts of England in the 1530s which were directed against real or imagined oppression by the government, and to a considerable extent led by the local gentry.

What then are the problems posed by peasant movements, and particularly by the large-scale movements of the later middle ages? We should remember the basic tensions in a society where peasants were the majority of the basic producers, but the course of each movement must be investigated separately. And although a mere narrative history of events will not in itself throw much light on the fundamentals of the movements, such a narrative history must be established in order to discover the existence (or otherwise) of a common pattern in the sequence of events. Emerging, too, from an examination of the sequence of events must come some notion of the organization of the movements, and of the degree to which they either arose spontaneously, or were carefully planned by groups or individual organizers. This brings us to the vital question of the social and intellectual origins of the leaders of the movements—a problem which once answered necessarily involves the allied problems of the social composition of the participating masses. These considerations will lead us to the problem of the ideas guiding the various elements involved; this is by no means the same problem as that of the immediate or long-term goals, which also need scrutiny.

Finally some assessment of the historical consequences must be undertaken, not simply in terms of success or failure in the realization of explicitly stated goals, but also in terms of such changes of direction in the history of society which peasant movements may effect. An examination of the major European movements in terms of the problems thus classified could in turn be used to look afresh at the history of the English rising of 1381—one of the most interesting and significant as well as the best documented of all medieval peasant rebellions.

It is, of course, insufficient to prove that peasants and landowners had incompatible interests in the division of the social product, and that peasants therefore had a propensity to withhold rents and services and come into juridical or even political conflict with their lords. The fact is that the traditional social relationships between peasant and lord in varying forms persisted in different parts of Europe, probably from the bronze age until the eighteenth or nineteenth century. Something more than the natural antagonism between an exploiting and exploited class must therefore have precipitated movements which often seemed to the participants on both sides a break in the "natural order" of things; this phrase gives us a clue to the outbreak of many of the more serious movements.

Peasants, even more than their lords, tended to cling to custom, even when, without knowing it, they were constantly seeking to mould custom to suit their own interests. Günther Franz, in his history of the peasants' war in Germany at the beginning of the sixteenth century, noticed that (at any rate to begin with) rebellious peasants saw themselves as defending "the old law."

And so it was innovation by the lords which (in peasant eyes) seemed to justify their own renunciation of their humble role in the social hierarchy. It was the imposition of the indemnity tax by the King of France to be collected by the officials of the Count of Flanders (who should have been their protector) which pushed the self-assertive, unservile peasants and artisans in the maritime districts of Flanders into rebellion; it was the requisitions for the victualling of the castles of the nobility in the region of Paris, done at the expense of the peasants in the surrounding villages, which provoked the Jacquerie in 1358; it was the insolent taxation imposed by the king's lieutenant, the Duke of Berry, on his subjects in central France, when he was unable to protect them from the English and their hired *routiers*, which began the equally serious, though less well-known, Jacquerie of the Tuchins; and it was the extra demands by the lords of Catalonia for the so-called *malos usos*, or "evil customs," which precipitated the long war of the *remensas*, the servile peasants.

In none of these cases can it be supposed that the breach of customary expectations was the only cause of the outbreak. There were important, indeed essential, predisposing factors. The resistance to the collection of the indemnity tax in Flanders in 1323 was not a sudden decision on the part of a normally passive population. This population was composed for the most part of descendants of free settlers in the coastal districts. Many of them were quite poor, although their leaders were among the richest of the peasants of the district, as is shown in the enumeration of the lands and goods of the dead after the defeat of the rising in 1327 at the battle of Cassel. Many of the peasants were involved in the textile trade, which was already spreading from town to country. Their obligations to their lords were mainly acquitted in money rent, and they were of free status, and made up a strong quasi-communal element in the organization of local government. Although presided over by the Count of Flanders' bailiff (usually a noble), the local courts were composed of jurors, *keuriers* or *échevins*, many of whom were peasants. And when the revolt reached fever pitch at the beginning of 1325, the peasants took over the existing organization and put their own captains in place of the count's bailiffs. Above all, there had existed since the beginning of the century a strong sentiment of hostility to the French-speaking nobility and their patrician allies among the great merchants of the towns. They had, for these reasons, supported the Count of Flanders so long as he resisted his suzerain, the King of France. No doubt they remembered the battle of Courtrai in 1302, when peasants and weavers defeated the mounted knights of France, but in spite of which they had had imposed upon them by the count's capitulation at Athis (1304) the first heavy indemnity payment to the French crown.

The general conditions in the area to the north, north-east and south of

Paris, in the spring of 1358, were even more likely than those in maritime Flanders to enable any extra oppression to spark off a rebellion. For a year, the hired soldiers of the French and English, now under truce, had been living off the countryside, and the peasants could no longer distinguish between their "own" and the enemy's supporters. The situation was further complicated by the entry into the game of Charles, King of Navarre, a possible pretender to the French throne, whose troops were as likely to be fighting for the English or for themselves, as for the Regent of France, the king being in prison in England. Furthermore, from March 1358, there had been civil war between the regent and his supporters, on the one hand, and a reforming party, on the other, led by Etienne Marcel, provost of the merchants of Paris.

The nobility was discredited, and unable to perform its traditional function of defending the other orders. Its landed income was insufficient, for rents were low; and the price of grain was low, while wages and other costs were high. Many of the male members of the nobility had to be ransomed. Hence, the nobles and their men-at-arms in the castles of the Île de France, were as likely to pillage and slay the local peasants as were the bands led by such foreign captains as the Englishman James Pipe, lieutenant of the King of Navarre, who was operating south of Paris. While the traditional explanation of the Jacquerie as a revolt against misery contains an element of truth, it is insufficient. Included in the rebellious area were prosperous villages, especially north of Paris, where exasperation at taxation and requisition, and disillusion with the collapse of the traditional social order, were combined with the economic grievances of the normally well-to-do cereal farmers who were unable to get a good price for their product. At the same time, the impoverished and badly harassed area to the south-west of the city—precisely where one would expect an explosion of pure misery—was virtually untouched by the rebellion.

A combination of pillaging by bands of soldiers, and heavy, even illegal, taxation was also responsible for the further and very different Jacquerie in the France of the Hundred Years' War—the counter-brigandage of the Tuchins. If the Jacquerie of 1358 in Paris gives the appearance (even if illusory) of being a short, sharp and elemental protest against miserable conditions, the Tuchins are the prototype of a very different form of poor people's protest, one which we have come to recognize as "social banditry." We find here no rising *en masse* of an outraged peasant population, but a cunning adoption by the mountain population of Auvergne, both the suburban artisans of towns like St Flour and the peasants of the district, of the pillaging habits of their erstwhile oppressors. From the early 1360s until the middle of the 1380s, the Tuchins troubled the authorities, while the Jacques around Paris were crushed after only two weeks by the noble companies under the command of the King of Navarre. All the same, the immediate causes were the same for both Jacqueries—the pillage of the military companies, and government taxation.

One of the most sustained of peasant wars was that of the Catalan *remensas*, or servile peasants, in the fifteenth century. Catalonia, compared with most other parts of Spain, was heavily seigneuralized, and the majority of peasants were unfree. Apart from the various rents and services which they owed to their lords, they were particularly restricted in their feedom of movement, and these restrictions had been strengthened from the thirteenth century—the lords' response to emigration southwards to colonize the newly conquered lands and to the growing cities. After the Black Death, there was a further seigneurial reaction, prompted by the fall in landed revenues, when extra rents in kind were demanded, and boon services were made compulsory.

All those peasants who were already forbidden to leave their holdings except on payment of a heavy redemption, the *remensas*, were now reckoned automatically liable to what had become known as the "five evil customs" (*malos usos*). These were: *intestia*, a death duty of one-third of movables payable in case of intestacy; *exorquia*, another death duty; *cugucia*, one-third or one-half of movables payable in case of a wife's adultery; *arsina*, a fine paid if the farm caught fire accidentally; and *firma d'espoli violenta*, a fine aimed at restricting the raising of a mortgage. These obligations were not new in the fifteenth century, but they had not been universally applicable. It was their generalization and imposition on all peasants liable to *remensas* and the fear of free tenants that they would spread to them which united the Catalan rural population against their lords. This resentment arose as much because these obligations were obvious earmarks of personal servility as because they were economically burdensome. But the search for freedom was, it seems, also exacerbated by a conflict with the lords over abandoned holdings (*casos ronecs*). The question was whether these should be shared among surviving tenants at low rents, or absorbed into demesne or let on lease on short terms at high rents.

Small-scale local revolts against the seigneurial reaction had already begun by the late 1380s, and continued into the early part of the fifteenth century. The *remensas* attempted to have the *malos usos* abolished by the crown, and offered enormous sums for their redemption. Their abolition was accepted by Alphonso V in 1455, under peasant pressure, and it was the refusal of the nobles, led by the Bishop of Gerona and the patricians of Barcelona, which precipitated the war of 1462. In this war the reactionary nobility and the urban patricians found themselves fighting not only the peasants but the king. A renewal of the war in 1483 was due entirely to an attempt by the nobility and the patricians to put the clock back to the pre-1455 situation, but social tensions became critical as a result also of the prolonged crisis of Catalonia's declining economy.

It will be seen that the immediate causes for some of the most serious of the mass movements were actions by landowners or governments, or both together, which altered the customary relationships or disappointed normal expectations, to the detriment of the peasant class as a whole, rich and poor. Although a heavy tax, or a requisition order, or the reversal of a concession might not in itself precipitate a rising, it might do so in the context of the strained social relationships which we find in each of the areas we have considered. This strain is normally seen by the peasants from an apparently conservative standpoint. They cannot accept the abandonment of traditional roles by any one of the orders of the society—whose basic structure they do not, to begin with, challenge. This seems always to be the most important factor, and the significance of precipitating causes (taxes, for example) is that, as they affect all, they unify all—and focus existing resentments.

If we can see common features in the causation of these movements, contrasts rather than similarities appear when we look at the pattern of events and the form of the struggle. The most obvious contrast is the duration of the rebellions. The rising which has bequeathed to history that most familiar name, the Jacquerie, and the supposedly typical characteristics of peasant rebellion—namely, extreme violence and a hatred of the nobility—was in fact the shortest and worst-organized. The first of the recorded conflicts between peasants and the plundering brigands, the nobles, was at St Leu d'Esserent, near Senlis, on 28 May 1358, though there were probably almost simultaneous outbreaks further west. The destruction of the main peasant army under Guillaume Cale by the King of Navarre near Mello occurred on 10 June and the peasants who were helping the Parisians in their siege of the royalist nobles in the fortress at Meaux were defeated and slaughtered on the following day. The Jacquerie began and was militarily defeated in a fortnight.

On the other hand, the armed revolt of the peasants of maritime Flanders which began in 1323 did not end until June 1328, when the King of France and the Flemish nobility defeated the peasants and artisans at Cassel. The Tuchins began their independent operations as groups of "social bandits" in the mountains of Auvergne in 1363 and were not destroyed as a social force until the summer of 1384. Even after their defeat at Mentières, sporadic bands were operating until the general amnesty of 1381, and there was a brief revival in the early fifteenth century. The struggle of the remensas was even longer lived, if we count the earliest sporadic outbreaks as occurring from 1388. The mass campaigns lasted from 1462 until 1471, and from 1484 until 1486—though there is some difficulty here in separating the peasant war for the abolition of the malos usos from the civil war which involved the crown, the nobility and the bourgeoisie.

It must be due partly to a failure in organization when a mass peasant movement is as quickly suppressed as the Jacquerie: a failure to organize according to the needs of the situation, the known strength of the enemy and the reliability of the allies. The Jacques gathered in village groups and operated separately. Owing to the surprise experienced by the nobles at this sudden insubordination, the rebels, with some assistance from the Parisians, managed to destroy a considerable number of castles, along with the records which the owners kept of the peasants' obligations to them. In common with other rural risings, the example of rebellion rapidly spread by word of mouth from village to village, without the separate bands concerting a common policy. Eventually, their most experienced captain, Guillaume Cale, managed to get together a force of several thousands; but this numerical strength gave an illusion of power which Cale tried to dispel. Militarily inexperienced, the fact that they had come together to present a single target for the knights and men-at-arms under Charles of Navarre led to their downfall. Special methods of fighting were needed for peasants to defeat armed horsemen in pitched battle, as the Taborites with their battlewagons made from farm carts were to show after 1420 in Bohemia. Even the successors of the victors of Courtrai were defeated in the end by an army of French chivalry at Cassel, although they had, it seems, succeeded for a time in organizing themselves on the basis of the existing administrative framework of the *ambachten* or castleries.

The most successful peasant military organization (if we put on one side the Hussite armies as not being the product of a specifically peasant movement) was undoubtedly that of the *remensas*. They had already begun to meet in assemblies in the 1440s, in order to discuss the redemption of the *malos usos*, and when the peasant army was eventually organized in the 1460s, their leader Francisco Verntallat did so by recruiting one man from every three households. The removal at the end of the first *remensa* war of peasant garrisons from castles shows that they had learnt the importance of fortification, and a later royal veto, on the eve of the second war, on peasants or artisans having riding horses, shows that they must have learnt, too, this other aspect of medieval armed combat. Above all, the peasant army rested on the basis of sworn association, the *sacramental*, created in the peasant assemblies.

This, then, was one way of organizing: the creation of a military force based on a form of political and social institution, the village or district assembly. It was more successful in Catalonia than in maritime Flanders; but the Tuchins show that it was not the only way in which peasants and plebeians could organize to harass the authorities. Here we return to the more elemental form of organization in small bands, but in the case of the Tuchins there was no attempt to engage in head-on conflict with the military forces of the nobility or the crown. Continuing with their ordinary agricultural or artisan occupations in village or suburb, these bands of twenty or thirty men, or occasionally more—associates, bound together by terrible oaths—organized themselves for the pillage of livestock, valuables or cash, and for the capture of churchmen, gentry or merchants for the purposes of ransom. In Auvergne, between the 1360s and the 1380s, the habitual prey of the Tuchins were the English or Gascon *routiers*, who were despoilers of the countryside but whose booty was then looted by the Tuchins like wolves drawn to the sheepfold.

The Tuchins were able to play an intricate political game. Local authorities, such as the consuls of St Flour, made truces with the English in order to be left at peace, while the Tuchins robbed the English, and so embroiled the local notables whom the English suspected of breaking the truce. In the eyes of the royal government, however, such truces were illegal, and the peasant and artisan brigands came almost to appear—quite unintentionally as far as they were concerned—as patriots. The Tuchins kept going as long as conditions favoured them, that is, while disorder created by the operations of the *routiers* and general hostility among peasants and town artisans to the nobles and to the authorities, resulting from the failure to defend them from the Anglo-Gascons and from the excessive taxation of the king's lieutenant, lasted. When relative peace and stability returned, the Tuchins' bands could only prey on the mass of the peasantry, so losing their support.

The Tuchins were not all peasants. Artisans from the suburbs of St Flour and elsewhere were also involved. Furthermore, the leaders of the bands were often members of the nobility. Even so, it is by no means the case that we should not examine the Tuchinat as a peasant movement. For there were, in fact, very few "pure" peasant movements, at any rate on a mass scale, in the sense that the participants and leaders were exclusively of peasant origin. The number of nobles in the leadership of the Tuchins is not difficult to explain. In the first place, they were often outcasts from their own class, sometimes using the Tuchins only for their own purposes, but used by the Tuchins in turn, who found it convenient to employ the military skills of the class which still regarded itself, by profession as well as status, primarily as a warrior class.

Thus, Mignot de Cardaillac, a Tuchin leader in the Paulhac region in the 1360s, was a bastard of a prominent noble family involved in disputes with other nobles over succession to property. Pierre de Brugère (or de Brès), a Tuchin leader during the 1380s, was connected by family ties with many leading families of Auvergne and Languedoc, and probably joined the Tuchins after robbing his relative, the Bishop of Albi, and perhaps because of domestic troubles when his squire became his wife's lover. After Pierre was killed, other gentry leaders appeared, such as the Lord of Pertus and Jean de Dienne. At the fag-end of the Tuchin movement, Jean de Chalus, returning to Auvergne from Agincourt in 1415, was captured by a band of Tuchins and forced to join them, to take part in their assemblies and to bind himself to them by swearing an oath.

The leadership of peasant bands by members of the nobility, even for quite specifically peasant objectives, was not as rare as one might imagine. Even in a movement as frankly hostile to the nobility as a class as the Jacquerie of 1358, some nobles, as well as bourgeois, were engaged on the side of the peasants. The three or four whose names we know from letters of pardon issued afterwards by the king, naturally sought to excuse themselves, alleging that they had been forced to become leaders of the peasants' bands. This may, indeed, have been true, though we can never know what private or political rancours might have determined an individual to abandon his apparent class interest. The interest of the peasants in securing the leadership of locally prominent individuals is more explicable. In the case of the Montmorency district, we even find them asking Simon de Bernes, provost and captain of the county of Beaumont, for permission to choose a leader, a choice which fell on Jacques de Chennevières, who afterwards pretended to have accepted against his wishes and to have attempted to moderate the peasants' violence. As we have already suggested, some peasants may have been conscious of their lack of military expertise. The question also arises as to what extent the concept of the gentry as the natural leaders of the peasants still persisted, even when the conflict of interest between the two classes seemed absolute.

It will not do to overemphasize the part played by gentry in the leadership of peasants' movements. There is the abundant evidence from the earlier period of peasant leadership of small-scale movements which we have already examined, and this source of leaders by no means dried up. Lack of contrary indication would suggest that Guillaume Cale of Mello must have been a well-to-do peasant, and Clais Zannekin, who began to play a leading role in the rising of maritime Flanders from 1324, appears as one of the better-off peasants with a holding of between thirty-five and forty acres of arable land, although it has been suggested that he had property in Bruges. In addition, was not Francisco Verntallat really a peasant, in spite of his poor *hidalgo* ancestors on one side of the family, and his promotion and enrichment by the king after the end of the first war of the *remensas*? And the more radical Père Jean Sala likewise? The same kind of background was probably true of most of the minor leaders in all of the movements. Their names tend not to be recorded. Fewer but more exceptional individuals are mentioned by chroniclers or appear in the records precisely because their participation was unexpected.

A frequently noticed source of outside leaders of peasant and other plebeian movements of the Middle Ages is the clergy, particularly the lesser clergy. Various explanations are given, such as that which states that the participating clerics may have been of peasant origin, and that their lowly position at the bottom of the ecclesiastical hierarchy made them resentful of the existing social order, and that, further, they were influenced by the radical, egalitarian element in the Christian tradition. The lesser clergy, as we have seen, often occupied an important position of leadership in the people's crusades and in heretical movements with peasant and artisan followings. On the whole, the clerics' presence is most frequent where movements have aims going well beyond the satisfaction of immediate social and political demands or the expression of immediate resentment of social oppression. Thus, even if the fight of the Apostles in northern Italy at the beginning of the fourteenth century had any of the characteristics of a peasant movement, by reason of its class composition, its aims were apocalyptic and were inevitably articulated by a man with a clerical background. Similarly, the extreme Taborites or Pikarts around the year 1420 in Bohemia—whatever the temporary practice of a sort of "war communism" might have implied about their social views—were also apocalyptic visionaries, and their leaders tended to be priests, like the Moravian, Martin Huska. Similarly the views of the Taborite centre, of Waldensian inspiration, were articulated by priests such as Jan Zelivsky.

Those movements, however, which we have taken to be typical, where not only was the mass of participants drawn from the peasantry, but where they were reacting against social pressures on them as peasants, and were seeking a peasant solution, had a remarkably weak priestly participation. The one important exception to this is to be found in England in 1381, and will be considered later in detail. Not only were there no priests in the leadership of the rebellion in maritime Flanders, but there is evidence of strong anticlericalism. The refusal to pay tithes, for example, in the area of Ghent, shows a clear anti-clerical disposition, though this could have been compatible with a certain type of radical clerical inspiration. But under the later leadership of Jacques Peyt, anti-clericalism sharpened. In November 1325 an interdict had been placed on Flanders, and Peyt and his successors had forced priests either to perform their office or to emigrate. Peyt was said to have wished to do away with all priests. Some evidence of a minor participation by a few clerics in the Jacquerie of 1358 can be shown, but there is no leadership. The Tuchins not only had no leaders from the clerical order, but at times show signs of anti-clericalism. In the 1380s, for instance, clerics in Tuchin-dominated areas thought it prudent to disguise themselves as laymen (in areas of military operations it was usually the other way round); a Trinitarian friar so disguised was killed when he was captured.

Nor does the *remensas* movement reveal any clerical participation or direction. It is true that one of the earliest rebellious actions of some of the *remensas* was participation in the anti-Jewish pogroms of 1391, in which there was clerical direction and which assumed a social character unexpected by some of these clerical agitators. *Remensas* were also involved in a jointly antisemitic and anti-landowner action in Gerona in 1415. But the essential movement against the *malos usos* had no clerical or even religious inspiration. Indeed the historian of the movement, J. V. Vives, particularly noticed how little religion there was in its ideology. This, he discovered, was mainly of juridical inspiration, namely the idea that by natural law all men are free and have the right to be protected by the king against the nobles. It was the jurisconsult Thomas Mieres, not a cleric, who voiced these views. . . .

In spite of the considerable differences between these late-medieval peasant movements, there was one prominent feature which they had in common: the emergence, among some of the participants, of a consciousness of class. It was, however, a negative class consciousness in that the definition of class which was involved was that of their enemies rather than of themselves: in other words, the nobility. Henri Pirenne, writing about the revolt of maritime Flanders in his introduction to the list of confiscations after Cassel, insisted on its social character. It was, he wrote, "a class war between the peasants and the nobility." This anti-noble characteristic was to the fore already in 1323 in an attack on members of local courts, the *keuriers*, who were of noble or patrician origin. Under the leadership of Jacques Peyt, in 1326, after the reimposition of an indemnity payable to the King of France at the so-called peace of Arques, this deep emotion developed into a terror directed against both the nobility and their supporters. The peasant rebels were said by the official chronicler of the counts of Flanders to have threatened the rich with death, saying to them: "you love the nobles more than you do the commons from whom you live."

This conscious hostility towards the noble class was very prominent during the Jacquerie of 1358. Without any declaration of aims, its existence could be concluded from the fact that the objects of the peasants' attacks were exclusively knights, squires and ladies, along with the castles in which they lived. A recent historian, commenting on the fiscal and other pressures on the peasants which were particularly irksome after the battle of Poitiers, goes so far as to say that "the quick irritation that Jacques Bonhomme experienced in the face of these exactions was nothing compared with his permanent rage against the nobles whom he blamed, as a whole, for not having fulfilled their duty of protection which tradition and mutual obligation demanded of them." Froissart, at the beginning of his account of the Jacquerie, reports a discussion among the peasants (no doubt imagined):

> . . . one of them got up and said that the nobility of France, knights and squires, were disgracing and betraying the realm, and that it would be a good thing if they all destroyed. At this they all shouted: "He's right! He's right! Shame on any man who saves the gentry from being wiped out."

And again Froissart says (somewhat illogically) that when the peasants were asked the reason for their violent actions, "they replied that they did not know; it was because they saw others doing them that they copied them. They thought that by such means they could destroy all the nobles and gentry in the world, so that there would be no more of them."

Jean de Venette emphasizes the same element of class hatred:

> . . . the peasants . . . seeing that the nobles gave them no protection, but rather oppressed them as heavily as the enemy, rose and took arms against the nobles of France . . . the number of peasants eager to extirpate the nobles and their wives and to destroy their manor houses grew until it was estimated at five thousand.

The social bandit, as compared with the peasants engaged in mass risings, operated mostly with a less precise consciousness of his position of social antagonism to his opponents. Any bird was worth the plucking, and if he did not pluck his own kind it was because there was little or nothing to be had. All the same, awareness of social conflict was not altogether missing. The evidence for the greatest degree of class consciousness comes from the last major phase of Tuchin activity, that of the 1380s, when, according to the life of Charles VI in the St Denis chronicle, the terrible mutual oaths of the Tuchin bands included the promise never more to submit to taxation, but only to keep the ancient liberty of their country (*patrie antiquam servantes libertatem*). The social bandit's chosen prey were men of the church, the nobles, and the merchants. One of their captains, the renegade noble, Pierre de Brugère, gave orders to his lieutenants that no one with smooth, uncalloused hands or who by gesture, clothing or speech showed courtliness or elegance should even be admitted to their company, but rather slain. Such remarks about the Tuchins come from a hostile writer, writing no doubt like Froissart from hearsay evidence. But even taking exaggeration into account, the element of conscious class antagonism which is suggested may well have been present.

The ferocity which, rightly or wrongly, was attributed to the French rebels by the aristocratic chroniclers does not appear in the Catalan wars unless we can glimpse it in the physical demonstrations by some of the *remensas* peasants at the turn of the fourteenth century, when in order to intimidate the landowners, and perhaps unwelcome lessees of the lapsed holdings, they dug ditches and put up crosses and other signs, the *senyals mort*, threatening death. There may have been some diversion from possible class antagonism on the peasants' part by the attitude evinced by the monarchy from time to time, and expressed in its strongest terms perhaps by Queen Maria de Luna in letters to Pope Benedict XIII. In these letters she describes the peasants' servile obligation as "evil, detestable, pestiferous, execrable, and abominable . . . against God and justice, perilous to the soul and leading to the infamy of the Catalan nation." Whether or not such strong words reached the peasants themselves and perhaps counteracted the impression of later more ambivalent royal attitudes to the conflict, the fact remains that the peasants from the beginning made a distinction between rents payable simply for the use of land, which many of them were prepared to pay, and dues which resulted from the special jurisdictional power of the nobles as feudal lords, which they rejected as being "against the natural justice of the liberty of man." In the last phase of the *remensas* war under the leadership of Sala, the most radical demanded the end of all rent and the establishment of absolute peasant property rights. All this implies a generally radical outlook with respect to the institutions which underpinned medieval society, but one without a specific commitment to the eradication of the nobility as a class.

The "moderates" among the Catalan peasants negotiated a settlement by which not only the *malos usos* were to be abolished together with compensation to the lords, but serfdom and the lords' right to impose their will by force (*ius maletractandi*). Perhaps this settlement, like other half-way agreements, would never have been embodied in the *Sentenciae Arbitral de Guadalupe* (1486), had it not been for the pressure of the extremists. The *remensas* became almost peasant-proprietors and for some time enjoyed a relative prosperity, compared with their contemporaries in Aragon and Castile. This success was unique and undoubtedly due to the social and economic crises of fifteenth-century Catalonia and to the need of the crown of Aragon for allies against the Catalan nobility and the patrician government of Barcelona. No other mass-movement, with the possible exception of the English peasants after 1381, achieved a comparable success. We have seen that the Flemish peasants were bloodily defeated, and Flanders entered on a prolonged period of crisis. The peasants of northern France were also crushed in 1358, and were to continue to suffer the main brunt of the Anglo-French wars until the final defeat of the English in 1453. And although we have not found it possible to accept the struggles of the Taborites in Bohemia as other than a national and social movement with peasant support, it must be admitted that in Bohemia in the long run, the position of the peasants, in a society whose structure was not fundamentally changed, worsened rather than improved. The successors of the Taborites adopted a pacifist and quietist position in politics which enabled the lords to bring to Bohemia the deteriorating conditions suffered by peasants all over eastern Europe.

Feudal War in Practice

JOHN KEEGAN

Many books and articles have been devoted to the study of warfare in the Middle Ages and to individual battles and campaigns, but the great majority of these works focus on the art of war rather than on the actual conduct of operations. The military predominance of the heavily armed knight, and the great body of contemporary literature promulgating the ideal of knightly life, have influenced the historiography of warfare so as to emphasize the role of the knight. Medieval chroniclers, too, focused on the aristocratic mounted soldiers, but recent studies show that the major portion of most medieval armies was an infantry force.

Recognition of the composite nature of medieval armies, with its attendant appreciation for the tactics of such forces, does not, however, satisfy the British historian John Keegan. He asserts that historians of modern wars and armies, where the composition of the troops has not been in question, nonetheless give a distorted history of campaigns and battles because they see them from the standpoint of generals and politicians. Keegan points out the defects of this sort of military history and suggests that we will not get a fair view of war unless we look at battles and campaigns against the background of the societies in which they occurred. How violent or sacrificial was the society that produced the army and its generals? What impact did contemporary ideas of mortality have? Questions such as these would enlarge the field of military history and make it part of the general historiography on any period or society. Keegan himself wants to do something more specific, however. He wants to focus on battle itself, but to see it from the standpoint of the common soldier. He asks: What was the common experience of war in medieval and modern Europe? He explains his approach this way: "I do not intend to write about generals or generalship, except to discuss how a commander's physical presence on the field may have influenced his subordinates' will to combat. I do not intend to say anything of logistics or strategy and very little of tactics in the formal sense. And I do not intend to offer a two-sided picture of events, since what happened to one side in any battle I describe will be enough to convey the features I think are salient. On the other hand, I do intend to discuss wounds and their treatment, the mechanics of being taken prisoner, the nature of leadership at the most junior level, the role of compulsion in getting men to stand their ground, the incidence of accidents as a cause of death in war and, above all, the dimensions of the danger which different varieties of weapons offer to the soldier on the battlefield. . . . my purpose [is]

. . . to suggest how and why the men who have had (and do have) to face these weapons control their fears, staunch their wounds, go to their deaths. It is a personal attempt to catch a glimpse of the face of battle" (*The Face of Battle*, p. 78). What follows is Keegan's description and explanation of the battle of Agincourt, October 25, 1415, one of the principal battles of the Hundred Years' War.

The army embarked in the second week of August at Portsmouth and set sail on August 11th. It had been gathering since April, while Henry conducted deliberately inconclusive negotiations with Charles VI, and now numbered about ten thousand in all, eight thousand archers and two thousand men-at-arms, exclusive of camp followers. A good deal of the space in the ships, of which there were about 1,500, was given over to impedimenta and a great deal to the expedition's horses: at least one for each man-at-arms, and others for the baggage train and wagon teams. The crossing took a little over two days and on the morning of August 14th the army began to disembark, unopposed by the French, on a beach three miles west of Harfleur. Three days were taken to pitch camp and on August 18th the investment of the town began. It was not strongly garrisoned but its man-made and natural defences were strong, the Seine, the River Lézarde and a belt of marshes protecting it on the south, north and east. An attempt at mining under the moat on the western front was checked by French counter-mines so the small siege train, which contained at least three heavy guns, undertook a bombardment of that section of the walls. It lasted for nearly a month, until the collapse of an important gate-defence, the repulse of a succession of sorties and the failure of a French relieving army to appear, convinced the garrison that they must surrender. After parleys, the town opened its gates to Henry on Sunday, September 22nd.

He now had his base, but was left with neither time nor force enough to develop much of a campaign that year; at least a third of his army was dead or disabled, chiefly through disease, and the autumnal rains were due. Earlier in September he had set to paper his intention of marching down the Seine to Paris and thence to Bordeaux as soon as Harfleur fell; that had clearly become unfeasible, but honour demanded that he should not leave France without making a traverse, however much more circumspect, of the lands he claimed. At a long Council of War, held on October 5th, he convinced his followers that they could both appear to seek battle with the French armies which were known to be gathering and yet safely out-distance them by a march to the haven of Calais. On October 8th he led the army out.

His direct route was about 120 miles and lay across a succession of rivers, of which only the Somme formed a major obstacle. He began following the coast as far as the Béthune, which he crossed on October 11th, revictualling his army at Arques. The following day he crossed the Bresle, near Eu, having made eighty miles in five days, and on October 13th swung inland to cross the Somme above its estuary. On approaching, however, he got his first news of the enemy and it was grave; the nearest crossing was blocked and defended by a force of six thousand. After discussion, he rejected a retreat and turned south-east to follow the line of the river until he found an unguarded ford. For the next five days, while his army grew hungrier, the French kept pace with him on the northern bank until on the sixth, by a forced march across the plain of the Santerre (scene of the great British tank battle on August 8th, 1918), he got ahead of them and found a pair of unguarded though damaged causeways at Bethencourt and Voyennes. Some hasty sappering made them fit for traffic and that evening, October 19th, the army slept on the far bank. Henry declared October 20th a day of rest, which his men badly needed, having marched over two hundred miles in twelve days, but the arrival of French heralds with a challenge to fight was a reminder that they could not linger. On October 21st they marched eighteen miles, crossing the tracks of a major French army and, during the three following days, another fifty-three. They were now within two, at most three, marches of safety. All were aware, however, that the French had caught up and were keeping pace on their right flank. And late in the day of October 24th scouts came back with word that the enemy had crossed their path and were deploying for battle ahead of them. Henry ordered his men to deploy also but, as darkness was near, the French eventually stood down and withdrew a little to the north where they camped astride the road to Calais.

The English army found what shelter it could for the night in and around the village of Maisoncelles, ate its skimpy rations, confessed its sins, heard Mass and armed for battle. At first light knights and archers marched out and took up their positions between two woods. The French army, composed almost exclusively of mounted and dismounted men-at-arms, had deployed to meet them and was in similar positions about a thousand yards distant. For four hours both armies held their ground. Henry apparently hoped that the French would attack him; they, who knew that sooner or later he would have to move—either to the attack, which suited their book, or to retreat, which suited them even better—stood or sat idle, eating their breakfasts and calling about cheerfully to each other. Eventually Henry decided to up sticks (literally: his archers had been carrying pointed stakes to defend their lines for the last week) and advance on the French line. Arrived within three hundred yards—extreme bowshot—of the army, the English archers replanted their stakes and loosed off their first flights of arrows. The French, provoked by these arrow strikes, as Henry intended, into attacking, launched charges by the mounted men-at-arms from the wings of the main

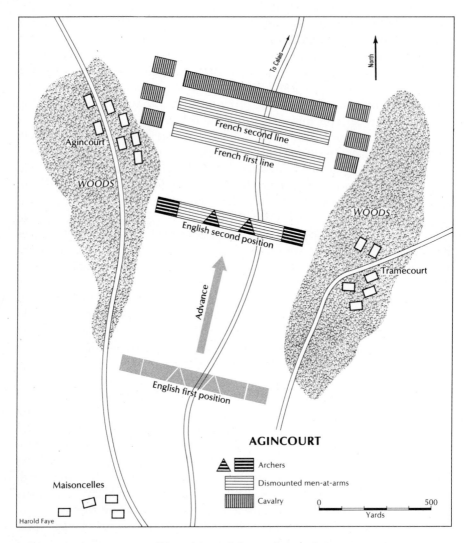

THE BATTLE OF AGINCOURT: Disposition of the English and French forces

body. Before they had crossed the intervening space they were followed by the dismounted men-at-arms who, like them, were wearing full armour. The cavalry failed to break the English line, suffered losses from the fire of the archers and turned about. Heading back for their own lines, many riders and loose horses crashed into the advancing line of dismounted men-at-arms. They, though shaken, continued to crowd forward and to mass their attack against the English men-at-arms, who were drawn up in three groups, with archers between them and on the right and left flank. Apparently disdaining battle with the archers, although they were suffering losses from their fire, the French quickened their steps over the last few yards and crashed into the middle of the English line. For a moment it gave way. But the French were so tightly bunched that they could not use their weapons to widen the breach they had made. The English men-at-arms recovered their balance, struck back and were now joined by numbers of the archers who, dropping their bows, ran against the French with axes, mallets and swords, or with weapons abandoned by the French they picked up from the ground. There followed a short but very bloody episode of hand-to-hand combat, in which freedom of action lay almost wholly with the English. Many of the French armoured infantrymen lost their footing and were killed as they lay sprawling; others who remained upright could not defend themselves and were killed by thrusts between their armour-joints or stunned by hammer-blows. The French second line which came up, got embroiled in this fighting without being able to turn the advantage to their side, despite the addition they brought to the very great superiority of numbers the French already enjoyed. Eventually, those Frenchmen who could disentangle themselves from the mêlée made their way back to where the rest of their army, composed of a third line of mounted men-at-arms, stood watching. The English who faced them did so in several places, over heaps of dead, dying or disabled French men-at-arms, heaps said by one chronicler to be taller than a man's height. Others were rounding up disarmed and lightly wounded Frenchmen and leading them to the rear, where they were collected under guard.

While this went on, a French nobleman, the Duke of Brabant, who had arrived late for the battle from a christening party, led forward an improvised charge; but it was broken up without denting the English line, which was still drawn up. Henry had prudently kept it under arms because the French third line—of mounted men—had not dispersed and he must presumably have feared that it would ride down on them if the whole English army gave itself up to taking and looting prisoners. At some time in the afternoon, there were detected signs that the French were nerving themselves to charge anyhow; and more or less simultaneously, a body of armed peasants, led by three mounted knights, suddenly appeared at the baggage park, inflicted some loss of life and stole some objects of value, including one of the King's crowns, before being driven off.

Either that incident or the continued menace of the French third line now prompted Henry to order that all the prisoners instantly be killed. The order was not at once obeyed, and for comprehensible reasons. Even discounting any moral or physical repugnance on the part of their captors, or a misunderstanding of the reason behind the order—that the prisoners might

attack the English from the rear with weapons retrieved from the ground if
the French cavalry were suddenly to attack their front—the poorer English
soldiers, and perhaps not only the poorer, would have been very reluctant to
pass up the prospects of ransom which killing the prisoners would entail.
Henry was nevertheless adamant; he detailed an esquire and two hundred
archers to set about the execution, and stopped them only when it became
clear that the French third line was packing up and withdrawing from the
field. Meantime very many of the French had been killed; some of the
English apparently even incinerated wounded prisoners in cottages where
they had been taken for shelter.

The noblest and richest of the prisoners were, nevertheless, spared and
dined that evening with the King at Maisoncelles, his base of the previous
evening, to which he now returned. En route he summoned the heralds of
the two armies who had watched the battle together from a vantage point,
and settled with the principal French herald a name for the battle: Agincourt,
after the nearest fortified place. Next morning, after collecting the army,
marshalling the prisoners and distributing the wounded and the loads of loot
among the transport, he marched the army off across the battlefield towards
Calais. Numbers of the French wounded had made their way or been
helped from the field during the night; those still living, unless thought
ransomable, were now killed. On October 29th, the English, with two thousand prisoners, reached Calais. The King left for England at once, to be
escorted into London by an enormous party of rejoicing citizens.

These are the bare outlines of the battle, as recorded by seven or eight
chroniclers, who do not materially disagree over the sequence, character or
significance of events. Of course, even though three of them were present at
the scene, none was an eye-witness of everything, or even of very much, that
happened. An army on the morrow of a battle, particularly an army as small
as that of Agincourt, must, nevertheless, be a fairly efficient clearing-house of
information, and it seems probable that a broadly accurate view of what had
happened—though not necessarily why and how it had happened—would
quickly crystallize in the mind of any diligent interrogator, while a popularly
agreed version, not dissimilar from it, would soon circulate within, and outside, the ranks. It would seem reasonable therefore to believe that the narrative of Agincourt handed down to us is a good one; it would in any case be
profitless to look for a better.

The Battle

What we almost completely lack, though, is the sort of picture and
understanding of the practicalities of the fighting and of the mood, outlook
and skills of the fighters which were themselves part of the eye-witness
chroniclers' vision. We simply cannot visualize, as they were able to do, what

the Agincourt arrow-cloud can have looked, or sounded, like; what the armoured men-at-arms sought to do to each other at the moment of the first clash; at what speed and in what density the French cavalry charged down; how the mêlée—the densely packed mass of men in hand-to-hand combat—can have appeared to a detached onlooker, say to men in the French third line; what level the noise of the battle can have reached and how the leaders made themselves heard—if they did so—above it. These questions lead on to less tangible inquiries: how did leadership operate once the fighting had been joined—by exhortation or by example? Or did concerted action depend upon previously rehearsed tactics and corporate feeling alone? Or was there, in fact, no leadership, merely every man—or every brave man— for himself? Less tangible still, what did "bravery" mean in the context of a medieval fight? How did men mentally order the risks which they faced, as we know it is human to do? Were the foot more likely to be frightened of the horses, or of the men on them? Were the armoured men-at-arms more or less frightened of the arrows than of meeting their similarly clad opponents at a weapon's length? Did it seem safer to go on fighting once hard pressed than to surrender? Was running away more hazardous than staying within the press of the fighting?

The answers to some of these questions must be highly conjectural, inter-esting though the conjectures may be. But to others, we can certainly offer answers which fall within a fairly narrow bracket of probability, because the parameters of the questions are technical. Where speed of movement, density of formations, effect of weapons, for example, are concerned, we can test our suppositions against the known defensive qualities of armour plate, pene-trative power of arrows, dimensions and capacities of the human body, carry-ing power and speed of the horse. And from reasonable probabilities about these military mechanics, we may be able to leap towards an understanding of the dynamics of the battle itself and the spirit of the armies which fought it.

Let us, to begin with, and however artificially, break the battle down into a sequence of separate events. It opened, as we know, with the armies forming up in the light of early morning: whether that meant just after first light, or at the rather later hour of dawn itself—about 6:40 a.m.—is a point of detail over which we cannot expect the chroniclers to meet Staff College standards of precision. Nor do they. They are even more imprecise about numbers, particularly as they concern the French. For though there is agree-ment, supported by other evidence, that Henry's army had dwindled to about five or six thousand archers and a thousand men-at-arms, the French are variously counted between 10,000 and 200,000. Colonel Burne convincingly reconciles the differences to produce a figure of 25,000, a very large propor-tion of which represented armoured men-at-arms. Of these, about a thousand brought their horses to the battlefield; the rest were to fight on foot.

The two armies initially formed up at a distance of some thousand yards from each other; at either end of a long, open and almost flat expanse of ploughland, bordered on each side by woodland. The width of the field, which had recently been sown with winter wheat, was about twelve hundred yards at the French end. The woods converged slightly on the English and, at the point where the armies were eventually to meet, stood about nine hundred to a thousand yards apart. (These measurements suppose—as seems reasonable, field boundaries remaining remarkably stable over centuries— that the outlines of the woods have not much changed.)

The English men-at-arms, most of whom were on foot, took station in three blocks, under the command of the Duke of York, to the right, the King, in the centre, and Lord Camoys, on the left. The archers were disposed between them and also on the flanks; the whole line was about four or five deep. The archer flanks may have been thrown a little forward, and the archers of the two inner groups may have adopted a wedge-like formation. This would have made it appear as if the men-at-arms were deployed a little to their rear. Opposite them, the French were drawn up in three lines, of which the third was mounted, as were two groups, each about five hundred strong, on the flanks. The two forward lines, with a filling of crossbowmen between and some ineffectual cannon on the flanks were each, perhaps, eight thousand strong, and so ranked some eight deep. On both sides, the leaders of the various contingents—nobles, bannerets and knights—displayed armorial banners, under which they and their men would fight, and among the French there was a great deal of tiresome struggling, during the period of deployment, to get these banners into the leading rank.

Deployed, the armies were ready for the battle, which, as we have seen, resolved itself into twelve main episodes: a period of waiting; an English advance; an English arrow strike; a French cavalry charge; a French infantry advance; a mêlée between the French and English men-at-arms; an intervention in the mêlée by the English archers; the flight of the French survivors from the scene of the mêlée; a second period of waiting, during which the French third line threatened, and a small party delivered, another charge; a French raid on the baggage park; a massacre of the French prisoners; finally, mutual departure from the battlefield. What was each of these episodes like, and what impetus did it give to the course of events?

The period of waiting—three or four hours long, and so lasting probably from about seven to eleven o'clock—must have been very trying. Two chroniclers mention that the soldiers in the front ranks sat down and ate and drank and that there was a good deal of shouting, chaffing and noisy reconciliation of old quarrels among the French. But that was after they had settled, by pushing and shoving, who was to stand in the forward rank; not a real argument, one may surmise, but a process which put the grander and the braver in front of the more humble and timid. There is no mention of the English imitating them, but given their very real predicament, and their much thinner line of battle, they can have felt little need to dispute the place of honour among themselves. It is also improbable that they did much eating or drinking, for the army had been short of food for nine days and the archers are said to have been subsisting on nuts and berries on the last marches. Waiting, certainly for the English, must then have been a cold, miserable and squalid business. It had been raining, the ground was recently ploughed, air temperature was probably in the forties or low fifties Fahrenheit and many in the army were suffering from diarrhoea. Since none would presumably have been allowed to leave the ranks while the army was deployed for action, sufferers would have had to relieve themselves where they stood. For any afflicted man-at-arms wearing mail leggings laced to his plate armour, even that may not have been possible.

The King's order to advance, which he gave after the veterans had endorsed his guess that the French would not be drawn, may therefore have been generally and genuinely welcome. Movement at least meant an opportunity to generate body heat, of which the metal-clad men-at-arms would have dissipated an unnatural amount during the morning. Not, however, when the moment came, that they would have moved forward very fast. An advance in line, particularly by men unequally equipped and burdened, has to be taken slowly if order is to be preserved. The manœuvre, moreover, was a change of position, not a charge, and the King and his subordinate leaders would presumably have recognized the additional danger of losing cohesion in the face of the enemy who, if alert, would seize on the eventuality as an opportune moment to launch an attack. Several chroniclers indeed mention that on the King's orders a knight, Sir Thomas Erpingham, inspected the archers before they marched off in order to "check their dressing," as a modern drill sergeant would put it, and to ensure that they had their bows strung. The much smaller groups of men-at-arms would have moved as did the banners of their lords, which in turn would have followed the King's.

The army had about seven hundred yards of rain-soaked ploughland to cover. At a slow walk (no medieval army marched in step, and no modern army would have done so over such ground—the "cadenced pace" followed from the hardening and smoothing of the surface of roads), with halts to correct dressing, it would have reached its new position in ten minutes or so, though one may guess that the pace slackened a good deal as they drew nearer the French army and the leaders made mental reckoning of the range. "Extreme bowshot," which is the distance at which Henry presumably planned to take ground, is traditionally calculated at three hundred yards. That is a tremendous carry for a bow, however, and two hundred and fifty yards would be a more realistic judgment of the distance at which he finally halted his line from the French. If, however, his archer flanks were thrown a little forward, his centre would have been farther away; and if, as one chronicler suggests, he had infiltrated parties of bowmen into the woods, the gap between the two armies might have been greater still. Something between two hundred and fifty and three hundred yards is a reasonable bracket therefore.

There must now have ensued another pause, even though a short one. For the archers, who had each been carrying a stout double-pointed wooden stake since the tenth day of the march, had now to hammer these into the ground, at an angle calculated to catch a warhorse in the chest. Once hammered, moreover, the points would have had to be hastily resharpened. Henry had ordered these stakes to be cut as a precaution against the army being surprised by cavalry on the line of march. But it was a sensible improvisation to have them planted on the pitched battlefield, even if not a wholly original one. The Scots at Bannockburn, the English themselves at Crécy and the Flemings at Courtrai had narrowed their fronts by digging patterns of holes which would break the leg of a charging horse; the principle was the same as that which underlay the planting of the Agincourt archers' fence. Though it is not, indeed, possible to guess whether a fence was what the archers constructed. If they hammered their stakes to form a single row, it supposes them standing for some time on the wrong side of it with their backs to the enemy. Is it not more probable that each drove his in where he stood, so forming a kind of thicket, too dangerous for horses to penetrate but roomy enough for the defenders to move about within? That would explain the chronicler Monstrelet's otherwise puzzling statement that "each archer placed before himself a stake." It would also make sense of the rough mathematics we can apply to the problem. Colonel Burne, whose appreciation has not been challenged, estimates the width of the English position at 950 yards. Given that there were a thousand men-at-arms in the line of battle, ranked shoulder to shoulder four deep, they would have occupied, at a yard of front per man, 250 yards. If the five thousand archers, on the remaining seven hundred yards, planted their stakes side by side, they would have formed a fence at five-inch intervals. That obstacle would have been impenetrable to the French—but also to the English archers;* and *their* freedom of movement was, as we shall see, latterly an essential element in the winning of the battle. If we want to picture the formation the archers adopted, therefore, it would be most realistic to think of them standing a yard apart, in six or seven rows, with a yard between them, also disposed chequerboard fashion so that the men could see and shoot more easily over the heads of those in front: the whole forming a loose belt twenty or thirty feet deep, with the stakes standing obliquely among them.

What we do not know—and it leaves a serious gap in our understanding of the mechanics of the battle—is how the archers were commanded. The men-at-arms stood beneath the banners of their leaders, who had anyhow

---

* Indeed, they could not have got back *behind* it after they had driven their stakes in.

mustered them and brought them to the war, and the larger retinues, those of noblemen like the Earl of Suffolk, also contained knighted men-at-arms, who must have acted as subordinate leaders. There is thus no difficulty in visualizing how command was exercised within these fairly small and compact groups—providing one makes allowances for what a modern officer would regard as the unsoldierly habit in the man-at-arms of seeking to engage in "single combat" and of otherwise drawing attention to his individual prowess and skill-at-arms. But if the "officer class," even though the expression has a very doubtful meaning in the medieval military context, was wholly committed to the leadership of a single component of the army, who led the rest? For it is not naïve, indeed quite the contrary, to suppose some sort of control over and discipline within the archers' ranks. Had the groupings into twenties under a double-pay "vintenar" and of the twenties into hundreds, under a mounted and armoured "centenar," which we know prevailed in the reign of Edward I, at the beginning of the fourteenth century, persisted into the fifteenth? That would be probable. But we cannot tell to whom the "centenars" were immediately answerable, nor how the chain of command led to the King. We can only feel sure that it did.

Archers versus Infantry and Cavalry

The archers were now in position to open fire (an inappropriate expression, belonging to the gunpowder age, which was barely beginning). Each man disposed his arrows as convenient. He would have had a sheaf, perhaps two, of twenty-four arrows and probably struck them point down into the ground by his feet. The men in the front two ranks would have a clear view of the enemy, those behind only sporadic glimpses: there must therefore have been some sort of ranging order passed by word of mouth. For the archers' task at this opening moment of the battle was to provoke the French into attacking, and it was therefore essential that their arrows should "group" as closely as possible on the target. To translate their purpose into modern artillery language, they had to achieve a very narrow 100° zone (i.e. that belt of territory into which *all* missiles fell) and a Time on Target effect (i.e. all their missiles had to arrive simultaneously).

To speculate about their feelings at this moment is otiose. They were experienced soldiers in a desperate spot; and their fire, moreover, was to be "indirect," in that their arrows would not depart straight into the enemy's faces but at a fairly steeply angled trajectory. They need have had no sense of initiating an act of killing, therefore; it was probably their technical and professional sense which was most actively engaged in an activity which was still preliminary to any "real" fighting that might come.

They must have received at least two orders: the first to draw their bows, the second to loose their strings. How the orders were synchronized between different groups of archers is an unanswerable question, but when the shout went up or the banner down, four clouds of arrows would have streaked out of the English line to reach a height of a hundred feet before turning in flight to plunge at a steeper angle on and among the French men-at-arms opposite. These arrows cannot, however, given their terminal velocity and angle of impact, have done a great deal of harm, at least to the men-at-arms. For armour, by the early fifteenth century, was composed almost completely of steel sheet, in place of the iron mail which had been worn on the body until fifty years before but now only covered the awkward points of movement around the shoulder and groin. It was deliberately designed, moreover, to offer a glancing surface, and the contemporary helmet, a wide-brimmed "bascinet," was particularly adapted to deflect blows away from the head and the shoulders. We can suppose that the armour served its purpose effectively in this, the opening moment of Agincourt. But one should not dismiss the moral effect of the arrow strike. The singing of the arrows would not have moved ahead of their flight, but the sound of their impact must have been extraordinarily cacophonous, a weird clanking and banging on the bowed heads and backs of the French men-at-arms. If any of the horses in the flanking squadrons were hit, they were likely to have been hurt, however, even at this extreme range, for they were armoured only on their faces and chests, and the chisel-pointed head of the clothyard arrow would have penetrated the padded cloth hangings which covered the rest of their bodies. Animal cries of pain and fear would have risen above the metallic clatter.

Cavalry versus Infantry

We can also imagine oaths and shouted threats from the French. For the arrow strike achieved its object. How quickly, the chroniclers do not tell us; but as a trained archer could loose a shaft every ten seconds we can guess that it took at most a few minutes to trigger the French attack. The French, as we know, were certain of victory. What they had been waiting for was a tactical pretext; either that of the Englishmen showing them their backs or, on the contrary, cocking a snook. One or two volleys would have been insult enough. On the arrival of the first arrows the two large squadrons of horse on either flank mounted—or had they mounted when the English line advanced?—walked their horses clear of the line and broke into a charge.

A charge at what? The two chroniclers who are specific about this point make it clear that the two groups of cavalry, each five or six hundred strong, of which that on the left hand was led by Clignet de Brébant and Guillaume de Saveuse, made the English archer flanks their target. Their aim, doubtless, was to clear these, the largest blocks of the enemy which immediately threatened them, off the field, leaving the numerically much inferior centre of English men-at-arms, with the smaller groups of their attendant archers, to be overwhelmed by the French infantry. It was nevertheless a strange and dangerous decision, unless, that is, we work on the supposition that the archers had planted their stakes among their own ranks, so concealing that array of obstacles from the French. We may then visualize the French bearing down on the archers in ignorance of the hedgehog their ranks concealed; and of the English giving ground just before the moment of impact, to reveal it.

For "the moment of impact" otherwise begs an important, indeed a vital question. It is not difficult to picture the beginning of the charge: the horsemen booting their mounts to form line, probably two or three rows deep, so that, riding knee to knee, they would have presented a front of two or three hundred lances, more or less equalling in width the line of the archers opposite, say three hundred yards. We can imagine them setting off, sitting (really standing) "long" in their high-backed, padded saddles, legs straight and thrust forward, toes down in the heavy stirrups, lance under right arm, left free to manage the reins (wearing plate armour obviated the need to carry a shield); and we can see them in motion, riding at a pace which took them across all but the last fifty of the two or three hundred yards they had to cover in forty seconds or so and then spurring their horses to ride down on the archers at the best speed they could manage—twelve or fifteen miles an hour.*

So far so good. The distance between horses and archers narrows. The archers, who have delivered three or four volleys at the bowed heads and shoulders of their attackers, get off one more flight. More horses—some have already gone down or broken back with screams of pain—stumble and fall, tripping their neighbours, but the mass drive on and . . . and what? It is at this moment that we have to make a judgment about the difference between what happens in a battle and what happens in a violent accident. A horse, in the normal course of events, will not gallop at an obstacle it cannot jump or see a way through, and it cannot jump or see a way through a solid line of men. Even less will it go at the sort of obviously dangerous obstacle which the archers' stakes presented. Equally, a man will not stand in the path of a running horse: he will run himself, or seek shelter, and only if exceptionally strong-nerved and knowing in its ways, stand his ground. Nevertheless, accidents happen. Men, miscalculating or slow-footed, and horses, confused or maddened, do collide, with results almost exclusively unpleasant for the man. We cannot therefore say, however unnatural and exceptional we recognize collisions between man and horse to be, that

---

* The horses were probably a big hunter type, not the carthorse of popular belief, and the weight they had to carry some 250 lbs (man 150 lbs, armour 60 lbs, saddle and trappings 40 lbs).

nothing of that nature occurred between the archers and the French cavalry at Agincourt. For the archers were trained to "receive cavalry," the horses trained to charge home, while it was the principal function of the riders to insist on the horses doing that against which their nature rebelled. Moreover, two of the eye-witness chroniclers, St Remy and the Priest of the Cottonian MS, are adamant that some of the French cavalry did get in among the archers.

The two opposed "weapon principles" which military theorists recognize had, in short, both failed: the "missile" principle, personified by the archers, had failed to stop or drive off the cavalry; they, embodying the "shock" principle, had failed to crush the infantry—or, more particularly, to make them run away, for the "shock" which cavalry seek to inflict is really moral, not physical in character. It was the stakes which must have effected the compromise. The French, coming on fast, and in great numbers over a short distance, had escaped the deaths and falls which should have toppled their charge over on itself; the English, emboldened by the physical security the hedgehog of stakes lent their formation, had given ground only a little before the onset; the horses had then found themselves on top of the stakes too late to refuse the obstacle; and a short, violent and noisy collision had resulted.

Some of the men-at-arms' horses "ran out" round the flanks of the archers and into the woods. Those in the rear ranks turned their horses, or were turned by them, and rode back. But three at least, including Guillaume de Saveuse, had their horses impaled on the stakes, thumped to the ground and were killed where they lay, either by mallet blows or by stabs between their armour-joints. The charge, momentarily terrifying for the English, from many of whom French men-at-arms, twice their height from the ground, and moving at ten or fifteen miles an hour on steel-shod and grotesquely caparisoned war-horses, had stopped only a few feet distant, had been a disaster for the enemy. And as they rode off, the archers, with all the violent anger that comes with release from sudden danger, bent their bows and sent fresh flights of arrows after them, bringing down more horses and maddening others into uncontrolled flight.

Infantry versus Infantry

But the results of the rout went beyond the demoralization of the survivors. For, as their horses galloped back, they met the first division of dismounted men-at-arms marching out to attack the English centre. Perhaps eight thousand strong, and filling the space between the woods eight or ten deep, they could not easily or quickly open their ranks to let the fugitives through. Of what happened in consequence we can get a clear idea, curiously, from a cinema newsreel of the Grosvenor Square demonstration against the Vietnam war in 1968. There, a frightened police horse, fleeing the demonstrators, charged a line of constables on foot. Those directly in its path, barging sideways and backwards to open a gap and seizing their neighbours, set up a curious and violent ripple which ran along the ranks on each side, reaching policemen some good distance away who, tightly packed, clutched at each other for support, and stumbled clumsily backwards and then forwards to keep their balance. The sensations of that ripple are known to anyone who has been a member of a dense, mobile and boisterous crowd and it was certainly what was felt, to a sudden and exaggerated degree, by the French men-at-arms in the face of that involuntary cavalry charge. As in that which had just failed against the archers, many of the horses would have shied off at the moment of impact. But those that barged in, an occurrence to which the chroniclers testify, broke up the rhythm of the advance and knocked some men to the ground, an unpleasant experience when the soil is wet and trampled and one is wearing sixty or seventy pounds of sheet metal on the body.

This interruption in an advance which should have brought the French first division to within weapon's length of the English in three or four minutes at most gave Henry's men-at-arms ample time to brace themselves for the encounter. It also gave the archers, both those in the large groups on the wings and the two smaller groups in the central wedges, the chance to prolong their volleying of arrows into the French ranks. The range was progressively shortened by the advance, and the arrows, coming in on a flat trajectory in sheets of five thousand at ten-second intervals, must have begun to cause casualties among the French foot. For though they bowed their heads and hunched their shoulders, presenting a continuous front of deflecting surface (bascinet top, breastplate, "taces"—the overlapping bands across the stomach and genitals—and leg-pieces) to the storm, some of the arrows must have found the weak spots in the visor and at the shoulders and, as the range dropped right down, might even have penetrated armour itself. The "bodkin-point" was designed to do so, and its terminal velocity, sufficient to drive it through an inch of oak from a short distance, could also, at the right angle of impact, make a hole in sheet steel.

The archers failed nevertheless to halt the French advance. But they succeeded in channelling it—or helping to channel it—on to a narrower front of attack. For the French foot, unlike the cavalry, apparently did not make the archers' positions their objective. As their great mass came on, their front ranks "either from fear of the arrows . . . or that they might more speedily penetrate our ranks to the banners (of the King, the Duke of York and Lord Camoys) . . . divided themselves into three . . . charging our lines in the three places where the banners were." We may also presume that the return of their own cavalry on the flanks would have helped to compress the infantry mass towards the centre, a tendency perhaps reinforced (we really cannot judge) by the alleged unwillingness of men-at-arms to cross weapons with archers, their social inferiors, when the chance to win glory, and prisoners, in combat with other men-at-arms presented itself. Whatever the play of forces at work on the movement of the French first division, several narrators testify to the outcome. The leading ranks bunched into three assaulting columns and drove into what Colonel Burne, in a topographical analogy, calls the three "re-entrants" of the English line, where the men-at-arms were massed a little in rear of the archers' staked-out enclosures.

Their charge won an initial success, for before it the English men-at-arms fell back "a spear's length." What distance the chronicler means by that traditional phrase we cannot judge, and all the less because the French had cut down their lances in anticipation of fighting on foot. It probably implies "just enough to take the impetus out of the onset of the French," for we must imagine them, although puffed by the effort of a jostling tramp across three hundred yards of wet ploughland, accelerating over the last few feet into a run calculated to drive the points of their spears hard on to the enemy's chests and stomachs. The object would have been to knock over as many of them as possible, and so to open gaps in the ranks and isolate individuals who could then be killed or forced back on to the weapons of their own comrades; "sowing disorder" is a short-hand description of the aim. To avoid its achievement, the English, had they been more numerous, might have started forward to meet the French before they developed impulsion; since they were so outnumbered, it was individually prudent and tactically sound for the men most exposed to trot backwards before the French spearpoints, thus "wrong-footing" their opponents (a spearman times his thrust to coincide with the forward step of his left foot) and setting up those surges and undulations along the face of the French mass which momentarily rob a crowd's onrush of its full impact. The English, at the same time, would have been thrusting their spears at the French and, as movement died out of the two hosts, we can visualize them divided, at a distance of ten or fifteen feet, by a horizontal fence of waving and stabbing spear shafts, the noise of their clattering like that of a bully-off at hockey magnified several hundred times.

In this fashion the clash of the men-at-arms might have petered out, as it did on so many medieval battlefields, without a great deal more hurt to either side—though the French would have continued to suffer casualties from the fire of the archers, as long as they remained within range and the English had arrows to shoot at them (the evidence implies they must now have been running short). We can guess that three factors deterred the antagonists from drawing off from each other. One was the English fear of quitting their solid position between the woods and behind the archers' stakes for the greater dangers of the open field; the second was the French certainty of victory; the third was their enormous press of numbers. For if we accept that they had now divided into three *ad hoc* columns and that the head of each matched in width that of the English opposite—say eighty yards—with intervals between of about the same distance, we are compelled to visualize, taking a bird's-eye viewpoint, a roughly trident-shaped formation, the Frenchmen in the prongs ranking twenty deep and numbering some five thousand in all, those in the base a shapeless and unordered mass amounting to, perhaps, another three thousand—and all of them, except for the seven or eight hundred in the leading ranks, unable to see or hear what was happening, yet certain that the English were done for, and anxious to take a hand in finishing them off.

No one, moreover, had overall authority in this press, nor a chain of command through which to impose it. The consequence was inevitable: the development of an unrelenting pressure from the rear on the backs of those in the line of battle, driving them steadily into the weapon-strokes of the English, or at least denying them that margin of room for individual manœuvre which is essential if men are to defend themselves—or attack—effectively. This was disastrous, for it is vital to recognize, if we are to understand Agincourt, that all infantry actions, even those fought in the closest of close order, are not, in the last resort, combats of mass against mass, but the sum of many combats of individuals—one against one, one against two, three against five. This must be so, for the very simple reason that the weapons which individuals wield are of very limited range and effect, as they remain even since missile weapons have become the universal equipment of the infantryman. At Agincourt, where the man-at-arms bore lance, sword, dagger, mace or battleaxe,* his ability to kill or wound was restricted to the circle centred on his own body, within which his reach allowed him to club, slash or stab. Prevented by the throng at their backs from dodging, side-stepping or retreating from the blows and thrusts directed at them by their English opponents, the individual French men-at-arms must shortly have begun to lose their man-to-man fights, collecting blows on the head or limbs which, even through armour, were sufficiently bruising or stunning to make them drop their weapons or lose their balance or footing. Within minutes, perhaps seconds, of hand-to-hand fighting being joined, some of them would have fallen, their bodies lying at the feet of their comrades, further impeding the movement of individuals and thus offering an obstacle to the advance of the whole column.

This was the crucial factor in the development of the battle. Had most of the French first line kept their feet, the crowd pressure of their vastly superior numbers, transmitted through their levelled lances, would shortly have forced the English back. Once men began to go down, however—and perhaps also because the French had shortened their lances, while the English

---

* A category which includes glaive, bill, and similar weapons.

had apparently not—those in the next rank would have found that they could get within reach of the English only by stepping over or on to the bodies of the fallen. Supposing continuing pressure from the rear, moreover, they would have had no choice but to do so; yet in so doing, would have rendered themselves even more vulnerable to a tumble than those already felled, a human body making either an unstable fighting platform or a very effective stumbling block to the heels of a man trying to defend himself from a savage attack to his front. In short, once the French column had become stationary, its front impeded by fallen bodies and its ranks animated by heavy pressure from the rear, the "tumbling effect" along its forward edge would have become cumulative.

Cumulative, but sudden and of short duration: for pressure of numbers and desperation must eventually have caused the French to spill out from their columns and lumber down upon the archers who, it appears, were now beginning to run short of arrows. They could almost certainly not have withstood a charge by armoured men-at-arms, would have broken and, running, have left their own men-at-arms to be surrounded and hacked down. That did not happen. The chroniclers are specific that, on the contrary, it was the archers who moved to the attack. Seeing the French falling at the heads of the columns, while those on the flanks still flinched away from the final flights of arrows, the archers seized the chance that confusion and irresolution offered. Drawing swords, swinging heavier weapons—axes, bills or the mallets they used to hammer in their stakes—they left their staked-out positions and ran down to assault the men in armour.

This is a very difficult episode to visualize convincingly. They cannot have attacked the heads of the French columns, for it was there that the English men-at-arms stood, leaving no room for reinforcements to join in. On the flanks, however, the French cannot yet have suffered many casualties, would have had fairly unencumbered ground to fight on and ought to have had no difficulty in dealing with any unarmoured man foolish enough to come within reach of their weapons. The observation offered by two chroniclers that they were too tightly packed to raise their arms, though very probably true of those in the heart of the crowd, cannot apply to those on its fringes. If the archers did inflict injury on the men-at-arms, and there is unanimous evidence that they did, it must have been in some other way than by direct assault on the close-ordered ranks of the columns.

The most likely explanation is that small groups of archers began by attacking individual men-at-arms, infantry isolated by the scattering of the French first line in the "reverse charge" of their own cavalry or riders unhorsed in the charge itself. The charges had occurred on either flank; so that in front of the main bodies of archers and at a distance of between fifty and two hundred yards from them, must have been seen, in the two or three minutes after the cavalry had ridden back, numbers of Frenchmen, prone, supine, half-risen or shakily upright, who were plainly in no state to offer concerted resistance and scarcely able to defend themselves individually. Those who were down would indeed have had difficulty getting up again from slithery ground under the weight of sixty or seventy pounds of armour; and the same hindrances would have slowed those who regained or had kept their feet in getting back to the protection of the closed columns. Certainly they could not have outdistanced the archers if, as we may surmise, and St Remy, a combatant, implies, some of the latter now took the risk of running forward from their stakes to set about them.*

"Setting about them" probably meant two or three against one, so that while an archer swung or lunged at a man-at-arms' front, another dodged his sword-arm to land him a mallet-blow on the back of the head or an axe-stroke behind the knee. Either would have toppled him and, once sprawling, he would have been helpless; a thrust into his face, if he were wearing a bascinet, into the slits of his visor, if he were wearing a closed helmet, or through the mail of his armpit or groin, would have killed him outright or left him to bleed to death. Each act of execution need have taken only a few seconds; time enough for a flurry of thrusts clumsily parried, a fall, two or three figures to kneel over another on the ground, a few butcher's blows, a cry in extremis. "Two thousand pounds of education drops to a ten rupee . . ." (Kipling, "Arithmetic on the Frontier"). Little scenes of this sort must have been happening all over the two narrow tracts between the woods and the fringes of the French main body within the first minutes of the main battle being joined. The only way for stranded Frenchmen to avoid such a death at the hands of the archers was to ask for quarter, which at this early stage they may not have been willing to grant, despite prospects of ransom. A surrendered enemy, to be put hors de combat, had to be escorted off the field, a waste of time and manpower the English could not afford when still at such an apparent disadvantage.

But the check in the front line and the butchery on the flanks appear fairly quickly to have swung the advantage in their favour. The "return charge" of the French cavalry had, according to St Remy, caused some of the French to retreat in panic, and it is possible that panic now broke out again along the flanks and at the front.† If that were so—and it is difficult otherwise to make sense of subsequent events—we must imagine a new tide of movement within the French mass: continued forward pressure from those at the back who could not see, a rearward drift along the flanks of the columns by those who had seen all too clearly what work the archers were at, and

---

* "Soon afterwards, the English archers perceiving this disorder of the advance guard . . . and *hastening to the place where the fugitives came from*, killed and disabled the French." (Author's italics.) Nicolas, *The History of the Battle of Agincourt*, p. 268.
† The sight of archers killing men-at-arms might either have provoked a counter-attack from the Frenchmen on the flanks *or* persuaded them individually that Agincourt had become no sort of battle to get killed in. There was no reputation to be won in fighting archers.

a reverse pressure by men-at-arms in the front line seeking, if not escape, at least room to fight without fear of falling, or being pushed, over the bodies of those who had already gone down. These movements would have altered the shape of the French mass, widening the gaps between its flanks and the woods, and so offering the archers room to make an "enveloping" attack. Emboldened by the easy killings achieved by some of their number, we must now imagine the rest, perhaps at the King's command, perhaps by spontaneous decision, massing outside their stakes and then running down in formation to attack the French flanks.

"Flank," of course, is only the military word for "side" (in French, from which we take it, the distinction does not exist) and the advantage attackers enjoy in a flank attack is precisely that of hitting at men half turned away from them. But presumably the state in which the archers found the French flanks was even more to their advantage than that. On the edge of the crowd, men-at-arms were walking or running to the rear. As they went, accelerating no doubt at the sight of the English charging down on them, they exposed men deeper within the crowd who would not until then have had sight of the archers, who were not indeed expecting yet to use their arms and whose attention was wholly directed towards the banging and shouting from their front, where they anticipated doing their fighting. Assaulted suddenly at their right or left shoulders, they can have had little chance to face front and point their weapons before some of them, like those already killed by the English men-at-arms, were struck down at the feet of their neighbours.

If the archers were now able to reproduce along the flanks of the French mass the same "tumbling effect" which had encumbered its front, its destruction must have been imminent. For most death in battle takes place within well-defined and fairly narrow "killing zones," of which the "no-man's-land" of trench warfare is the best known and most comprehensible example. The depth of the killing zone is determined by the effective range of the most prevalent weapon, which, in infantry battles, is always comparatively short, and, in hand-to-hand fighting, very short—only a few feet. That being so, the longer the winning side can make the killing zone, the more casualties can it inflict. If the English were now able to extend the killing zone from along the face to down the sides of the French mass (an "enveloping" attack), they threatened to kill very large numbers of Frenchmen indeed.

Given the horror of their situation, the sense of which must now have been transmitted to the whole mass, the French ought at this point to have broken and run. That they did not was the consequence, once again, of their own superiority of numbers. For heretofore it had only been the first division of their army which had been engaged. The second and the third had stood passive, but as the first began to give way, its collapse heralded by the return of fugitives from the flanks, the second walked forward across the wet and trampled ground to lend it support. This was exactly not the help needed at that moment. Had the cavalry, in third line, been brought forward to make a second charge against the archers, now that they were outside the protection of their stakes and without their bows, they might well have achieved a rescue. But they were left where they were, for reasons impossible to reconstruct.* Instead, the second division of infantrymen arrived and, thrusting against the backs of their tired and desperate compatriots, held them firmly in place to suffer further butchery.

From what the chroniclers say, we can suppose most of those in the French first line now to be either dead, wounded, prisoner or ready to surrender, if they could not escape. Many had made their surrender (the Priest of the Cottonian MS cattily reports that "some, even of the more noble . . . that day surrendered themselves more than ten times"); some had not had it accepted: the Duke of Alençon, finding himself cut off and surrounded in a dash to attack the Duke of Gloucester, shouted his submission over the heads of his attackers to the King, who was coming to his brother's rescue, but was killed before Henry could extricate him. Nevertheless, very large numbers of Frenchmen had, on promise of ransom, been taken captive, presumably from the moment when the English sensed that the battle was going their way. Their removal from the field, the deaths of others, and the moral and by now no doubt incipient physical collapse of those left had opened up sufficient space for the English to abandon their close order and penetrate their enemy's ranks.

This advance brought them eventually—we are talking of an elapsed time of perhaps only half an hour since the first blows were exchanged—into contact with the second line. They must themselves have been tiring by this time. For the excitement, fear and physical exertion of fighting hand-to-hand with heavy weapons in plate armour quickly drained the body of its energy, despite the surge of energy released under stress by glandular activity. Even so, they were not repulsed by the onset of the second line. Indeed, its intervention seems to have made no appreciable impact on the fighting. There is a modern military cliché, "Never reinforce failure," which means broadly that to thrust reinforcements in among soldiers who have failed in an attack, feel themselves beaten and are trying to run away is merely to waste the newcomers' energies in a struggle against the thrust of the crowd and to risk infecting them with its despair. And it was indeed in congestion and desperation that the second line appear to have met the English. The chroniclers do not specify exactly what passed between them, presumably because it was so similar to what had gone on before during the defeat of the first line. Though we may guess that a large number of the second line, as soon as they became aware of the disaster, turned their backs and ran off the way they had come; some were dragged out by their pages or servants.

What facts the chroniclers do provide about this, the culmination of the

* But probably having to do a) with the lack of effective overall command in the French army, b) with the difficulty of seeing from the third line (c. 500 yards from the "killing zone") what was happening at the front.

hand-to-hand phase, are difficult to reconcile. The English appear to have had considerable freedom of movement, for they were taking hundreds prisoner and the King and his entourage are reported to have cut their way into the second line (it may have been then that he took the blow which dented the helmet which is still to be seen above his tomb in Westminster Abbey). And yet in at least three places, suggested by the priest's narrative to have been where the enemy columns initially charged the English men-at-arms, the bodies of the French lay piled "higher than a man." Indeed the English are said to have climbed these heaps "and butchered the adversaries below with swords, axes and other weapons."

This "building of the wall of dead" is perhaps the best known incident of the battle. If it had occurred, however, we cannot accept that the King and his armoured followers were able to range freely about the field in the latter stages, since the heaps would have confined them within their own positions. Brief reflection will, moreover, demonstrate that the "heap higher than a man" is a chronicler's exaggeration. Human bodies, even when pushed about by bulldozers, do not, as one can observe if able to keep one's eyes open during film of the mass-burials at Belsen, pile into walls, but lie in shapeless sprawling hummocks. When stiffened by rigor mortis, they can be laid in stacks, as one can see in film of the burial parties of a French regiment carting its dead from the field after an attack in the Second Battle of Champagne (September 1915). But men falling to weaponstrokes in the front line, or tripping over those already down, will lie at most two or three deep. For the heaps to rise higher, they must be climbed by the next victims: and the "six-foot heaps" of Agincourt could have been topped-out only if men on either side had been ready and able to duel together while balancing on the corpses of twenty or thirty others. The notion is ludicrous rather than grisly.

The dead undoubtedly lay thick at Agincourt, and quite probably, at the three places where fighting had been heaviest, in piles. But what probably happened at those spots, as we have seen, is that men-at-arms and archers achieved an envelopment of the heads of the French columns, hemmed in and perhaps completely surrounded groups of the enemy, toppled them over on top of each other with lance thrusts and killed them on the ground. The mounds thus raised were big and hideous enough to justify some priestly rhetoric—but not to deny the English entry into the French position.

The Killing of the Prisoners

Indeed, soon after midday, the English men were "in possession of the field"—by which soldiers would understand that they were able to move freely over the ground earlier occupied by the French, of whom only dead, wounded, and fugitives were now to be seen. Fugitives too slow-footed to reach hiding in the woods, or sanctuary among the cavalry of the still un-committed third division, were chased and tackled by bounty-hunters; others, greedy for ransom, were sorting through the recumbent bodies and pulling "down the heaps . . . to separate the living from the dead, proposing to keep the living as slaves, to be ransomed." At the back of the battlefield the most valuable prisoners were massed together under guard. They were still wearing their armour but had surrendered their right gauntlets to their captors, as a token of submission (and subsequent reidentification), and taken off their helmets, without which they could not fight.

Henry could not allow each captor individually to sequester his prisoners because of the need to keep the army together as long as the French third division threatened a charge. So while small parties, acting both on their own behalf and that of others still in the ranks, reaped the rewards of the fight, the main bodies of men-at-arms and archers stood their ground—now about two or three hundred yards forward of the line on which they had received the French charge. Henry's caution was justified. Soon after midday, the Duke of Brabant, arriving late, half-equipped, and with a tiny following, charged into these ranks. He was overpowered and led to the rear. But this gallant inter-vention inspired at least two French noblemen in the third division, the Counts of Masle and Fauquemberghes, to marshal some six hundred of their followers for a concerted charge. They could clearly be seen massing, two or three hundred yards from the English line, and their intentions were obvious. At about the same time, moreover, shouting from the rear informed the English of a raid by the enemy on the baggage park, which had been left almost unguarded.

It was these events which precipitated Henry's notorious order to kill the prisoners. As it turned out, the charge was not delivered and the raid was later revealed to have been a mere rampage by the local peasantry, under the Lord of Agincourt. The signs were enough, however, to convince Henry that his victory, in which he can scarcely have yet believed, was about to be snatched from him. For if the French third division attacked the English where they stood, the archers without arrows or stakes, the men-at-arms weary after a morning of hacking and banging in full armour, all of them hungry, cold, and depressed by the reaction from the intense fears and elations of combat, they might easily have been swept from the field. They could certainly not have withstood the simultaneous assault on their rear, to which, with so many inadequately guarded French prisoners standing about behind them on ground littered with discarded weapons, they were likely also to have been subjected. In these circumstances, his order is comprehensible.

Comprehensible in harsh tactical logic; in ethical, human, and practical terms much more difficult to understand. Henry, a Christian king, was also an experienced soldier and versed in the elaborate code of international law

governing relations between a prisoner and his captor. Its most important provision was that which guaranteed the prisoner his life—the only return, after
all, for which he would enter into anything so costly and humiliating as a
ransom bargain. And while his treachery broke that immunity, the mere
suspicion, even if well-founded, that he was about to commit treason could
not justify his killing. At a more fundamental level, moreover, the prisoner's
life was guaranteed by the Christian commandment against murder, however
much more loosely that commandment was interpreted in the fifteenth century. If Henry could give the order and, as he did, subsequently escape the
reproval of his peers, of the Church, and of the chroniclers, we must presume
it was because the battlefield itself was still regarded as a sort of moral no-
man's-land and the hour of battle as a legal *dies non*.

His subordinates nevertheless refused to obey. Was this because they felt
a more tender conscience? The notion is usually dismissed by medieval
specialists, who insist that, at best, the captors obejcted to the King's interference in what was a personal relationship, the prisoners being not the King's
or the army's but the vassals of those who had accepted their surrender; that,
at worst, they refused to forgo the prospect of so much ransom money (there
being almost no way for a man of the times to make a quick fortune except
on the battlefield). But it is significant that the King eventually got his order
obeyed only by detailing two hundred *archers*, under the command of an
esquire, to carry out the task. This may suggest that, among the captors, the
men-at-arms at any rate felt something more than a financially motivated
reluctance. There is, after all, an important difference between fighting with
lethal weapons, even if it ends in killing, and mere butchery, and we may
expect it to have been all the stronger when the act of fighting was as
glorified as it was in the Middle Ages. To meet a similarly equipped opponent
was the occasion for which the armoured soldier trained perhaps every day of
his life from the onset of manhood. To meet and beat him with a triumph,
the highest form which self-expression could take in the medieval nobleman's
way of life. The events of the late morning at Agincourt, when men had leapt
and grunted and hacked at each other's bodies, behaving in a way which
seems grotesque and horrifying to us, was for them, therefore, a sort of
apotheosis, giving point to their existence, and perhaps assuring them of
commemoration after death (since most chroniclers were principally concerned to celebrate individual feats of arms). But there was certainly no
honour to be won in killing one's social equal after he had surrendered and
been disarmed. On the contrary, there was a considerable risk of incurring
dishonour, which may alone have been strong enough to deter the men-at-
arms from obeying Henry's order.

Archers stood outside the chivalric system; nor is there much to the
idea that they personified the yeoman virtues. The bowmen of Henry's
army were not only tough professional soldiers. There is also evidence that

many had enlisted in the first place to avoid punishment for civil acts of violence, including murder. The chroniclers also make clear that, in the heat of combat, and during the more leisurely taking of prisoners after the rout of the French second division, there had been a good deal of killing, principally by the archers, of those too poor or too badly hurt to be worth keeping captive. The question of how more or less reluctant they were to carry out the King's command need not therefore delay us.

But the mechanics of the execution do demand a pause. Between one and two thousand prisoners accompanied Henry to England after the battle, of whom most must have been captured before he issued his order to kill. The chroniclers record that the killers spared the most valuable prisoners and were called off as soon as Henry assured himself that the French third division was not going to attack after all. We may take it therefore that the two hundred archers whom he detailed were heavily outnumbered by their victims, probably by about ten to one. The reason for wanting them killed, however, was that they were liable to re-arm themselves from the jetsam of battle if it were renewed. Why did they not do so when they saw themselves threatened with death, for the announcement of the King's order "by trumpet" and the refusal of their captors to carry it out can have left them in no doubt of the fate he planned for them? And how were the archers able to offer them a match? It may have been that they were roughly pinioned (some contemporary pictures of battle show prisoners being led away with their hands bound); but in that case they offered no proper—or a very much reduced—menace to the army's rear, which in turn diminishes the justification for Henry's order. And even if they were tied, their actual killing is an operation difficult to depict for oneself. The act of surrender is notably accompanied by the onset of lassitude and self-reproach. Is it realistic to imagine, however, these proud and warlike men passively awaiting the arrival of a gang of their social inferiors to do them to death—standing like cattle in groups of ten for a single archer to break their skulls with an axe?

It does seem very improbable, and all the more because what we know of twentieth-century mass-killing suggests that it is very difficult for small numbers of executioners, even when armed with machine-guns, to kill people much more defenceless than armoured knights quickly and in large numbers. What seems altogether more likely, therefore, is that Henry's order, rather than bring about the prisoners' massacre, was intended by its threat to terrorize them into abject inactivity. We may imagine something much less clinical than a *Sonderkommando* at work: the captors loudly announcing their refusal to obey the proclamation and perhaps assuring their prisoners that they would see them come to no harm; argument and even scuffling between them and members of the execution squad; and then a noisy and bloody cattle-drive to the rear, the archers harrying round the flanks of the crowd of armoured Frenchmen as they stumbled away from the scene of fighting and its dangerous debris to a spot nearer the baggage park, whence they could offer no serious threat at all. Some would have been killed in the process, and quite deliberately, but we need not reckon their number in thousands, perhaps not even in hundreds.

The killing, moreover, had a definite term, for Henry ordered it to end when he saw the French third division abandon their attack formation and begin to leave the battlefield. The time was about three o'clock in the afternoon, leaving some two hours more of daylight. The English began at once to spread out over the field looking for prisoners and spoil in places not yet visited. The King made a circuit and, on turning back for his quarters at Maisoncelles, summoned to him the French and English heralds.

The Wounded

The heralds had watched the battle in a group together and, though the French army had left, the French heralds had not yet followed them. For the heralds belonged not to the armies but to the international corporation of experts who regulated civilized warfare. Henry was anxious to hear their verdict on the day's fighting and to fix a name for the battle, so that its outcome and the army's exploits could be readily identified when chroniclers came to record it. Montjoie, the principal French herald, confirmed that the English were the victors and provided Henry with the name of the nearest castle—Agincourt—to serve as eponym.

That decision ended the battle as a military and historical episode. The English drove their prisoners and carried their own wounded back to Maisoncelles for the night, where the twenty surgeons of the army set to work. English casualties had been few: the Duke of York, who was pulled from under a heap of corpses, dead either from suffocation or a heart-attack, and the Earl of Suffolk were the only notable fatalities. The wounded numbered only some hundreds. What were their prospects? In the main, probably quite good. The English had not undergone an arrow attack, so most of the wounds would have been lacerations rather than penetrations, clean even if deep cuts which, if bound up and left, would heal quickly. There would also have been some fractures; depressed fractures of the skull could not be treated—the secret of trepanning awaited rediscovery—but breaks of the arm and lower leg could have been successfully set and splinted. The French wounded enjoyed a much graver prognosis. Many would have suffered penetrating wounds, either from arrows or from thrusts through the weak spots of their armour. Those which had pierced the intestines, emptying its contents into the abdomen, were fatal: peritonitis was inevitable. Penetrations of the chest cavity, which had probably carried in fragments of dirty clothing, were almost as certain to lead to sepsis. Many of the French would have suffered depressed fractures of the skull, and there would have been broken backs caused by falls from horses in armour at speed. Almost all of these injuries we may regard as fatal, the contemporary surgeons begin unable to treat them. Many of the French, of course, had not been collected from the battlefield and, if they did not bleed to death, would have succumbed to the combined effects of exposure and shock during the night, when temperatures might have descended into the middle-30s Fahrenheit. It was, therefore, not arbitrary brutality when, in crossing the battlefield next morning, the English killed those whom they found alive. They were almost certain to have died, in any case, when their bodies would have gone to join those which the local peasants, under the supervision of the Bishop of Arras, dug into pits on the site. They are said to have buried about six thousand altogether.

The Will to Combat

What sustained men in a combat like Agincourt, when the penalty of defeat, or of one's own lack of skill or nimbleness was so final and unpleasant? Some factors, either general to battle—as will appear—or more or less particular to this one are relatively easy to isolate. Of the general factors, drink is the most obvious to mention. The English, who were on short rations, presumably had less to drink than the French, but there was drinking in the ranks on both sides during the period of waiting and it is quite probable that many soldiers in both armies went into the mêlée less than sober, if not indeed fighting drunk. For the English, the presence of the King would also have provided what present-day soldiers call a "moral factor" of great importance. The personal bond between leader and follower lies at the root of all explanations of what does and does not happen in battle: and that bond is always strongest in martial societies, of which fifteenth-century England is one type and the warrior states of India, which the British harnessed so successfully to their imperial purpose, are another. The nature of the bond is more complex, and certainly more materialistic than modern ethologists would like to have us believe. But its importance must not be underestimated. And though the late-medieval soldier's immediate loyalty lay towards his captain, the presence on the field of his own and his captain's anointed king, visible to all and ostentatiously risking his life in the heart of the mêlée, must have greatly strengthened his resolve.

Serving to strengthen it further was the endorsement of religion. The morality of killing is not something with which the professional soldier is usually thought to trouble himself, but the Christian knight, whether we mean by that the ideal type as seen by the chroniclers or some at least of the historical figures of whom we have knowledge, was nevertheless exercised by it. What constituted unlawful killing in time of war was well-defined, and carried penalties under civil, military, and religious law. Lawful killing, on the other hand, was an act which religious precept specifically endorsed, within the circumscription of the just war; and however dimly or marginally religious doctrine impinged on the consciousness of the simple soldier or more unthinking knight, the religious preparations which all in the English army underwent before Agincourt must be counted among the most important factors affecting its mood. Henry himself heard Mass three times in succession before the battle, and took Communion, as presumably did most of his followers; there was a small army of priests in the expedition. The soldiers ritually entreated blessing before entering the ranks, going down on their knees, making the sign of the cross and taking earth into their mouths as a symbolic gesture of the death and burial they were thereby accepting.

Drink and prayer must be seen, however, as last-minute and short-term reinforcements of the medieval soldier's (though, as we shall see, not only his) will to combat. Far more important, and, given the disparity of their stations, more important still for the common soldier than the man-at-arms, was the prospect of enrichment. Medieval warfare, like all warfare, was about many things, but medieval battle, at the personal level, was about only three: victory first, of course, because the personal consequences of defeat could be so disagreeable; personal distinction in single combat—something of which the man-at-arms would think a great deal more than the bowman; but, ultimately and most important, ransom and loot. Agincourt was untypical of medieval battle in yielding, and then snatching back from the victors the bonanza of wealth that it did; but it is the gold-strike and gold-fever character of medieval battle which we should keep foremost in mind when seeking to understand it.

We should balance it, at the same time, against two other factors. The first of these is the pressure of compulsion. The role which physical coercion or force of unavoidable circumstance plays in bringing men into, and often through, the ordeal of battle is one which almost all military historians consistently underplay, or ignore. Yet we can clearly see that the force of unavoidable circumstances was among the most powerful of the drives to combat at work on the field of Agincourt. The English had sought by every means to avoid battle throughout their long march from Harfleur and, though accepting it on October 25th as a necessary alternative to capitulation and perhaps lifelong captivity, were finally driven to attack by the pains of hunger and cold. The French had also hoped to avoid bringing their confrontation with the English to a fight; and we may convincingly surmise that many of those who went down under the swords or mallet-blows of the English had been drawn into the battle with all the free-will of a man who finds himself going the wrong way on a moving-staircase.

The second factor confounds the former just examined. It concerns the commonplace character of violence in medieval life. What went on at Agin-

court appals and horrifies the modern imagination which, vicariously accustomed though it is to the idea of violence, rarely encounters it in actuality
and is outraged when it does. The sense of outrage was no doubt as keenly
felt by the individual victim of violence five hundred years ago. But the
victim of assault, in a world where the rights of lordship were imposed and
the quarrels of neighbors settled by sword or knife as a matter of course, was
likely to have been a good deal less surprised by it when it occurred. As the
language of English law, which we owe to the Middle Ages, reveals, through
its references to "putting in fear," "making an affray," and "keeping the
Queen's peace," the medieval world was one in which the distinction between
private, civil, and foreign war, though recognized, could only be irregularly
enforced. Thus battle, though an extreme on the spectrum of experience, was
not something unimaginable, something wholly beyond the peace-loving individual's ken. It offered the soldier risk in a particularly concentrated form; but
it was treatment to which his upbringing and experience would already have
partially inured him.

The Organization of
the Late Medieval City

GERALD STRAUSS

There is a currently prevalent image of the medieval and early modern city as having crowded, noisy streets, filth, and a lack of sunlight and open space. This image has been engraved on our minds by films like *Becket* and *Tom Jones;* the filmmakers took their notion of the city from historians who themselves had based their descriptions on engravings of cities produced in the sixteenth and seventeenth centuries. The impression is reinforced when we enter the older parts of European and some American cities, where the streets are narrow, crooked, and apparently laid out in a haphazard pattern. Compared with the gridlike plans favored by modern city planners, these remains of earlier urban life seem confused and crowded; but the builders of premodern cities were not abdicating their duties, and they were not incompetent. The picture of their efforts should be much brighter than it is painted.

Cities were planned for two purposes—defense and trade. In most cases, these two functions together determined the plans, but defensibility was the greater value. Study of most European cities will reveal a plan of streets radiating out from the central point, which once contained, and sometimes still contains, the fortress. In some cities, the cathedral usurped the position of the citadel, since the bishops were the lords of those places. Thus, in Toledo or Chartres or Durham, the cathedral holds the heights and could, with its strong walls and high towers, also have functioned as a fortress when necessary.

Not only were medieval cities well planned for their needs, they were also full of open spaces. The urban population grew rapidly from the twelfth century on, but houses were built close together, leaving gardens and even pastures within the city walls. The new urban families came from the countryside (mostly from the area immediately surrounding the town), and it took some time for them to lose their penchant for farming. City dwellers supplemented their diets by growing their own vegetables and milking their own cows; "truck farming" was rather primitive in most places. The open spaces were gradually filled, however, and the cities became increasingly crowded despite efforts in some places to limit the population by law. It was only the plague that brought an end to the growth, and the population decline continued long after the epidemics subsided. It is estimated, for example, that between 1494 and 1520, one eighth to one seventh of the houses in the German city of Freiburg were demolished and turned back into gardens.

City dwellers and city fathers knew that only by careful regulation could they avoid the hygienic problems of urban life while enjoying its commercial and cultural advantages. In this selection, Gerald Strauss describes the precautions taken in Nuremberg to ensure public safety from crime, fire, and disease. Strauss also reveals the pattern of daily life in the city, which was one of the most prosperous in Germany and which exerted great cultural influence in eastern Europe as well as within its own country. At the same time, the selection deals with many topics treated by N. J. G. Pounds in his piece on Rome and Roman cities in Part 1, and it therefore provides a means for assessing both development and continuity in the history of the European city.

"A city is an assembly of men brought together to live happily." Thus said Giovanni Botero in 1588 in his treatise on the place of cities in European society. Botero's definition really illustrates the shift of perspective away from the self-governing commune toward the all-powerful state, which had taken place by the late sixteenth century. To Botero a city was a place where population and money proliferated, where industrial power was gathered, and where a country's economic, social, and cultural resources were concentrated. ("And greatness of a city," he continues, "is termed not the spaciousness of situation or the compass of walls, but the multitude of inhabitants and their power.") There is nothing in Botero's book to suggest that a city should or could have a purpose distinctly its own, different from, perhaps at odds with, the objectives of the territorial state. But for the independent city this is just what the struggle of the past three-and-a-half centuries had been about. A municipal polity and a civic ethic had been created and maintained against king, prince, and baron. Botero did not understand this. He and his book speak for the nascent age of absolutism and mercantilism. A citizen of Nuremberg reading *The Greatness of Cities* in the last decade of the sixteenth century must have put it down with an uneasy apprehension of how times were changing.

Still, there is nothing wrong with the statement that men are gathered in cities "to live happily." As an empirical observation of the rewards of civic life it is unobjectionable. By and large, urban life was pleasant, and urban institutions were designed to make it so. No one has ever invented a device for measuring happiness, but where the material conditions were never less than adequate, where society provided not only security but purpose and direction as well, and where work and pleasure coincided, there was bound to be at least contentment. But let us go behind the generalizations and test Botero's statement by trying to find out what it was like to live and work in Nuremberg in the sixteenth century.

For administrative purposes the city was divided into quarters but not, as the name might suggest, into four quarters. Nuremberg had five quarters in the fourteenth century, six in 1400, and from 1449 on, eight: four each in the Sebald and Lorenz parishes. Originally the quarter organization had served military purposes, and the two quartermasters (Viertelmeister) of each of the sections were directly responsible to the three captains general of the city. Their most important duty had always been the mobilization of the residents of their district in the event of siege or attack. But the quarters were used for other civic purposes as well: taxing, census taking, fire fighting, enrolling men for forced labor duty. Quartermasters were helped by street captains, each taking charge of a block of houses. The citizen swore an oath of obedience to his street captain and furnished him with lists of possessions useful to the city in case of emergencies and liable to requisition: arms and ammunition, grain reserves, carts and horses, lanterns, ladders, spare rooms, and so on. The quartermaster coordinated these lists, thus providing the Council with an up-to-date inventory of men and material available when the need arose.

The most dreaded emergency and the most disruptive of civic affairs was, of course, a sudden predatory strike by some rural war lord or a protracted siege by a hostile prince, though Nuremberg's splendid defenses and her reputation for wealth and diplomatic skill discouraged most of the kinds of capricious assaults suffered by lesser cities. But one had to be prepared and Nuremberg was. However, the most frequent use to which the quarter organization was put was not mobilization but fire fighting. News of fires turns up monotonously in the chronicles of the city. Sometimes a single house burned down, often a whole block was reduced to cinders. To the medieval town these fires were anything but ordinary. Every city had its great conflagrations when whole sections of the town were destroyed, with incalculable loss of property and income. In Nuremberg the great fire of 1340 was still remembered after two centuries; starting in the kitchen of a widow's home, it had quickly spread to nearby structures, and two days and nights later more than 400 houses lay in ashes. Next to the dreaded plague, the worst catastrophe that could hit a medieval community was a fire burning out of control. Its destructiveness often remained evident for decades, for, without insurance, few people could put their hands on enough money to rebuild a razed home and workshop. This fact explains the prevalence of clear spaces and garden spots in medieval towns. Houses had once occupied many of these, but fire had gutted them, and the ground had come into the hands of neighbors who preferred to keep it open.

By the fourteenth century most governments had learned to meet the dangers of fire with statutes concerning building materials and space utilization. But little could be done in a country where lumber was cheap and customary and where every householder liked to store his own supplies of wood in his shed and grain under his roof. Not many residences were really well built, and the annals make frequent mention of houses collapsing of their own weight or falling apart when an adjacent structure was damaged. The only practical precaution was to have an effective fire fighting organization. In Nuremberg the quarter administration enabled authorities to call out a large number of men within minutes of the alarm, each prepared to do an assigned job and familiar with the equipment. The public baths were required to keep large vats filled with water mounted on carts ready to go, and every quarter had two hand pumps with adjustable brass nozzles. Fire hooks, leatherbuckets, ladders and axes were mounted on designated houses in each block. Fitted boards to dam up the *Fischbach*, which ran through the center of the city, were in readiness for creating a reservoir from which to deploy bucket brigades. Rewards went to the four carters first to bring water to the scene and to the first three men up the fire ladders. Everything was precisely regulated: responsibility for refilling the vats and cleaning the pumps, guarding the charred site for twenty-four hours, repairing damaged ladders, and so on. The system worked so well in Nuremberg that none of the innumerable isolated fires of which we read became a major conflagration.

The same can be said of security arrangements to control nighttime horseplay and hooliganism. Though these measures were not foolproof, and the courts were kept busy enough sentencing nocturnal brawlers, the worst of the trouble makers were probably discouraged by the precautions taken against them. Once the curfew bell had rung two hours after sunset, everyone was expected to be off the streets unless he had valid business. Patricians were permitted in their *Herrentrinkstube* after dark, and they could also play cards and dice there, but only until the hour before midnight. If legitimately abroad, a man must carry a lighted torch (the streets themselves were dark); failing to do so he was liable to arrest by the city's men at arms who patrolled the streets at night. If upon questioning a person was able to make himself known, he was let go after payment of a fine. "But any citizen, resident, or visitor who cannot establish his identity or provide a credible sponsor will be taken to prison." After midnight the fines doubled, and knives or other weapons found on the suspect, even a lute if he had been out serenading, were confiscated.

Inns closed at sundown, and a traveller lodging for a night could get nothing to drink once the curfew had sounded. If for any reason a tumult got under way, the government was prepared for it. Lanterns and torches were mounted on designated houses, and residents instructed to light them when they heard noise or sensed trouble. Most streets could be blocked off with iron chains drawn across the road from house to house; main thorough-fares were guarded by sets of double or triple chains. Ordinarily these chains were wound on drums enclosed in locked cases, but when trouble began and a crowd gathered, the street captains drew the chains out, making a clatter frightening enough to dishearten at least some of the ruffians. Endres Tucher, the city architect in the 1460's and 1470's . . . lists the location of all these chains. There were 420 of them in 1475. Like all other public property, the chains were maintained in good working order, oiled regularly, locks tested, and the drums inspected. No doubt the idea for this system occurred to the Council in the unhappy days of the Rebellion of 1349. It became a standard security device soon after that, always kept in readiness.

The streets themselves were in good condition, well surfaced, and, by and large, clean. This may be a difficult fact for the modern reader to accept, irreconcilable as it is with the commonly held image of mud, filth, and debris in medieval towns. But the evidence to the contrary is conclusive. Nurem-berg's unpleasantly wet climate (every visitor complained of the frequent downpours and the ankle-deep mud on country roads) makes it easy to imagine what the city would have looked like had its streets not been properly sur-faced. Stone paving was therefore introduced as early as the middle of the fourteenth century and from 1368 on proceeded systematically. The city architect had charge of this work, which was carried on by several paving masters, assisted by journeymen and apprentices and a detachment of day laborers. Streets were paved at public expense to within four feet of the door-step of a private house. The remaining distance was paved at the home owner's expense. Work was governed by exact regulations. Size and quality of paving stones were determined by the architect, as was the minimum num-ber of blows each stone had to receive from the pounder. The architect noted defective surfaces on his daily tours about the city and ordered immediate repairs.

More difficult was the problem of keeping streets free of trash and refuse, and the most determined measures were required to induce householders to surrender their time-honored right to allow pigs to forage freely on the streets—a practice not only unsightly in itself but also bound to encourage the dumping of garbage onto the streets to feed the scavengers. In 1475 the Council forbade the free circulation of pigs, confining them to sites in front of or behind houses. Once a day they could be driven to the Pegnitz to drink, but their droppings had to be swept up at once and thrown into the river.

The Pegnitz provided a ready receptacle for anything unwanted, from

wilted cabbage leaves to cattle carcasses, but here also the Council was determined to prevent the worst of abuses. It ordered the *Fischbach* kept entirely free of refuse, but the very repetition of warnings, threats, and exemplary
penalties issuing from the Council Chamber are sad evidence of the inveterate
habit of discarding rubbish where most convenient. In the Pegnitz, dumping
was permitted only at certain places downstream, set aside for the disposal
of the foulest matter, including the contents of the fifty or so public privies
located about the city. (Privy cleaning was a job in the hands of skilled
technicians called *Nachtmeister* and their helpers, supervised and inspected
by the city architect and confined to certain times in the year when the Pegnitz was sufficiently high and swift). Industrial waste, sweepings from the
workshops, and harmful chemicals used by tinsmiths and etchers and others
were to be taken to the same spot, and care was urged on apprentices to see
that nothing was dropped or spilled on the way. Householders were instructed
to keep servants from emptying slops into the street and were held liable for
infractions. Carcasses had to be taken to a field beyond the gates and buried
there. Building sites were to be tidied as soon as construction had come to an
end to keep loose soil and mortar from running into the streets. No great accumulation of trash was permitted in front of houses "so that the rains may
not wash it into the streets." Small compost heaps were permitted, but these
had to be renewed once a week.

The very punctiliousness of these laws and their constant reiteration suggest that citizens tended to take the Council's warnings lightly. There must
certainly have been more dirt around than the regulations allowed. . . .
"Bathing money" constituted a regular part of a man's salary, paid weekly,
usually on Saturdays. Municipal building workers left work one hour early
once a week to go bathing. Like every other profession, the bathing masters
had their official *Ordnung*, periodically revised and augmented by Council
decrees. Professional bath attendants were trained in the technique of sanitary
and medicinal bathing, also in hair cutting and depilation and in simple
medical operations, notably blood letting with suction cups. It took three
years of apprenticeship to become a journeyman in the craft and seven more
years of journeyman's work around the country before one could qualify as a
master. During the sixteenth century, Nuremberg had fourteen licensed
baths, all located on or near the Pegnitz and the *Fischbach*, whence the water
was drawn by means of wooden pipes, then heated over wood fires. Prices of
admission to the baths were kept low by Council order so that very nearly
every person in the city could go. (Children were admitted free if accompanied by parents.) The usual Council-appointed inspectors went from bath
to bath to ensure cleanliness and expert performance. If one paid for the full
treatment one was in for an elaborate ritual. It opened with a trumpet or bell
signal to indicate that the water was hot and the bath was open. Once inside
and stripped of one's clothes, one began with foot washing, then the body

was scoured and slapped with a sheaf of twigs, next steam bathing and rubbing to induce perspiration, swatting the skin with wet rags, scratching (for the pleasure of it; bathing masters and employees were obligated to provide this service), hair washing and cutting, combing, lavendering, blood letting, and finally a nap to recuperate from the exertion.

As for medical services, Nurembergers were professionally attended by at least half a dozen doctors, a team of midwives, and several apothecaries. Municipal physicians had practiced in the city since before 1400; they were paid by the Council for the treatment of poor folk, but charged fees for visiting the rich. In the late sixteenth century the medical doctors organized themselves into a *collegium medicum* to suppress quacks and regulate fees; one gulden was charged for the first housecall, a quarter gulden for each subsequent visit, with higher fees for the treatment of infectious diseases. Even in a time of inflation these were high prices, and some kind of free or low-cost medical care was obviously needed. Midwives were salaried, and their activities supervised by several matrons of good family who had a charitable concern for pregnant women, helping out where assistance was called for. Apothecaries were bound by oath to fill prescriptions faithfully. Periodic inspection by two Council members and one or two doctors ascertained that everything was done properly and the scales were accurate.

For the seriously and incurably sick and the very poor, there existed a number of free hospitals, all of them charitable foundations dating back hundreds of years: St. Elisabeth's built by the Johannite Order just outside the walls, near the gate named for it; the so-called "New Hospital" of the Holy Ghost, originally a refuge for the poor but turned into a place for the sick in the 1480's; the Hospital of the Holy Cross in the western part of the city, set aside for syphillitics at the end of the fifteenth century; St. Sebastian's for plague patients and St. John's, St. Leonard's, and St. Jobst's for sufferers from infectious and loathsome diseases. The Hospital of Sts. Peter and Paul accommodated foreign lepers. Persons judged to be mentally ill were incarcerated along with prisoners of war and common criminals in a tower in the *Burg*. . . .

In fact, there was hardly an ill fortune not mitigated by some sort of charitable establishment. Unwanted children found a refuge in privately endowed, but publicly supervised, foundling homes. Nuremberg had one for girls and another for boys. They apparently were decent places. A visitor to the girls' home in 1537 described "a large room wherein I saw forty-six foundling girls, the foundling father and mother, and a few servants. On the walls were racks for drying laundry in winter. Adjacent, a chamber with beds for the children, another for the master and mistress, also a kitchen, a place for firewood, a bath outside, and stables." The children were taught to read and write and kept busy with simple work.

Grown to adolescence, poor children had recourse to several sources of help. Honest girls of poor families could apply to one of a number of foundations for sums up to twenty gulden to buy a trousseau. Serving maids with years of household service behind them might procure a dowry from Andreas Oertel's Marriage Endowment. Older women who had neither prospects of marriage nor sufficient means to enter one of the better convents found a haven in the *Seelhaus* (founded by a well-to-do merchant to speed the salvation of a soul in purgatory). Rehabilitated prostitutes were accommodated in homes maintained, until the Reformation, by the two convents. Other funds provided help for women after childbirth, granted scholarships to poor boys to study at home or abroad, helped men who had met misfortune in business or fallen into debt because of illness. One of the handsomest foundations in the city offered free lodging and board to twelve retired master artisans who had not been able to save enough for a dignified life in their declining years.* And for the really poor there was the so-called Rich Alm, an endowment established privately in 1388, the interest from which bought every Sunday enough bread, meat, flour, herrings, and seasonal vegetables to feed the city's needy during the week. This charity was directly administered by the Council, whose agents compiled fresh lists of the poor and indigent every three months, to make sure that, on the one hand, no one undeserving got on the list and, on the other, no needy person had to do without these basic means to a civilized life.

Occasionally a single case reveals the quality of the Council's concern for its cocitizens. In 1555 the goldsmith Niklas Sailer, despondent over ill health and poor business, made a halfhearted attempt at suicide, but failed. The incident was brought to the Council's attention and investigated. Convinced that the man was at the end of his wits through no moral fault of his own, the Council granted him a weekly subsidy of one gulden, and in order not to humiliate him with this handout, it was arranged that a third person would receive the gulden and turn it over to Sailer without naming the source. The case illustrates the combination of administrative efficiency and personal solicitude characteristic of Nuremberg's government. A similar concern was reflected in the new beggars' regulation of 1522, where special provisions were made for "poor people who feel ashamed to beg and wear the beggar's badge, either because they think it a disgrace to their parents or a dishonor to their craft." . . .

A few observations may illustrate the conditions of material life as enjoyed in Nuremberg at the beginning of the sixteenth century. Almost every family, from patrician to journeyman, had its own house. Statistics from

---

* This was Konrad Mendel's *Zwölfbrüderstiftung*, founded in 1388. It was remarkable for its *Memorial Book* containing portraits of nearly all the members through the centuries, showing each at his craft or trade.

the middle of the fifteenth century show that the largest number of buildings in the city accommodated no more than three or four persons plus a servant girl or two and an apprentice. In time of war, especially when the city was under siege, the picture changed, of course. Rural residents, territorial officials, and even peasants whose farms had been destroyed or occupied sought refuge in the city and were quartered in burgher houses. In fact this need for occasional quartering is one reason for the lack of crowding in normal times: the Council liked to know that space was available for the accommodation of territorial subjects if the need should arise.

Dwellings were places of work as well as of residence. Ground-floor rooms never accommodated living quarters but provided space for workshops, storage, and such. During working hours and unless the weather was inclement, work spilled over into the street; in fact, fire regulations obliged all activities causing sparks or fumes to be carried on outside. Upstairs, even the least pretentious house had enough bedrooms to separate children from parents and servants from their employers. It is interesting to note from the available statistics that the proportion of residents and households to buildings increased as the centuries advanced toward the industrial age. In 1500 few families were crowded close on one another. Tenements did not exist. Even factory workers, the surviving information suggests, were housed in comfortable quarters. To give an example of this: there was a combined copper and iron hammer and flour mill on the bank of the Pegnitz just outside the city. It turned out wire, brass, and metal foil, as well as flour for bread. Workers' residences were attached to the factory, the whole establishment forming a closed rectangle of buildings and sheds. The residences, two rows of attached one-story houses, consisted, each, of a living room, one or two bedrooms, and a kitchen. A small stable for a goat or two and a sty for the inevitable pig were adjacent. All this was provided rent free. Every spring the houses were whitewashed, and stoves and other equipment were maintained at the factory-owner's expense. Workers' widows moved to smaller houses in the colony but could live rent free until their deaths. For the children there was a schoolhouse with a salaried master. Probably not all the workers employed in the city's hammer and paper mills lived quite so nicely. But in general the description accords with local expectations of acceptable conditions of work and residence.

This was true also of the amount and variety of food consumed by Nurembergers. All available information, and there is an enormous lot of it for all periods and for all segments of society, indicates that people ate well and abundantly—superabundantly, if one is to believe the many sermons and verses that portrayed Germans as uncontrollable gluttons and guzzlers. Rich and poor ate differently, of course, then as now, not only because of differences in purchasing power but because each estate had its inherited tastes and preferences and its own occasions for eating. . . .

Life was by no means unremitting toil. There were many holidays, even after the Reformation, for people to enjoy leisure, and enough free entertainment to give everyone something to do. But hard and dedicated work was a way of life for merchant and artisan alike, and it is clear that labor and achievement in one's calling came first in the scale of values. The working day varied in length according to the season, as is only natural where so much work is done outside and where artificial illumination is costly. Nuremberg, along with many south German cities, went by the so-called Great Clock, which counted the hours consecutively from sunrise to sunset: the first hour after daybreak was one hour of the day ("when the clock strikes one"), the first hour after sunset was one hour of the night, the second hour was two of the night, and so on. When the day was shortest it had eight hours, and the night sixteen; from the winter solstice on, the relation changed until it was reversed. Regiomontanus worked out the system scientifically for Nuremberg in 1488. Before that the days for changing the count had been determined by rule of thumb.

During the day, watchmen went about the city and rang the bells to indicate the hours of the clock. Working hours followed the length of the day, the working day being longer in summer than in winter. To quote from the regulations governing building workers:

> When the clock strikes eight or nine hours in the day [i.e., when the day is eight or nine hours long] be at work when the last hour of the night is over. When it strikes three [i.e., 11 o'clock by the modern clock, the day having begun at 8 a.m.], go to have your midday meal, and return to work at four, until the last hour of the day is over. When the clock strikes fourteen hours in the day, be at work when the clock strikes one [6 a.m.], have your breakfast at three [8 a.m.], return to work at four, take your midday meal at seven [noon], return at eight, have your Vesper at ten [3 p.m.], return at eleven, and leave work for the night when it strikes one of the night [7 p.m.].

Thus the shortest work day was seven hours in length, not counting meal times, the longest thirteen. The elongation of the working day to correspond to daylight hours may explain the proliferation of holidays and half-holidays during the Middle Ages. Reformers disapproved of these, not only on theological grounds, but one wonders how the public responded to the cancellation of so many feasts when the change brought abolition of most of the days that could be spent at games or sports while the weather was good. Since so many people were paid by the day and since prices were always on the rise, the grief over missed shooting matches and rope pulls probably was mitigated by the expectation of more pay at the end of the week. But it gives us pause for thought today that a work week of six days and a work day in spring and summer of from twelve to sixteen hours, including mealtimes, left very little occasion for diversion and recreation.

In winter the problem was the reverse: what to do with all the dark hours before bedtime. Most likely people slept much longer in the winter season; there was little else they could do, since no one was expected to be about the streets after it had gotten fully dark. The inns closed down, most convivial occasions were confined to daytime hours, and theatrical plays were not performed in the evenings. Card playing was probably the great favorite for whiling away time; it had been forbidden for some years in the fourteenth century, along with other games of chance, but in the fifteenth, cards reappeared on a list of licit games that also included chess and other board games. Nuremberg had several well-known card makers, artisans who hand painted expensive playing cards and also turned out cheap decks of block-printed cards. Dice throwing was outlawed, as were other means of gambling ("games in which one wins or loses one's pennies" in the official language of the decree), but it is clear from the constant repetition of the ban that it was largely ignored, even though the law specifically included private homes in the injunction.

The Relevance of a University Education in Fourteenth-Century England

GUY F. LYTLE

In the twentieth century, the position of universities has see-sawed. The steady growth in enrollments and in the importance of university-trained people in American society that can be perceived in the early part of the century ended during the Depression, when graduates found that their education did not open up job opportunities, and when many people could not afford even to enter the university. After the Second World War, growth began again and continued at a very rapid rate until recently. In the past decade, economic problems have again disappointed the aspirations of graduates, inflation has put a severe strain on university budgets, and slower population growth has contributed to a decline in enrollments. This pattern of growth and contraction of enrollments can also be seen in the history of the medieval universities, but the nodal points of the rise and decline are spread over centuries rather than decades. In the first two centuries of their existence, the great universities of Paris, Bologna, and Oxford played an important role in society and politics. Kings took an active interest in university affairs and relied on them for the civil servants who built their bureaucratic regimes. University-trained teachers began to dominate the growing educational system of Europe and to participate in the spread of literacy. The universities even acted as arbiters in local and international disputes within the Church, and political issues often affected the internal affairs of the faculty and student organizations. The apex of the universities' political involvement in the Church occurred during the great schism of the late fourteenth century.

The university system also provided an avenue for social mobility in the late medieval community—a community in which the lines of class division were progressively hardening. The values of the educational system cut across economic and social-class boundaries—although it would be wrong to overestimate the egalitarianism of the system. There were a significant number of poor boys in the schools and universities, but for individual members of the lower classes, gaining entry to the university must have appeared a formidable task whose successful achievement depended on luck and really extraordinary ability.

Between 1340 and 1430, however, the steady growth in enrollments and increasing influence and wealth of the universities turned around. Study of university records of this period shows that the institutions were in decline—losing students, political and social power, and income and endowment. In this selection, Guy F. Lytle argues that, in England at least, this reversal of fortunes was caused by a lack of jobs for university graduates, and that it led to significant changes in the structure of the universities of Oxford and Cambridge.

Both the semi-autonomy the university enjoyed and the not infrequent official trouble it experienced can be more clearly seen in the light of the overlapping jurisdictions and rival powers of patronage which formed the structure of medieval society. The universities of medieval northern Europe were nurtured originally within the culture of international Christendom, as the special children of a centralizing papacy. As they grew they produced theologians, canon lawyers, and educated priests who could defend and advance both the faith and the church. But if in the early years the papacy was usually a friend to the schools, the bishops often were not. In order to counter this and other localized interference, the universities turned to the king, who responded with a wide-ranging set of exemptions and privileges. As an indirect reward the universities produced anti-papal civil lawyers and chauvinistic bureaucrats and, by the late 15th and early 16th centuries, a class of educated laymen and troubled clerics who would lead in the struggle to redefine the church and state of Reformation Europe.

Oxford found that it could get into trouble with both ecclesiastical and royal patrons when its educational process produced a brilliant heretic, such as John Wyclif, and gave him a forum for his opinions. But more often the university faced the ambiguity of the church (pope, archbishop, or bishop) and the state both appealing to it or threatening it from opposite sides of a conflict. In 1487, and again in 1495, the king demanded that Oxford yield up to his courts a bishop and some students who were using the university as sanctuary while they were seeking justice under its ecclesiastical law. Letters from the university to all the concerned parties show the agony of her indecision, caught in the middle of royal pressure, threats of censure from the church, and the necessity to safeguard her own privileges.

But all of these matters, which might be called the macrostructure of patronage, are well known and yet difficult to analyze briefly. This essay is more concerned with the microstructure: how the attitudes and practices

Excerpt from Guy Fitch Lytle, "Patronage Patterns and Oxford Colleges, c. 1300–c. 1530," in *The University in Society*, Vol. 1: *Oxford and Cambridge from the 14th to the Early 19th Century*, edited by Lawrence Stone (Copyright © 1974 by Princeton University Press), pp. 112–40. Omission of footnotes. Reprinted by permission of Princeton University Press.

of a society based on patronage affected the internal organization of the university and the careers of its graduates.

Between about 1340 and 1430 in England, there was a serious crisis of patronage for the university and its students which had its roots in demography, war, nationalism, religion, and especially the growing conflict between different types of patrons. At about the same time, Oxford and Cambridge underwent notable institutional changes in which, among other things, *colleges* emerged as the primary administrative, physical, social, and educational focus, at the expense of the older *halls*. There is no simple correlation between these complex events; but, by considering them together, the need for, and the contribution of, the colleges becomes somewhat clearer. The colleges provided one important means of solving the patronage crisis for many students, a solution which reflected basic assumptions and realities of English society in the late Middle Ages. It could be argued that their position as dispenser of various kinds of patronage was not by itself a sufficient cause for the rise of colleges to their preeminence within Oxford in the 16th century and later, but the patronage role was certainly a necessary cause, and patronage considerations strongly affected the process by which the change took place. . . .

The Principle of Patronage and English Society 1300–1530

Patronage, in one sense, is simply a matter of who got what jobs for whom and how this was accomplished. As such, the problem can be classified, quantified, and if the data exists, fairly easily determined.

But in another sense patronage may imply a great deal more. In the hierarchical world that was England from the feudal era to the time of Jane Austen and beyond, patronage was the mode in which all society functioned and by which all men, if they could, advanced. As a social principle, however, patronage has always contained numerous ambiguities. On the one hand, it was the working out in practice of the principle and rewards of hierarchy; on the other hand, it was the only counterbalance to hierarchical privilege for those whose ambition exceeded their birth. The patron–client relationship involved a pattern of both exploitation and benevolence on the part of the lord, with the former usually more prominent; but it also established a system which fulfilled many genuine needs for mutual support felt by socially superior men as well as by their inferiors. The client acknowledged subordinance or lack of power (at least in a certain context) in return for material gains and protection. The patron enjoyed a sense of status and munificence, as well as the political influence implicit in large retinues of loyal followers. But perhaps more importantly in the bilateral social relationships which remained as the remnant of an earlier feudal society, lordship implied responsibility. One of the most significant of these obligations was the exercise of the ideal of "public generosity," the distribution of largesse which was demanded by the chivalric ideology and which was institutionalized in patronge.

The many forms and functions of patronage embodied social, political, moral, psychological, legal, religious, and aesthetic realities. They generally acted to bind society together, although abuses were far from being uncommon. Patronage in late medieval society in fact had many of the same attributes that anthropologists find in the "gift-relationship" both in primitive and in sophisticated cultures. Professor Richard Titmuss has described how "in some societies, past and present, gifts to men aim to buy peace; to express affection, regard, or loyalty; to unify the group; to bind the generations; to fulfill a contractual set of obligations and rights; to function as acts of penitence . . . and to symbolize many other human sentiments." Gifts, or patronage, may be economic commodities of some sort which are being used "as vehicles and instruments for realities of another order." One common feature of all these roles is the lack of anonymity. The human relationships were intensely personal (although they produced a feeling of belonging rather than individualism), and neither the patron nor the client could effectively generate a social identity without the other. Another aspect of the social code and structure of chivalry, loyalty, was by these means strengthened.

Patronage both formalized and provided a means for expressing many connections and obligations the society had otherwise imposed. First among these was probably one's duties to his family and kin. Advancement of the family's fortune and honor was a prime consideration in everything from marriage to the need for education, to the appointment of the local vicar; and it would be to a prosperous relative that a youth would most often look for a scholarship or some other patronage. Loyalty to a particular geographical region would often involve a lord, bishop, or official in the advancement of people from that area, and the obligation and satisfaction of this patronage was especially felt when the patron and client were closely allied by reciprocal economic ties, as a landlord and his tenant would be. As we shall see, each of these connections would affect the colleges and their students in the 14th and 15th centuries.

The two greatest sources of patronage were of course the crown and the church. They were approached continuously by suitors, and in turn responded often, since their influence reached every facet of late medieval life. Universities and masters were among the more ardent pleaders, and they received perhaps more than their fair share of the available benefits. University authorities were allowed to control most of the judicial and financial matters in which students and graduates might be involved. Time after time during the Middle Ages the townsmen of Oxford learned, to their discomfort, the extent of these privileges. Not only the members of the university, but also their families, servants, and university employees received special rights. Tax exemptions were forthcoming for students and colleges, and in general the concern shown, and the patronage offered, by the English monarchs for the welfare of the country's scholars was unmatched anywhere in Europe at the time. Nor was the papacy to be outdone in granting favors, and enough immunities and special rulings were issued to set scholars apart as a privileged elite within the already well-protected clergy. . . .

Patronage, as a social principle, always involves a process of reciprocity although the items in that process are usually unequal, intangible, or immeasurable. What would the medieval patron expect and receive? Without going into detail, we can point to service both in war and in peace (chaplains might well serve abroad during times of fighting, just as knights might well represent a lord in Parliament during periods of peace) and to public deference and support as the chief social and political obligations of the client. In the course of the 15th century, many university graduates would find themselves acting as lawyers, secretaries, tutors, chaplains, and administrators in the households of the king, noblemen, and bishops. For this service most of them received ecclesiastical benefices. The reciprocal nature of the arrangement, however, might be carried further. In 1439, the Bishop of Chichester rewarded Thomas Bekynton, a New College graduate and a prominent bureaucrat, with a canonry in his cathedral. Bekynton wrote to the bishop, whom he called his "most beloved father," to thank him for his patronage. No mere words, he said, were sufficient to express his gratitude for the bishop's favor to him, and he desired nothing more than the opportunity to repay these favors. In the meantime, he wished the bishop to know that he had told the king all about the patronage. The patron might receive monetary payment (e.g., from his tenant–clients), but this form of reciprocity did not affect students who had only "human capital" to offer. More common was the proposal of spiritual benefits. Many wills of late medieval Oxford students close by bequeathing the residue of the testator's possessions for the good of his soul and the souls of his benefactors. Many patrons drew up contracts with the recipient of their favors (frequently institutions such as Oxford colleges) both to foster their worldly designs and to assure their own future commemoration.

Finally, we must note that there are many different types of patron–client connections. If "patronage" is to be useful for explaining many of the aspects of medieval history, scholars who use it must distinguish the similarities and differences between, say, a landlord's dealings with a peasant or some other tenant and the same lord's relationship to a knight, a servant, or the local vicar. Almost all of the anthropological literature on patronage has stressed the "dyadic" nature of the contract, the personal tie between two individuals, not between an individual and a collectivity (or an institution). It is clear that this narrow definition will not account for many relationships within medieval society. The undying, corporate lords of the church, such as monasteries, were a serious social and political problem in the eyes of Edward I in the late 13th century. This paper will show how institutions could function not only as direct patrons in a variety of ways, but also as "patronage brokers" to link individuals either with each other (even across several intervening generations) or with the supernatural.

Much research and analysis remains to be done before the precise nature and all the ramifications of medieval patronage become clear. Recent findings, however, have demonstrated that much more than the formal, legal ties of fiefs, fiefe-rentes, and indentures must be considered. We must study the many informal patronage connections, with their social, economic, political, personal, and ritual aspects, which acted to coordinate a complex social and cultural system. Only in this way can we gradually supersede our vague vision of "feudal society."

In 1338, the sheriff of Suffolk found that he could not assemble a jury of knights to examine a petition from several lords because there were none in the county who "was not a tenant or of the blood or of the fee or of the robes of one of the aforesaid" lords. As George Holmes has said, " 'Bastard feudalism' was well established both as a normal network of relationships and as a possible element in wild disorder." Large retinues made civil war possible. The personal nature both of patronage and a state based on it put great stake in a strong and yet generous monarch; and thus when a weak king such as Henry VI lost control of his patronage, both the opportunity and even the necessity of open conflict emerged. In this paper we are not so much concerned with the more spectacular confrontations such as the "Wars of the Roses," but rather with some of the details of how both the system and the principle of patronage worked with regard to university students.

The Crisis of Patronage, c. 1340–c. 1430

The complaint that unworthy men received promotion while learned doctors and masters were being ignored was one of the commonplace themes of medieval authors. Chaucer's "clerk of Oxenford"

> . . . he was not right fat, I undertake.
> But looked holwe, and thereto soberly.
> Ful thredbare was his overeste courtepy;
> For he hadde geten hym yet no benefice,
> No was so worldly for to have office. . .

was certainly not the only lean student waiting for a church living in later 14th century England. It is impossible to judge for sure the effect of his own frustration in seeking ecclesiastical promotion on the direction of some of

John Wyclif's thought, but certainly he reflects the conflict between lay and papal power over patronage and attacks simony and other related abuses. In a long sermon to the university on the "seven streams of Babylon," Chancellor Thomas Gascoigne discussed absenteeism, pluralism, appropriation of rectories, indulgences, dispensations, and abuses of absolution; but he opened his diatribe with "the unworthy and scandalous ordination and institution of bishops, rectors, and officials which is called promotion," or the various aspects of ecclesiastical patronage.

But few students were as unworldly as Chaucer's clerk, as radical as Wyclif, or as reform-minded as the wealthy Gascoigne. The later Middle Ages in England have been called an "age of ambition," and the universities were competing with warfare, marriage, and trade to be the best avenue of social mobility and thus to attract students. In the early 1400s, a manifesto declared that "knights, esquires, merchants, and the entire community of the realm prefer to make their sons or kinsmen apprentices in some . . . secular craft rather than to send them to the university to become clerks." A proverb, in about 1450, gave as the motive for studying:

> I have heard said in old Romance,
> He that in youth will do his diligence
> To learn, in age it will him advance
> To keep him from all indigence.

The need for promotion as an encouragement to dedicated learning was reiterated by Edmund Dudley, an important civil servant under Henry VII, in a book addressed to the aristocracy:

> Favor your cunning clerks and promote them with promotions. . . . Make them your archdeacons and deans, and give them your prebends . . . exhort all others in your diocese that have promotions in likewise to order themselves. . . . How much shall your promoting of virtuous and cunning clerks in great number encourage the students of your universities to take pain and diligence to increase in virtue and cunning.

If a university degree could not assure students of good jobs after they graduated, the institutions faced imminent decline. The figures . . . show that there was a significant decline in the number of university graduates gaining advancement in the church in the later 14th and early 15th centuries. The resulting crisis in the universities caused general alarm.

The dioceses here listed represent a variety of geographical regions and conditions, and yet they clearly indicate a similar pattern of graduate employment. At some point in the second quarter of the 14th century, the percentage of graduates receiving positions turned downward. This trend was accentuated in the latter half of that century, and recovery was slow until the 1430s when the crisis ended. . . .

During this same period, Oxford saw its student body decrease sharply in size: there may have been some 1500 students in the early 14th century and no more than 1000 by 1438. A shrinking of the pool of graduates available to fill the same number of clerical jobs may well explain the pattern, but we must examine the causes of this contraction and not accept too easily a purely demographic explanation for complex social developments.

The demographic and economic changes which affected the whole of Europe after the famines and plagues of the first half of the 14th century undoubtedly had some direct and indirect impact on late medieval Oxford. About 1379, William of Wykeham stated that his foundation of New College was intended to "relieve in part, though in truth we cannot wholly cure, the general disease of the clerical army, which we have seen grievously wounded through want of clergy caused by plagues, wars, and other miseries of the world." Indeed New College was built on a site which had been decimated by plague and which had perhaps served as a plague-pit, or burial ground. Toward the middle of the next century, Gascoigne touched on this cause, among others, for the decline of the state of the church:

> Before the great pestilence in England there were few quarrels among the people and few lawsuits . . . and few lawyers in Oxford, when there were 30,000 scholars at Oxford, as I saw in the rolls of the ancient chancellors of Oxford when I was chancellor there. And the promotion of good men and their residence in their parishes and the fact that churches were sufficiently endowed and not appropriated . . . were the causes why few quarrels then occurred in the parishes and few errors when compared with . . . the errors which occur in the present day.

Gascoigne's statistics are absurd, but the list of causes in the rest of his argument may have substantial merit.

The town of Oxford, situated on the London–Gloucester–Bristol trade route, was certainly hit by plague, but its impact on the university remains an open question. Salter, in an account of his survey of some hall rentals, suggested only a 5 percent falling-off at mid-century; and the general scope of mortality due to the "black death" has been called into question by recent research. In addition, we know that at a later date both the university and the colleges made provisions to carry on academic work away from Oxford in case of plague, and the members of the university never hesitated to disperse at the slightest rumor of a possible outbreak. Unpublished research, however, now indicates that Salter seriously underestimated the decay of the halls and the decline of students, and contemporary founders of colleges usually listed plague as a cause for the decline of educated clergy. The psychological reactions to the "black death" and the consequent growth in chantry endowments may have been a very significant factor in the ultimate solving of the university patronage crisis. But we cannot allow demographic factors to explain wholly these complex developments, since the chronology of the demographic and patronage curves fails to fit in at least one crucial respect: while the decline may have commenced at roughly the same time in each case, the increase in the percentage of university men finding church positions preceded the rise in the number of students entering Oxford by one generation and the recovery of population growth in the country as a whole by two generations.

If we follow Gascoigne, the possibility that changes in patronage patterns explain the fall and rise of student numbers, rather than vice versa, must be considered. University officials at Oxford were certainly of this opinion in the 15th century. In 1438, they claimed that, while students had once flocked there from every country and all the faculties had flourished, now no students came, the buildings were in ruins, and the schools were in danger of closing. These conditions had been caused by war, scarcity of both food and money, and the lack of adequate reward for merit. The ignorant were being promoted in the church and elsewhere, while even those who studied until their old age still could find no positions. The university cited the example of earlier days, the warnings of the Bible, and the dangers facing the faith, and then begged the Archbishop of Canterbury and others for help. In all of this, there was no mention of plague. Although much less credence can be given to a similar complaint in 1471, again it was the furious opposition of the world against both Oxford and the Christian faith, and the continued promotion of unlettered men instead of graduates, which was said to have kept the university half-empty. The effects of this situation, according to the officials, were disastrous for the country, since insubordination and wickedness were spreading quickly and would destroy the order of the realm. The latter concluded with a recommendation that, in order to obtain divine favor for the whole kingdom, special prayers should be widely said for the intercession of Oxford's patron saint, St. Frideswide. Plague and demographic change, fluctuations in the economy, and extended warfare all were crucial factors in the social history of late medieval England; but in order to account fully for the crisis of the universities, it would seem necessary to pursue further this question of patronage.

Universities and graduates had traditionally looked to Rome to solve their patronage problems. The papacy had sheltered the nascent *studia generale* and later used their graduates in its expanding bureaucracy. Since the popes had supported the growth of the institutions, it was only natural that their graduates would expect papal patronage. Because of the long years they had to spend in the schools and away from their local region, students often lost contact with potential patrons; only when they could obtain the intervention of the international papal authority were they able to redress the balance in their favor in the face of "the localization and preponderance of personal influence in the disposal of benefices." The universities became even more dependent on the process of papal patronage when they began to follow the example of other petitioners and to submit to the pope *rotuli*, or lists of graduates seeking positions or reservations of benefices. These rolls, which reflect the hierarchy of university degrees and the hostility of rival faculties, were compiled by the University of Oxford from 1317 until the early 15th century. Even though a successful petition depended as much on luck as on real desert, and while grants became less and less effective as time passed, as late as 1417 Oxford authorities still hoped that the practice might be renewed as an important facet of patronage.

An indication of the role of papal patronage in the careers of some Oxford students can be found in the following figures. Between 1301 and 1350, some 48 percent of those graduates who had careers in the church received at least one papal presentation or reservation. About 26 percent of the graduates had received their first known benefice by this means. In the second half of the century, these figures declined to 40 percent and 16 percent respectively. After the final Oxford *rotulus* in 1404, papal patronage virtually ceased. While too much weight should not be placed on these numbers, they do suggest that papal provision was very important in the hopes of students and was perhaps especially important in securing their first job.

During the late 14th and early 15th centuries, direct papal presentations to church livings in England gradually came to a halt, although popes continued their formal provision of bishops and maintained their powers of dispensation. This decline was primarily the result of an increasingly hostile lay public opinion, which was articulated in large part by those groups who were feeling the patronage squeeze in society most severely, the lords and knights, many of whom sat in Parliament. As early as the Parliament at Carlisle in 1307, strong opposition to the pope was being voiced. It had increased further by 1351 when Parliament passed the Statute of Provisors, which greatly limited papal influence on patronage in England. Common themes which ran throughout these documents, as well as those acts which would come later, "the neglect of divine service, hospitality, alms, . . . the frustration of the founders' intentions and the destruction of patrons' rights; the exportation of treasure to enemies; the lack of councillors and betrayal of the kingdom's secrets." They show the growing chauvinism of English attitudes combined with the insistent need to find ways to pay for the new social relationships of the "bastard feudal" or patronage society. Periodic relaxations of these new laws, and the attempts both by Edward III (in 1376) and by Richard II (in 1399) to reach a concordat with Rome, were offset by the passing of a much more stringent Statute of Provisors in 1390 and the annulment by the Lancastrians of Richard II's agreement.

Claims and counterclaims interspersed with years of amiable dealings characterized the relationship between the English rulers and the popes up to the Reformation, but Rome had ceased permanently to be a major patron in the English church. The papal power of patronage, however, had not really collapsed until after 1400; the patronage crisis had begun before 1350 and thus before the first Statute of Provisors, and it was ending just as papal provisions were disappearing. Certain individuals, and probably certain whole classes of scholars, were adversely affected by this change, but it can hardly have been, as many thought, the sole cause.

The decline of papal patronage should be seen as a symptom or a consequence of a more fundamental social change which was occurring in the later Middle Ages. To fulfill the obligations of the indentures they had signed, lords needed all the patronage they could muster, and they could not afford to exclude the church from this quest. It can be proved that many university graduates were involved in this contractual system of secular employment, but contemporary critics often saw that system as detrimental to the advancement in the church of poor but worthy students. According to John Audelay,

> Now if a poor man sends his son to Oxford to school,
> Both the father and the mother, hindered they shall be;
> And if there falls a benefice, it shall be given a fool,
> To a clerk of a kitchen or of the chancery.

Hoccleve, Dudley, Barclay, and Saint-German, among others, repeat this accusation up to the early 16th century.

As the remaining tables in this paper all show, laymen already controlled a significant amount of religious patronage; but as the social system grew in elaboration, so the demands for even more were intensified. Many contemporary letters, petitions, and lawsuits show the king, the queen, the Prince of Wales, royal officials, and other laymen trying to gain control over ecclesiastical presentations. Monasteries, another source of considerable patronage, could often be bullied or bribed into allowing a layman or the king to dictate a presentation or they might do so to reciprocate for some other favor. The papacy, however, was less pliable, and it had been only a matter of time until its claims to English patronage were successfully attacked. It would not be until the middle of the 15th century when the universities had adjusted themselves to the new ways of society (especially by the foundations of more colleges) and when university training and the students it produced were satisfying more of the secular and spiritual needs of their society that graduates found increasingly good markets for employment and ecclesiastical preferment at the hands of new patrons. . . .

Responses to the Crisis

Before this gradual change had reached fruition, individuals and committees of all sorts had suggested and tried a number of specific remedies to aid university graduates.

In 1392, the House of Commons authorized Richard II and his council to modify the Statute of Provisors and requested that they "d'avoir tendrement au coer en ceste Ordinance l'estat & relievement des Universitees d'Oxenford' & de Cantebrigg." In 1400, exemptions were asked both for an individual graduate and for the universities and graduates as a whole. In 1415, the Commons laid the blame for almost all the nation's evils, including rebellion, heresy, and "the extinction of the universities," on the Statute of Provisors, which they acknowledged their own predecessors had devised. Seldom can a university have received such accolade as that which marks the beginning of that Commons' petition to the king. . . . But, the Commons went on, now to the contrary because "l'estatuit de Provision & encountre Provisours fuit fait per Parlement, le Clergie en les ditz Universitees lamentablement est extincte" and because no one had any incentive to study, the church and the realm were falling into ruin for lack of guidance. The king referred the matter to the lords spiritual, the bishops who sat in Parliament.

At times the king intervened personally. In 1399, Richard II granted permission to the Chancellor and graduates of Oxford to seek and accept letters of provision from the pope, notwithstanding all contrary laws, and Henry IV allowed a similar relaxation in 1403, at the special request of his queen. A year earlier, Henry had supported a plan, drawn up by the Convocation of Canterbury at the request of "doctors and other graduates" of Oxford and Cambridge, which required all spiritual patrons to notify a commission composed of the Bishops of Exeter, Hereford, and Rochester of the names, values, and conditions of the benefices in their gift, so that the commission could recommend graduates to the patrons for appropriate promotion. The Bishop of Exeter received the king's Privy Seal letter and passed it on to his vicar-general, but this scheme apparently produced no jobs for the graduates, and it vanished without a further trace from the records. (It is illuminating to notice that when the same vicar-general, Robert Rygge, an Oxford doctor of theology, later wished to make large donations to aid the university and its students, he did so by adding to the endowment of two colleges, Merton and Exeter.)

The church attempted in other ways to relieve the plight of university men. In addition to their responses to the rotuli when they were allowed to be sent, popes from time to time issued special directives. In 1382, Urban VI urged the Archbishop of Canterbury to appoint doctors, masters, and bachelors to dignities in the great cathedrals. Churchmen who attended the General Councils like the one at Constance in the early 15th century were consulted, and patronage considerations were high on the agenda for reform. In the list of forty-six articles which Oxford sent to that council, the fourth one contained a plea for the promotion of her graduates; and in a separate list, one Oxford graduate, Richard Ullerston, asked for the special advancement of theologians. The English position was best summed up in the avisamentum "de collacionibus beneficiarum pro nacione Anglicana" [concerning the granting of benefices in the English nation]. The *avisamentum* lamented the decline of the church, which it blamed on the lack of good preachers, and then presented a program for making certain that graduates obtained useful benefices. It was more realistic than many of the other remedies proposed, since it very clearly took into account the changing situation and attitudes of both the church and society in late medieval England. It mentioned the pope only once, and rather concentrated on the diocesan bishop as the crucial administrative figure in any new patronage reform. These episcopal patrons were to collate one noncathedral living to every umpromoted graduate with an M.A. or higher degree who had been born in the diocese in question. Whenever there were any graduates born in a bishop's or archbishop's diocese, they were to be given at least one in every four cathedral dignities and canonries; and the universities, to facilitate these presentations, would compile a list of alumni arranged according to place of birth. By focusing directly on one type of powerful patron, and by allowing for the functioning of regional biases which were very strong in that patronage-based society, this proposal ought to have had some chance of success. But the *avisamentum* does not appear in any administrative records, and it therefore seems not to have been implemented.

Similar proposals were discussed by the English clergy themselves in the Convocations of Canterbury in 1417, 1421, and again in 1438. Nothing came of the first two ordinances because of a long-standing conflict between Oxford and the religious orders. In 1438, Pope Eugenius ordered the universities to send delegations to the Council of Ferrara. Oxford alleged that it was too poor to support such a delegation, and the Archbishop of Canterbury was asked to relieve this poverty by a more systematic enforcement of the earlier ordinances for the promotion of graduates. In return for a few concessions from Oxford, Convocation reissued the 1421 plan. All of these schemes put great emphasis on the role of the bishops, and they did in fact become the patrons most favorable toward graduates. In part this can be explained by the rise in the percentage of bishops who were themselves graduates: from roughly 50 percent in the reign of Henry III in the 13th century, to 70 percent under Edward III, to over 90 percent in the 15th century. Moreover, most bishops were very practical men, and they too were using more graduates in their administrations and had to reward them as best they could. As we shall see below, not all graduates had an equal chance to obtain some of this episcopal largesse.

All of these remedies show an awareness by contemporaries of the problem then facing the universities. But most of the responses either answered one small request for one given year or relied on exhortation and other soft pressure. The question remains, therefore, whether in the late 14th and early 15th centuries there was not some firmer, institutional response to the crisis which both aided some pressing university problems and brought the university more into line with prevailing social conditions and attitudes. Clues toward an answer can be found by studying the early history of some colleges founded in that period, especially that of New College.

Oxford Colleges and Patronages, c. 1350–c. 1530

The employment of her graduates was not the only problem facing Oxford in the late Middle Ages and early Renaissance which required new institutional solutions. In nearly every case, the changes which occurred in response to these problems meant that colleges took a more prominent role in the affairs of the university.

To counter the decline in the number of students attending Oxford in the later 14th century, new colleges were founded and older ones were expanded explicitly to recruit new undergraduates, not just to support graduate students as most colleges had previously done. Colleges offered a solution to the problem of financing an education in a period of some economic depression, and this internal patronage of its chosen members has remained the most significant long-term contribution of the colleges. In part because they were not endowed and thus could not fulfill the same patronage role for their students, the number of halls in the university steadily declined from some 120 around 1300 to only 69 in 1444. They fell further to 50 (in 1469), to 31 (in 1501), to 25 (in 1511), to 12 (in 1514), and finally to 8 by 1522. Although in the early 16th century, the halls still housed almost a third of the student body, the surviving halls were large and, since the passage of the various "aulerian" statutes in the 15th century, very collegiate in their structure. A number of colleges annexed or permanently gained control of halls in their immediate area, installed a college fellow as principal of the hall, and used the halls to house what was in effect their new undergraduate population. Because of this change, college men came to dominate the important university jobs, especially those of proctor and scribe. Moreover, as early as 1410, the heads of the colleges were being summoned, along with experts from the faculties, to make an important decision.

Oxford also faced problems in its primary responsibility of teaching. The Regent Master system was no longer producing either enough or the right kind of teachers, and new curricula interests forced many students and scholars to look outside the traditional statutory paths to find alternative methods of gaining and conveying knowledge. The advent of printing was of course crucial in this intellectual transformation, but one must not underestimate the importance of the colleges with their tutorials and endowed lectureships. New College was the first to appoint specific fellows as tutors for other members, but this form of academic and intellectual patronage soon spread to other colleges. New College also established early on a special teacher of Greek, but in this it was soon far surpassed by Magdalen and Corpus Christi.

But we must limit our detailed study of the colleges to the question of their role in ecclesiastical patronage. The university as a corporation tried, but evidently failed, to solve the patronage crisis of its graduates. Even by the middle of the 15th century, it did not hold the advowson, or right to present, to more than one or two livings. The official letter-books (*Epistolae Academicae Oxon.*) are crammed with letters of recommendation for graduates to all conceivable patrons, but, as with other forms of exhortation, these were seldom sufficient to get the person a job. With the cessation of the *rotuli*, not only were graduates obliged to turn away from their reliance on the pope and to look for a local patron, but also the university—the sponsor and compiler of the rolls and thus a collective, corporate lord—lost its only effective patronage function. Oxford tried to overcome this weakness by changing the nature of the chancellorship and substituting a bishop or a nobleman for the often outstanding theologians who had governed the university since the 13th century. This change aided the university as an institution, especially in some of its elaborate building projects, but it did little directly to help graduates secure jobs.

The halls had no answer to this patronage need. In a medieval formulary, there is a testimonial letter by the principal and fellows of a hall on behalf of one of their members. William Swan, a lawyer at the court of Rome in the early 15th century, replied to Master William Dogge's request for a new grace of provision that he would do all he could to help him for the sake of the time they spent together at Oxford in the same "dining hall" (*sala*). But the halls themselves had no patronage to offer and were even less effective than the university.

The colleges did have a solution, at least in part, for the patronage crisis. But in order to understand that solution more fully, we must examine the relationship between the colleges and late medieval society, some evidence of which can be gathered from the motives of the founders. While all colleges had philanthropic aspects, and many can be understood as extensions of a royal, noble, or episcopal "household" or court, all colleges were also chantries of more or less elaboration. All the founders accepted the implicit and explicit relationship between the principle of patronage in late medieval social organization and its spiritual manifestations. Archbishop Chichele demonstrated this attitude quite clearly in his statutes for All Souls College in the early 15th century. He lamented the decayed state of the "unarmed militia of clerics" because of their lack of promotion and their consequent destitutions; he also mourned the "armed militia . . . which has been very much reduced by the wars between the realms of England and France"; and then went on:

> we, therefore, pondering with tedious exercise of thought how . . . we
> may . . . spiritually or temporally . . . succor each aforesaid soldiery . . .
> [decided to found] one college of poor and indigent scholars, being clerks,
> who are constantly bound, not so much to attend therein to the various
> sciences and faculties, but with all devotion to pray for the souls of glorious
> memory . . . ,

especially those of the House of Lancaster (Chichele's patrons), those who
fell in the French wars, and all souls of the faithful departed. Other rubrics
of the statutes gave the details on the liturgy to be followed in the masses
for the dead. This function of the colleges was increased at the death of almost
every fellow, since most graduates would leave money or goods either to
specific friends at the college or to the college itself for the celebration of
obits and the increase of the college endowment. . . .

In order to fulfill their stated ambitions, the founders had to devise
some method not only to educate future priests, but also to find for them
effective parish and cathedral positions. The founders came up with an
excellent solution: they included as many advowsons as possible in the
endowment of the college, which gave the colleges direct control over a substantial amount of ecclesiastical patronage. Of the twenty-one manors which
Bishop Wykeham gave to New College, thirteen or fourteen included the
advowson of the local church, and two separate advowsons were also included.
Although it was wealthier than many other colleges, the pattern of the New
College endowment was not untypical. When the college fell into financial
difficulties in the 1430s, a former fellow and future bishop, Thomas Bekynton,
showed filial loyalty by persuading Henry VI to grant to the college the confiscated property of the alien priory of Longueville. This brought not only
six more manors, but also an additional nine units of church patronage. At
the Council of Constance there was some reformist pressure to abolish the
appropriation of such alien priory possessions to other owners in England. In
a letter from New College to Bishop Bubwith, who was at the council, the
concern of the college for the manors and the advowsons is evident:

> Some evil people . . . do not shrink . . . from making widows of the
> colleges and other institutions, established by pious founders, by the de-
> privation of their privileges and the taking away of their goods. . . .
> Growling with canine fury at the liberties and privileges granted to us by
> the Holy Roman Pontiff, they strive to destroy completely the unions of
> churches which our lord of holy memory canonically secured at great
> expense and by licence of the Apostolic See from the alien houses.

All Oxford colleges had much of their endowment in the form of income
from the great tithes of impropriated rectories; indeed at their foundation
Balliol, Exeter, and Oriel had little else. The income was crucial for the daily
operation of the colleges, but the patronage which came with these rectories
was also of great importance for starting their graduates on their careers.

Touring the Holy Land

H. F. M. PRESCOTT

Beginning in late imperial times, pilgrims traveled to shrines throughout Europe, and from the eleventh century on, many of them went to Jerusalem and the holy places in its vicinity. The establishment of the Latin kingdom of Jerusalem after the First Crusade (1099) facilitated the movement of pilgrims to that area, and in the twelfth century, the first of several knightly orders was formed to protect pilgrims on their way to and in the Holy Land. The first order was the Knights Templar, and they, in conjunction with other orders formed later, built a series of fortresses along the pilgrimage routes. Many of these still stand today.

In early times, pilgrims were probably the most numerous travelers in Europe—along with some of the Jewish merchants whose activities are described in Robert Chazan's "Jews in a Christian Society" in Part 2. By the later Middle Ages, commercial travelers were by far the most important group, although the number of pilgrims had also increased dramatically. The pilgrims followed the trade routes and in fact became an important part of the traffic going through the great Italian commercial centers. The seriousness with which the city fathers of Venice and other cities regarded the pilgrim trade is demonstrated by the elaborate controls they imposed on those who transported the travelers. It is clear that ship captains in the Italian cities maintained a regular transportation service for the pilgrims, and that the authorities wanted to ensure the continuation of the flow of pilgrim-tourists through their ports.

The pilgrims, in turn, have helped historians by leaving many accounts of their journeys across the Mediterranean. These travel diaries are the principal source of our knowledge of the conditions of transport and travel in the fifteenth and sixteenth centuries. The longest of the fifteenth-century accounts is by Friar Felix, a Dominican from Ulm in southern Germany, who made two trips, one in 1480 and one in 1483. Felix's diary serves as the basis of the following description by H. F. M. Prescott.

In the year 1480, just at that season in which, as Chaucer knew, men long to go on pilgrimage, namely on April 14, Felix, having preached his farewell sermon, mounted his horse, and with Prior Ludwich Fuchs set out for Memmingen, where he should meet "Master George." Of the start from the convent at Ulm he says nothing; the parting from Fuchs was what mattered; at Memmingen next morning the two friends kissed, not without tears, the Prior insisting that Felix should promise to remember him at the Holy Places, to write (if he might find a messenger), to come back soon. "Then sadly he left me, returning with the servant to Ulm, to his sons, my brothers there." That parting took away at a stroke all Felix's courage and all his delight in pilgrimage. "And I raged at myself for having entered upon it. All who would have dissuaded me I thought of now as my best counselors and true friends; those who had led me into it I reckoned my deadly enemies. At that moment I had rather look on Swabia than on the land of Canaan, Ulm was sweeter to me than Jerusalem; I was more frightened than ever about the sea, and . . ." (this is a most honest traveler) "if I had not been ashamed I should have hurried after Master Ludwig and gone back to Ulm with him, for that was what then I most longed for."

Shame, however, did prevent that flight from the unknown; Felix, with the young man and his servant, set out for Innsbruck, and by the time they reached the Alps the Friar is able to use one of his favorite words, for already they were traveling "merrily," having discovered, as they came to make each other's acquaintance, "that we and our tastes agreed well together." So that though they had lost their way, and though, having no common language with the people of the inn, they could use only signs, their night at Bassano, with as much of the local red wine as they liked to drink, must have been cheerful.

So much, without any information about mileages, or rates of exchange ("let those who want such, read other books of pilgrimages"), without even a mention of relics seen and revered upon the way, is all that Felix says of this first stage in their pilgrimage, which landed them at that great port of pilgrim travel—the city of Venice.

Even before the fifteenth century Venice had monopolized the pilgrim traffic to Jerusalem, and, as with her other concerns, had organized it with a thoroughness and precision which belong rather to the modern than to the medieval world, the state itself often fulfilling the functions both of the shipping company and the travel agency, and when allowing individual enterprise, minutely and jealously controlling it.

Directly he reached Venice the pilgrim found himself the object of almost fatherly care on the part of the state. There were inns for him to put up at, and license to keep such an inn must be sought from the Senate. But it was not enough that his lodging should be respectable; the crowds of pilgrims which poured into Venice each pilgrimage season must be shepherded about the strange city and protected from those who would exploit them. For this purpose, since a time long before that of Felix's pilgrimage, the Venetian State had regularly appointed officials called *Cattaveri*, and, under them, a number of "Piazza Guides." At the beginning of the century two of the twelve Piazza guides must be on duty during every week, keeping, from dawn to dusk, their station either on the Rialto or in the Piazza of St. Mark, and these two must have command of more than one foreign language between them. Human nature being what it is, these guides at one time began to make a practice of taking the dinner hour off. This would not do; it was enacted that while one dined the other must remain on duty; later the Senate softened, and the dinner hour was allowed.

The business of these officers was to interpret for the pilgrims, to help them to obtain the correct exchange for their money, to see that they were not fleeced in the shopping so necessary for the next stage of their journey, to bring them into contact with the captains of the pilgrim galleys, and to a certain extent advise them in the agreements which were then made. Over all these activities the Cattaveri kept a sort of watching brief; appeal could be made at any time to them, the contract between captain and pilgrims must be handed in at their office three days before it was signed.

The records of the Venetian Senate show what vigilance and ingenuity were needed in order that the profiteering tendencies of innkeepers and guides might be thwarted. But the battle against their peccadilloes was as nothing to that against the greed and insubordination to statute of the captains; all of them of the great noble houses of Venice, and by the circumstances of the case removed for the greater part of the voyage from supervision by the state.

From as far back as the early years of the thirteenth century the Senate had laid down regulations which, if observed, should insure the safety and comparative comfort of their pilgrim clients. Every pilgrim galley sailing from Venice must have a cross painted at a certain level on the hull; this served the same purpose as our Plimsoll mark, lading with relation to this cross being graded according to the age, and hence the seaworthiness, of the vessel. So many sailors, so many rowers, must be shipped; sailors in the earlier century, and again during the dangerous times of the Ottoman advance, must be provided with arms, must be over eighteen, must take an oath to look after ship and tackle, and not to steal more than five small soldis' worth. Captains must be at least thirty years old. In order to prevent these noble captains from merely painting up ancient and unseaworthy craft, the magistrates were instructed to send experts to inspect these before sailing, and the Venetian governors at various ports were made responsible for seeing that the captains of the pilgrim galleys did not load them up with any more merchandise than was agreed upon between captain and pilgrims. But this list of provisions, regulations, prohibitions could be prolonged almost indefinitely. Let us sum it up by saying that no possible opportunity seems to have been lost by the Venetian captains for making something "on the side" out of the pilgrim traffic, and that such sharp practice was nosed out and forbidden (as we shall see, vainly forbidden) by the state, through a period of more than three hundred years.

The great flow of Jerusalem pilgrims to Venice was accommodated for the journey in three different classes of vessels. For the rich, the "V.I.P.'s" of the period, there was the galley, hired out by the Venetian State to the noble pilgrim. For the poor there was the sailing ship. For the vast mass of pilgrims there was the regular service of galleys, timed to leave Venice at two seasons of the year, that is to say soon after Easter and soon after Ascension Day.

The practice of hiring a galley to persons of wealth and importance was considered by the Venetian State as part of their foreign policy. With the enlightened self-interest fitting in a nation of splendid shopkeepers, the Senate in 1392 declared that it was "wise and prudent to oblige the princes of the world . . . having in view the facilities and favors which our merchants trading in those ports may receive and obtain."

Though so candid about their motive, the Fathers of the State seem to have been less truthful about the terms of their bargain in this case. The minutes of their meeting state that the galley in which Henry of Lancaster, later Henry IV, passed oversea to the Holy Land was lent, furnished, and stocked free. The earl's account books tell another tale; a payment of 2,785 ducats goes down under the heading of "Skippagium" for the hire of the galley. However the Signory voted 300 ducats to be spent on a farewell entertainment before Henry sailed and another 100 for a similar function on his return. And, one way or another, the sprat caught its mackerel, for when Henry of Lancaster became Henry King of England in 1399 he promised to treat all Venetians as his own subjects.

Lancaster was by no means the only great noble to whom the Senate hired out their galleys for the Jerusalem journey. His enemy, Mowbray of Norfolk, in 1399; a Portuguese prince in 1406; and others throughout the fifteenth century made the pilgrimage in this way.

While the great went overseas, each with his own household, in a galley, lent or hired by the Venetian State, the poor would travel most cheaply in a sailing ship. When the writer of the *Informacōn for Pylgrymes* sailed with "Luke Mantell" each of forty-six pilgrims on board paid as he could afford 32, 26, or 24 ducats for his return fare to Jaffa, with food included. Devout captains sometimes carried friars "for the love of God." The less devout took them at a reduced rate, charging 15 to 20 ducats for the voyage out and back.

But the ordinary run of pilgrims traveled in the regular service of pilgrim galleys, though even among these ordinary pilgrims there were often to be found great men who, whether from motives of humility or parsimony, arrived in Venice and took their passage without advertising their wealth and rank. This practice caused the Signory considerable anxiety, ". . . on account of the abominable way in which princes, counts and other foreign noblemen who went disguised as pilgrims, to the Holy Sepulchre, on board our galleys, had been and were actually treated" by avaricious galley captains. What such treatment could be we shall see later, for Felix and his companions sailed with a captain notorious for his avarice and bad faith. The Venetian State, acutely sensitive to the opinion of such great persons, ". . . considering how much they can injure or aid those of our merchants and citizens who pass through their countries," could only continue its unending battle against the erring captains.

Apart from keeping constant watch over the condition of the pilgrim galleys, and this might mean, as in 1473, the condemning of a vessel which had seen twenty years' service, the state did what it could to protect the pilgrims in the formal contract, made between them and whatever captain was to carry them overseas. Enactment and re-enactment follow each other in the minutes of the Senate; but in spite of all, at the end of the century it was necessary to decree that captains must find four sureties to be bound to the amount of 250 ducats each for the observation of the contract; the injured pilgrims should be compensated by the sureties, and the defaulting captain punished by the state.

The pilgrims themselves, profiting by the long experience that lay behind them, did what they could, in these contracts, to safeguard themselves, and there is a common form which the contract usually follows. The fare was more or less fixed by custom. Surian, in 1500, says that pilgrims were charged according to their quality, and that the sums ranged from 30 to 60 ducats, with 13½ ducats for sight-seeing expenses in the Holy Land. In 1483 Bernhard von Breydenbach's party, which sailed with Agostino Contarini, paid 42 ducats each; Felix and his company, in the ship of Pietro Lando, paid 40. The *Informacōn for Pylgrymes* on the other hand says that you must pay 50 ducats for "freight and for meat and drink . . . for to be in a good honest place, and to have your ease in the galley and to be cherished." Casola, fourteen years later than Felix, but traveling with the captain of Felix's first pilgrimage, paid 60 gold ducats. But this was to cover his keep "by sea and land" and a place at the captain's table.

This fare covered more than the transport to and from Jaffa. On board ship the captain was to provide a hot meal twice a day with good wine (but, said the pilgrims, there was always plenty of water in it), and "to each of us a bicker or small glass of Malvoisie" every morning before breakfast. In port, on the voyage, pilgrims provided their own food, unless it were an "uninhabited harbour," where the captain must feed them. Once arrived at Jaffa it was the duty of the captain to arrange and pay for the transit of the pilgrims to Jerusalem; that is to say "all dues, all money for safe-conducts, and for asses and other expenses, in whatever names they may be charged . . . or in whatever place they have to be paid, shall be paid in full by the captain alone, on behalf of all the pilgrims without their being charged anything. . . ." The anxious precision of the clause indicates what pitfalls were known to lie in the path of overconfiding pilgrims.

This "lump sum" payment, satisfactory in one way to the pilgrim, had its drawbacks. It was necessary to stipulate that "the captain shall let the pilgrims remain in the Holy Land for the due length of time, and shall not hurry them through it too fast. . . ." The "due time" was a fortnight from landing to departure, and as we shall see, Felix in his first pilgrimage was denied even this short period.

Other clauses, among the twenty or so which may appear, seek to insure the pilgrims against the captain keeping them waiting, and wasting their money in Venice; against his calling at unnecessary, unusual, and strange ports on his way; against his trying to prevent them going out of Jerusalem to the Jordan. It is stipulated that he shall protect the pilgrims from the galley slaves; shall, if a pilgrim die on the journey return half the fare to his executors; shall not interfere with the goods of the dead man; and shall, if possible, put into port for the burial. A sick pilgrim shall be given a place to lie out of the "stench of the cabin"—but that might mean no better refuge than one of the rowers' benches. Not only the pilgrims but the Venetian State itself tried to prevent the captains of the pilgrim galleys from adding to their legitimate profits by private trading on the homeward run. In 1417 two captains were prosecuted for crowding the pilgrims with their merchandise; next year, though it was admitted that the officers and oarsmen had the right to trade, their merchandise must not overflow into the ship but must be contained in boxes; in 1440, and again twelve years later, trading was forbidden to the captains. But prohibitions and prosecutions were in vain.

On his first pilgrimage Felix sailed in the galley of one of the most notorious of these patrician profiteers. Agostino Contarini, Agostino dal Zaffo ("of Jaffa") as he came to be known, had already begun his long career as a pilgrim captain, and had begun it badly, since in his voyage of 1479 he had found himself succeeding to the inheritance of a nasty quarrel between the captain of the previous year and the Saracens. That had meant loss instead of profit; even in 1480 he thought it wiser to bring as a present to the Saracen governor of Syria one of the famous glass vessels of Murano. He was therefore determined to recoup himself. The state allowed him to raise his charges to 55 golden ducats for each pilgrim and throughout the voyage he saw to it that wherever he might he would spend a little less on, or wring a little more out of, the pilgrims; or would cheat the Saracens; or would do a little private trading on his own account.

At Ramle, when he must pay dues to the Saracens for every man who went up to Jerusalem, he tried to pass off fifteen of the pilgrims (without their knowledge of the deal) as sailors of the galley's crew, ". . . so that he should pay for them only half the tribute, although he had had from each 55 ducats. And certain of the pilgrims passed as crew, and the others were refused . . . and thus the said captain's trick failed, although he made a lot on those who passed."

At Jerusalem the pilgrims fell foul of him again, for he would not provide them with an escort to make the Jordan expedition, though this, they insisted, had been included in the contract. At Ramle on the way home he demanded a ducat and 8 *marcelins* from each of them for the hire of donkeys; those stouter spirits who refused, and who continued to refuse, were brought to order at Jaffa by the threat that they would be left behind.

When all were on board he kept the ship waiting at Jaffa from "Thursday to Friday evening" in order to trade; and his merchandise must have added to the discomfort of the pilgrims, for already "our whole galley was cluttered with the 600 or 800 ducats' worth of good Jaffa cotton" which was the result of the trading ventures of the officers and crew. Nor was the captain yet satisfied, for at Cyprus he loaded up with ". . . lovely salt, white as crystal . . . in fine pieces like tiles, four or six fingers thick . . ." from the salt lake at Larnaca.

Fourteen years later Agostino dal Zaffo, still in the pilgrim trade, had not changed his ways. Casola, a friendly critic, thought that the amount of Cyprus carob beans brought to the galley at Limasol was "stupendous. . . . sufficient to supply all the world . . ." At Crete, on the homeward run, the pilgrims, "satiated with so much malmsey and muscatel . . . began to say to the captain that he must take them away from there, and that if he wanted to trade in malmsey or anything else he could do it at his good pleasure, provided he sent the company to Venice."

Apart from the momentous affair of their agreement with the galley captain the pilgrims' most serious business in Venice was shopping for the voyage. It is remarkable and I think curious, that Felix himself, even in the full flood of his reminiscences of his second pilgrimage, says little of this, though quite a lot when he comes to describe the setting out from Jerusalem of the pilgrims for Sinai that same year. At Venice he briefly remarks that "we went to the market and bought all that we should need on our galley for the voyage—cushions, mattresses, pillows, sheets, coverlets, mats, jars, and so forth . . . I bade them buy a mattress for me stuffed with cows' hair, and I had brought woollen blankets with me from Ulm . . ."

Other pilgrims are far more particular in their lists and earnest in the advice that they give. You must have a feather bed and bedding, pillow slips and two pairs of sheets. You should buy the bed mattress and pillows from a man near St. Mark's. They will cost you 3 ducats, and when you come back you can sell them again, even if "broken and worn," for half that. You should also buy a chest and see that it has a lock and key. Buy barrels, two for wine and one for water. The best water for keeping is to be drawn at St. Nicholas, and when that is used up fill the barrel again at any port of call. As for wine, there is none so good for the voyage as that of Padua, "which is a little wine, bright red, and not strong." The wines that you will find on the voyage are so strong that they cannot be drunk (fearful things are said of the effect upon the inner man of Cyprian wine: drunk neat it will burn up the entrails, therefore dilute it with anything up to four quarts of water). A wise man will keep his Paduan wine to drink on the return voyage. It is well to have "a little caldron, a frying pan, dishes . . . saucers of tree [wood], cups of glass [an unexpected refinement] a grater for bread . . ."

Although the pilgrims while on board ship were provided with two meals a day by the captain, they did not build much upon these, "for some time ye shall have feeble bread and feeble wine and stinking water so that many times ye will be right fain to eat of your own." So, besides flour and firewood they would buy hams or salt ox-tongues; Englishmen took bacon; Italians would take "good Lombard cheese" and sausage; all would take cheese of some sort, eggs, bread, and biscuit, ". . . that is bread twice baked which keeps without going bad, and it is so well baked that it is as hard three days after as it is at the end of a year." Fruit was important, dried apples and dates, figs and raisins, spices too, unless you were prepared to eat tasteless food, so take "pepper saffron cloves and maces a few as ye think need, and loaf sugar also."

An Italian adds such refinements as sugar "of the best quality" and above all fruit syrup, ". . . for it is that which keeps a man going in that great heat . . ."; some syrup of ginger to be used, but with discretion, after seasickness; quinces, unspiced; "aromatics flavoured with rose and carnation," the necessity for which is made sufficiently clear by an Englishman's vivid description of the lower deck on a galley as a place "right evil and smoldering hot and stinking." The Italian adds also, with startling modernity, "some good milk products."

Besides all these it was well to "hire you a cage for half a dozen of hens or chickens to have with you. . . . And buy you half a bushel of millet seed at Venice for them." Nor would even this bulk of provision be sufficient: wherever the ship touches on the voyage the pilgrim "should furnish himself with eggs and fowls, bread, sweetmeats and fruit, and not count what he has paid to the captain, because" (it is a wealthy Italian speaking) "this is a journey on which the purse cannot be kept shut." In addition to all that he brought the rich and influential pilgrim might, while at Venice arrange, as von Harff did, for letters of credit.

Having provided as far as possible for all needs, the pilgrims almost always found themselves forced to wait upon, as they were convinced, the pleasure of the captain, or, as he regularly maintained, a favorable wind. This delay, during which the pilgrims fretted, and which the anxious state tried by successive legislation to restrict to reasonable dimensions, the pilgrims would fill in by sight-seeing, sacred or secular. But in 1480 Felix, still numbed by the "temptation" of homesickness, which "caused me to be dull and stupid both in viewing places of note . . . and also in writing accounts of them," says nothing at all about the beauties of that city, which his fellow pilgrim, the clerk from Paris, describes with such enthusiasm. Neither the curiosity and fascination of water instead of roadway, "the little barks and boats [which] go through the streets," nor the "twelve to fifteen hundred bridges, big and little, of stone or wood," nor "the fair houses which they call palaces," drew from Felix a word of notice. It is the Paris pilgrim who so carefully explains and so palpably admires the splendors of mosaic work: "the little pieces and bits of glass the size of a small silver penny . . . in gold and azure and other right rich colors . . . of these little bits are made the vaults and walls of the churches, all showing characters of the Old and New Testaments, and to each of these characters a writing, which describes the character, and the writing is made of the little bits, and the pavement is made up of small pieces of stone of all colors, in the shape of beasts, birds, and other most beautiful designs." It is the Paris pilgrim who describes the massed splendors of the treasure of St. Mark's displayed at Ascensiontide, the "images, angels, chalices, patens, vessels, and chandeliers, all of gold, huge, thick, massive, and garnished with precious stones of price inestimable and of every color." While the Paris pilgrim climbed the campanile and looked down upon "the sea and the town," and "round about the town, towers, castles, churches, abbeys, houses of Religious, monasteries, hospitals, and villages . . . all in the midst of the sea"; while he visited the Arsenal, and stared at the reception of the Turkish ambassador and admired the nightly illuminations on the towers of Venice, Felix, for all we know to the contrary, moped in the inn of St. George, yet making friends, in spite of his melancholy, with Master John, the innkeeper, and Mistress Margaret, and with the big black dog, all of whom were to welcome him so warmly on his arrival at Venice three years later.

With this heavy mood upon him Felix passes by his first visit to Venice without a word. He and Master George came there, made their agreement with Agostino Contarini, and waited for the day on which they might sail, as all the rest of the pilgrims then gathered in Venice must wait. This company, scattered as yet among the many inns, included noblemen of various countries, "priests, monks, laymen, gentle and simple, from Germany . . . and France, and especially two Bishops, that is of Orleans and of Le Mans," besides English, Scots, Spanish, and Flemings. To the disgust of some of the noblemen there were as well no less than six wealthy matrons, who, though "through old age scarcely able to support their own weight . . ." intended the pilgrimage.

When at last the ship was ready to sail, news came which, to the expectant pilgrims, was a heavy, almost a disabling blow. A ship arriving in Venice reported that the Grand Turk was besieging the Knights in Rhodes and that the seas of the Levant swarmed with his ships. Whether to go or stay became the question which sowed "troubles, discord and quarrels" among the pilgrims, especially as the Venetian Senate refused to guarantee in any way the safety of the pilgrims themselves, though it did not prohibit the voyage, the galley being covered by the Turkish safe-conduct.

It was therefore after a period of painful indecision that on Thursday,

June 7, "just before dinner time, all the pilgrims aboard, and the wind fair, the three sails were spread to the sound of trumpets and horns and we sailed out to the open sea. . . ."

When he came to write his book for the stay-at-home brethren at Ulm, Felix dealt thoroughly with the subject of ships, and from his account and that of Casola we learn much of the disposition of the pilgrim galleys and the routine of life aboard.

Felix, according to his custom, goes right back to the elements, and enumerates three kinds of ships "which are great, middle-sized and small ones," refers to the reputed invention of the first ship, and so, working his way gradually onward to the present and the particular, declares that he will deal only with the galley, "an oblong vessel which is propelled by sails and oars."

But here it is necessary to explain what is only implicit in the descriptions of the Friar and of Canon Casola. The pilgrim galleys formed part of the merchant fleet of Venice, and by this time were vessels of much greater draft than the fast war galleys. A large merchant galley could load two hundred and fifty tons of cargo below deck, so that she rode low in the water, and must depend for the greater part of the voyage upon her sails, being, in fact, practically a sailing ship, with the added convenience of oars for use in entering and leaving port. So Casola will state, though without explanation, that during his voyage the oars were little used, and Felix will remark that "when the sun rose, the galley slaves began to work the galley along with their oars," or that "before it was fully light the slaves rowed the galley out of the harbour as far as the corner of the mountain, where we committed her to the wind."

Again, though both Casola and Felix mention biremes and triremes, and Felix explains that one is "rowed by pairs and pairs of oars" and the other "by threes and threes of oars, because on each bench it has three oars and as many rowers," neither he nor Casola makes it clear that these benches were set at such an angle with the ship's side that the oar of the rower at the inboard end entered the water aft of that of his neighbor, and this man's oar aft of that of the rower nearest the gunwale.

Apart from this the two landsmen give a fairly exhaustive description of the galley. They speak of its narrow build, of the three masts, of the iron prow "made something like a dragon's head, with open mouth . . . wherewith to strike any ship which it may meet." Both were especially impressed by the ropes, "many, long, thick, and of manifold kinds. It is wonderful to see the multitude of ropes and their joinings and twinings about the vessel." Casola learnt with respect the price of the great anchor cable, and doubted whether "two Milanese waggons with two pairs of oxen to each could have carried all the ropes" in the galley.

Starting from the prow, with its small forecastle and sail, the two mention the rowers' benches, with the wide gangway between, laid upon chests of merchandise and running from prow to poop. Felix alone concerns himself with the rowers, most of them, he says, slaves of the captain, though there were others, wretched enough but free, from Albania, Macedonia, Illyria. They lived, ate, slept on the benches, if necessary chained there in port lest they should escape. "They are all big men; but their labours are only fit for asses. . . . They are frequently forced to let their tunics and shirts hang down by their girdles, and work with bare backs . . . that they may be reached with whips and scourges. . . . They are so accustomed to their misery that they work feebly . . . unless someone stands over them and beats them like asses and curses them." When not at work they would gamble with cards or dice, shocking the good Friar with the incessant foulness of their language. Some were craftsmen, plying such trades as that of the tailor or shoemaker; all were traders, keeping their merchandise under their benches to sell when the ship made harbor, or to the pilgrims; they sold, says Felix, excellent wine.

At the galley's stern rose the tall, three-storied poop, upon which "the flag is always hoisted to show which way the wind blows." When Casola made his pilgrimage the "castle" was hung with canvas and with curtains of red cloth embroidered with devices of the Holy Sepulcher and the Contarini arms. In a latticed chamber in the topmost story was the steersman "and he who tells the steersman how the compass points, and those who watch the stars and winds, and point out the way across the sea." Below, on the deck level, was the captain's cabin, and the place where "the tables are spread for meals." Below again, when Felix made his first pilgrimage, "the noble ladies were housed at night," and the captain kept his treasure. Casola describes this lowest compartment as without windows, and says that it was used for sleeping and for storing arms and tackle.

A little forward of the poop, toward the starboard side, was the captain's food store. Between this and the ship's side stood the kitchen, open to the air, with its "large and small cauldrons, frying-pans and soup-pots—not only of copper, but also of earthenware—spits for roasting and other kitchen utensils." There were three or four cooks, very hot-tempered men, said Felix, but excusably so, considering the restricted space, the number of pots and things to be cooked, the smallness of the fire, and the shouting that went on outside as men clamored to have things made ready; "besides that the labor of cooks is always such as moves one to pity." Close and handy to the kitchen were the pens for the wretched animals, carried for food, but so ill nourished that by the end of the voyage they were little but skin and bone.

The pilgrims' cabin, "a kind of hall . . . supported by strong columns," was reached by four hatchways, and with ladders of seven steps, from the rowers' deck. It was spacious but unlighted, and here the berth space of each pilgrim was chalked out on the deck; one and a half feet was looked on as a fair allowance. In two long lines, at the feet of the pilgrims, stood each man's chest, but in the daytime mattress, pillows, and all must be rolled up, roped, and hung from a nail above the berth.

Below the pilgrims' cabin was the sand ballast, and this the pilgrims found a convenience, for they could lift the planks and bury in the sand wine, eggs, or anything that needed to be kept cool. Quite a different matter was the bilge water below, the stench of which was a sore trial to the pilgrims. But it was only one trial in many, for besides this they must suffer such inconveniences as smoke from the kitchen, rats, mice, fleas, and other vermin, but not (Providence being merciful in this to sailors) scorpions, vipers, toads, poisonous snakes, or spiders.

Comfort, and even peace, were rare on shipboard. Meals were a scramble for all except those noblemen who had their own servants and ate either on deck near the mainmast or by lantern light in the cabin. The ordinary pilgrim, when the four trumpets sounded for meals, must "run with the utmost haste to the poop," if he wanted to get a place at the three tables laid there; if he came late he must be content with a place on the rowers' benches "in the sun, the rain, or the wind." Even those at table were served in a hurry; they had malvoisie as an apéritif, and with the meal "as much wine . . . as one can drink, sometimes good, sometimes thin, but always well mixed and baptized with water." The food was, of course, cooked Italian fashion; at dinner a salad of lettuce in oil if there was any greenstuff to be had, then mutton, and some sort of pudding of meal, bruised wheat or barley; or else panada and cheese. On fast days salt fish with oil and vinegar took the place of meat, and there was a spongecake and a pudding. There was fresh bread only in harbor, or for the few days after; otherwise that biscuit of which the Paris pilgrim spoke, and which Felix describes as "hard as stones."

No sooner had the pilgrims finished eating than the trumpets sounded again, and they must get up from table so that this could be cleared and laid again for the captain and the other Venetian noblemen on board; who, though their fare was more frugal than that of the pilgrims, ate from silver, "and his [the captain's] drink is tasted . . . as is done to princes in our own country."

In between mealtimes pilgrims often found time hang heavy on their hands. "Some . . . go about the galley inquiring where the best wine is sold, and there sit down and spend the whole day over their wine. This is usually done by Saxons, Flemings, and other men of a low class. Some play for money [it was the Frenchmen who, according to Felix, were "gambling morning, noon, and night"]. . . . Some sing songs, or pass their time with lutes, flutes, bagpipes, clavichords, zithers and other musical instruments. Some discuss worldly matters, some read books, some pray with beads; some sit still and meditate . . . some work with their hands, some pass almost the whole time asleep in their berths. Others run up the rigging, others jump, others show their strength by lifting heavy weights or doing other feats. Others accompany all these, looking on first at one, and then at another. Some sit and look at the sea and the land which they are passing, and write about them . . ." a feat of concentration upon which one at least of our authors, Santo Brasca, was rightly congratulated. *Mutatis mutandis*, the description would not be unapt for the passengers of many a liner today. One occupation, however, these later travelers are spared, which in Felix's day "albeit loathsome, is yet very common, daily, and necessary—I mean the hunting and catching of lice and vermin."

On deck, even in daytime, and whatever his occupation, the pilgrim must be on his guard. He must not meddle with ropes; he must not sit where a block will fall upon him; during this very voyage the chief officer himself was killed by a falling spar. Above all the landsman must not get in the way of the sailors, or, be he lord, bishop, or even officiating priest, they will throw him down and trample on him, so urgent is work at sea, to be done, as it were, "with lightning speed." If he sits down on the rowers' benches he is liable to be assaulted by these rough and desperate fellows.

His property, as well as his person, is always in danger. The rowers steal whatever they can lay hands on, but this is not so surprising as the strange habit of thieving which attacks even honest men at sea, "especially in the matter of trifles, such as kerchiefs, belts, shirts. . . . For example, while you are writing, if you lay down your pen and turn your face away, your pen will be lost, even though you be among men whom you know. . . . " And there are other lesser perils. The pilgrim must be careful "where he sits down . . . for every place is covered with pitch, which becomes soft in the heat of the sun." He must beware if he leans on the edge of the galley not to let anything of value slip from his hand into the sea, or he will lose it, as a nobleman talking to Felix lost a rosary of precious stones and Felix himself his Office Book.

If the day is full of discomforts and anxieties the night is worse. There is a "tremendous disturbance" while all are making their beds, with dust flying and tempers rising, till in disputes about the boundary for each man's berth "whole companies of pilgrims" take part, sometimes with swords and daggers. Even when most have settled down to sleep there will be latecomers who keep the rest awake by their talk and the lights they bring, which lights Felix had seen hot-tempered pilgrims extinguish, impolitely but effectively, with the contents of their chamber pots. And when all lights were out there were some incorrigible talkers who would "begin to settle the affairs of the world with their neighbours," continuing till midnight, and perhaps causing a fresh outbreak of noise and quarreling if some outraged companion called for silence.

For a man used to the quiet of his own cell rest was almost impossible. When all others slept Felix would be kept awake by the snoring of his fellows, the stamping of the penned beasts, and the trampling of the sailors on the deck above. The narrow bed, the hard pillow, the close proximity of his neighbors, the foul and hot air, the vermin, would drive him at last on deck, braving even the danger of being taken for a thief, to sit, "upon the wood-work at the sides of the galley, letting his feet hang down towards the sea, and holding on by the shrouds . . . . "

There, though waking, the pilgrim found some good moments, at least in fair weather, for "the ship runs along quietly, without faltering . . . and all is still, save only he who watches the compass and he who holds the handle of the rudder, for these by way of returning thanks . . . continually greet the breeze, praise God, the Blessed Virgin and the saints, one answering the other, and are never silent as long as the wind is fair." Their chant reminded the Friar of the cry of the night watchmen at home, "which cry hinders no one from sleeping, but sends many restless folk to sleep."

But the freedom from anxiety necessary for the enjoyment of such rare moments cannot have been possible for the pilgrims who sailed from Venice at Ascensiontide in 1480, bound for Corfu, where they should find the Vene-tian Captain of the Sea and ask his permission to proceed on their pilgrimage. At Parenzo, their first port of call, they heard "horrible tales about the Turks." At Zara they dared not touch, for they heard there was plague there. Lesina (Hvar) they passed by in order to take advantage of a good wind, which changed presently and brought them to an uninhabited harbor on the Croatian coast; going ashore for diversion they found upon the beach "a corpse cast up by the sea, putrid and rotten"; a sign, so the sailors at once declared, of approaching disaster. Yet when, three days later, and after many unsuccessful attempts, a fair wind took them from that inhospitable coast they learnt from a passing Venetian war galley with which they spoke that the contrary winds that had beaten them back into port had saved them from falling in with the Turkish fleet, even then on its way to sack Otranto.

The fear of the Turk was everywhere. At Curzola (Korčula) and Ragusa (Dubrovnik) they found that folk had either fled from, or hastily fortified, their towns. On the hills at night they saw the alarm beacons lit, and as they sailed along the wooded Albanian coast they might remember the strong places which Venice had held there, now in Turkish hands, and regret the days when timber from those forests was used to build Venetian galleys, but now served for the ships of the infidel. When they came to Corfu the Cap-tain of the Sea called them fools for their pains, advised them to turn back, and threatened that if they persisted they must make shift for themselves, for he would not allow a galley of St. Mark's to go into such dangers as those which lay ahead.

Small shame to the pilgrims had they yielded to such pressure. Many did yield, among whom were two of the greatest of the German nobles and the two French bishops. The rest, foolhardy or courageous but certainly ob-stinate, after a week of wrangling ignored both advice and prohibition. They had come, they told the captain, ". . . from France, Spain, England, Scotland, Flanders, Germany, and other regions and countries at great cost and outlay, determined to accomplish their pilgrimage or die, according as it was the will of God. . . . " They then made ready to leave and defiantly carried into the galley all that they had bought, but once on board, being solemnized by their peril, they took an oath not to gamble, swear, or quarrel any more, but to have litanies sung by the clerks on board. Next morning the trumpets were blown, the moorings cast off, and "with joy and singing" they left the harbor, where the other pilgrims laughed at them from the quay, those turning back being, doubtless, embittered by the fact that of each man's 55 ducats Contarini had repaid only 10.

Upon the remainder of the voyage out we need not linger. At Crete even the Turkish merchants trading there charitably advised them not to put to sea. They persisted, passed the dangerous proximity of Rhodes on a favorable gale, touched at Cyprus, and so on the third day out of Larnaca got their first sight of the Holy Land and came safe to Jaffa.

They had dared and suffered much but, as it proved, to little purpose. At Ramle Agostino Contarini was seized and kept in prison for four days, which time he, on his enlargement, took care to subtract from the pilgrims' time in Jerusalem, so that "we did not spend," says Felix, "more than nine days in the Holy Land, and in that time we rushed round the usual Holy Places in the utmost haste, making our pilgrimages both by day and night, and hardly given any time to rest. . . . When we had hurriedly visited the Holy Places . . . we were led out of the Holy City, by the same road by which we had come, down to the sea where our galley waited."

That was all, after six weeks at sea and many perils. Felix's first pilgrimage would have been a miserable failure but for one thing. When at Jerusalem the Friar "firmly determined that I would return again." It was this resolve which prevented him at once undertaking the journey to Mount Sinai in company with two English pilgrims who were setting out thither—that and not the fact that he and the Englishmen had no common language. It was also, I think, this resolve which restored Felix to himself, so that on the journey home he was able to observe, to savor experience, and to laugh.

He had in any case sufficiently recovered himself to be equal to snubbing an ecclesiastical superior, though certainly the occasion was just and the provocation extreme. The pilgrims, sick and weary for home, were held up for three days in the open roadstead of Larnaca; they were told that the galley must wait for two bishops of Cyprus who were to be passengers. When these arrived, with a great cavalcade and much gear, the pilgrims, crowded enough already, found themselves worse off than ever, and what made their discomforts harder to bear, they could not like their new companions. One of the two dignitaries Felix passes over in silence, but upon the other his eye was fixed with disapproval and growing indignation. For the bishop of Paphos, though a friar of Felix's own order, was "a young man, beardless and lady-faced, and behaving like any woman too." He wore a friar's gown, but it was of costly cloth, and colored "with a tail at the back like a woman"; his fingers were covered with jeweled rings; round his neck was a golden chain. Besides all this his manners were bad; he squabbled constantly with his servants and looked down on everyone, especially the pilgrims, whom he would not allow to sit down with him.

One day "a certain priest, chaplain to one of the pilgrim knights,"—the anonymity is not so consistently kept but that we may not recognize Felix himself—"a certain priest" asked the young man "to move up a little from where he sat." The bishop's only answer was a disdainful look. The priest, calling to mind how dearly he had paid for his berth and passage, determined to resist encroachment, and for a minute priest and bishop leaned heavily and angrily against each other in silence.

Then said the bishop, "How, you ass, can you dare to contend with me? Don't you know who I am?"

"I," replied Felix, "am not an ass but a priest. It would be wrong for me to scorn a priest or despise a bishop, but I know a proud monk and an irregular friar when I see one, and I will contend against such with all my might."

At this point the bishop, forgetful of episcopal dignity, made that gesture with his thumb, "which the Italians use when they want to be rude to anyone." This brought in "the priest's knight" and other young knights with him, all shouting and swearing, so that the bishop, choosing the wisest course, fled to the captain's cabin, and came no more among the pilgrims.

Felix certainly needed all his courage for the voyage that was before him. Worn out by their labors, by the heat, by having to sleep out-of-doors, by lack of wine and of good bread, by the hurry of their tour, the pilgrims returned to the galley in such a state that it "became like a hospital full of wretched invalids," and it was the old women who, of tougher fiber than any man, nursed those who had scorned their company.

Worse suffering was to come. Contrary winds kept them at sea even when, knowing that the Turk had given up the siege of Rhodes, they tried to make that port. Water ran short; the sailors now could sell any that was not foul, "albeit it was lukewarm, whitish, and discoloured," at a higher price than wine. Soon "even putrid stinking water was precious and the captain and all the pilots were scared that we should run out even of . . . that." No water at all could be spared for the beasts; and Felix watched them with pity as they licked the dew from the ship's timbers.

"During those days of suffering," says he, "I often wondered how any man living on earth can be so pampered as to worry almost the whole year about the Lent fast, and the bread and water of Good Friday." (Was it Felix himself who so worried?) Now he found himself longing for that "white bread, fresh and good, and for the water, clear, cold, sweet and clean. . . .

Often I suffered so from thirst, and so greatly desired cold water, that I thought, when I get back to Ulm I will climb up at once to Blaubüren and there sit down beside the lake which wells out from the depths until I have slaked my thirst." At last, however, they made the coast of the island, the sailors rowed ashore for water, the pilgrims drank, and at once, "like parched plants," revived.

They were held up in Crete by damage to the rudder. But Felix did not object to the delay. For one thing there was plenty for the pilgrims to watch. They might hang over the side and see the man who was to mend the rudder strip to his breeches and sink down into the water with hammer, nails, and pincers, to come up again, long after, with the work marvelously completed below the surface. Besides everything was cheap here, and especially that famous Cretan wine, malvoisie, "so we did not mind staying there, but enjoyed it."

That same Cretan wine was responsible for a number of laughable accidents which Felix recorded, because "as I promised . . . I often mix fun and amusement with serious matters." So, when the evening trumpet blew to recall the pilgrims to the ship, those already on board might be diverted by the sight of their fellows lined up on the quay, too drunk to risk the steps down to the boats. Once Felix enjoyed the spectacle of a drunken servingman who pitched headlong from the steps into the harbor; he had been carrying on his back his master's gear, and though he himself was soon fished out by the boatmen, "the loaves of bread and all that he was carrying floated over him, and were all utterly ruined."

Even ecclesiastics, losing their dignity, provided entertainment for the rest of the company. A Dalmatian priest with whom Felix had become friendly, returning late and "lit up" to the galley, lingered on deck till it was almost dark; then, deciding to go below, he made for the nearest hatchway, and, forgetting that the ladder was always removed at sunset, stepped down. At the crash of his fall "the whole galley shook, for he was a big man and fat," and for a moment the rest of the pilgrims, lying in their beds below, talking, were silent in horror, till they heard his voice, angry and stammering, but not that of one seriously injured.

"There!" said he, "I had the ladder under my feet and I went down three steps, and someone dragged it from under my feet and I fell down." He was told, "The ladder was taken away an hour ago," but he persisted. "That's not true, for I had gone down three steps already, and when I stood on the third it was dragged from under me."

At that the others began to laugh, and Felix loudest of all, for joy, he explains, that his friend had taken no harm in so great a fall.

"There!" cried the Dalmatian, "now I am sure that it was you, Brother Felix, who dragged the ladder from my feet. Be sure that I shall pay you out before you leave the galley," and the more Felix tried to clear himself the angrier grew the other, swearing to have his revenge the very next day. But, says Felix, by next morning all was forgotten, so potent is the wine of Crete.

After the pleasant days of Crete the pilgrims had yet another trial to face. Beyond Corfu they ran into a terrible storm, with wind and rain, lightning and thunder. Yet even here it is possible to discern in Felix that priceless gift, the enjoyment of mere experience.

"The rain . . . fell in such torrents as though entire rainclouds had burst and fallen upon us. Violent squalls kept striking the galley, covering it with water, and beating upon the sides of it as hard as though great stones from some high mountains were sent flying along the planks. I have often wondered when at sea in storms how it can be that water, being as it is a thin, soft and weak body, can strike such hard blows . . . for it makes a noise when it runs against the ship as though millstones were being flung against her. . . . Waves of sea-water are more vehement, more noisy, and more wonderful than those of other water. I have had great pleasure in sitting or standing on the upper deck during a storm, and watching the marvellous succession of gusts of wind and the frightful rush of the waters." But, as well as the interest of the thing, this storm drove them fast upon their course, so, though "our beds and all our things were sopping," bread and biscuit spoiled with salt water, no fire in the galley, the kitchen awash, and all the pilgrims seasick, they bore it with patience.

And, except for one bad time when the anchor dragged and they nearly fell upon the rocky Dalmatian coast, the storm was the last of their ill fortune. After five days at Parenzo, on Friday, October 21, "we reached the city of Venice and broke up our company, every man going to his own home," though Felix, ill and exhausted, spent a fortnight in bed at Venice and did not reach Ulm till November 16.

Part 5

THE RENAISSANCE AND REFORMATION

16th–17th Centuries

Bas relief of Florentine craftsmen by Nanni di Banco, Florence

The cultural and religious movements that gave their names to the Renaissance–Reformation period occurred against a social background that has become familiar through many historical studies. In Italy, urbanization combined with a rediscovery of classical Roman literature to create a new view of history and a new sense of national and human identity. Whereas medieval scholars and rulers had extolled the virtues of the Roman Empire and its autocratic government because they saw themselves as its continuators, the Italian humanists, who were both scholars and political figures, rediscovered the Roman Republic and made it their ideal. This shift of political consciousness necessitated a change in historical consciousness, because it made the humanists aware of historical discontinuity. For them, the study of Roman history could not be, as it had been for their medieval predecessors, a study of an earlier stage of their own development. Instead, it was the study of a civilization wholly separate from theirs. On the one hand, this historical consciounsess led them to attempt a revival of ancient culture. On the other hand, the rediscovery of the Republic brought into vogue republican political values, which were at odds with Roman and medieval imperial ideals, and a new appreciation for urban life. As the humanists gained sway in the intellectual and artistic world of Europe, their values became the dominant ones in politics and society. Two of the articles in this section deal with aspects of these changes. In "Cultural Patronage in Renaissance Florence," Gene Brucker discusses the connection between the powerful urban patriciate and the new intellectuals and artists in the most striking of the Renaissance city-states. In "Parent and Child in Renaissance Italy," James Bruce Ross reveals the patterns of child-rearing and family life in the urban middle class, who were already becoming the dominant social group in early modern Europe.

Just as the Italian Renaissance can be linked with renaissances of the Middle Ages—although fundamentally different from them—so the Reformation can be seen as yet another medieval reform movement—but it too differs fundamentally from its medieval counterparts. After Martin Luther's initial attempts to reform the Church and to reformulate its principles of belief, he and other Protestants succeeded in establishing new churches. The Protestant movement may have begun as a reform of the Church as an institution, but it soon turned to a complete reform of the religion itself. To what extent did the Reformation reflect social changes in late medieval Europe? What were the social consequences of the overhaul of Christianity? Natalie Z. Davis assesses the relationship between religious and social change in "City Women and the French Reformation."

The first article in this section deals with a different kind of movement in late medieval and early modern Europe—the movement of microorganisms. The bubonic plague was endemic in Europe from the middle of the fourteenth century to the middle of the seventeenth century, and communities had to develop plans and institutions to counter its periodic attacks. Carlo Cipolla describes the new institutions of public health in "A Community Against the Plague."

BIBLIOGRAPHY

For a look at the general problem of plagues and epidemics, see William H. McNeill, *Plagues and Peoples* (New York, 1976). See also, Hans Zinsser, *Rats, Lice and History* (Boston, 1935). Every history of the late Middle Ages contains sections on the plague, but for a general survey, see Philip Ziegler, *The Black Death: A Study of the Plague in 14th Century Europe* (New York, 1969). Very little has been written about health institutions, but see L. F. Hirst, *The Conquest of Plague* (Oxford, 1953).

On the social life and culture of sixteenth-century France, see Natalie Z. Davis, *Society and Culture in Early Modern France* (Palo Alto, Calif., 1975), from which the selection "City Women and the French Reformation" is taken. For general information, see Roland H. Bainton, *Women of the Reformation: In Germany and Italy* (Minneapolis, 1971) and *Women of the Reformation: In France and England* (Minneapolis, 1973). Bainton also wrote a good introduction to the Reformation as a whole, *The Reformation of the Sixteenth Century* (Boston, 1952). See also Robert Kingdon, *Geneva and the Consolidation of the French Protestant Movement* (Madison, Wis., 1967).

The classic work on Renaissance humanism is Jacob Burckhardt, *The Civilization of the Renaissance in Italy*, 2 vols. (New York, 1951 [originally published 1860]). The more recent classic of Hans Baron, *The Crisis of the Early Italian Renaissance*, rev. ed. (Princeton, 1966), deals specifically with the relationship between trends in humanist thought and politics. Denys Hay, *The Italian Renaissance in Its Historical Background* (Cambridge, Eng., 1965; 2nd ed., 1977), and L. Martines, *The Social World of the Florentine Humanists* (Princeton, 1963) deal with the subject of

Brucker's selection "Cultural Patronage in Renaissance Florence." See also Gene Brucker, *Florentine Politics and Society 1343–1378* (Princeton, 1963). For a penetrating study of humanist thinking, see P. O. Kristeller, *Renaissance Thought* (New York, 1961).

Some of the works cited above also relate to James Bruce Ross's study of the urban family. See, in addition, P. Jones, "Florentine Families and Florentine Diaries in the Fourteenth Century," in *Studies in Italian Medieval History Presented to Miss E. M. Jamison*, ed. P. Grierson and J. W. Perkins (Rome, 1956), pp. 183–205. See the articles in Anthony Molho, ed., *Social and Economic Foundations of the Italian Renaissance* (New York, 1969). For a general survey of life during the Renaissance, see John Gage, *Life in Italy at the Time of the Medici*, ed. Peter Quennell (New York, 1968). A new work on the subject of Ross's article is Francis William Kent, *Household and Lineage in Renaissance Florence: The Family Life of the Capponi, Ginori, and Rucellai* (Berkeley, 1978).

A Community Against the Plague

CARLO CIPOLLA

Public health is a prominent national and international issue in the twentieth century. In the United States, every city, county, and state has a large and active public health agency, and the federal government maintains national health centers for research on and control of disease, all of them under the giant, cabinet-level Department of Health, Education, and Welfare. The growth of this apparatus for the common good is not the result of modern medical science, but stems from the terrible experience of the late medieval plague epidemics. The plague attacked rural as well as urban areas, but its impact on the close and neighborly populations of the cities far exceeded the toll it took in rural districts. It exposed the vulnerability of life in close quarters, and people fled the cities in hopes of preserving their lives.

The retreat from urbanism was temporary, of course. After the epidemic subsided, people returned to the cities to pick up their careers and settle again into the best life they knew. City dwellers were innovators. They had left the tradition-bound life of the farm and had come to the city to build new lives. Just as they had learned to react to new commercial opportunities and deal with market changes, and just as they had readily received new artistic and intellectual movements, now they responded to the plague and created institutions of public health. In the selection that follows, Carlo Cipolla describes the health institutions of a small Italian city and its environs while telling the story of its battle against the plague epidemic of 1630. His story also reveals the relationship between town and country in late medieval and early modern Italy, and illustrates the hegemony exercised by the great cities, like Florence here, over the small ones.

Prato lies in a plain bordered on the west by the pleasant hills of Montalbano and on the north and the east by the "most stony and barren mountaines, which are called Apennine and divide the length of Italy." In that "most pleasant plain" vines and mulberry trees, cypresses and rosemary grew in the harmony of nature. . . .

Politically and administratively, Prato was part of the Grand Duchy of Tuscany whose capital was Florence. The town was administered by a Town Council led by the *Priori* and the *Gonfaloniere*. The central authority of the Grand Duke was locally represented by the *Podestà*. The local administration was closely controlled by the central government; however by the early seventeenth century the local administrators were ready to oblige and most willing to prove their deference and obedience to the *Signori* of Florence.

In the first decades of the seventeenth century Prato numbered about 6,000 souls within the walls and about 11,000 souls within its jurisdiction outside the gates. Today Prato boasts a thriving textile industry that exports its products to the four corners of the world. In the fifteenth century Prato was the base of a huge and thriving mercantile firm, the product of the enterprising and managerial genius of Francesco di Marco Datini, "the Merchant of Prato." At the beginning of the seventeenth century the great enterprise of Francesco had long since disappeared and the modern textile industry had not yet started. Robert Dallington visiting Prato in 1596 had a general impression of poverty. . . .

The first official warning of the danger of plague reached Prato toward the end of October 1629: a letter dated the 26th from the Health officers in Florence instructed the local administration to place guards for health controls. Only five days had passed since the news of the outbreak of plague on the northern side of Lake Como had reached Milan and the action of the Health Board in Florence could not have been more prompt.

In the absence of any knowledge about vaccination, the establishment of a sanitary cordon was the only preventive measure people could resort to besides prayers and processions. In response to the letter from Florence, the town Council of Prato, on October 27th promptly appointed four citizens to the position of "*Officiali di Sanità*" (Health officers).

All affairs pertaining to Public Health were placed in their hands and thus the positioning of the guards also. It was customary at the time to have two lines of defence: one at the borders of the territory, at mountain passes and at fords, and the other at the gates of the city. On November 1st, the Officers of Prato wrote to the Officers in Florence that they had complied with the general instructions received on October 26th. On December 27th, in consideration of the very cold weather, the officers ordered the construction of barracks for the guards at three of the five gates and also made provision of one *staio* of embers per day for the guards at each of the five gates. It was a small ration of fuel, but in those days people were accustomed to a harsh life. And so the winter passed.

In May 1630 the news from the north suddenly became very alarming: the plague had been identified in Bologna. The immediate reaction of the Health Board in Florence was to request that all people moving from one place to another should carry health passes. No one without such a certificate could be admitted into the territory of the State or into any walled place. On May 14th the Board instructed the Health officers in Prato to appoint a person who would issue the passes for the local people. Within two days the instructions were carried out.

In the meantime in Bologna the situation had deteriorated tragically, and on June 12th Florence rushed troops to the northern border of the Grand Duchy so that there would be one guard-post every three miles. On the following day, Bologna was put under a total ban, which meant that persons, merchandise and letters could not be received from that city even if accompanied by reassuring health passes. On the 16th all people living close to the border were requested to be on the alert: if they saw strangers crossing the border where there were no guards they had "to cry in chorus, ring the bells alarmingly and follow the trespassers until they were captured." As fear mounted, the activity of Health officers both central and local became feverish. June 16th: the officers of Prato added more guards at the gates and increased the wages of the guards as an obvious incentive to them to be more conscientious; June 22nd: the officers in Florence instructed the Health officers of all towns and walled villages of the Grand Duchy to use greater care in the issuing of health passes; July 1st: the Grand Duke rushed thirty horsemen of his personal guard to strengthen border control; July 6th: the officers in Florence instructed local officers to stop all movements of friars of any religious order; July 10th: in Prato the three most frequently used gates—Mercatale, Fiorentina and Pistoiese—were reinforced with barricades. All in vain.

The establishment of a sanitary cordon is a necessary but rarely sufficient measure. This was especially so in an age when the microbic enemy was unknown and invisible, when animal vectors were not recognized as such and when the reliability and competence of the guards were questionable.

The precautionary measures of the Health officers did not stop the advance of the enemy. By July, the plague had invaded Trespiano, a village four miles north of Florence on the road to Bologna, and by August it had entered the city of Florence and Tavola, a little village in the jurisdiction of Prato. Both Trespiano and Tavola were isolated, and in Florence a number of houses were quarantined.

There was resistance to the facts. Physicians kept debating whether it was plague or not, and the Health officers in Florence, pending a final decision, distributed reassuring bulletins deluding themselves and others. But day by day the awful truth became more tragically obvious.

During the months of July and August 1630, mortality in Prato seems to have been higher than normal, and in September there were a number of cases of death and illness of a suspicious nature. The local physicians and surgeons were uncertain in their diagnosis: official confirmation of the plague was resisted because of its disastrous implications, yet the local administration grew increasingly nervous. On August 3rd, 1630, the town council decided to raise the number of the Health officers from four to eight, and about one month later the officers wrote to the Health Board in Florence asking for authorization to prepare a pest-house as a precautionary measure. This was an excellent idea but unfortunately the officers in Florence, in their eagerness to prevent panic and avoid the banning of Tuscany by other states, discouraged the initiative. They pointed out that Florence was very close and could easily provide advice and assistance; moreover, the recent rains—they added—by refreshing the air, were bound to have beneficial effects.

Their optimism was ill founded. One man, Niccolò Bardazzi, attendant in the hospital of the Misericordia in Prato, was in charge of those cases of death or sickness which looked suspicious. On September 16th the man fell sick and he died on the 19th. This time the physicians had no doubts: it was the plague. The same day the officers of Prato hurriedly reported the facts to those in Florence. On the following day, September 20th, the Florentine officers promptly responded with a letter of instructions which is exemplary in its precision and conciseness. In its almost telegraphic style one perceives the officers' concern to prevent misunderstanding, to avoid delays, to empha- size the need for precise and effective action:

> you must straightway order that the persons of the family of the deceased be confined to the house. The household items used by the deceased must be separated from the others. You must bar the door of the house from the outside. The family of the deceased must receive victuals through the win- dows. Make sure that no one comes out. All members of the family have to be provided with victuals for the amount of one *giulio* per day. The money will be paid by the officer who pays the guards at the gates and it will be credited to him. All the above to be ordered and carried out at once. You will inform us of what follows.

Unfortunately what followed was not good. With a letter dated October 2nd, 1630, the Health officers of Prato reported to the Board in Florence that the town was a prey to the plague.

The first round of the battle had been lost. The invisible and pitiless enemy was within the walls claiming lives at a dreadful rate. People were religious and superstitious and they placed much faith in the Divine Provi- dence. Although perfectly aware of how dangerous it was to gather in large groups, they organized processions and other religious ceremonies on October 8th, on October 28th and then again in November. People however, were also practical and while stubbornly hoping for help from God or some other holy Dignitary, they knew that they had to help themselves in their own way.

There were two hospitals in Prato: the hospital *della Misericordia* and the hospital of San Silvestro, both of which were under the same administration. The governor was appointed by the Grand Duke and held office for a period of three years at the end of which he could be reappointed. Over the centuries, these two hospitals had been endowed with property by various citizens and as their income was derived from such properties, their financial situation was largely dependent upon the level of agricultural prices. Around 1630, in normal years, the income of the two hospitals fluctuated around 5,500–7,500 ducats. In a year of exceptionally low agricultural prices, such as 1634, the income of the two hospitals could drop as low as 2,500 ducats.

The hospital regularly received patients for treatment, but this was only incidental. According to an old tradition of medieval origin, the hospitals of Prato like most European hospitals, were devoted to charity at large rather than to the specific task of attending the sick. Between July 1st, 1631 and June 30th, 1632 for example, the two hospitals received 292 patients for a total of 3,692 patient-days, which meant an average permanence of about 13 days per patient. This was approximately equivalent to having had 10 patients for the 365 days of the year. For the 365 days of the year the hospital *della Misericordia* kept 182 abandoned adolescents (128 girls and 54 boys) and also cared for about 100 foundlings. Although the hospital had resident wet nurses, most of the foundlings were given out to non resident wet nurses who of course received compensation for their services. In 1630 the ratio of foundlings kept in the hospital to those given out was 8 to 98. All the above figures conform with a normal pattern, and they clearly show that the vast majority of the resources of the two hospitals was devoted to the care of abandoned youth.

Normally Prato could also count on the services of a number of surgeons and physicians. Early in September 1630, the Health officers of Florence wanted to know the strength of the medical profession in Prato and complying with their request the administration of Prato reported the following:

> . . . The Community of Prato keeps two physicians as *medici condotti*. One is ser Latanzio Magiotti, aged about 40, bachelor, very good doctor, patrician, native of Montevarchi. The other is messer Giobatta Serrati, native of Castiglione Fiorentino, aged 30 with wife and one daughter and is a good doctor. Native of this place is messer Pierfrancesco Fabbruzzi, who has a private practice, is 70 years of age, married with children, a good doctor if he were not so old. In addition there is messer Giuliano Losti, a young man of 25 years of age. He obtained his doctorate in medicine this year and thus far has not put his knowledge into practice. There is also messer Jacopo Lionetti, aged 60, with wife and children who, however, has never practiced.
>
> Although you did not request information about either the quantity

or quality of the surgeons, we inform you that there are three surgeons, two of which are in *condotta*: they are Master Michele Cepparelli, native of this place, aged 60, with great experience and without wife or children and Master Antonio Gramigna, native of this place, aged 50, with wife and children, one of whom is at present learning the art from his father. There is also Master Tiburzio, native of this place, who has a private practice, aged 60 with wife and children.

It might be mentioned here that in Italy since the thirteenth century, first in the cities and later also in the villages of some importance, it had become customary to hire physicians and surgeons at the expense of the community. These physicians (and surgeons) were either called *medici* (and *chirurghi*) *condotti* or also *medici* (and *chirurghi*) *del pubblico*. Receiving a regular monthly salary they were to reside in the community, never to leave without permission and to cure without charge all those in need of medical care who could not afford its cost. On occasion, when treating people of some means, they were allowed to receive an extra fee. Besides these doctors and surgeons there were the physicians and surgeons with private practices. According to the report cited above, Prato had two physicians *condotti* and two physicians with private practice as well as one man who held a doctorate but never practiced. Moreover, there were two surgeons *condotti* and one with private practice. This gives a grand total of seven active medical men for a population of about 17,000 souls—definitely a high ratio for the time. Whether a relatively high number of doctors was beneficial to the health of the population is another matter.

When the plague broke out in the town, the ordinary medical structure of Prato had to be reorganized and strengthened. The Health officers of Prato informed the Board in Florence that their town was a prey of the plague on October 2nd; that same day they hurriedly decided to transform one of the two hospitals into a pest-house. Since the hospital *della Misericordia* housed the children, the officers selected the hospital of San Silvestro with the annexed church of San Silvestro. The hospital *della Misericordia* however, had to provide the hospital of San Silvestro with the food, the medicines, the fuel, the beds and the other equipment necessary to operate as a pest-house. The town was to cover the expenses for the personnel.

The officers appointed a confessor, a surgeon and a number of attendants to serve in the pest-house. They also appointed gravediggers, guards, a messenger, a man to deliver the victuals to those confined in their homes and a man to carry the necessities from the hospital *della Misericordia* to the hospital of San Silvestro. Including the physicians, the surgeons, the vice-chancellor who issued the passes, the gravediggers, the chief constable and his men, those who in one way or another fought the plague in Prato under the orders of the Health officers, numbered about twenty-five at the peak of their strength.

The physicians were persons of rank. The surgeons were on a markedly lower social level. At one point, some of the guards at the gates were put in jail, which proves that their conduct was not always exemplary. The grave-diggers were an unpleasant and mercenary group and the nicknames given to some of them clearly indicate vulgar and brutal people. On one occasion we know that a convict was enlisted as a gravedigger because of lack of regular help. This was the army which the Health officers led in their fight against the plague—a small army and a very heterogeneous one, which included physicians as well as constables, friars as well as convicts.

It was not easy to keep this small army at full strength. The plague claimed lives among those who served the Public Health as well as among those who were served by it. . . .

City Women
and the French Reformation

NATALIE Z. DAVIS

How much did the Reformation revolutionize European life? Clearly, it made a very great difference in the religious life and institutions of Europeans, in their political life, and perhaps in their intellectual life. In the religious sphere, the reformers raised questions about the structure, authority, and beliefs of the universal church of the Middle Ages. Few of these questions were unfamiliar—they had been raised many times by medieval reformers and dissenters—but they now became the foundation for new ecclesiastical structures. These new churches institutionalized the changes desired by their founders, and, presumably, life in such churches differed in significant ways from life in the Catholic Church. The differences were most prevalent in those cities, such as Geneva, where the reformers gained complete political control and established a society organized by the new church—the better to accomplish its goal of salvation. The changes did not, of course, affect the material aspects of life, but they did profoundly change the relationship between people by changing the authority structure of the ecclesiastical community, by encouraging literacy and the independent reading of the scriptures, and by reviving strong currents of piety and religious feeling in a whole population, making it both more cohesive and less tolerant than it had been under the old Catholic regime.

The purpose of this selection is to investigate the impact of the Protestant Reformation on society. Of course, comparison of Protestant and Catholic communities, where one or the other side was overwhelmingly victorious, will not reveal the reformation experience of most sixteenth-century people. In most places, Protestants and Catholics coexisted, although the coexistence was not usually very peaceful, and it is in these places of contact and conflict that Natalie Z. Davis seeks the answer to the question posed above. The Reformation in France was short-lived, but it split ancient communities and disrupted them. Moreover, women had the most to gain from change, so that focusing on them exposes the promise and performance of the reformed communities and churches. Did people join these churches only for theological or religious reasons, or were there other, social grounds? Did the Reformation change people's social position or the quality of their lives?

[I]

The growing cities of sixteenth-century France, ranging from ten thousand inhabitants in smaller places to sixty thousand in Lyon and a hundred thousand in Paris, were the centers of organization and dissemination of Protestantism. The decades in question here are especially those up to the Saint Bartholomew's Day Massacre of 1572—the years when it still seemed hopeful, in the words of a female refugee in Geneva, that the new Christians might deliver their cities from the tyranny and cruelty of the papist Pharaohs. For a while they were successful, with the growth of a large Protestant movement and the establishment in 1559 of an official Reformed Church in France. After 1572, the Huguenot party continued to battle for survival, but it was now doomed to remain a zealous but small minority.

Apart from the religious, almost all adult urban women in the first half of the sixteenth century were married or had once been so. The daughter of a rich merchant, lawyer, or financial officer might find herself betrothed in her late teens. Most women waited until their early twenties, when a dowry could be pieced together from the family or one's wages or extracted from a generous master or mistress.

And then the babies began and kept appearing every two or three years. The wealthy woman, with her full pantry and her country refuge in times of plague, might well raise six or seven children to adulthood. The artisan's wife might bury nearly as many as she bore, while the poor woman was lucky to have even one live through the perils of a sixteenth-century childhood. Then, if she herself had managed to survive the first rounds of childbearing and live into her thirties, she might well find that her husband had not. Remarriage was common, of course, and until certain restrictive edicts of the French king in the 1560's a widow could contract it quite freely. If she then survived her husband into her forties, chances are she would remain a widow. At this stage of life, women outnumbered and outlived men, and even the widow sought after for her wealth might prefer independence to the relative tutelage of marriage.

With the death rate so high, the cities of sixteenth-century France depended heavily on immigration for their increasing populations. Here, however, we find an interesting difference between the sexes: men made up a much larger percentage of the young immigrants to the cities. The male immigrants contributed to every level of the vocational hierarchy—from notaries, judges, and merchants to craftsmen and unskilled day laborers. And although most of the men came from nearby provinces, some were also drawn from

Excerpted from *Society and Culture in Early Modern France: Eight Essays by Natalie Zemon Davis* by Natalie Zemon Davis, pp. 68–83, 86–95, with the permission of the publishers, Stanford University Press. © 1973, 1975 by Natalie Zemon Davis.

faraway cities and from regions outside the kingdom of France. The female immigrants, on the other hand, clustered near the bottom of the social ladder and came mostly from villages and hamlets in surrounding provinces to seek domestic service in the city.

Almost all the women took part in one way or another in the economic life of the city. The picture drawn in Renaissance courtesy books and suggested by the quotation from Robert Mandrou—that of women remaining privily in their homes—is rather far from the facts revealed by judicial records and private contracts. The wife of the wealthy lawyer, royal officer, or prosperous merchant supervised the productive activities of a large household but might also rent out and sell rural and urban properties in her own name, in her husband's name, or as a widow. The wives of tradesmen and master craftsmen had some part in running the shops, not just when they were widowed but also while their husbands were alive: a wife might discipline apprentices (who sometimes resented being beaten by a woman's hand), might help the journeymen at the large looms, might retail meats while her husband and his workers slaughtered cattle, might borrow money with her husband for printing ventures, and so on.

In addition, a significant proportion of women in artisanal families and among the menu peuple [lower classes] had employ on their own. They worked especially in the textile, clothing, leather, and provisioning trades, although we can also find girls apprenticed to pinmakers and gilders. They sold fish and tripe; they ran inns and taverns. They were painters and, of course, midwives. In Paris they made linen; in Lyon they prepared silk. They made shoes and gloves, belts and collars. In Paris, one Perette Aubertin sold fruit at a stall near the Eglise des Mathurins while her husband worked as a printer. In Lyon, one Pernette Morilier made and sold wimples while her husband worked as a goldsmith. And in an extraordinary document from Lyon, a successful merchant-shoemaker confesses that his prosperity was due not so much to his own profits as to those made by his wife over the preceding 25 years in her separate trade as a linen merchant.

Finally, there were the various semiskilled or unskilled jobs done by women. Domestic service involved a surprisingly high number of girls and women. Even a modest artisanal family was likely to have a wretchedly paid serving girl, perhaps acquired from within the walls of one of the orphan-hospitals recently set up in many urban centers. There was service in the bath-houses, which sometimes slid into prostitution. Every city had its filles de joie, whom the town council tried to restrict to certain streets and to stop from brazenly soliciting clients right in front of the parish church. And there was heavy work, such as ferrying people across the Saône and other rivers, the boatwomen trying to argue up their fares as they rowed. If all else failed, a woman could dig ditches and carry things at the municipal construction sites. For this last, she worked shoulder to shoulder with unskilled male day workers, being paid about one-half or two-thirds as much as they for her pains.

This economic activity of women among the *menu peuple* may explain in part the funny nicknames that some of them had. Most French women in the sixteenth century kept their maiden names all their lives: when necessary, the phrase "wife of" or "widow of" so-and-so was tacked on. Certain women, however, had sobriquets: *la Capitaine des vaches* (the Captain of the cows) and *la reine d'Hongrie* (the queen of Hungary) were nicknames given to two women who headed households in Lyon; *la Catelle* was a schoolmistress in Paris; *la Varenne*, a midwife in Le Mans; and *la Grosse Marguerite*, a peddler of Orléans. Such names were also attached to very old women. But in all cases, we can assume not only that these women were a little eccentric but also that these names were bestowed on them in the course of public life—in the street, in the marketplace, or in the tavern.

The public life of urban women did not, however, extend to the civic assembly or council chamber. Women who were heads of households do appear on tax lists and even on militia rolls and were expected to supply money or men as the city government required. But that was the extent of political participation for the *citoyenne*. Male artisans and traders also had little say in these oligarchical city governments, but at least the more prosperous among them might have hoped to influence town councillors through their positions as guild representatives. The guild life of women, however, was limited and already weaker than it had been in the later Middle Ages. In short, the political activity of women on all levels of urban society was indirect or informal only. The wives of royal officers or town councillors might have hoped to influence powerful men at their dining tables. The wives of poor and powerless journeymen and day laborers, when their tables were bare because the city fathers had failed to provide the town with grain, might have tried to change things by joining with their husbands and children in a well-timed grain riot.

What of the literacy of urban women in the century after the introduction of printing to Europe? In the families of the urban elite the women had at least a vernacular education—usually at the hands of private tutors—in French, perhaps in Italian, in music, and in arithmetic. A Latin education among nonnoble city women was rare enough that it was remarked—"learned beyond her sex," the saying went—and a girl like Louise Sarrasin of Lyon, whose physician–father had started her in Hebrew, Greek, and Latin by the time she was eight, was considered a wondrous prodigy. It was women from these wealthy families of bankers and jurists who organized the important literary salons in Paris, Lyon, Poitiers, and elsewhere.

Once outside these restricted social circles, however, there was a dramatic drop in the level of education and of mere literacy among city women. An examination of contracts involving some 1,200 people in Lyon in the 1560's and 1570's to see whether those people could simply sign their names reveals that, of the women, only 28 percent could sign their names. These were almost all from the elite families of well-off merchants and publishers, plus a few wives of surgeons and goldsmiths. All the other women in the group—the wives of mercers, of artisans in skilled trades, and even of a few notaries— could not sign. This is in contrast to their husbands and to male artisans generally, whose ability to sign ranged from high among groups like printers, surgeons, and goldsmiths, to moderate among men in the leather and textile trades, to low—although still well above zero—among men in the food and construction trades. Thus, in the populous middle rank of urban society, although both male and female literacy may have risen from the mid-fifteenth century under the impact of economic growth and the invention of printing, the literacy of the men increased much more than that of the women. Tradesmen might have done business with written accounts; tradeswomen more often had to use finger reckoning, the abacus, or counting stones. Only at the bottom of the social hierarchy, among the unskilled workers and urban gardeners, were men and women alike. As with peasants, there were few of either sex who were literate.

And where would women of artisanal families learn to read and write if their fathers and husbands did not teach them? Nunnery schools received only a small number of lay girls, and these only from fine families. The municipal colleges set up in the first half of the sixteenth century in Toulouse, Nîmes, and Lyon were for boys only; so were most of the little vernacular schools that mushroomed in even quite modest city neighborhoods during these years. To be sure, a few schoolmistresses were licensed in Paris, and there were always some Parisian schoolmasters being chided for illegally receiving girls along with their boy pupils. But in Lyon, where I have found only five female teachers from the 1490's to the 1560's, I have come upon 87 schoolmasters for the same decades.

Thus, in the first half of the sixteenth century, the wealthy and well-born woman was being encouraged to read and study by the availability to her of printed books; by the strengthening of the image of the learned lady, as the writings of Christine de Pisan and Marguerite de Navarre appeared in print; and by the attitude of some fathers, who took seriously the modest educational programs for women being urged by Christian humanists like Erasmus and Juan Luis Vives. Reading and writing for women of the *menu peuple* was more likely to be ridiculous, a subject for farce.

All this shows how extraordinary was the achievement of Louise Labé, the one lowborn female poet of sixteenth-century France. From a family of Lyon ropemakers, barber-surgeons, and butchers, in which some of the women were literate and some (including her own stepmother) were not, Louise was beckoned to poetry and publication by her talent and by profane love. Her message to women in 1555 was "to lift their minds a little above their disstaffs and spindles . . . to apply themselves to science and learning . . . and to let the world know that if we are not made to command, we must not for that be disdained as companions, both in domestic and public affairs, of those who govern and are obeyed."

[II]

The message of Calvinist reformers to women also concerned reading and patterns of companionship. But before we turn to it, let us see what can be said about the Catholic religious activity of city women on the eve of the French Reformation.

In regard to the sacramental life of the church, the women behaved very much like their husbands. The prominent families, in which the husband was on the parish building committee, attended mass and confession with some regularity. The wealthiest of them also had private chapels in their country homes. Among the rest of the population attendance was infrequent, and it was by no means certain that all the parishioners would even get out once a year to do their Easter duty of confession and communion. (The clergy itself was partly to blame for this. Those big city parishes were doubling and even tripling in size in these decades, and yet the French Church took virtually no steps to increase accordingly its personnel in charge of pastoral functions or even to guarantee confessors who could understand the language and dialect of the parishioners.) Baptism was taken more seriously, however, as were marriage and extreme unction. Every two or three years the husband appeared before the curé with the new baby, bringing with him one or two godfathers and up to five godmothers. The wife was most likely at home, waiting till she was ready to get up for her "churching," or purification after childbirth (the *relevailles*). Moreover, the wills of both men and women show an anxious preoccupation with the ceremonial processions at their funerals and masses to be said for the future repose of their souls. A chambermaid or male weaver might invest many months' salary in such arrangements.

In regard to the organizational and social aspects of Catholic piety on the eve of the Reformation, however, the woman's position was somewhat different from the man's. On the one hand, female religious life was less well organized than male religious life; on the other, the occasions in which urban women participated jointly with men in organized lay piety were not as frequent as they might have been.

To be sure, parish processions led by the priests on Corpus Christi and at other times included men, women, and children, and so did the general processions of the town to seek God's help in warding off famine or other disasters. But the heart of lay religious activity in France in the early sixteenth century was in the lay confraternities organized around crafts or around some devotional interests. Here laymen could support common masses, have their own banquets (whose excesses the clergy deplored), and mount processions on their own saints' days—with "blessed bread," music, costumes, and plays. City women were members of confraternities in much smaller numbers than men at this period. For instance, out of 37 confraternities at Rouen in the first half of the sixteenth century, only six mention female members, and these in small proportion. Women were formally excluded from the important Confraternity of the Passion at Paris, and some confraternities in other cities had similar provisions. Young unmarried men were often organized into confraternities under the patronage of Saint Nicholas; young unmarried women prayed to Saint Catherine, but religious organizations of female youth are hard to find.

Even the convents lacked vitality as centers of organization at this time. Fewer in number than the male religious houses in France and drawing exclusively on noble or wealthy urban families for their membership, the convents were being further isolated by the "reform" movements of the early sixteenth century. Pushed back into arid enclosure, the nuns were cut off not only from illicit love affairs but also from rich contact with the women in the neighborhoods in which they lived. Nor in France during the first part of the sixteenth century do we hear of any new female experiments with communal living, work, and spiritual perfection like the late medieval Beguinages or the imaginative Ursuline community just then being created in an Italian city.

Thus, before the Reformation the relation of Catholic lay women to their saints was ordinarily private or informally organized. The most important occasions for invoking the saints were during pregnancy and especially during childbirth. Then, before her female neighbors and her midwife, the parturient woman called upon the Virgin, or, more likely, upon Saint Margaret, patron of pregnant women—that God might comfort her peril and pain and that her child might issue forth alive.

Into this picture of city women separated from their parish clergy and from male religious organizations, one new element was to enter, even before the Reformation. Women who could read or who were part of circles where reading was done aloud were being prompted by vernacular devotional literature and the Bible to speculate on theology. "Why, they're half theologians," said the Franciscan preachers contemptuously. They own Bibles the way they own love stories and romances. They get carried away by questions on transubstantiation, and they go "running around from . . . one [male] religious house to another, seeking advice and making much ado about nothing." What the good brothers expected from city women was not silly reasoning but the tears and repentance that would properly follow a Lenten sermon replete with all the rhetorical devices and dramatic gestures of which the Franciscans were masters.

Even a man who was more sympathetic than the Franciscans to lettered females had his reservations about how far their learning should take them.

A male poet praised the noble dame Gabrielle de Bourbon in the 1520's for reading vernacular books on moral and doctrinal questions and for composing little treatises to the honor of God and the Virgin Mary. But she knew her limits, for "women must not apply their minds to curious questions of theology and the secret matters of divinity, the knowledge of which belongs to prelates, rectors and doctors."

The Christian humanist Erasmus was one of the few men of his time who sensed the depths of resentment accumulating in women whose efforts to think about doctrine were not taken seriously by the clergy. In one of his *Colloquies*, a lady learned in Latin and Greek is being twitted by an asinine abbot (the phrase is Erasmus'). She finally bursts out, "If you keep on as you've begun, geese may do the preaching sooner than put up with you tongue-tied pastors. The world's a stage that's topsy-turvy now, as you see. Every man must play his part—or exit."

[III]

The world was indeed topsy-turvy. The Catholic Church, which Erasmus had tried to reform from within, was being split by Protestants who believed that man was saved by faith in Christ alone and that human work had nothing to do with it, who were changing the sacramental system all around and over-throwing the order of the priesthood. Among this welter of new ideas, let us focus here on the new image of the Christian woman as presented in Calvinist popular literature.

We can find her in a little play dated around 1550. The heroine is not a learned lady but a pure and simple woman who knows her Bible. The villain is not a teasing, harmless abbot but a lecherous and stupid village priest. He begins by likening her achievements to those of craftsmen who were meddling with Scripture, and then goes on: "Why, you'll even see a woman / Knock over your arguments / With her responses on the Gospel." And in the play she does, quoting Scripture to oppose the adoration of Mary and the saints and to oppose the power of the popes. The priest can only quote from glosses, call her names, and threaten to burn her.

Wherever one looks in the Protestant propaganda of the 1540's to the 1560's, the Christian woman is identified by her relation to Scripture. Her sexual purity and control are demonstrated by her interest in the Bible, and her right to read the New Testament in the vernacular is defended against those who would forbid it to her, as to such other unlearned persons as merchants and artisans. The author of the pamphlet *The Way to Arrive at the Knowledge of God* put the matter sharply enough: "You say that women who want to read the Bible are just libertines? I say you call them lewd merely because they won't consent to your seduction. You say it's permitted to women to read Boccaccio's *Flamette* or Ovid's *Art of Love* . . . which teach them to be adulterers, and yet you'll send a woman who's reading a Bible to the flames. You say it's enough for a woman's salvation for her to do her housework, sew and spin? . . . Of what use then are Christ's promises to her? You'll put spiders in Paradise, for they know how to spin very well."

The message was even put to music during the First Religious War in the 1560's. The Huguenot queen of Navarre sings:

> Those who say it's not for women
> To look at Holy Writ
> Are evil men and infamous
> Seducers and antichrist.
> Alas, my ladies.
> Your poor souls
> Let them not be governed
> By such great devils.

And in reality as well as in popular literature Protestant women were freeing their souls from the rule of priests and doctors of theology. Noble churchmen were horrified at the intemperance with which Protestant females abused them as godless men. The pages of Jean Crespin's widely read *Book of the Martyrs*, based on the real adventures of Protestant heretics, record the story of one Marie Becaudelle, a servant of La Rochelle who learns of the Gospel from her master and argues publicly with a Franciscan, showing him from Scripture that he does not preach according to the Word of God. A bookseller's wife disputes doctrine in a prison cell with the bishop of Paris and with doctors of theology. An honest widow of Tours talks to priests and monks with the witness of Scripture: "I'm a sinner, but I don't need candles to ask God to pardon my faults. You're the ones who walk in darkness." The learned theologians did not know what to make of such monstrous women, who went against nature.

To this challenge to the exclusion of women, the Catholic theologians in mid-century responded not by accommodating but by digging in their heels. It wasn't safe, said an important Jesuit preacher, to leave the Bible to the discretion of "what's turning around in a woman's brain." "To learn essential doctrine," echoed another cleric, "there is no need for women or artisans to take time out from their work and read the Old and New Testament in the vernacular. Then they'll want to dispute about it and give their opinion . . . and they can't help falling into error. Women must be silent in Church, as Saint Paul says." Interestingly enough, when a Catholic vernacular Bible was finally allowed to circulate in France at the end of the sixteenth century, it did not play an important role in the conversion or devotional life of Catholic leaders like Barbe Acarie and Saint Jeanne Frances de Chantal.

Thus, into a pre-Reformation situation in which urban women were estranged from priests or in tension with them over the matter of their theological curiosity, the Protestant movement offered a new option: relations with the priestly order could be broken, and women, like their husbands (indeed *with* their husbands), could be engaged in the pure and serious enterprise of reading and talking about Scripture. The message being broadcast to male artisans and lesser merchants was similar but less momentous. In the first place, the men were more likely already to be literate; and anyway, the only natural order the men were being asked to violate was the separation between the learned and unlearned. The women were *also* being called to a new relation with men. It is worth noting how different is this appeal to women from that which Max Weber considered most likely to win females over to a new religion. Rather than inciting to orgy and emotion, it was summoning to intellectual activity and self-control.

How was the appeal received? France never became a Protestant kingdom, of course, and even in cities where the movement was strong only one-third to one-half of the population might be ardent Calvinists. City men who became caught up in Protestantism ranged from wealthy bankers and professionals to poor journeymen, but they were generally from the more skilled and complex, the more literate, or the more novel trades and occupations. A printer, a goldsmith, or a barber–surgeon was more likely to disobey priests and doctors of theology than was a boatmaster, a butcher, or a baker.

What of the Calvinist women? As with the men, they did not come from the mass of poor unskilled people at the bottom of urban society, although a certain percentage of domestic servants did follow their masters and mistresses into the Reformed Church. The Protestant women belonged mostly to the families of craftsmen, merchants, and professional men, but they were by no means exclusively the literate women in these circles. For all the female martyrs who answered the Inquisitors by citing Scripture they had read, there were as many who could answer only by citing doctrines they had heard. It is also clear that in Lyon in the 1570's, more than a decade after the Reformed Church had been set up, a significant percentage of Reformed women still could not write their names. For this last group, then, the Protestant path was not a way to express their new literacy but a way finally to associate themselves with that surge of male literacy already described.

But there is more that we can say about city women who turned Protestant. A preliminary examination of women arrested for heresy or killed in Catholic uprisings in many parts of France, of women among the Protestant suspects in Toulouse in 1568–69, and of a very large sample of Protestant women in Lyon (about 750 women) yields three main observations. First, there is no clear evidence either that the wives mainly followed their husbands into the movement or that it worked the other way around.* We can find women converted by their husbands who became more committed than their men; we can find wives who converted while their husbands remained "polluted in idolatry" and husbands who converted while their wives lagged behind. Second, the Protestant women seemed to include more than a random number of widows, of women with employ of their own—such as dressmakers, merchants, midwives, hotel-keepers, and the like—and of women with the curious nicknames associated with public and eccentric personalities. But finally, the Protestant movement in the sixteenth century did not pull in the small but significant group of genuinely learned women in the city—neither the patronesses of the literary salons nor the profane female poets. Louise Labé, who pleaded with women to lift their heads above their distaffs, always remained in the church that invoked the Virgin, although one of her aunts, a female barber, joined the Calvinists.

What do these observations suggest about the state of life of city women before their conversion to the new religion? They do not indicate a prior experience of mere futility and waste or restrictive little family worlds. Rather, Protestant religious commitment seems to have complemented in a new sphere the scope and independence that the women's lives had already had. Women already independent in the street and market now ventured into the male preserve of theology. And yet the literary woman, already admitted to the castle of learning, does not seem to have needed the Religion of the Book. A look at developments within the Reformed Church will indicate why this should have been so.

[IV]

After 1562 the Reformed Church of France started to settle into its new institutional structures and the promise of Protestantism began to be realized for city women. Special catechism classes in French were set up for women, and in towns under Huguenot control efforts were made to encourage literacy, even among all the poor girls in the orphanages, not just the gifted few. In certain Reformed families the literate husbands finally began teaching their wives to read.

Some Protestant females, however, had more ambitious goals. The image of the new Christian woman with her Bible had beckoned them to more than catechism classes or reading the Scriptures with their husbands. Consider Marie Dentière. One-time abbess in Tournai, but expelled from her convent

---

* Nancy Roelker found a different pattern among Huguenot noblewomen, who more often than their husbands took the first step toward conversion ("The Appeal of Calvinism to French Noblewomen in the Sixteenth Century," *The Journal of Interdisciplinary History* 2 [1972]: 402). Class differences help explain this contrast, such as the more significant roles in public life enjoyed by noblewomen than those allowed to city women.

in the 1520's because of heresy, Dentière married a pastor and found her way to Geneva during its years of religious revolution. There, according to the report of a nun of the Poor Clare order, Marie got "mixed up with preaching," coming, for instance, to the convent to persuade the poor creatures to leave their miserable life. She also published two religious works, one of them an epistle on religious matters addressed to Princess Marguerite de Navarre. Here Dentière inserted a "Defense for Women" against calumnies, not only by Catholic adversaries but also by some of the Protestant faithful. The latter were saying that it was rash for women to publish works to each other on Scriptural matters. Dentière disagreed: "If God has done the grace to some poor women to reveal to them by His Holy Scriptures some good and holy thing, dare they not write about it, speak about it, and declare it, one to the other? . . . Is it not foolishly done to hide the talent that God has given us?"

Dentière maintained the modest fiction that she was addressing herself only to other females. Later women did not. Some of the women prisoners in the French jails preached to "the greater consolation" of both male and female listeners. Our ex-Calvinist jurist Florimond de Raemond gave several examples, both from the Protestant conventicles and from the regular Reformed services as late as 1572, of women who while waiting for a preacher to arrive had gone up to pulpits and read from the Bible. One *théologienne* even took public issue with her pastor. Finally, in some of the Reformed Churches southwest of Paris—in areas where weavers and women had been early converts—a movement started to permit lay persons to prophesy. This would have allowed both women and unlearned men to get up in church and speak on holy things.

Jean Calvin, Théodore de Bèze, and other members of the Venerable Company of Pastors did not welcome these developments. The social thrust of the Reformation, as they saw it, was to overthrow the hierarchical priestly class and administer the church instead by well-trained pastors and sound male members of the Consistories. That was enough topsy-turvy for them. And like Catholic critics who had quoted Paul's dictum from I Corinthians that "women keep silence in the churches" against Protestants who were reading and talking about the Bible, now the Reformed pastors quoted it against Protestant women who wanted to preach publicly or have some special vocation in the church. Pierre Viret explained in 1560 that the elect were equal in that they were called to be Christian and faithful—man and woman, master and servant, free and serf. But the Gospel had not abolished within the church the rank and order of nature and of human society. God created and Christ confirmed that order. Even if a woman had greater spiritual gifts than had her husband, she could not speak in Christian assembly. Her task, said Pastor Viret, was merely to instruct her children in the faith when they were young; she might also be a schoolteacher to girls if she wished. . . .

[V]

An examination of a few other areas of Protestant reform reveals the same pattern as in reading Scripture and preaching: city women revolted against priests and entered new religious relations that brought them together with men or likened them to men but left them unequal.

The new Calvinist liturgy, with its stress on the concerted fellowship of the congregation, used the vernacular—the language of women and the unlearned—and included Psalms sung jointly by men and women. Nothing shocked Catholic observers more than this. When they heard the music of male and female voices filtering from a house where a conventicle was assembled, all they could imagine were lewd activities with the candles extinguished. It was no better when the Protestant movement came into the open. After the rich ceremony of the mass, performed by the clergy with due sanctity and grandeur, the Reformed service seemed, in the words of a Catholic in Paris in the 1560's, "without law, without order, without harmony." "The minister begins. Everybody follows—men, women, children, servants, chambermaids. . . . No one is on the same verse. . . . The fine-voiced maidens let loose their hums and trills . . . so the young men will be sure to listen. How wrong of Calvin to let women sing in Church."

To Protestant ears, it was very different. For laymen and laywomen in the service the common voice in praise of the Lord expressed the lack of distance between pastor and congregation. The Catholic priests had stolen the Psalms; now they had been returned. As for the participants in the conventicles, the songs gave them courage and affirmed their sense of purity over the hypocritical papists, who no sooner left the mass than they were singing love songs. The Protestant faithful were firmly in control of their sexual impulses, they believed, their dark and sober clothes a testimonal to their sincerity. And when the women and men sang together in the great armed street marches of the 1560's, the songs were a militant challenge to the hardened Catholics and an invitation to the wavering listeners to join the elect.

For the city women, there was even more novelty. They had had a role smaller than men's in the organized lay ceremonial life of the church, and the confraternities had involved them rather little. Previously, nuns had been the only women to sing the office. Now the confraternities and the convents would be abolished. The ceremonial was simplified and there was only one kind of group for worship, one in which men and women sang together. For Protestant tradesmen, many of whom were immigrants to the city, the new liturgical fellowship provided religious roots they had been unable to find in the inhospitable parishes. For Protestant women, who were not as likely to have been immigrants, the new liturgy provided roots in religious organizations with men.

But this leveling, this gathering together of men and women, had its limits. Singing in church did not lead women on to preaching or to participating in the Consistory any more than Bible-reading had. Furthermore, there was some effort by the pastors to order the congregations so as to reflect the social order. In Geneva, special seats were assigned to minimize the mingling of the sexes. And in some Reformed churches the sexes were separated when communion was taken: the men went up first to partake of the Holy Supper.

Psalms were added to the religious life of the Protestants and saints were taken away—from prayer, image, and invocation. Here the matter of sex was indifferent: Saint Damian departed as did Saint Margaret; Saint Nicholas departed as did Saint Catherine. Protestant men and women affirmed before the Inquisition that one must not call upon the Virgin, for, blessed though she was, she had no merit. And when the magistrates were slow to purify the churches of their idolatrous statues, zealous members of the menu peuple smashed the saints. Females were always included in these crowds. Indeed, like the armed march of the psalm-singers, the iconoclastic riot was a transfer of the joint political action of the grain riot into the religious sphere.

But the loss of the saints affected men and women unequally. Reformed prayer could no longer be addressed to a woman, whereas the masculine identity of the Father and Son was left intact. It may seem anachronistic to raise the matter of sexual identity in religious images during the Reformation, but it is not. Soon afterward, the Catholic poet Marie le Jars de Gournay, friend and editor of Montaigne, was to argue in her Equality of the Sexes that Jesus' incarnation as a male was no special honor to the male sex but a mere historical convenience; given the patriarchal malice of the Jews, a female savior would never have been accepted. But if one were going to emphasize the sex of Jesus, then it was all the more important to stress the perfection of Mary and her role in the conception of our Lord. So, if the removal from Holy Mother Church cut off certain forms of religious affect for men, for women the consequences for their identities went even deeper. Now during their hours of childbirth—a "combat," Calvin described it, "a horrible torment"—they called no more on the Virgin and said no prayers to Saint Margaret. Rather, as Calvin advised, they groaned and sighed to the Lord and He received those groans as a sign of their obedience.

Obedience to the Lord was, of course, a matter for both men and women. But women had the additional charge of being obedient to their husbands. The Reformed position on marriage provides a final illustration of the pattern "together but unequal."

The Protestant critique of clerical celibacy involved first and foremost a downgrading of the concept that the male had a greater capacity than the female to discipline his sexual impulses. Since the time of the Greeks, physicians had been telling people that physiology made the female the more lustful, the more uncontrollable sex. As Doctor François Rabelais put it, there are many things a man can do, from work to wine, to control "the pricks of venery"; but a woman, with her hysteric animal (the womb) within, could rarely restrain herself from cuckolding her husband. Given these assumptions, clerical celibacy for the superior sex had been thought a real possibility whereas for the female it had appeared an exceptional achievement.

The Reformers' observation that continence was a rare gift of God and their admonition "Better to marry than to burn" were, then, primarily addressed to the numerous male clergy and less to the small fraction of female religious. Indeed, sermons on clerical marriage stressed how the groom would now be saved from fornication and hellfire but said little of the soul of the bride. It is surely significant, too, that male religious joined the Reformation movements in proportionately larger numbers than did female. The nuns were always the strong holdouts, even when they were promised dowries and pensions. Though some of them may have been afraid to try their chances on the marriage market, many simply preferred the separate celibate state and organizations. When Marie Dentière tried to persuade the nuns of the Poor Clare order at Geneva to end their hypocritical lives and marry, as she had, the sisters spat at her.

The argument for clerical marriage, then, equalized men and women somewhat in regard to their appetites. It also raised the woman's status by affirming that she could be a worthy companion to a minister of God. The priest's concubine, chased from his house in ignominy by Catholic reformers and ridiculed as a harlot by Protestants, could now become the pastor's wife! A respectable girl from a good city family—likely, in the first generation, to be the daughter of a merchant or prosperous craftsman—would be a helpful companion to her husband, keeping his busy household in order and his colleagues entertained. And she would raise her son to be a pastor and her daughter to be a pastor's wife.

Since marriage was now the only encouraged state, the Reformers did what they could to make it more tolerable according to their lights. Friendship and companionship within marriage were stressed, as many historians have pointed out, although it is a mistake to think that this was unique to Protestant thought. Catholic humanist writers valued these relations within marriage as well. In other ways, the Reformed position was more original.*

* It does not seem justified to argue, as does Roelker, that Calvin's position on divorce "advanced women to a position of equality with their husbands." "By permitting wives as well as husbands to instigate divorce proceedings," she maintains, "Calvin elevated their dignity and increased their legal rights. Enacted into Genevan law, this could not help but raise the position of women to a higher level" ("The Appeal of Calvinism," p. 406). The institution of divorce with permission to remarry in cases of adultery or very prolonged absence was, of course, an important innovation by Calvin and other Protestant reformers. But this change did not remedy an *inequality* in the existing marriage law. The canon law had long allowed either male or female the right to initiate proceedings in an ecclesiastical court for separation in case of the partner's adultery, as well as for annulment and dissolution in certain circumstances. What determined whether men and women in

A single sexual standard would now be enforced rather than talked about; and the victorious Huguenot Consistories during the Wars of Religion chased out the prostitutes almost as quickly as they silenced the mass. The husband would be compelled insofar as possible to exercise his authority, in Calvin's words, "with moderation and not insult over the woman who has been given him [by God] as his partner." Thus, in a real innovation in Christian Europe, men who beat their wives were haled before Consistories and threatened with denial of communion. The men grumbled and complained—"I beat my wife before and I'll beat her again if she be bad," said a Lyon typecaster— but the situation had improved enough in Geneva by the end of the century that some called it "the women's Paradise."

But despite all this, the Reformed model of the marriage relation subjected the wife to her husband as surely as did the Catholic one. Women had been created subject to men, said Calvin, although before the fall "this was a liberal and gentle subjection." Through sin, it had become worse: "Let the woman be satisfied with her state of subjection, and not take it amiss that she is made inferior to the more distinguished sex." Nor was this view restricted to pastors. There are many examples from sixteenth-century France of Protestant husbands instructing their wives, "their dear sisters and loyal spouses," telling them of their religious duties, telling them of their responsibilities toward their children, warning them that they must never do anything without seeking advice first. And if Protestant wives then told their husbands to go to the devil or otherwise insulted them so loudly that the neighbors heard, the women might soon find themselves brought before the Consistories and even punished (as the criminal records of Geneva reveal) by three days in prison on bread and water.

Undoubtedly there were many Reformed marriages in commercial and artisanal circles where the husbands and wives lived together in peace and friendship. And why not? Women had joined the Reformation to rebel against priests and pope, not to rebel against their husbands. Although they wanted certain "masculine" religious activities opened to them, Calvinist wives— even the most unruly of them—never went so far as to deny the theory of the subjection of women within marriage. The practice of subjection in individual

---

fact had equal access to separation or divorce before or after the Reformation was, first, the informal operation of the double standard, which tolerated the husband's adultery more readily than the wife's, and, second, the relatively greater economic difficulty faced by the single woman supporting herself and her children in the interval before she was able to remarry. For all but the very wealthy man or woman, divorce or legal separation was an unlikely possibility. In any case, the exhaustive research of René Stauffenegger has shown that divorces were very rarely granted in Geneva in the late sixteenth and early seventeenth centuries—pastors and Consistory always pressing for couples to solve their disputes. See Keith Thomas, "The Double Standard," *Journal of the History of Ideas* 20 (1959): 200–202; John T. Noonan, Jr., *Power to Dissolve* (Cambridge, Mass., 1972), chaps. 1–3, 7; R. Stauffenegger, "Le mariage à Genève vers 1600," *Mémoires de la société pour l'histoire du droit* 27 (1966): 327–28.

marriages during those heroic decades of the Reformation may have been tempered by two things: first, the personality of the wife herself, which sustained her revolt against priestly power and her search for new relations with books and men; and second, the common cause of reform, which for a while demanded courageous action from both husbands and wives.

And what could a city woman accomplish for the cause if she were not rich and powerful like a noblewoman? On a Catholic feast day, she could defy her Catholic neighbors by sitting ostentatiously spinning in her window. She could puzzle over the Bible alone or with her husband or with Protestant friends. If she were a printer's wife or widow, she could help get out a Protestant edition to spread the word about tyrannical priests. She could use her house for an illegal Protestant conventicle or assembly. She could put aside her dissolute hoop skirts and full gowns and start to wear black. She could harangue priests in the streets. She could march singing songs in defiance of royal edicts. She could smash statues, break baptismal fonts, and destroy holy images. She could, if persecution became very serious, flee to London or Geneva, perhaps the longest trip she had ever taken. She could stay in France and dig the foundations for a Reformed temple. She could even fight—as in Toulouse, where a Huguenot woman bore arms in the First Religious War. And she could die in flames, shouting to her husband, as did one young wife of Langres, "My friend, if we have been joined in marriage in body, think that this is only like a promise of marriage, for our Lord . . . will marry us the day of our martyrdom."

Many of these actions, such as Bible-reading, clearly were special to Protestant city women. A few were not. The Catholic city women in Elizabethan England, for instance, hid priests in their quarters and, if captured, went to the "marriage" of martyrdom as bravely as did any Huguenot. It was the same among the radical Anabaptists. One kind of action, however, seems to have been special to Catholic city women (as also to the radical Quaker women of the seventeenth century): organized group action among women. On the highest level, this was expressed in such attempts to create new forms of common life and work among females as the Ursulines and the Sisters of Charity and the Christian Institutes of Mary Ward. On the lowest level, this was reflected in the violent activity of all-female Catholic crowds— throwing stones at Protestant women, throwing mire at pastors, and, in the case of a group of female butchers in Aix-en-Provence, beating and hanging the wife of a Protestant bookseller.

These contrasts can point the way to some general conclusions about the long-range significance of the Reformed solution for relations between the sexes. In an interesting essay, Alice Rossi suggests three models for talking about equality. One is assimilationist: the subordinate group is somewhat raised by making it like the superior group. A second is pluralistic: each group is allowed to keep its distinctive characteristics but within a context of society at large that is still hierarchical. The third is hybrid (or, better, transformational), involving changes within and among all groups involved. Whatever transformations in social relations were accomplished by either the Reformation or the Counter-Reformation, it seems that as far as relations between the sexes go the Reformed solution was assimilationist; the Catholic solution, with its female saints and convents, was pluralistic. Neither, of course, eliminated the subject status of women.*

Is one position clearly better than the other? That is, within the context of the society of the sixteenth and seventeenth centuries did one solution seem to offer greater freedom to men and women to make decisions about their lives and to adopt new roles? One important school of sociologists always answers such questions in favor of Protestantism. It is the superior sect: its transcendent and activist Father, less hierarchical religious symbolism, and this-worldly asceticism all make for a more evolved religion, facilitating the desacralization of society. More different choices are also facilitated, so this argument goes, and more rapid social change.

Certainly it is true that the Reformed solution did promote a certain desexualization of society, a certain neutralizing of forms of communication and of certain religious places so that they became acceptable for women. These were important gains, bringing new tools to women and new experience to both sexes. But the assimilationist solution brought losses, too. This worldly asceticism denied laymen and laywomen much of the shared recreational and festive life allowed them by Catholicism. It closed off an institutionalized and respectable alternative to private family life: the communal living of the monastery. By destroying the female saints as exemplars for both sexes, it cut off a wide range of affect and activity. And by eliminating a separate identity and separate organization for women in religious life, it may have made them a little more vulnerable to subjection in all spheres.

As it turned out, women suffered for their powerlessness in both Catholic and Protestant lands in the late sixteenth to eighteenth centuries as changes in marriage laws restricted the freedoms of wives even further, as female guilds dwindled, as the female role in middle-level commerce and farm direction contracted, and as the differential between male and female wages increased. In both Catholic France and Protestant England, the learned lady struggled to establish a role for herself: the female schoolteacher became a familiar figure, whether as a spinster or as an Ursuline; the female dramatist

---

* The same point can be made in regard to class relations within the two Reformations, the Reformed Church assimilating artisans and even peasants upward in styles of religious behavior and the Catholic allowing greater scope to "peasant religion." Although Calvinism reduced the levels of angelic and ecclesiastical hierarchy, neither church challenged the *concept* of social hierarchy.

scrambled to make a living, from the scandalous Aphra Behn in the seventeenth century to the scandalous Olympe de Gouges in the eighteenth.

Thus it is hard to establish from a historical point of view that the Reformed assimilationist structure always facilitated more rapid and creative changes in sex roles than did the relatively pluralistic structure found in the Catholicism of the sixteenth and seventeenth centuries. Both forms of religious life have contributed to the transformation of sex roles and to the transformation of society. In the proper circumstances, each can serve as a corrective to the other. Whatever long-range changes may be achieved, the varied voices heard in this essay will have played their part: the immodest Louise Labé telling women to lift their minds a little above their distaffs, the servant Marie Becaudelle disputing with her priest, the ex-nun Marie Dentière urging women to speak and write about Scripture, and yes, the Catholic Marie le Jars de Gournay reminding us that, after all, it was only a historical accident that our Lord Jesus Christ was born a male.

Cultural Patronage
in Renaissance Florence

GENE BRUCKER

How do artists and intellectuals get the time and freedom to pursue their crafts, and is such time and freedom justified? This question is a perennial one. It calls for an assessment of the cultural ideals and institutions of the society about which it is asked, and it has special importance when the society in question has had a particularly brilliant cultural life, as did Periclean Athens, Augustan Rome, Carolingian and twelfth-century Europe, and Renaissance Florence. In all these times and places, hardheaded men of commerce and politics invested in the patronage of artists and scholars. The additional question must always be asked: Why then and not at other times? In part, the answer may be found by reference to historical conditions. It is not surprising that art and intellect do not flourish in times of war, migration, or severe deprivation. The civil wars following Julius Caesar's murder, the Germanic invasions, the dislocations caused by Viking and Magyar attacks were not conducive to patronage of artistic and intellectual culture, which costs a great deal in materials and in the manpower of the most talented members of society. Yet, once we have noted that high culture requires relative peace and prosperity, we must still explain why Athens and not Corinth, why Charlemagne's court and not Offa's in England, why Florence and not Milan, became centers where artists and intellectuals found patrons.

In the following selection, Gene Brucker examines the relationship between Florence's leadership in business and politics and the artistic and intellectual community it supported.

Foundations and Premises

For two centuries, from the age of Dante and Giotto to that of Machiavelli and Michelangelo, Florence was one of Latin Europe's most dynamic and creative centers of intellectual and artistic activity. This chapter will attempt to define the nature of that cultural achievement, and to relate it to the city's institutions and values, and to her experience. Perhaps no problem of historical analysis is so challenging and provocative, and so beset with pitfalls, as the attempt to explain the relationship between social and cultural phenomena. Every student of Florentine history is confronted by these questions. Why was this society so creative, and so receptive to change and innovation? Of all the major Italian cities, why did Florence—and not Milan or Genoa or Venice—achieve the greatest distinction in art and learning during these centuries? . . .

The most distinctive feature of Florentine intellectual life was not its variety and complexity—which was matched, to some degree, by Milan, Venice, and Naples—but rather the unusually close rapport between these cultural traditions. Contributing to this atmosphere of free communication was the social structure, perhaps the most flexible of any major Italian city. But another important factor was the towering figure of Dante Alighieri. The poet represented a crucial stage in the fusion of the universalist, hierarchical ideals of the classic-Christian tradition with the parochial values and interests of the local milieu. In the Florentine schools and *studia* (and perhaps also at the University of Bologna), Dante had absorbed those universal ideals which had been summarized so brilliantly by Thomas Aquinas. The poet wrote scholastic treatises, and he also composed essays praising the Christian virtues. His political ideas, his veneration for the Empire and the values of ancient Rome, were likewise universal and hierarchical. Yet his *Divine Comedy* was written in the local Tuscan dialect, not in Latin. And although this work contains the universal concepts of the classical and Christian traditions, it is also a Florentine poem, replete with the particular values, emotions, and concerns of that community. The poet did not succeed in reconciling all of the contradictions between the two traditions, but his genius enabled him to surmount these discordant elements, and to create a magnificent synthesis combining ideal and reality, the universal and the particular. He also established a lofty standard of excellence, to serve as challenge and inspiration for later generations of Florentine intellectuals.

In the realm of the visual arts, Giotto di Bondone (d. 1337) filled a role similar to Dante's in literature. Giotto's subject matter was traditionally Christian; he learned to paint in the Byzantine style of the thirteenth century. His great contribution to fresco painting was to humanize the wooden, stylized figures of Byzantine art, to create scenes that were naturalistic and lifelike but also grandiose and monumental. His fresco cycle in Padua of Christ's life and the scenes in S. Croce from the life of St. Francis are supreme statements of these qualities in Giotto's art, worthy of comparison with the *Divine Comedy*. Certain attempts have been made to identify the sources of Giotto's inspiration and genius, for example, in the Franciscan emphasis upon Christ's humanity, and the striving for a more intense religious experience. Rather less persuasive is that interpretation which depicts him as a representative of the Florentine bourgeoisie, whose monumental human figures reflect the self-confidence of a rising social class, emancipating itself from subjection to the church and the feudal nobility. Giotto's fame during his lifetime was enormous, although his reputation declined during the second half of the fourteenth century. But his frescoes made a profound impact upon the revolutionary generation of Florentine artists in the early Quattrocento, who recovered Giotto's sense of the monumental, which had disappeared from the Florentine art of the preceding age.

Complexity of social structure, variety of intellectual interests, a history of fruitful intercourse between different traditions—these are some factors which fostered cultural vitality and innovation in Florence. The aristocracy did not merely patronize art and learning; it was actively involved in the city's cultural life. Nearly every prominent family counted a lawyer and a cleric among its number; and by the middle of the fifteenth century, many houses —Strozzi, Corbinelli, Rossi, Medici, Davanzati, Alessandri—could also boast of a humanist scholar. The intellectual interests of many Florentines cut across cultural and disciplinary barriers. Cosimo de' Medici is a good example: banker, statesman, scholar, a friend and patron of humanists (Bruni, Niccoli, Marsuppini, Poggio), artists (Donatello, Brunelleschi, Michelozzo), and learned clerics (Ambrogio Traversari, Pope Nicholas V). The library of a wealthy merchant, Piero di Duccio Alberti, was inventoried in 1400; it contained a large number of business papers and ledgers, a book of hours, several Latin grammars and works by the classical authors Aesop, Cicero, Seneca, Eutropius, and Vigentius. A notary, Ser Matteo Gherardi, died in 1390, leaving a collection of legal treatises (decretals, commentaries, works on canon law), but also a nucleus of religious works (a book of homilies, a psalter, a prayer collection, and a Bible), and the writings of Aesop and Boethius. Lapo Mazzei's letters to Francesco Datini contain references to the Bible and to Christian authors (St. Augustine, St. Bernard, St. Francis, St. Thomas Aquinas), to ancient writers (Cicero, Seneca, Sallust, Horace, Livy, Vergil, Valerius Maximus, Boethius), and to the vernacular works of Dante, Jacopone da Todi, and the Vallombrosan hermit Giovanni dalle Celle. In a treatise on the subject of fortune written about 1460, Giovanni Rucellai incorporated citations from an unusually wide range of classical, Christian, and Italian authors: Aristotle, Epictetus, Sallust, Cicero, Seneca, St. Bernard, Dante, Petrarch, and a Florentine theologian, Leonardo Dati.

Communication between merchants, politicians, artists, and scholars was also facilitated by certain attitudes and conventions, to some degree institutionalized, of this society. Wealthy banker and poor artisans sat together as equals in the Signoria, a political tradition which must have facilitated intellectual discourse between aristocratic patrons and the sculptors, painters and other craftsmen they employed to build their palaces and decorate their chapels. The open and candid discussions about the problems of cathedral construction (in which bankers, lawyers, friars, and craftsmen participated) also cut across social and professional barriers. Among the citizens invited to counsel the Signoria were men representing all of the major professions and occupations (with the sole exception of theology). These included the lawyers Filippo Corsini, Lorenzo Ridolfi, and Giuliano Davanzati; the physician Cristofano di Giorgio; the humanists Leonardo Bruni, Palla Strozzi, and Agnolo Pandolfini, who were thus provided with an arena for voicing their political opinions and for publicizing ideas and perspectives derived from their disciplines. This forum may have stimulated interest in classical antiquity, and thus contributed to Florence's precocious adoption of humanism as a moral and educational system.

Another device for promoting communication between men of diverse disciplines and cultural interests was the Florentine version of the salon. One of these meetings was described in the *Paradiso degli Alberti* by Giovanni da Prato; other groups gathered around the Augustinian friar Luigi Marsili, the humanist chancellor Coluccio Salutati, and the Camaldolese prior of S. Maria degli Angeli, Ambrogio Traversari. Scholars have also discovered references to an informal gathering which met in the early 1400s under the Tettoio dei Pisani, a pavilion adjacent to the Piazza della Signoria, and another two decades later organized by the Augustinian scholars, Fra Evangelista of Pisa and Fra Girolamo of Naples. . . .

The Florentine sense of quality was a product of the city's craft tradition and the exceptional skills of her artisans. The industrial and craft guilds had developed a system of quality control to protect their trades; every Florentine realized that the maintenance of high standards benefited the city's economy. This appreciation of quality, and a corresponding disdain for the shoddy and the inferior, became a characteristic feature of the Florentine mentality and mode of perception. It is revealed in this letter written by a lawyer, Rosso Orlandi, to a friend in Venice, Piero Davanzati, about a very small problem, the purchase of a piece of cloth:

> I received your letter in which you instruct me to buy and send you twelve yards of good blue cloth. One of my neighbors is a good friend and a cloth expert. First we looked around in the cloth factories, where occasionally one may find some nice remnants at a discount, but we didn't see anything we liked. Then we visited all of the retail shops which sell for cash. It is not their custom to allow buyers to examine and compare the cloth of one shop with that of another. However, we did find a way to examine the finest and most beautiful cloth in each shop, and we also seized the opportunity to compare these pieces side by side. From them all, we chose a cloth from the shop of Zanobi di Ser Gino. There were none that were better woven or more beautifully dyed. Furthermore, the cloth was nearly a foot wider than the others, even after it had been washed and trimmed. Since the

Florentine shearers do better work than those in Venice, I have had the cloth washed and trimmed here. When you see it, I believe that you will be pleased with it. You will like it even better after you have worn it for several months; for it is a cloth which will wear extremely well.

The Florentine esthetic sense was derived from this appreciation for quality; it is stamped upon the physical city and upon the rural landscape, fashioned by generations of men who prized beauty. It is revealed too in contemporary writing, for example, in a letter from a banker, Jacopo Pazzi, to his friend Filippo Strozzi in Naples (1464), thanking him for a consignment of gold coins: "They are so beautiful that they give me great pleasure, because I love coins which are well designed; and you know that the more beautiful things are, the more they are cherished." Writing in his diary in the 1460s, Giovanni Rucellai described "the most attractive and pleasing aspects" of his villa at Quarachi, a few miles west of Florence near the Arno. He mentioned the house, the garden planted with fruit trees, the fish pond surrounded by fir trees, and another wooded grove at the edge of the garden adjacent to the road. "This park is a source of great consolation," Rucellai wrote, "not only to ourselves and our neighbors, but also to strangers and travelers who pass by during the heat of summer . . . who can refresh themselves with the clear and tasty water. . . . And no traveler passes who does not stop for a quarter of an hour to view the garden filled with beautiful plants. So I feel that the creation of this park . . . was a very worthy enterprise." Also illustrating the Florentine concern for esthetic values is a document in the files of the republic's diplomatic correspondence. During a crucial period of the Milanese war (December 1400), the Signoria wrote to the general of the Camaldolese order concerning the sale of a grove of fir trees which were to be cut down, near the ancient monastery of Camaldoli in the Apennines. Expressing their shock and dismay at this vandalism, the priors reminded the general that the trees had been planted and nourished by his predecessors "for the consolation of the hermits and the admiration of the visitors." Four years later (September 1404) the commune again raised this issue, urging the general to cease the despoliation of the monastic patrimony, whose beauty was as pleasing to God as to man.

Florentines were usually sensitive to physical environment, and they possessed a rare talent for communicating their perceptions. They were also intensely aware of other men: their features and habits, their character, their virtues and vices. This curiosity led them ultimately to develop an introspective interest in themselves. Professor Kristeller has noted that humanist writing is characterized by "the tendency to express, and to consider worth expressing, the concrete uniqueness of one's feelings, opinions, experiences and surroundings. . . ." These qualities are displayed in Latin treatises and letters, and also in the diaries and private correspondence of ordinary Florentines. Even such prosaic documents as tax declarations are frequently couched in very expressive language, as they describe the topography of a hill farm or the antipathetic character of a surly peasant. This appreciation of the concrete, the specific, and the unique was fostered not only by the literature of antiquity, but also by the social and intellectual climate of Renaissance Florence.

Cultural Patronage in Renaissance Florence: Structures, Motivations, Trends

Renaissance culture, so the textbooks assert, was subsidized by a new social class, the urban bourgeoisie. Replacing the nobility and the clergy as the dominant group in society, the bourgeoisie also supplanted them in their traditional role as patrons of culture. With the wealth gained from their mercantile, banking, and industrial enterprises, they were able to hire the poets, scholars, and artists whose brilliant achievements brought fame and glory to them and their city. Through these intellectuals and artists, their employees and agents, the bourgeoisie were able to express their own ideals and values. Stated so simply and crudely, this analysis is valid, but it does require elaboration, qualification, and refinement. One must examine the methods and techniques by which this society encouraged and nourished— materially and psychologically—its intellectuals. How was talent recognized and merit rewarded? What were the peculiar and unique opportunities Florence offered for creative achievement? How effectively were the city's intellectual resources exploited, and how much talent was attracted from abroad? Finally, how were changes in the structure and values of the society reflected in different forms of patronage?

Intellectual activity in medieval and Renaissance Florence was predominantly—almost exclusively—functional; it was related to specific vocational and professional purposes, and directed toward the satisfaction of social needs. The educational system was organized to train some boys for mercantile careers and others for professional careers in law, the notarial discipline, medicine, and theology. In his statistical survey of Florence prior to the Black Death, Giovanni Villani cites some interesting figures on school enrollment. In a population of approximately 100,000, between 8000 and 10,000 youths were enrolled in the city's private schools. While the majority attended elementary schools, which taught the rudiments of the vernacular, 1000 advanced students went to special schools to learn the mathematics necessary for a business career, and another 500 enrolled in preprofessional academies which taught Latin grammar, rhetoric, and logic. Although these figures may be inflated, they do indicate the great value attached to education in Florence, and also the unusually high literacy rate, perhaps one-fourth or one-third of the male population. A basic knowledge of reading, writing, and arithmetic was an essential prerequisite for a business career, even in one of the artisan trades. An incident described in the protocols of the Merchants' Court illustrates this recognition of the value of education among the city's underprivileged. A young emigrant from the Perugian *contado*, Antonio di Manno, instituted a lawsuit for the recovery of a gold florin which he had paid in advance for some elementary instruction. Antonio worked as an apprentice in a shoemaker's shop where a fellow employee, Miniato, agreed to teach him reading and writing for a year, but then broke his promise when he left the shop.

The size and quality of Florence's educational system (which included conventual *studia* and a university as well as primary and secondary schools) was one factor in the city's ability to attract talent from abroad. Alongside the institutions which provided formal schooling were the guilds with their system of instruction for apprentices. Young artists like Giotto from the Mugello and Masaccio from S. Giovanni Valdarno came to Florence to study in the workshops of the great masters, to live and work in a stimulating intellectual environment, and to gain wealth and fame in a community which subsidized the arts. The city's attraction for men with professional training is documented by the unending flow of petitions from foreign lawyers, notaries, and physicians who sought Florentine citizenship. In 1381 a young physician, Ugolino of Montecatini, had just begun his professional career in Pisa, where he had a small practice and a lectureship in the university. He was then invited to become the town physician of Pescia in the Valdinievole. The most compelling reason for abandoning his teaching post at Pisa to accept this offer was the opportunity to pursue his medical studies in Florence, to take part in disputations, and to enlarge his experience. Ugolino admitted that the move to Pescia would not redound to his honor, but he believed that it would benefit his career. Apparently, his ultimate goal was to practice medicine in Florence and lecture in the university, but he was realistic about the difficulties confronting him. It required years to build a medical reputation, and then the physician had to endure the jealousy of his colleagues. But Ugolino was willing to accept the challenge of the metropolis, aware that "our profession is one of those influenced by fortune." In 1429, a young Lucchese lawyer, Filippo Balducci, was contemplating a move to Florence from Siena, where he taught and practiced law. To a Florentine acquaintance he wrote: "Since I have always had a great affection for that magnificent and glorious city, which I consider one of the three [greatest] in the world, I would rather be there than here, even though I will earn less."

Public recognition of distinguished achievement in Florence took various forms. The most tangible mark of distinction was the bestowal of a public office, a university professorship, or an artistic commission upon the meritorious, and these were distributed quite generously to prominent scholars and artists. In 1375, Coluccio Salutati became the first humanist chancellor of the republic; his successors in that office were men of great learning and reputation: Leonardo Bruni, Poggio Bracciolini, Carlo Marsuppini. In 1300, the commune granted a tax exemption to the architect Arnolfo di Cambio, "since this master is the most renowned and the most expert in church construction of any other in these parts; and that through his industry, experience and genius, the Florentine commune . . . from the magnificent beginning of this church . . . hopes to have the most beautiful and the most honorable cathedral in Tuscany." A century and a half later, Leonardo Bruni and Poggio Bracciolini obtained similar exemptions; Poggio had claimed that "he cannot pay the assessments levied against citizens who have profited from trade and the emoluments of public service, since he plans to devote all of his energies to study. . . ." Although Filippo Brunelleschi obtained no tax exemption from the state, he did receive a rare public acknowledgment of his talent. Described in a provision of June 1421 as a "man of the most perspicacious intelligence and admirable industry," he was granted a three-year patent on a boat he had invented, which apparently reduced the costs of transporting goods on the Arno. In reserving all benefits for this invention to Brunelleschi, the law stated that its objective was to prevent "the fruits of his talents and virtue from accruing to another," and also "to stimulate him to greater activity and even more subtle investigations. . . ."

During his lifetime, Dante Alighieri received no accolades from his native city, but after the poet's death, the Florentines made some belated gestures of apology. Giovanni Villani wrote that "because of the virtues and knowledge and worthiness of this citizen, it seems proper to grant him perpetual memory in our chronicle, even though his own noble works, which he has left to us in writing, bear witness to him and bring renown to our city." Giovanni Boccaccio's appointment (1373) as the commune's official lecturer on the Divine Comedy was an unprecedented sign of Dante's exalted reputation. Twenty-three years later, the councils passed a law authorizing the officials in charge of the cathedral to arrange for the return of the bodies of five illustrious Florentines who had died and been buried abroad. Munificent tombs were planned for these men in the cathedral, where no other interments were to be permitted. Four of the charter members of this Pantheon—Dante, Petrarch, Boccaccio, and Zanobi da Strada—were literary men, and the fifth was a distinguished lawyer named Accursius (d. 1260?) who taught for many years in the University of Bologna. This project failed completely, for the guardians of these bodies refused to surrender them. In 1430, the Signoria again appealed to the lord of Ravenna for Dante's remains. "Our people," so the official letter read, "harbor a singular and particular affection for the glorious and undying memory of that most excellent and renowned poet, Dante Alighieri; the fame of this man is such that it redounds to the praise and splendor of our city. . . ."

Not every distinguished citizen remained home to adorn his native city with his talents. Petrarch was never attracted to Florence, nor was Boccaccio an enthusiastic admirer of the city. After 1400, however, the pendulum swung quite decisively in Florence's favor, and during the first half of the Quattrocento, her cultural magnetism was particularly intense. Native artists and writers—Masaccio, Brunelleschi, Ghiberti, Manetti—stayed home and made only brief excursions abroad, while their ranks were supplemented by foreigners: Bruni, Poggio Bracciolini, Gentile da Fabriano. S. Croce, not the cathedral, became Florence's Pantheon, and the tombs in that Franciscan basilica are visual evidence of the magnitude of Florentine genius, and also of the city's inability to retain and exploit that genius fully. Dante, Petrarch, and Boccaccio are still missing, although Dante is commemorated by an ugly modern cenotaph. From an esthetic viewpoint, the two most noteworthy tombs are those of the humanists Bruni and Marsuppini, both of whom received imposing state funerals. Lorenzo Ghiberti, Niccolò Machiavelli, and Michelangelo are all buried in S. Croce, although Michelangelo died where he had lived and worked, in Rome. His body was spirited away to Florence by agents of Duke Cosimo I. Some distinguished Florentines of the Quattrocento are not interred in S. Croce. These include Palla Strozzi, who died in Padua while living in involuntary exile, Leon Battista Alberti, who died in Rome in 1472, and Leonardo da Vinci, who abandoned both Florence and Italy to spend his last years at the French court of Francis I.

The official recognition of intellectual and artistic distinction was one aspect of the collective, public nature of artistic and scholarly patronage in early Renaissance Florence. The great architectural monuments of the fourteenth and fifteenth centuries were supervised by commissions of operai selected by the guilds. In 1402, Lorenzo Ghiberti won a commission for the Baptistery doors in a public competition organized by the consuls of the Calimala guild, and judged by a special committee of thirty-four painters, sculptors, and goldsmiths. In the realm of letters and scholarship, official patronage was also important and useful, generally assuming the form of a communal office or a university professorship. The bestowal of the chancellor's office upon distinguished humanists like Salutati and Bruni was a reward for their fame and reputation, as well as payment for services rendered to the republic. By the middle of the fifteenth century, however, public subsidy of culture was declining, and the role of the private patron, and of culture created exclusively for private needs, now assumed greater importance than before. This trend can be charted in two quite different contexts: in the history of the Florentine Studio, and in Medicean patronage of the arts.

The fortunes of the city's major institution of higher learning provide a valuable corrective to the idealized picture of this society as totally committed to intellectual distinction, and willing to make heavy sacrifices to achieve and maintain excellence. From the beginning, Florence's efforts to create a university of the first rank met with very limited success. In 1321, a *studium generale* was established by the commune; it never flourished and ceased to function in the 1330s. But even before the Black Death had run its course, a courageous and imaginative Signoria enacted a decree (August 26, 1348) which authorized the reopening of the Studio, and bravely proclaimed that "from the study of the sciences, the city of Florence will receive an increase in honors and a full measure of wealth. . . ." Although the circumstances of its foundation could not have been less promising, the university did survive and gradually developed a modest reputation. But its existence was never secure, and it limped along on the rather meager resources which the commune grudgingly provided. Records of the deliberations on the university's budget in the 1360s reveal that some citizens doubted whether the school was worth its cost. During its most flourishing period, in the 1380s, the university operated with a substantial budget of 3000 florins, which paid for a staff of twenty-four professors. But one consequence of the debilitating wars with Giangaleazzo Visconti was the closing of the university in 1406; it did not reopen again until 1413. Thereafter, its budget was repeatedly cut during the Milanese wars of the 1420s; it was finally reduced to 200 florins in 1426. Four years later, the Studio governors candidly admitted that the university was in a parlous state. "It grieves us sorely," they announced, "that this glorious republic, which has surpassed the rest of Italy and all previous centuries in beauty and splendor, should be surpassed in this one respect by some of our neighboring cities, which in every other way are inferior to us."

This failure of the university to achieve the distinction which its founders and supporters envisaged is perhaps the crucial factor in the reluctance of Florence's ruling class to provide adequate and sustained support. The solid reputations of Bologna and Padua were never really challenged by the Studio, and shrewd politicians may have realized that no amount of money would change that fact. Patrician interests were not affected adversely by the mediocre quality of Studio instruction; wealthy citizens could send their sons to other Italian universities, and particularly to Bologna, to acquire the skills and the degrees needed to further their professional careers. Also contributing to the declining importance of the university was the tendency, in Florence and elsewhere, for humanistic studies—rhetoric, moral philosophy, poetry—to flourish outside of the university. Although these subjects were offered regularly in the Studio, occasionally by such distinguished scholars as Chrysoloras, Filelfo and Marsuppini, most teaching in the humanities occurred in a private context; tutors instructing students in their homes, scholars assembling in monasteries or in private palaces to discuss classical texts. Like other facets of patrician life in Quattrocento Florence, learning and education were becoming more private, aristocratic, and exclusive.

The most renowned institution of higher learning in Florence in the second half of the fifteenth century was not the Studio, but the Platonic Academy, an informal coterie of scholars and students united by an interest in Platonic philosophy. Its leader was Marsilio Ficino, whose translations of Platonic writings were subsidized by the Medici. The Academy had a geographical focus in Ficino's villa at Careggi outside of Florence, but it possessed no formal organization, nor did it provide any regular instruction. Its only scheduled events were irregular lectures by Ficino and occasional banquets and symposia held infrequently at the Careggi villa. Ficino did provide loose and informal guidance to his disciples and to visiting scholars like Pico della Mirandola and Jacques Lefèvre d'Étaples. But the essential qualities of this community were privacy, intimacy, and learning pursued for its own sake, without any concern for vocational or practical benefits.

This shift in the form and object of patronage from the public-corporate to the private sphere also occurred in the plastic arts. Communal and guild patronage was at its height between 1375 and 1425, when the Loggia dei Lanzi and the cathedral dome were built, when guilds were commissioning Baptistery doors and statues for Orsanmichele and erecting new headquarters for themselves. In these decades, too, private subsidy of the arts was largely (although not exclusively) directed toward public enterprises. The first architectural projects financed by Cosimo de' Medici were reconstructions of churches and monasteries: S. Lorenzo, S. Marco, the Badia of Fiesole, and the church of S. Francesco in Bosco in the Mugello. This pattern was sanctioned by tradition, and so too was its collective form, since other families were involved in several of these projects. If only because of his superior resources, Cosimo's voice in these collective enterprises tended to predominate; S. Lorenzo, for example, was finally completed with Medici money twenty years after the project had been initiated. Cosimo's reluctance to finish this work earlier was apparently due to his unwillingness to appear too bold and ambitious as a patron. His plan to rebuild S. Marco was thwarted when other families with burial rights in the convent refused to surrender them.

Despite these limitations imposed upon Cosimo's patronage by community sentiment and tradition, and by his own sense of propriety, his total contribution was impressive. His greatest achievement was, of course, the palace on the Via Larga, and it was within the confines of that structure that later Medici generations satisfied their esthetic needs. Lorenzo was recognized as the premier connoisseur of the arts in Italy, and his advice on painters and architects was sought by princes throughout the peninsula. As one dimension of his foreign policy, he sent Florentine artists to work for those rulers whose favor he desired. But Lorenzo's material subsidy of the arts in Florence was niggardly. Most of his money for this purpose was spent not on ecclesiastical or civic projects, but on his private collection of precious gems and antique art. This had been assembled for his enjoyment, and for that of close friends and visiting dignitaries, whose appreciation of the gesture might be politically advantageous as well as personally gratifying. Lorenzo's collection of objets d'art was the esthetic counterpart of the Platonic Academy.

Parent and Child in Renaissance Italy

JAMES BRUCE ROSS

Before the development of modern psychology, before it was fashionable to collect children's verses, artwork, and opinions, our only knowledge of childhood and the perceptions and experiences of children was derived from the recollections of adults. In the earlier selection on parents and children in the Middle Ages, Mary Martin McLaughlin relied on the reminiscences of Guibert of Nogent and on biographical works (saints' lives) that probably preserve some recollections by their subjects themselves. In addition, McLaughlin found occasional contemporary admonitions to parents that, by implication at least, give us some idea about how children were treated and what was expected of them. By a bit of imagination, the historian can describe the child's experience of such expectations and treatment, but the skimpiness of our knowledge is all too plain. In dealing with parent and child in the civilization of Renaissance Italy, James Bruce Ross has used sources similar to McLaughlin's, but the literate urbanites of the sixteenth century produced many more reminiscences than did medieval people. The relatively rich sources make it possible for Ross to construct a fairly complete portrait of children's experience in that period. He can describe the system of child-rearing, establish a general chronology of young life, and present contemporary ideas about family life, because many treatises and personal letters dealing with these subjects survive.

A brief review of the history of the family in medieval Europe will serve as background for Ross' article and as reflection on McLaughlin's article. We sometimes speak of the emergence of the family in the fifteenth and sixteenth centuries, and this way of speaking may seem rather strange. After all, medieval society derived from Germanic and Roman society, and both of these were wholly based on the family. But the growth of feudalism during the Middle Ages had a profound effect on the family. The family system of primitive Germanic society broke down as feudalism became the organizing principle of European society. Feudal lords could effectively control the political position of the family by controlling the marriage of their vassals. Likewise, feudal law restricted the role of families in the system of power by insisting on primogeniture: While younger sons could receive fiefs from their fathers, and daughters could be given dowries, there were strict limitations on the size of these donations. A man could not disinherit his eldest son, nor could he leave his heir so little land that the heir could not fulfill his obligations to his lord.

Families did, of course, occasionally gain a powerful position within the feudal hierarchy. The famous Clares of England used the favor of the English kings to spread through the baronage of the kingdom. Their success is indicated by their position within the party of rebellious barons that won the Magna Carta from King John in 1215. Of the twenty-four barons chosen to look after the royal government on behalf of the rebels, sixteen were members of the Clare family. Yet it is significant that the power of the family consisted in its success in infiltrating the feudal structure rather than opposing it. One Clare, for example, married the great William Marshal (see "The Training of a Knight" in Part 3). Feudal rank, not family connections, determined a person's place in the community.

Another indication of the declining importance of the family in medieval England is found in the common law of property. Progressively during the twelfth and thirteenth centuries, family rights of property—and the concomitant inability of the head of the family to alienate property—devolved on the paterfamilias. In 1225, the royal court decided that a man could alienate land and deprive his heirs of any right to it. Family rights of property had become individual rights.

Cases before the royal court did not much affect life in the peasant villages, which was in all likelihood much more traditional and thus more family-oriented than life among the upper classes. Yet the conclusions to be drawn from the documents of the upper classes are strikingly confirmed by another sort of evidence that was more popular, or at least more public, in character. The art of the cathedrals often portrayed aspects of everyday life, especially peasant life, but the family did not figure in these representations.

It can be argued that these medieval representations only reveal the life of the rural aristocracy and peasants, and that we should not take them as a reflection of urban family life. This is true; the rural society of feudal barons set the standards of medieval social and family life. In turning to look at the families of Renaissance Italy, we see a life style similar to that of medieval urban populations; but now middle-class urbanites were becoming the dominant group in European society. The difference in focus between McLaughlin's and Ross' articles is not merely the result of the historian's personal interest or the survival of particular sources; it represents an actual, major change in early modern society.

"I called to mind when, the exact hour and moment, and where and how he was conceived by me, and how great a joy it was to me and his mother; and soon came his movements in the womb which I noted carefully with my hand, awaiting his birth with the greatest eagerness. And then when he was born, male, sound, well-proportioned, what happiness, what joy I experienced; and then as he grew from good to better, such satisfaction, such pleasure in his childish words, pleasing to all, loving towards me his father and his mother, precocious for his age."

Giovanni Morelli

What was it like to be a middle-class child in the urban centres of northern and central Italy in the period of "the Renaissance," from about 1300 to the early sixteenth century? The life of the peasant child and of the proletarian urban child remains almost wholly obscure, but thanks to the articulate impulses of the mercantile and professional classes, and the remarkable number of their extant records, we can gain some understanding of the upbringing of their children. Although no voices of children reach us directly, we can hear them, faintly and imperfectly to be sure, through the media of those who controlled their lives or observed their development. Fathers of families sometimes recall their own early years and usually record with care the vital data of their offspring; moralists and preachers admonish parents in traditional Christian terms; educators create an ideal ethic of pedagogy, from classical sources; physicians and artists observe and comment upon the child in particular ways. A few exceptional individuals write their own life history, transmuting their childhood experience in their old age. All of these adults draw from the accumulated wisdom of the past but reflect as well the power of prevailing custom and the peculiar strains of an aggressive and competitive society subject to physical disasters, plague, famine and flood, as well as civil violence and war.

In pursuit of evidence for this elusive subject the modern scholar must search widely, examining masses of diverse materials, published and unpublished, in order to find even a few fragments or tessera with which to construct some kind of mosaic. The shapes that emerge will be faulty, the colors dim, but perhaps the whole may make some sense to the modern student of childhood, past and present. Deeper psychological insight, more lively historical imagination, as well as the fruits of contemporary quantitative studies, will enrich and doubtless modify the tentative conclusions of this short essay, but the evidence presented, almost wholly from the sources, will, I hope, remain valuable to the future inquirer.

From "The Middle-Class Child in Urban Italy, Fourteenth to Early Sixteenth Century" by James Bruce Ross, in *The History of Childhood*, edited by L. deMause (New York: The Psychohistory Press, 1974), pp. 183–216. Reprinted by permission of The Psychohistory Press.

Because the Tuscans, and especially the Florentines, were more articulate than any other people in Italy at this time and their records richer and more accessible than those of other areas, their voices are heard most clearly in this essay. The political fragmentation of the peninsula of Italy, only a geographical expression until the mid-nineteenth century, precludes the characterization of any child as "Italian," and the uneven cultural development of the major parts makes questionable any generalization beyond the limits of a single territorial entity. It seems valid, however, to consider as a whole the experience of the middle-class child in central and northern Italy. "The City" (Rome) was distinct in every way, and "The Kingdom" (Naples, with or without Sicily) was overwhelmingly rural, retarded in social and cultural development, and therefore relatively inarticulate for our purposes.

The First Two Years: Mother or Nurse?
The Balia: Ideal and Actual

What were the infant's first contacts with the world outside the womb? Birth in the parental bed, bath in the same room, and baptism in the parish church were followed almost at once by delivery into the hands of a *balia* or wet-nurse, generally a peasant woman living at a distance, with whom the infant would presumably remain for about two years or until weaning was completed. Immediate separation from its mother, therefore, was the fate of the new-born child in the middle-class families of urban Italy in the period of our study. It became wholly dependent for food, care and affection upon a surrogate, and its return to its own mother was to a stranger in an alien home, to a person with whom no physical or emotional ties had ever been established. Clearly the *balia* looms large in any discussion of the young child in Italy.

The antiquity of the institution of the wet-nurse is well known to all students of pediatrics. Of interest to us here is the continuity of a body of injunctions concerning the choice of a wet-nurse and the performance of her basic functions, especially as they had been formulated by the physician Soranus of Ephesus (96–138 A.D.). This core of material seems to be the source of most of the didactic treatises on the care of infants that were written in our period although the lines of transmission are not clear. Of equal interest in these Italian writings is the persistence of the advocacy of maternal feeding, but in ambivalent terms similar to those of Soranus:

> Other things being equal, it is better to feed the child with maternal milk; for this is more suited to it, and the mothers become more sympathetic towards the offspring, and it is more natural to be fed from the mother after parturition, just as before parturition. But if anything prevents it one

must choose the best wet-nurse, lest the mother grow prematurely old, having spent herself through the daily suckling. . . . The mother will fare better with a view to her own recovery and to further child-bearing, if she is relieved of having her breasts distended. . . .

Among the Italian writers of the fourteenth century the wet-nurse is accepted as a matter of course. For example, the mother is relegated to a minor role by the leading authority on the subject, the poet-notary, Francesco da Barberino, who urges that the wet-nurse be as much like the mother as possible, and that if she falls sick, she should take the infant to its mother, "who, if she wishes and it is convenient, will be able to suckle it with fine milk; though it is true that in the beginning the milk of another is better than hers." Much the same attitude is shown by the Tuscan merchant Paolo da Certaldo in his collection of moral admonitions written after 1350. Not mentioning the mother at all, he calls for great care in the choice of a wet-nurse:

She should be prudent, well-mannered, honest, not a drinker or a drunkard, because very often children draw from and resemble the nature of the milk they suck; and therefore be careful the wet nurses of your children aren't proud and don't have other evil traits. . . .

The fate of the child put out with a *balia* depended upon many variables including the duration of the stay. Supposedly it lasted for two years or until weaning, which was obviously abrupt in many cases; Barberino says about two years and warns against sudden weaning. Actually it varied considerably, as a few examples will show. A girl child in the Florentine Sassetti family was returned in 1370 after twenty-nine months by her *balia* with whom the parents remained on good terms "although the child was in rather poor shape, but in truth more from illness than from poor care." The fortunate illegitimate daughter of Datini (by a slave-girl) was taken in by his wife in 1395 and brought "home" at six years from her *balia* whose husband wrote saying that he and his wife had loved her like a daughter, and "because she is a good girl and very fearful," he hoped they would be kind to her. The father of Giovanni Morelli was left by his father with a *balia* in the country until he was "ten or twelve," perhaps because his parent "had so many grown children, or because his wife being dead and he an old man, he didn't want the trouble of bringing up the child, or the expense." The grown man remembered this *balia* as "the most awful bestial woman that ever was," who had given him so many blows that the mere thought of her so enraged him that he would have killed her if he could have laid hands on her. A branch of the Adriani family of Florence in 1470 received their son back from his *balia* at fifteen months and were told he had been "eight days without the breast" because she had become pregnant.

In general, it seems clear that the pregnancy of the *balia* more frequently terminated the stay than the early death of the child. The causes of the latter are rarely made clear. Did illegitimate infants die more frequently and earlier than legitimate babies in the care of a *balia*? Infanticide veiled as "smothering" may well have occurred more frequently than we know though there were more humane ways of disposing of unwanted children, legitimate and illegitimate. The foundling hospitals received a steady stream of the latter. But the danger of "smothering" is made clear by Barberino's injunction: "don't let the baby lie with you in such a way that you might roll over on top of him." (It is worth noting that the "layettes" sent with infants by Rustichi and others included a cradle with coverlet and pillow.)

Few explicit references to "smothering," however, have been found. Among the many deaths of young children noted by Morelli in his review of three generations, only one, a nephew, was thought to have been "suffocated" at the home of the *balia*; the great killer in this family was the Black Death in the recurrent waves of 1363, 1374, 1400. Another instance is found in an early life of the humanist Marsiglio Ficino; his grandmother appeared to his mother in a dream, grieving, on the seventeenth day after the birth of a child, and "the next day countrymen brought back her child suffocated by her nurse." And a few days after Cellini visited his natural son he received word the child was dead, "smothered" by his nurse. The question arises, however, why a *balia* would deliberately "smother" a child or carelessly run the risk of doing so. The child's death would mean the end of an arrangement profitable to her and to her husband. And the penalties for infanticide might be harsh.

The Return of the Native: From About Two to Seven
Child and Mother: Care in Theory and Practice

The return of the child to its native home after some two years forced upon him another severe adjustment; now displaced from the only "mother" he had ever known he must find his true mother in the midst of a strange household, an urban "family" which might be large and complex in composition. If the trend may have been towards the smaller "nuclear" family there is plenty of evidence of the persistence of the large "family" in the fourteenth and fifteenth centuries, that is, in the sense defined by Alberti as "children, wife, and other members of the household, both relatives and servants. . . . I would want all my family to live under one roof, to warm themselves at one hearth and to seat themselves at one table."

A few examples of the size and composition of households may be helpful.

One of the Peruzzi, Florentine merchants, notes in his "secret book" for 1314 the expenses incurred for half of the cost of "the house and family" which he had in common with his brother; he himself had twelve children. Two other merchants in the Florentine tax records of 1427 claim substantial reductions on the basis of large households, one noting a household of fifteen members, including two married sons and their families, as well as five adolescent sons, the other listing twelve dependents, wife, sister and nine children. In praising his wife in the late fourteenth century another merchant, Velluti, says she is a big, beautiful woman of fifty, wise, understanding, tireless, and splendid as a nurse, "and that's not to be wondered at, considering how many she's had to manage, husbands, sons, brothers and other persons." A mixed household under the roof of a widow is described in 1442 as containing her husband's two natural children, her own three sons, her daughters, the wives of two sons and three children of one of them. A similar composite household is that of Paoli Niccolini, wool merchant of the mid-fifteenth century; it included his children by two wives, the sons of one wife by her first husband and two of his sons by a slave whom he freed and kept in residence.

Discord in such households was inevitable. San Bernardino notes what a bride might expect on arrival in her new home, such as the enmity of step-children: ". . . and she has no love for them and can scarcely bear for them to have enough to eat. And they are often so knowing as to perceive that she doesn't wish them well and would like for her to have nothing at all to eat." And if she finds another daughter-in-law in the house, "there will soon be an end to peace and concord," and if a mother-in-law, "I'll say no more!" Morelli describes admiringly the way in which his sister "Mea," married at fifteen into a large, disorderly and quarrelsome household, imposed peace upon old and young by her grace and virtue.

The child returning from the *balia*, therefore, might have to compete for the attention of his mother, or some adult woman, not only with his own siblings but with half-brothers and sisters, legitimate or illegitimate, some obviously of alien blood, or with cousins under the tutelage of their fathers. Illegitimate children were sometimes even brought home from overseas, as in the case of Gregorio Dati, who, in 1391 had a child by a Tartar slave in Valencia, whom he sent back to Florence to be reared at three months. A member of the Velluti family brought back from Sicily in 1355 his dead brother's illegitimate daughter, age ten, although he was at first dubious about her parentage, "and I welcomed her, and I and my family . . . treated her as though she were my own daughter." The numbers of children might even be augmented by little slave-servants, especially girls of eleven or twelve, Tartars, Slavs, or "Arabs," whom Datini and other merchants bought to use as household drudges or little nurses. These children were distinguished from the others by looks, speech, manners and the clothes they were required to wear, marked with black, as were the older slave-servants in the house.

If it was difficult for the returning child to win a place in his mother's affections in such households, perhaps he attached himself at first to an older sister or brother, to an uncle or an aunt or grandparent living in the house. When a well-known Florentine widow was looking for a bride for one of her sons, she commented favorably on a girl who was "responsible for a large family (there are twelve children, six boys and six girls) and the mother is always pregnant and is not very competent." The grandmothers in the Medici family seem to have been active in the upbringing of children in that restless clan as they moved from city to villa, villa to villa, to escape the plague, bad weather and other troubles. In a well-known picture, Ghirlandaio conveys the feeling of intimacy which a child might develop towards a grandfather.

We shall never know what impressions of his family a child actually formed but some early adult memories, recorded in different ways, may be helpful. A study of Leonardo da Vinci, an illegitimate child who was successively part of several family groups, makes suggestive use of the drawings of heads, mostly in profile, dating perhaps from as early as the artist's sixteenth year. By means of verbal portraits the Florentine Giovanni Morelli in his private journal, written mostly in his thirties, evokes vivid images of those whom he loved most in the family constellation, treating as shadowy figures the others. He idealizes his father, whom he lost at three years, as a "poor abandoned boy," left at the balia's until ten or twelve years, who never saw his father, but who by courage and virtue triumphed over paternal neglect and fraternal indifference to become head of the family. Married at twenty-eight to Telda, "thirteen and beautiful," he sired five children before he died in the plague of 1374, leaving four surviving children, two girls, nine and six, and two boys, four and three, at the mercy of "a cruel mother" who soon re-married and turned them over to her parents. For a brief period an heroic young cousin served as a father figure to the child in a large family group which fled to Bologna to escape the plague but this admirable young man who skilfully managed the large household soon died. The child's next attachment was to his older sister, Mea, beautiful, gifted and gay, but she married at fifteen and died in childbirth at twenty-two. For Giovanni the loss of his father was irreparable, "so great is the benefit the child receives from a living father," his hourly guidance and good counsel; his first duty should be to insure that in case of his death the wife does not remarry and leave their children, "for there is no mother so bad that she isn't better for her children than any other woman." . . .

In Alberti's dialogue on the family, the characters, married and unmarried, place upon the father the weight of responsibility for the upbringing of children after infancy, "that tender age . . . more properly assigned to women's quiet care." They debate the balance of paternal joys and sorrows and seem to ignore or denigrate the mother's role, stressing the father's love as "more unshakable, more constant, more vast, more complete" than any other. Even they, however, reveal certain circumstances which diminished his role and enhanced the mother's, such as his absences from home and his greater age. Recent demographic studies, especially of the Florentine area, have established statistically a striking disparity in age between husband and wife and a consequent remoteness of the father from the child. Some social and cultural implications of the close proximity of mother and child have also been suggested.

The relative closeness in age of the young mother to the child was often enhanced by frequent absences, even prolonged, of mercantile fathers, and by political exile following upon sudden reversal of party controls, such as the return of the Medici to Florence in 1434. San Bernardino sharply warns against the long absences of merchants and encourages wives to try to force them to return: "I'm not speaking of a week or two weeks or even a month . . . but to stay two years or three is not rational and hence displeasing to God." Such practices, a normal aspect of mercantile activity, were probably more disruptive of family life than political exile. Many young women of prominent families, however, were made "widows" by the exile of their husbands. Vespasiano, the Florentine book-seller and biographer, pays tribute to some of these illustrious women, noting their careful administration of the household, their solicitude for their children; he admires especially those who, as real widows, remained celibate and devoted themselves wholly to their souls and their children.

"Young widows" were, in fact, a common social phenomenon and concern for their welfare, fiscal and moral, and that of their children pervades many kinds of sources. The preacher-prophet of Florence, Savonarola (1452–1498), devotes a whole treatise to widowhood in which he analyzes the motives for remarrying or remaining chaste. He does not condemn those young widows who remained unmarried not for love of God but "rather for human reasons such as the love of their children," from whom they cannot bear to separate themselves. San Antonino of Florence (1389–1459), in his letters of guidance to a young widow, urges her to try to be both father and mother to her children, "a father in punishing and training them, a mother in nourishing them, not with dainties or too many indulgences as do carnal mothers but not spiritual ones; for children need both bread and blows." And San Bernardino, "let the widow learn to rear her family" and be especially watchful of daughters.

Anxiety for the welfare of children whose widowed mothers remarry is expressed in many ways. Paolo da Certaldo urges fathers

> to avoid like fire leaving your goods and children only in the hands of your wife. . . . In many ways and for many reasons, it may happen that she'll

leave your children and rob them of their patrimony or treat them badly or see someone else abuse them and remain silent. . . .

The provisions of many wills contain a clause "if she remains a widow and lives with her children" qualifying legacies to daughters and wives. In his history of his family, Morelli, abandoned at four by a "cruel mother," notes in every case whether a widow remarried or stayed with her children. He gives elaborate directions to his heirs how to ensure in their wills that the mother should not leave the offspring, listing several provisions which he grades in terms of the husband's confidence in his wife's devotion to their children. . . .

The age between two and about seven was the period when the child of either sex must have known most closely the mother's care and developed its first emotional bond with her, a bond which might be enhanced by the youth of the mother, the age and absences of the father, or the widowhood of the mother. Perhaps the earlier deprivation suffered by both child and mother deepened this relationship and helps to explain the sustained devotion of many adult males to their mothers. It is doubtful whether this period was at first one "full of delight and accompanied by general laughter at the child's first words," as Alberti suggests. San Bernardino evokes a different kind of welcome when he attacks the odious "putting out" system: "and when he comes home to you, you say, 'I don't know whom you are like, certainly none of us!'" But time tempered the strangeness on both sides, and San Bernardino shrewdly notes the different qualities with which a mother looks at her own children ("with the eye of the heart"), those of her neighbor ("with pleasant mien"), and those of her enemies ("with a stern eye and scowl").

The predominant role of the mother is implicit in the treatise of the Dominican Giovanni Dominici (c. 1356 to c. 1420), himself the son of a widow, written for a lady who was "almost a widow," to advise her about the daily life of the child as well as its moral training: "one can effectively control children until they are grown up to about the age of twelve, then they begin to throw off the maternal yoke." The mother should adorn the house with pictures and statues "pleasing to childhood," such as "a good representation of Jesus nursing, sleeping in His mother's lap or standing courteously before Her," or one in which "he sees himself mirrored in the Holy Baptist . . . a little child who enters the desert, plays with birds" or "of Jesus and the Baptist pictured together. . . ." She should dress both sexes simply, in decent attire and modest colors; "from three years on" the son is to

know no distinction between male and female other than dress and hair. From then on let him be a stranger to being petted, embraced and kissed by you until after the twenty-fifth year. Granted that there will not take place any thought or natural movement before the age of five . . . do not be less solicitous that he be chaste and modest always and, in every place, covered as modestly as if he were a girl.

As for sleeping, she should not allow him after three years to "sleep on one bed or on one pillow with his sisters or romp too much with them during the day." Rear them separately if possible. "He should sleep clothed with a night shirt reaching below the knees. . . . Let not the mother nor the father, much less any other person, touch him."

"Do not forbid them to play games. . . . Growing nature makes the child run and jump." As long as they play these simple games "you play with them and let them win." If they hurt one another, chide the wrongdoer but moderately so the injured one won't delight in revenge.

To prepare them for adversity the mother should inure them to hardships, putting the boy to sleep sometimes dressed, "once a week on a couch, occasionally on a chest, and with the windows open," treating him "somewhat as if he were the son of a peasant." And "accustom them to eat bitter things, such as peachstones, horehound, strong herbs and fritters" and occasionally "certain harmless little remedies like purgatives" to prepare them for future sickness. And in anticipation of poverty, "children should be accustomed to eat coarse food, to wear cheap and common clothing, to go on foot. . . ."

From other kinds of sources it is clear that Dominici's prescriptions reflect religious attitudes and sexual fears more than the secular reality he observes and deplores:

> At present how much you work and strive to lead them about the whole day, to hug and kiss them, to sing them songs, to tell them foolish stories, to scare them with a dozen bogies, to deceive them, to play hide and seek with them and to take pains in making them beautiful, healthy, cheerful, laughing and wholly content according to the sensual!

His advice raises many questions, few of which can be answered. How was it possible to separate boys and girls at such an age, to prevent them from seeing and touching one another as they romped in the confines of an urban house and courtyard? The everyday garment of both sexes in the early years seems to have been a short tunic of wool, loose or belted, with little underneath.

Close relations between the sexes in childhood are evident in some sources, for example, in Morelli's account of trying to marry a young girl whom he had wanted for a wife from the time she was a tiny child. Also, a member of the Valori family in 1452 chose as his wife the one of two sisters whom he knew well "because up to the age of twelve we had been brought up almost together." A mixed group of lively children is pictured in a letter of Piero, age eight, to his father, Lorenzo de' Medici, in 1479:

We are all well and studying. Giovanni [four] is beginning to spell. . . . Giuliano [the baby] laughs and thinks of nothing else, Lucrezia [nine] sews, sings and reads. Maddalena [six] knocks her head against the wall. . . . Luisa [two] begins to say a few little words. Contessina [over a year] fills the house with her noise.

Spontaneous play by young children is recognized as natural even by the austere Dominici who sees no good in toys, such as "little wooden horses, attractive cymbals, imitation birds, gilded drums, and a thousand different kinds of toys, all accustoming them to vanity." In pictures of the period, little children playing spontaneously are most often shown in the persons of the Christ Child and little St. John, reaching out to each other, sometimes embracing, sometimes with a lamb, lively and responsive. They are also represented in dozens of ways, singly, in two's and larger groups, as tiny "angel-children," called putti or amorini, usually winged, nude, appealing. One of the most playful groups is that of the very young and chubby, winged male amori by Agostino di Duccio who are frantically engaged in a variety of activities on land and sea, shooting, boating, swimming on sea monsters, playing musical instruments. More realistic, perhaps, is the representation of seven nude putti in a drawing by Raphael who are acting out with glee a specific game, "judge and prisoner."

But all these putti are ideal, not real, infants inspired clearly by classical forms though doubtless influenced by observation of living children; their robust forms, angelic faces, fantastic activities, can hardly be considered as typical of actual children. And the same is true of the most famous examples of older children, some adolescent, on the two singers' pulpits created for the cathedral in Florence. The grace and dignity of the classically clad, almost sexless children of Luca della Robbia in their dancing and music-making convey the character of a heavenly, not earthly, choir, though the faces may resemble those of Tuscan boys, then and now. And the almost Bacchic abandon of the winged wreath dancers in Donatello's frieze seems even more remote from the homes and streets of Italian cities. What did these ideal children mean to those who created them or those who looked at them, children and adults? What were real children doing at these ages in the home, or school or shop? About the homely activities of the child, where and how he ate, slept, defecated, played, we know very little. Even surviving domestic architecture reveals little about the use of living space for intimate purposes.

The moralists tell us little, the ricordi almost nothing. Paolo da Certaldo is succinct, as always: "Feed the boy well and dress him as well as you can, I mean in good taste and decently. . . . Dress the girl well but as for eating, it doesn't matter as long as it keeps her alive; don't let her get fat."

And Dominici, with future poverty in mind:

Children should be accustomed to eat coarse food, to wear cheap and common clothes. . . . They should also learn to wait on themselves, and to use as little as possible the services of maid or servant, setting and clearing the table, dressing and undressing themselves, putting on their own shoes and clothes and so forth.

Did children eat, standing up, scraps from the table, while serving or later? (Seated children are generally seen only in school-room scenes.) Filarete, the humanist-architect, writing in the 1460's about an "ideal school," warns that children should not eat too much; let them be given tough meat so they won't bolt their food, and, up to the age of twenty, stand to eat while one child reads aloud. They should not sleep more than six to eight hours. If one may judge from the slender young children in the family portraits of the age, even the children of the rich were not over-fed; though well-formed they look less amply fed than the chubby babies or the plump *putti* of the artists.

In general, the didactic treatises of the humanist educators, inspired by classical authorities, call for a regime of austerity tempered by reason and concern for the individual. The most celebrated teacher of the age, Vittorino da Feltre (1378–1446), wrote no treatises but put the prevailing principles of classical-Christian education into effect in his boarding school for children of the ruling family of Mantua and other deserving children of varying ages, some as young as six or seven. "The Pleasant House" was governed by the ever-watchful ascetic eye of the celibate master who permitted no coddling in habits of eating, clothing or sleeping, obviously guided by sexual fears. Few mothers of busy households could have supervised the daily habits of the children as effectively as Vittorino. . . .

From Father to Master: The Father's Role
Discipline and Instruction

During the younger years of the child the father's responsibility seems to have been limited primarily to periods of illness and disaster except where the poor health of the mother or poverty made his attention indispensable. One of the married Alberti family members speaks of the anguish of the father during the first period of life which "seems to be almost nothing but attacks of smallpox, measles, and rose rash. It is never free of stomach trouble, and there are always periods of debility." These and dozens of other kinds of diseases of children are described in the Italian medical treatises of the sixteenth century but few are clearly identified in the sources. In the *ricordi* the fact of death is usually simply stated and dated by the father, especially with reference to cases of very early mortality at the home of the *balia*.

Morelli, in reviewing his own life, notes his "illness" at four years, "long serious illness" at seven, "smallpox" at nine, and a grave illness and fever at twelve. He describes much more fully the mortal illness of his son, Alberto, in 1406:

> He fell ill with a flow of blood from the nose. It happened . . . three times before we noticed that he had fever, and then Monday morning when he was at school, the fever seized him, the blood burst from his nose and stomach and body, and, as it pleased God, he lived sixteen days . . . in great torment and agony. . . .

Further details of the child's suffering make it clear that Alberto's father rarely, if ever, left the child during this time; he includes his wife, however, in this account and in the description of their common grief that followed.

Strenuous efforts to keep alive a baby of six months, the illegitimate son of Datini, were made by his friends in Prato in communication with the father in Florence. The child, afflicted by "seizures," perhaps due to the "humidity," and fever, died after a few days despite the use of medicines, ointments and "incantations"; the "beaver's fat" sent from Florence by his father arrived too late. He had been removed from the house of his *balia* so that he might receive better care. Lapo Mazzei writes to Datini that he took his little son afflicted with epilepsy into his own bed with him.

The harsh treatment received by the young Cardan from both parents perhaps intensified the night terrors and sweats from which he suffered, as well as the hallucinations he experienced from four to seven and found agreeable while resting in bed until his father permitted him to get up. His treatment of his own children seems to have been little better; his older son was given out to a dissolute *balia* and barely survived the illnesses of his third and fourth years. . . .

In theory the father was considered to be directly responsible for the son's education but even the members of the Alberti family agree that "if the father is not himself capable of teaching, or is too busy with more important tasks (if anything is more important than the care of one's children)," let him find a tutor. Seven is often termed the suitable age at which to begin formal education but Palmieri, and similarly Rucellai, suggest starting earlier to teach the child his letters at home, making use of little devices such as forming letters in fruits and sweetmeats and giving them to him if he can recognize S, O, C and other letters. Dominici also mentions the value of little inducements or rewards, such as new shoes, an inkstand, a slate and so on. Vegio stresses parental responsibility in the early years of schooling, proposing the use of a relative or older brother as a mentor and the participation of the parents in hearing the child recite what he has supposedly learned.

Most middle-class children first encountered formal instruction at the age of seven or earlier in the schools of the commune. These "common schools" were deplored by Dominici as places where "a multitude of wicked, dissolute persons assemble, facile in evil or difficult to control"; all the parents could do was to fortify the child morally. Vegio sees a positive advantage in sending the child out of the home for his schooling, among his peers and away from women and servants, but the parents should get to know the teachers, pay them well and beware of over-crowded classrooms and frequent changes of teachers.

Some records of actual experience may prove useful. A succinct account of his education is given by a member of the Valori family of Florence, born 1354:

> In 1363, when the plague stopped, I Bartolomeo, was put to learn grammar at the school of Master Manovello and I stayed there up to 1367 through the month of May. And then in June of the same year I was put to learn abacus to know how to keep accounts, with Master Tomaso . . . , and I stayed there up to February, 1368. And on the same day I was sent to the bank of Bernardo. . . .

Though his schooling was delayed by the plague, this boy went through the three stages which were the normal progression in a mercantile society, learning to read, learning to do accounting and then apprenticeship in a bank or shop.

Morelli, without a father's guidance, went to school at five where he suffered "many blows and frights" in subjection to his master. At eight he was put under a master in the house whose discipline by day and night he found "displeasing to childish freedom." And at eleven to twelve after a severe case of smallpox, he suffered from a master of unusual harshness. His little son, Alberto, was more precocious; at four he wanted to go to school, at six he knew "Donatus" (primary Latin grammar), and at eight the Psalter, at nine he studied Latin and learned to read mercantile letters. The father reproaches himself bitterly after the child's death for having "worn him out at school and with many and frequent harsh blows."

Antonio Rustichi recorded the early education of his sons as conscientiously as their births. He sent Lionardo at five and Stefano at four to primary school in 1422, changed them to a second master in 1423, and soon shifted to a master in the house, who was given his keep but "no salary, or shoes or clothes." The latter lasted only a few weeks, going off to Pisa to study. In 1425 Antonio sent Stefano (seven), and Marabottino (four) to a teacher at Or San Michele "to learn to read," adding a third son in 1427. But he shifted all three to another master in 1428 because the teacher "was not instructing them well." They were moved again "to learn to read" in 1431, and in 1432 sent to learn the abacus. And so on. This over-burdened father clearly tried to find not only the most economical way of educating his sons, sending them in groups and experimenting with a house tutor, but was also determined that they should be well taught. The frequent changes of teachers recall the similar shifts of *balias* from which his children had suffered earlier. . . .

In summary, the life of the ordinary urban middle-class child in the period of the Renaissance seems to have been marked by a series of severe adjustments, both physical and emotional. The first and most significant of these was the almost immediate displacement of the infant from its mother's bosom to that of a *balia*; the second was the return of the young child, after some two years of absence, to a strange mother and an unknown home; the third was the projection of the boy of about seven into the classroom, and later the shop, and of the young girl at nine or ten into a nunnery or, often before sixteen, into marriage. These major displacements of the child might be supplemented by minor ones, of flight with one's family from the plague into another house, to the country or to another city, or departure from the native city with one's exiled father. Disturbing as these changes might be they did not require separation of the child from the mother as did the first displacement or as the remarriage of the mother might do.

In the first period of its life the child, handed over to a surrogate, was deprived of the love and care of both parents; in the next period he was probably drawn most closely under the mother's wing; in the next the boy came under the tutelage of the father and his surrogate, the master, while the girl remained under the mother's close supervision until her fate was determined. The first stage seems to me the most crucial and the least recognized or understood. It poses an historical question of absorbing interest: how could the deprived and neglected infants of the middle classes develop into the architects of a vigorous, productive and creative era which we call "the Renaissance"? The enigma will probably remain with us but at least we are asking new questions and devising new methods of inquiry. It seems likely to me that the approach of the psychologist and psychoanalyst will prove most fruitful in illuminating the long-range consequences of emotional deprivation.

For the social historian the best focus of attention may be the second stage, the young child's life from about two to about seven years when circumstances forced upon him an extraordinary adjustment to a strange environment. For this period a greater volume of positive evidence can be found through the use of unpublished materials and the critical re-examination of what we already have at hand. Although the walls of the *balia*'s house will stand forever between us and the swaddled infant, perhaps we can learn how to look more sharply through the doors and windows of the urban home and see the child in his intimate activities and relationships. In our efforts we can make fuller use, among other materials, of the vast resources left to us by Italian architects, painters, sculptors and craftsmen whose work has rarely been subjected to psychohistorical analysis.